My Love Mix-Up!

4

Art by **Aruko**
Story by **Wataru Hinekure**

Contents

Aoki borrows an eraser from his unrequited crush, Hashimoto. He finds the name "IDA♡" written on the eraser, and his hopes are dashed. Then Ida sees him holding that very eraser, and thinks Aoki is in love with him. While attempting to resolve the misunderstanding, Aoki ends up falling for Ida. Though Aoki is still reeling from his own emotions, the school trip spurs him to confess his feelings. He's ready for rejection from Ida...only to find Ida wants to start dating instead?! Meanwhile, Hashimoto is encouraged by Aoki's own perseverance and confesses her feelings to Aida! But she is rejected. After hearing Aida's early impressions of her, she declares she'll try harder to let Aida get to know her.

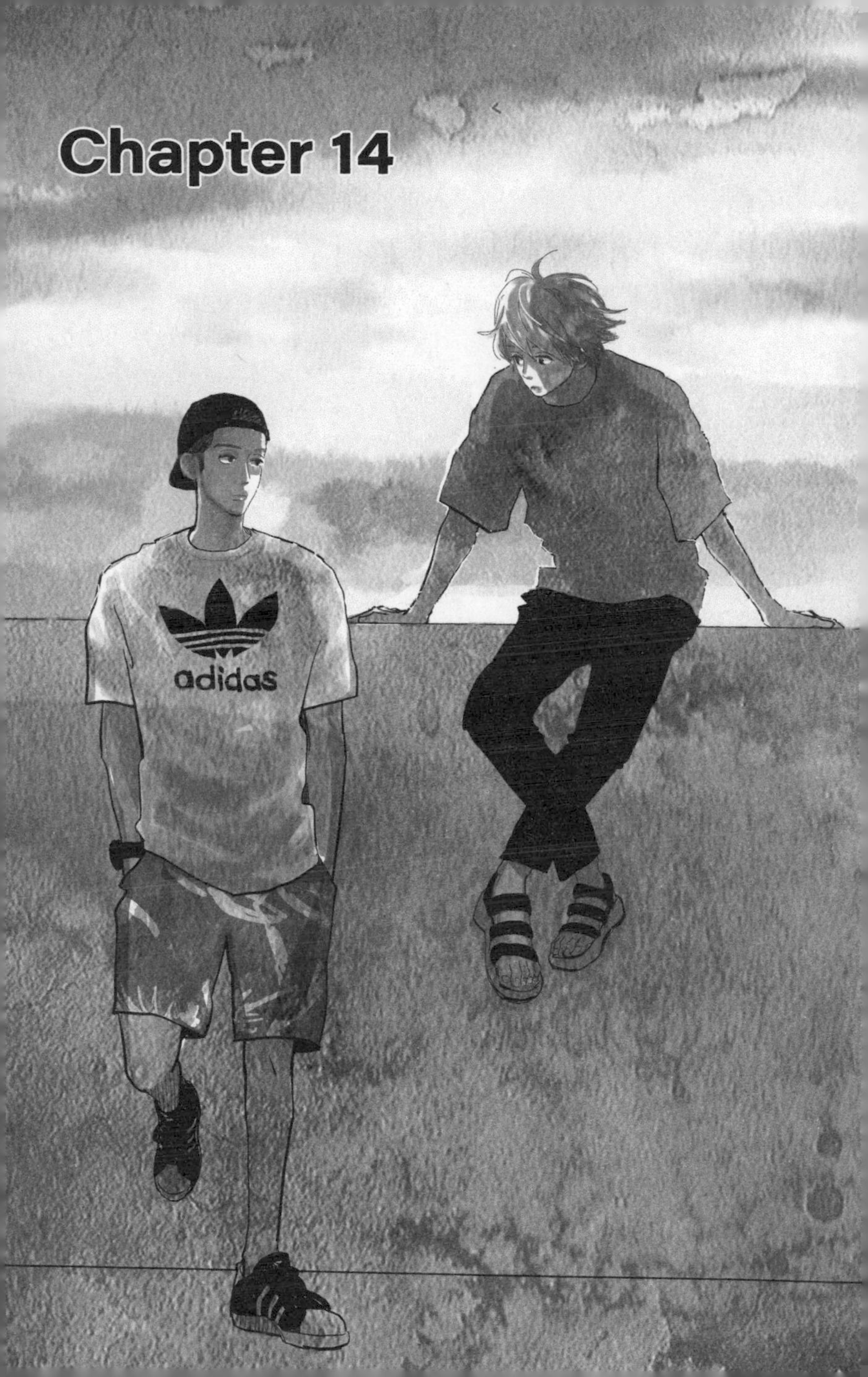
Chapter 14
adidas

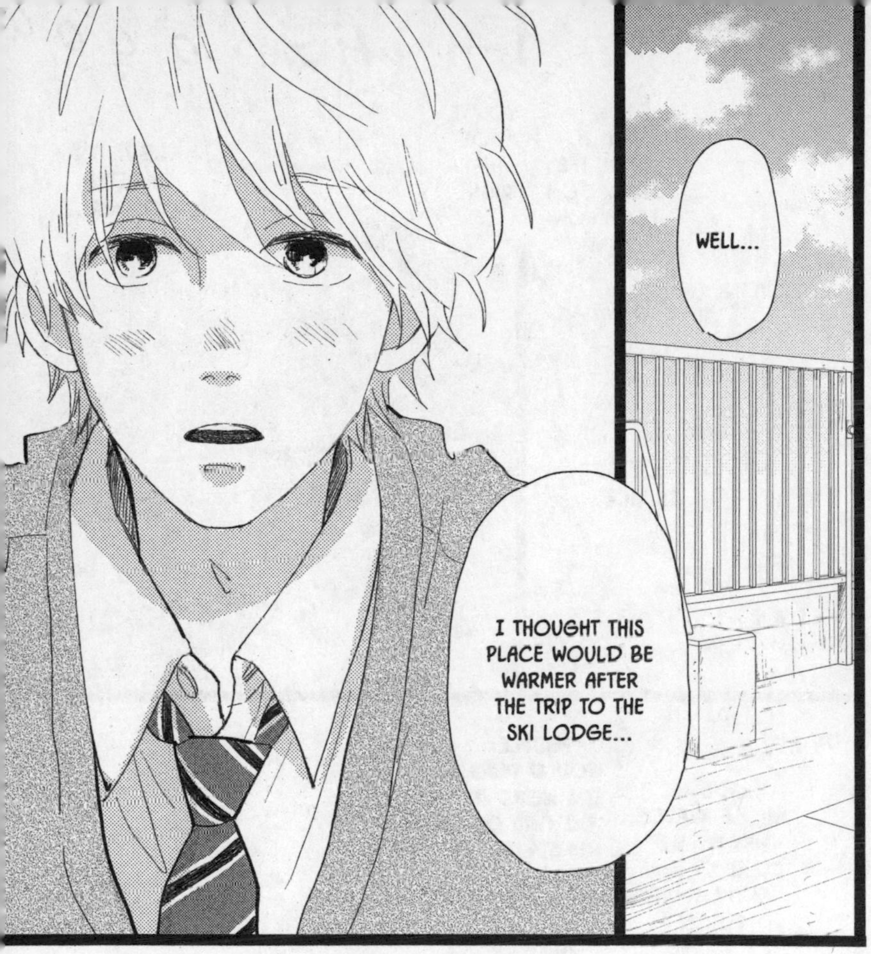
WELL...
I THOUGHT THIS PLACE WOULD BE WARMER AFTER THE TRIP TO THE SKI LODGE...

My Love Mix-Up!

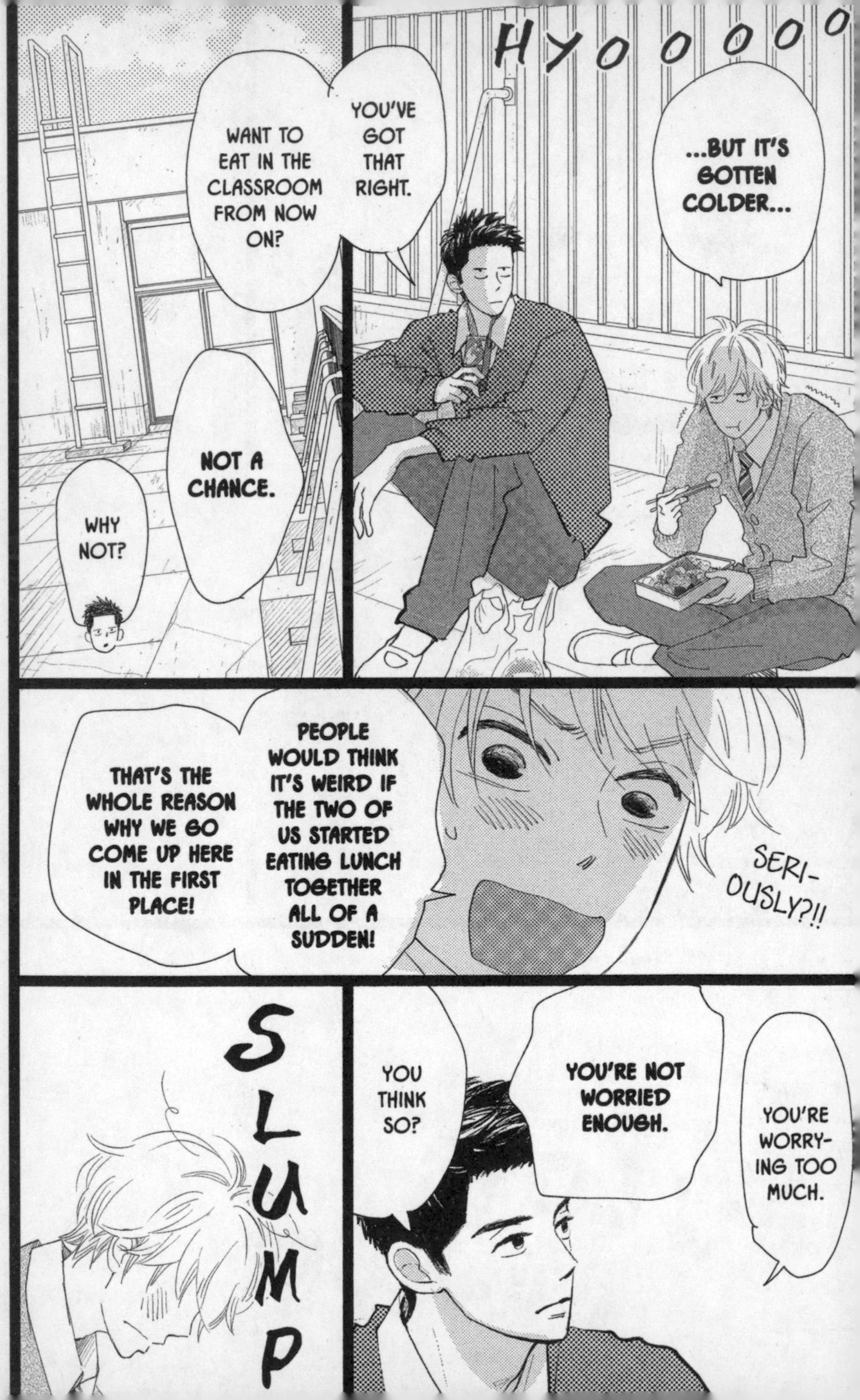
HYOOOOO
...BUT IT'S GOTTEN COLDER...
YOU'VE GOT THAT RIGHT.
WANT TO EAT IN THE CLASSROOM FROM NOW ON?
NOT A CHANCE.
WHY NOT?
SERI-OUSLY?!!
PEOPLE WOULD THINK IT'S WEIRD IF THE TWO OF US STARTED EATING LUNCH TOGETHER ALL OF A SUDDEN!
THAT'S THE WHOLE REASON WHY WE GO COME UP HERE IN THE FIRST PLACE!
YOU'RE WORRY-ING TOO MUCH.
YOU'RE NOT WORRIED ENOUGH.
YOU THINK SO?
SLUMP

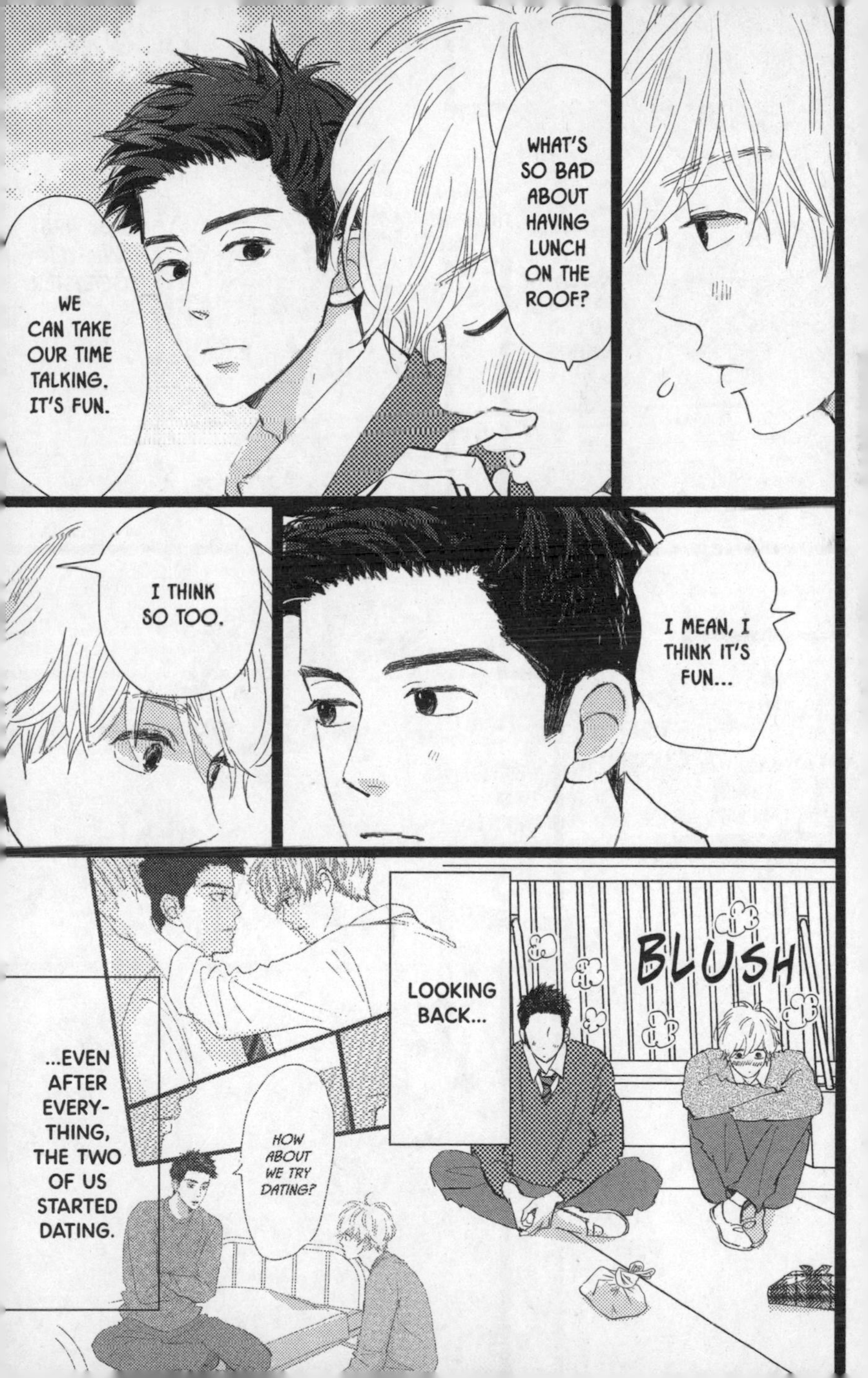
WHAT'S SO BAD ABOUT HAVING LUNCH ON THE ROOF?
WE CAN TAKE OUR TIME TALKING. IT'S FUN.
I MEAN, I THINK IT'S FUN...
I THINK SO TOO.
BLUSH
LOOKING BACK...
HOW ABOUT WE TRY DATING?
...EVEN AFTER EVERY-THING, THE TWO OF US STARTED DATING.

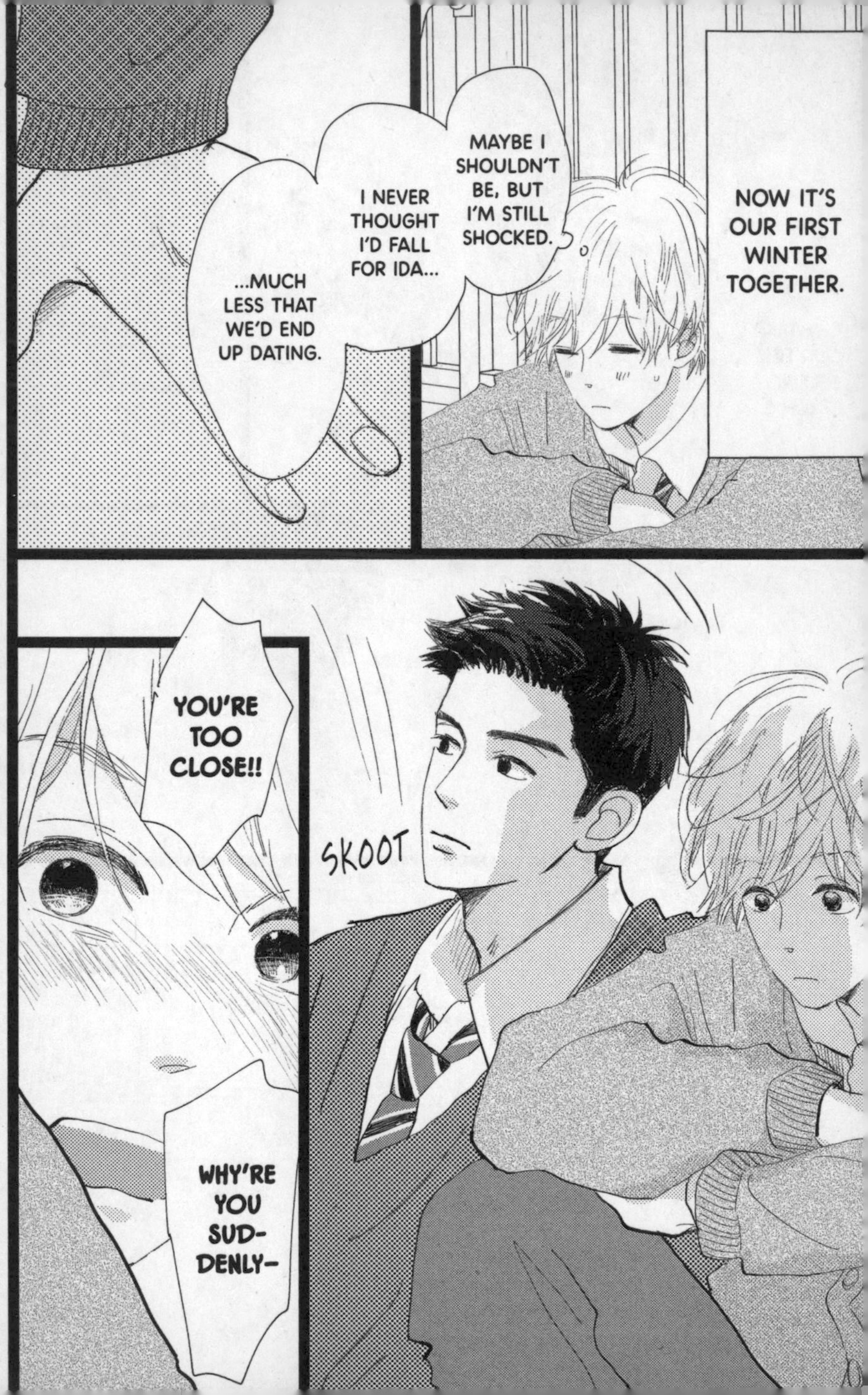
NOW IT'S OUR FIRST WINTER TOGETHER.
MAYBE I SHOULDN'T BE, BUT I'M STILL SHOCKED.
I NEVER THOUGHT I'D FALL FOR IDA...
...MUCH LESS THAT WE'D END UP DATING.
SKOOT
YOU'RE TOO CLOSE!!
WHY'RE YOU SUD-DENLY-

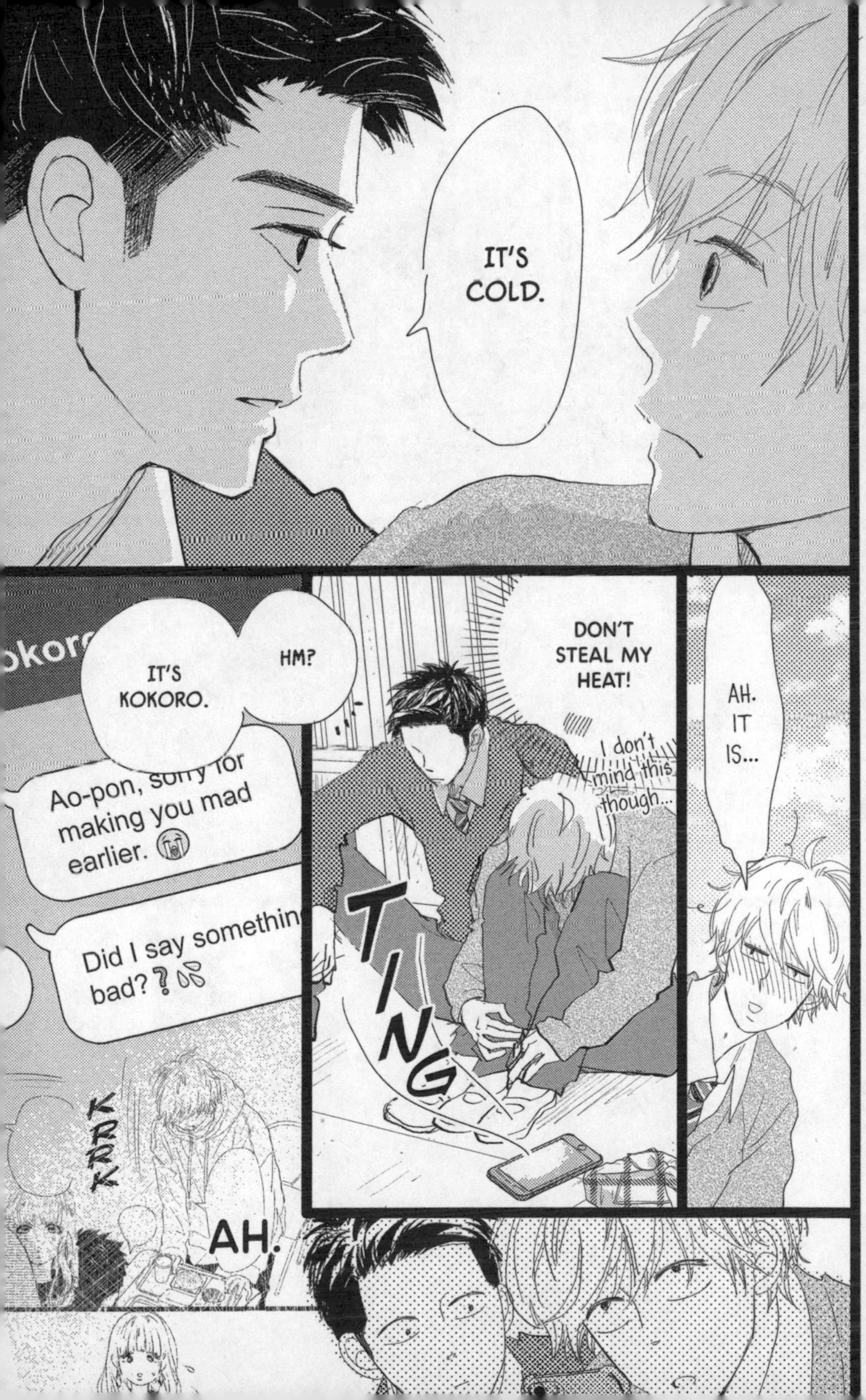
IT'S COLD.
AH. IT IS...
DON'T STEAL MY HEAT!
I don't mind this though...
TING
AH.
HM?
IT'S KOKORO.
kokoro
Ao-pon, sorry for making you mad earlier.
Did I say somethin bad?
KRRK

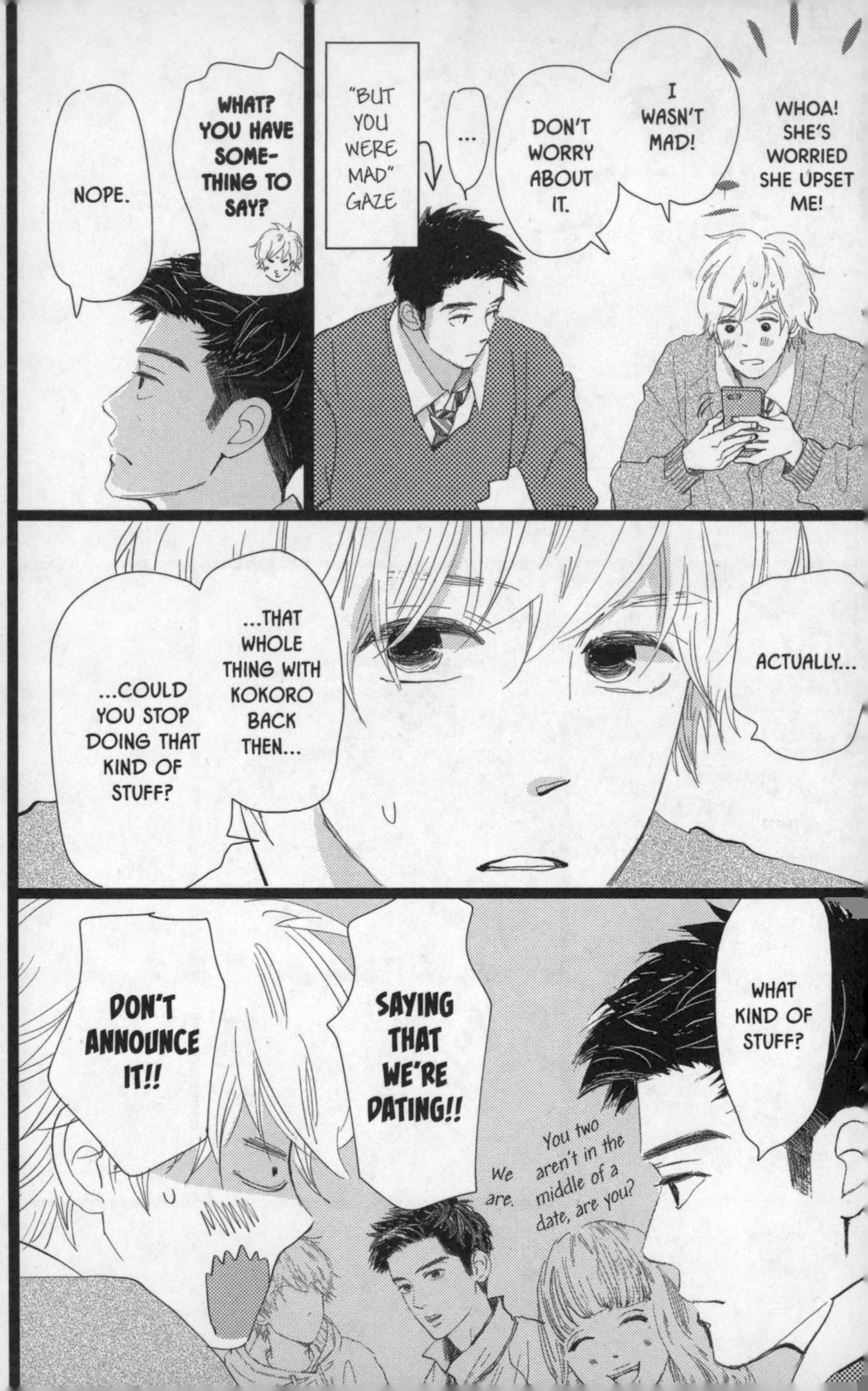
WHOA! SHE'S WORRIED SHE UPSET ME!
I WASN'T MAD!
DON'T WORRY ABOUT IT.
...
"BUT YOU WERE MAD" GAZE
WHAT? YOU HAVE SOME-THING TO SAY?
NOPE.
ACTUALLY...
...THAT WHOLE THING WITH KOKORO BACK THEN...
...COULD YOU STOP DOING THAT KIND OF STUFF?
WHAT KIND OF STUFF?
You two aren't in the middle of a date, are you?
We are.
SAYING THAT WE'RE DATING!!
DON'T ANNOUNCE IT!!

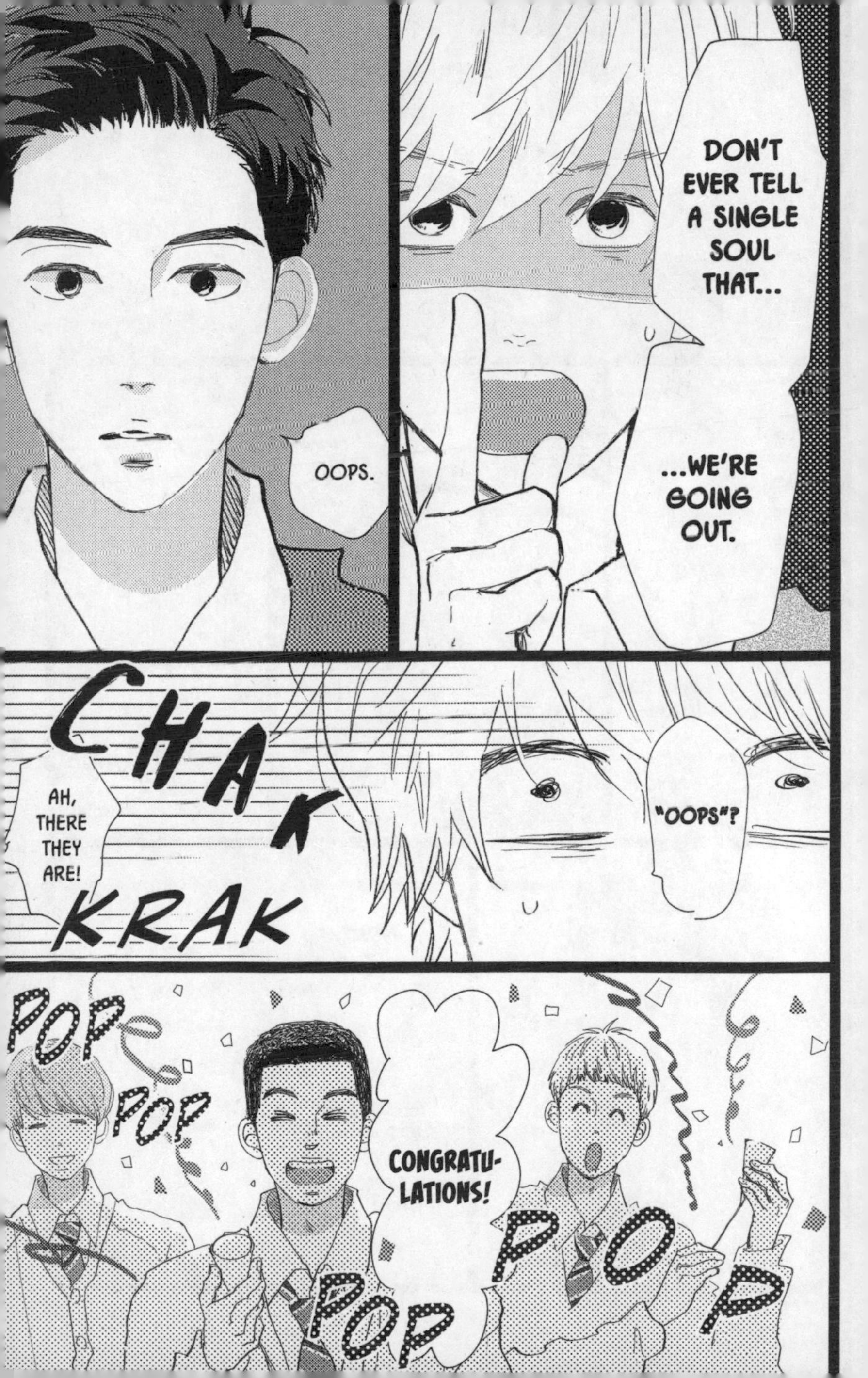
DON'T EVER TELL A SINGLE SOUL THAT...
...WE'RE GOING OUT.
OOPS.
"OOPS"?
CHAK KRAK
AH, THERE THEY ARE!
POP POP
CONGRATU-LATIONS!
POP
POP POP
POP

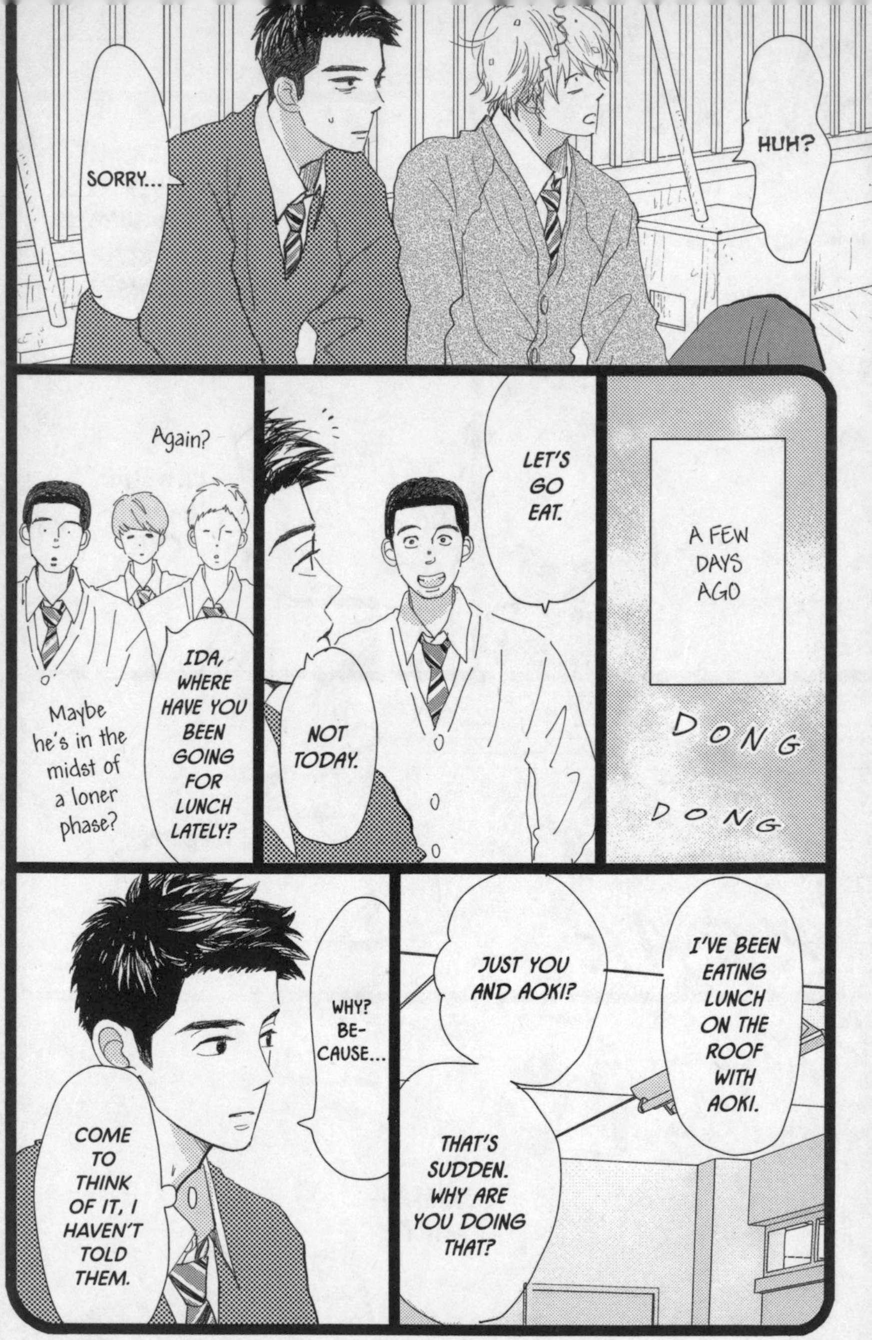
HUH?
SORRY...
A FEW DAYS AGO
DONG
DONG
LET'S GO EAT.
NOT TODAY.
Again?
IDA, WHERE HAVE YOU BEEN GOING FOR LUNCH LATELY?
Maybe he's in the midst of a loner phase?
I'VE BEEN EATING LUNCH ON THE ROOF WITH AOKI.
JUST YOU AND AOKI?
THAT'S SUDDEN. WHY ARE YOU DOING THAT?
WHY? BE-CAUSE...
COME TO THINK OF IT, I HAVEN'T TOLD THEM.

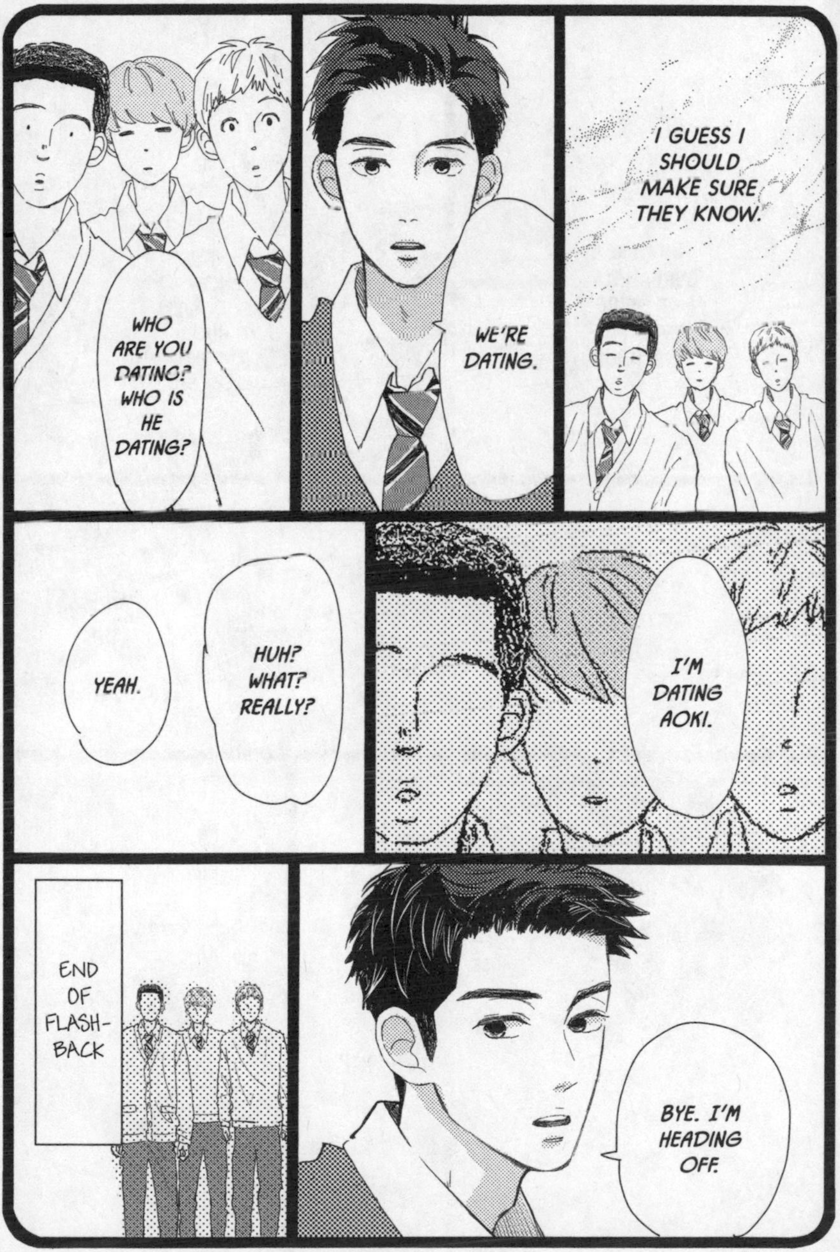
I GUESS I SHOULD MAKE SURE THEY KNOW.
WE'RE DATING.
WHO ARE YOU DATING? WHO IS HE DATING?
I'M DATING AOKI.
HUH? WHAT? REALLY?
YEAH.
BYE. I'M HEADING OFF.
END OF FLASH-BACK

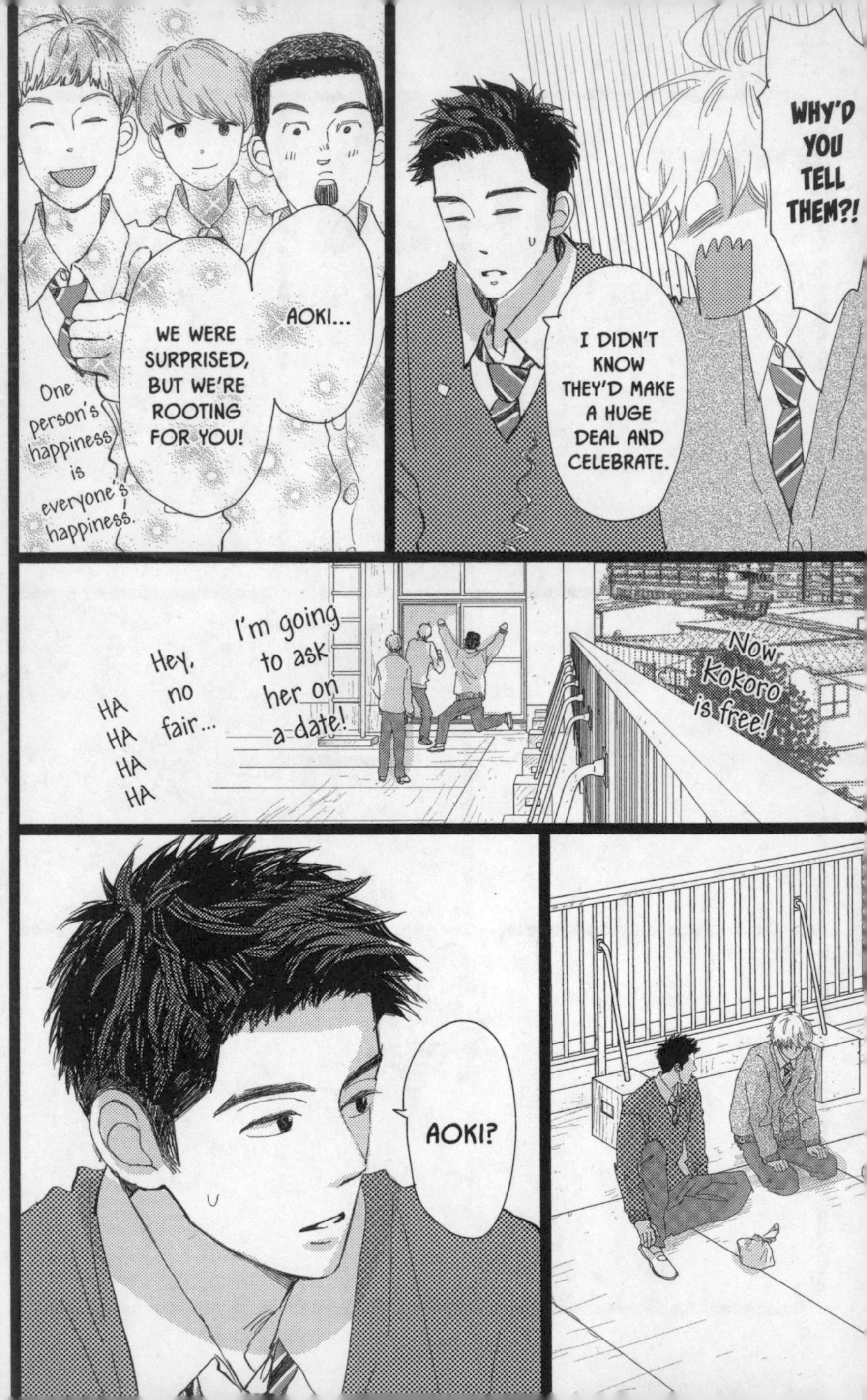
WHY'D YOU TELL THEM?!
I DIDN'T KNOW THEY'D MAKE A HUGE DEAL AND CELEBRATE.
AOKI...
WE WERE SURPRISED, BUT WE'RE ROOTING FOR YOU!
One person's happiness is everyone's happiness.
Now Kokoro is free!
I'm going to ask her on a date!
Hey, no fair...
HA HA HA HA
AOKI?

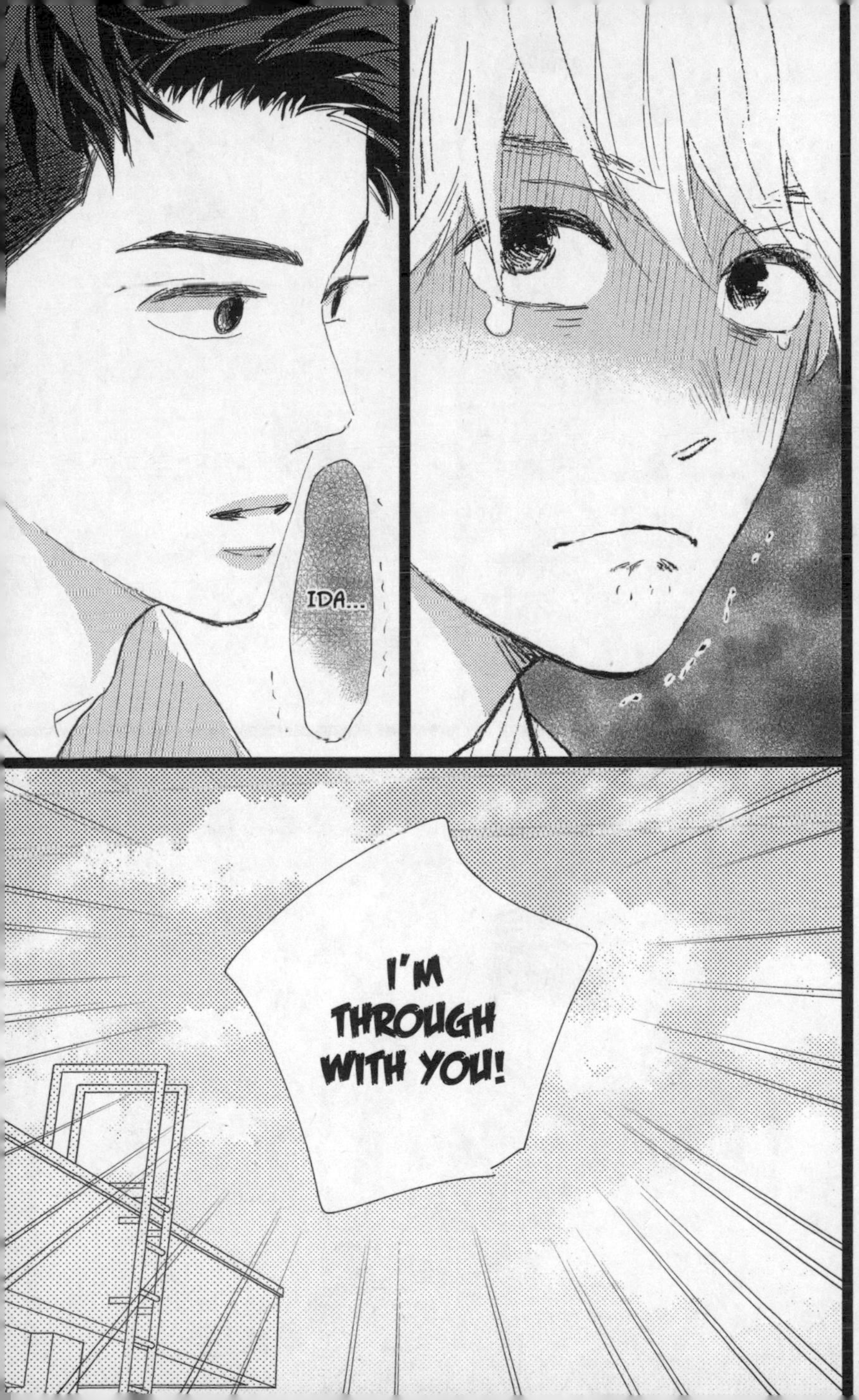
IDA...
I'M THROUGH WITH YOU!

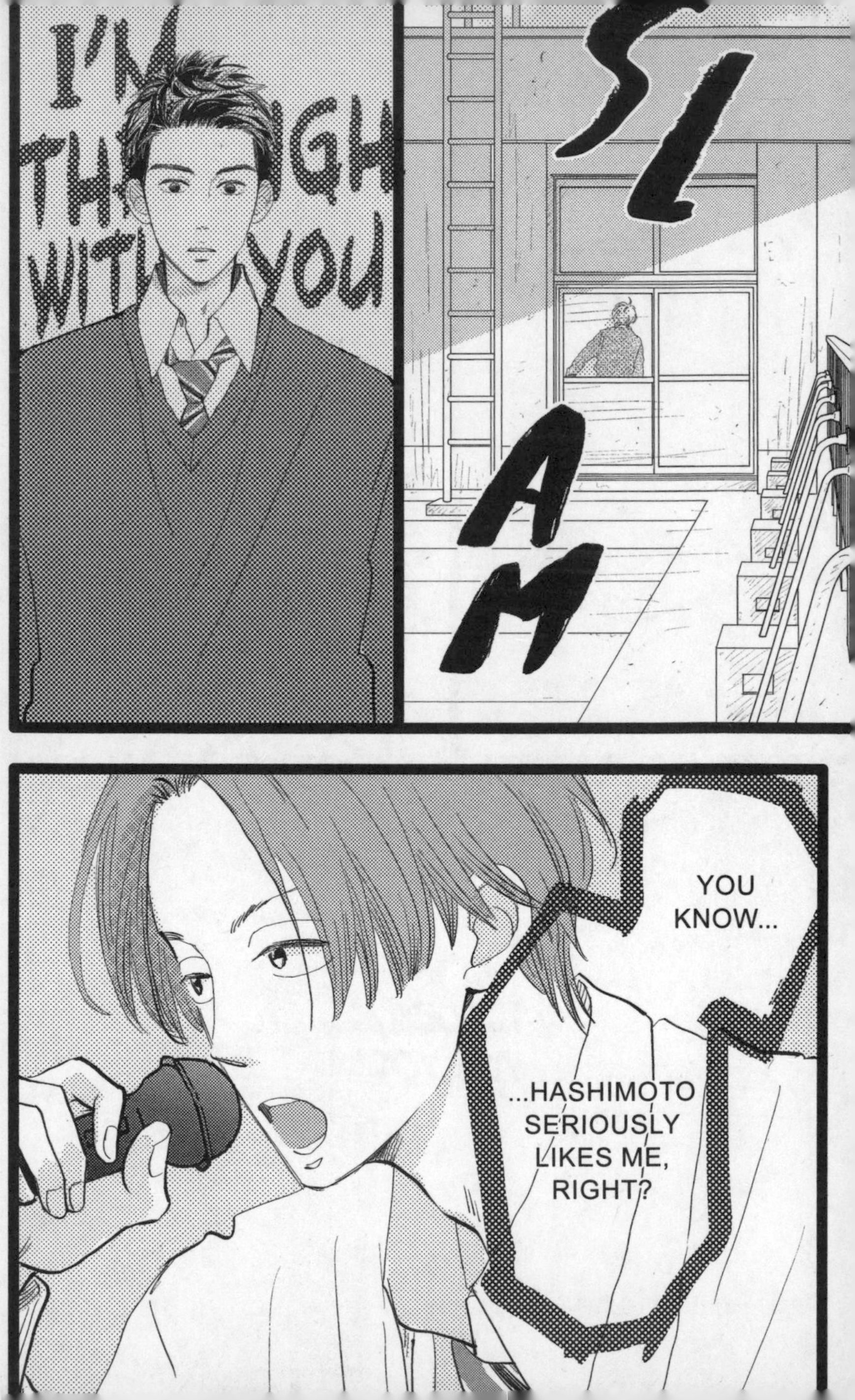
SLAM
I'M TH IGH WIT YOU
YOU KNOW...
...HASHIMOTO SERIOUSLY LIKES ME, RIGHT?

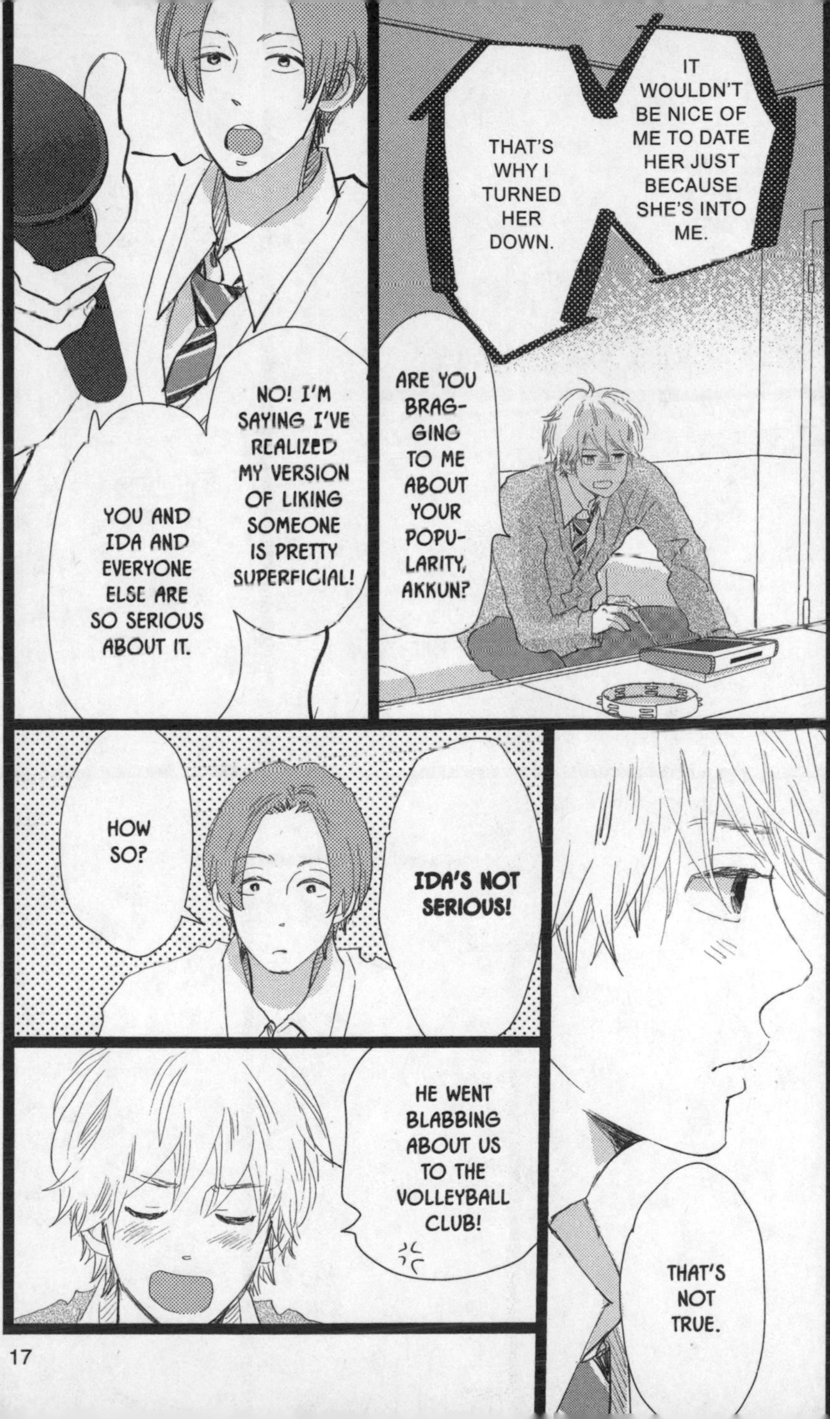
IT WOULDN'T BE NICE OF ME TO DATE HER JUST BECAUSE SHE'S INTO ME.
THAT'S WHY I TURNED HER DOWN.
ARE YOU BRAG-GING TO ME ABOUT YOUR POPU-LARITY, AKKUN?
NO! I'M SAYING I'VE REALIZED MY VERSION OF LIKING SOMEONE IS PRETTY SUPERFICIAL!
YOU AND IDA AND EVERYONE ELSE ARE SO SERIOUS ABOUT IT.
THAT'S NOT TRUE.
IDA'S NOT SERIOUS!
HOW SO?
HE WENT BLABBING ABOUT US TO THE VOLLEYBALL CLUB!

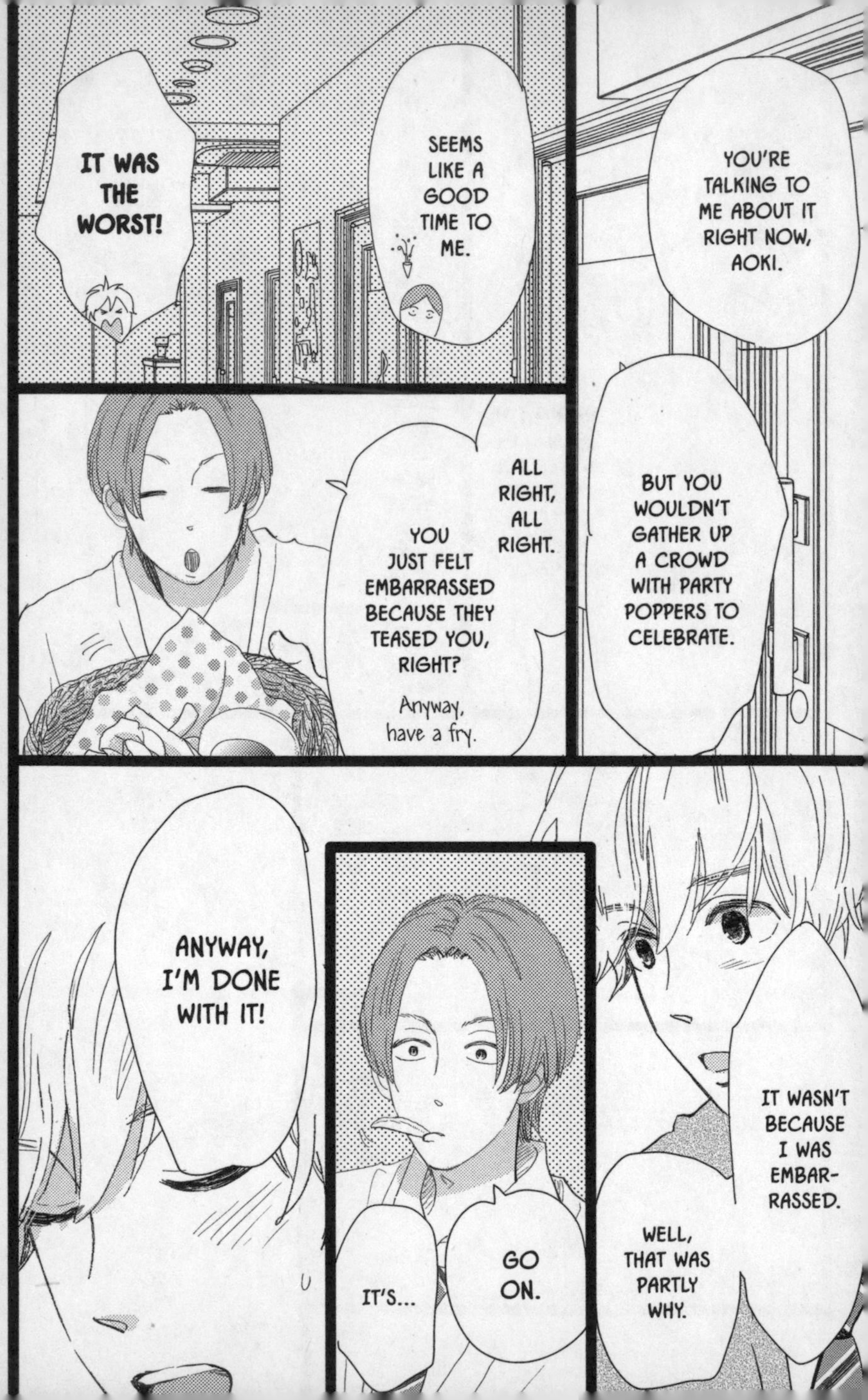
YOU'RE TALKING TO ME ABOUT IT RIGHT NOW, AOKI.
BUT YOU WOULDN'T GATHER UP A CROWD WITH PARTY POPPERS TO CELEBRATE.
SEEMS LIKE A GOOD TIME TO ME.
IT WAS THE WORST!
ALL RIGHT, ALL RIGHT.
YOU JUST FELT EMBARRASSED BECAUSE THEY TEASED YOU, RIGHT?
Anyway, have a fry.
IT WASN'T BECAUSE I WAS EMBAR-RASSED.
WELL, THAT WAS PARTLY WHY.
GO ON.
IT'S...
ANYWAY, I'M DONE WITH IT!

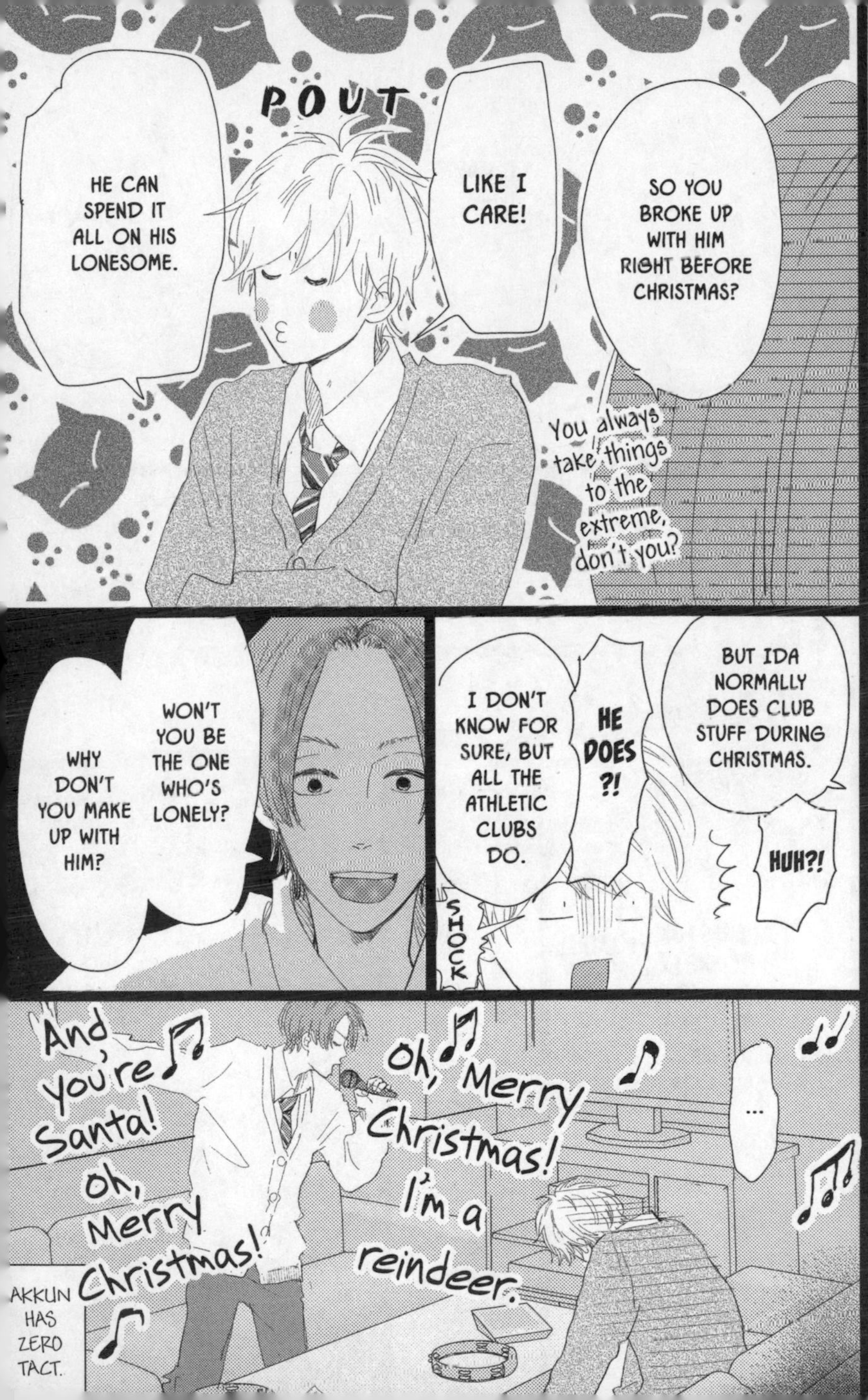
SO YOU BROKE UP WITH HIM RIGHT BEFORE CHRISTMAS?
You always take things to the extreme, don't you?
LIKE I CARE!
POUT
HE CAN SPEND IT ALL ON HIS LONESOME.
BUT IDA NORMALLY DOES CLUB STUFF DURING CHRISTMAS.
HUH?!
HE DOES?!
I DON'T KNOW FOR SURE, BUT ALL THE ATHLETIC CLUBS DO.
SHOCK
WON'T YOU BE THE ONE WHO'S LONELY?
WHY DON'T YOU MAKE UP WITH HIM?
...
Oh, Merry Christmas! I'm a reindeer.
And, you're Santa! Oh, Merry Christmas!
AKKUN HAS ZERO TACT.

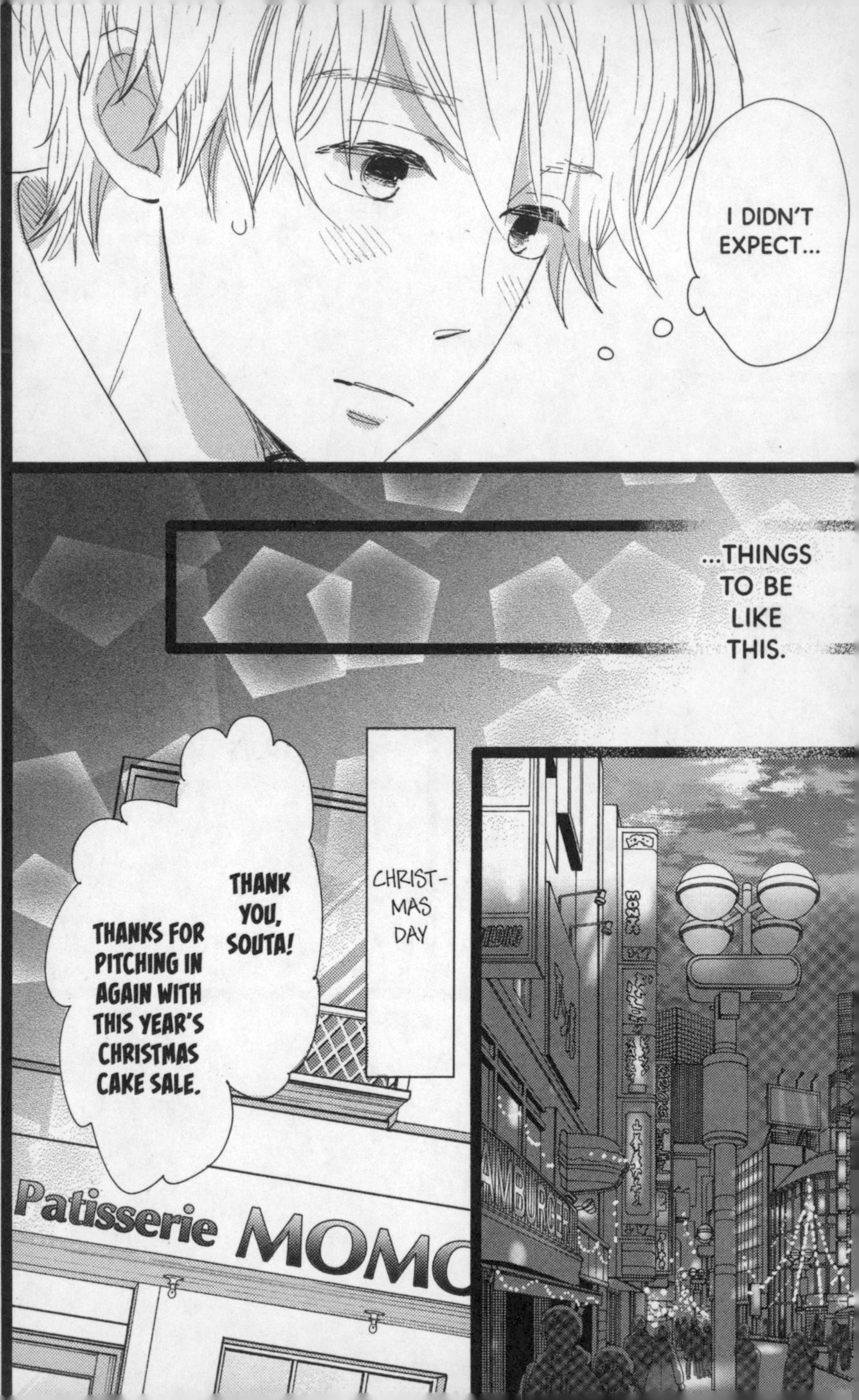
I DIDN'T EXPECT...
...THINGS TO BE LIKE THIS.
AMBURGER
CHRIST-MAS DAY
THANK YOU, SOUTA!
THANKS FOR PITCHING IN AGAIN WITH THIS YEAR'S CHRISTMAS CAKE SALE.
Patisserie MOM

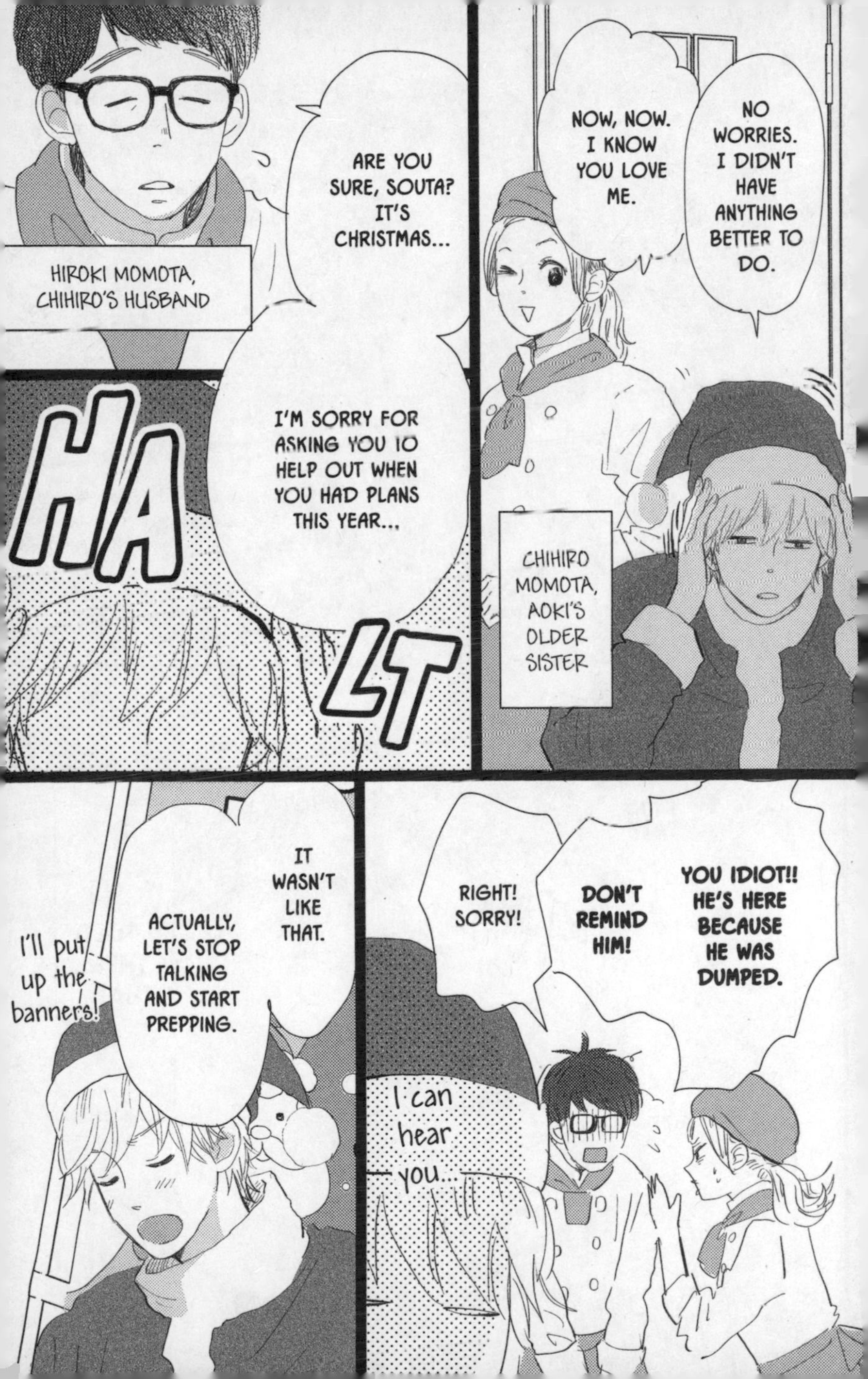
NO WORRIES. I DIDN'T HAVE ANYTHING BETTER TO DO.
NOW, NOW. I KNOW YOU LOVE ME.
CHIHIRO MOMOTA, AOKI'S OLDER SISTER
ARE YOU SURE, SOUTA? IT'S CHRISTMAS...
HIROKI MOMOTA, CHIHIRO'S HUSBAND
I'M SORRY FOR ASKING YOU TO HELP OUT WHEN YOU HAD PLANS THIS YEAR...
HALT
YOU IDIOT!! HE'S HERE BECAUSE HE WAS DUMPED.
DON'T REMIND HIM!
RIGHT! SORRY!
I can hear you...
IT WASN'T LIKE THAT.
ACTUALLY, LET'S STOP TALKING AND START PREPPING.
I'll put up the banners!

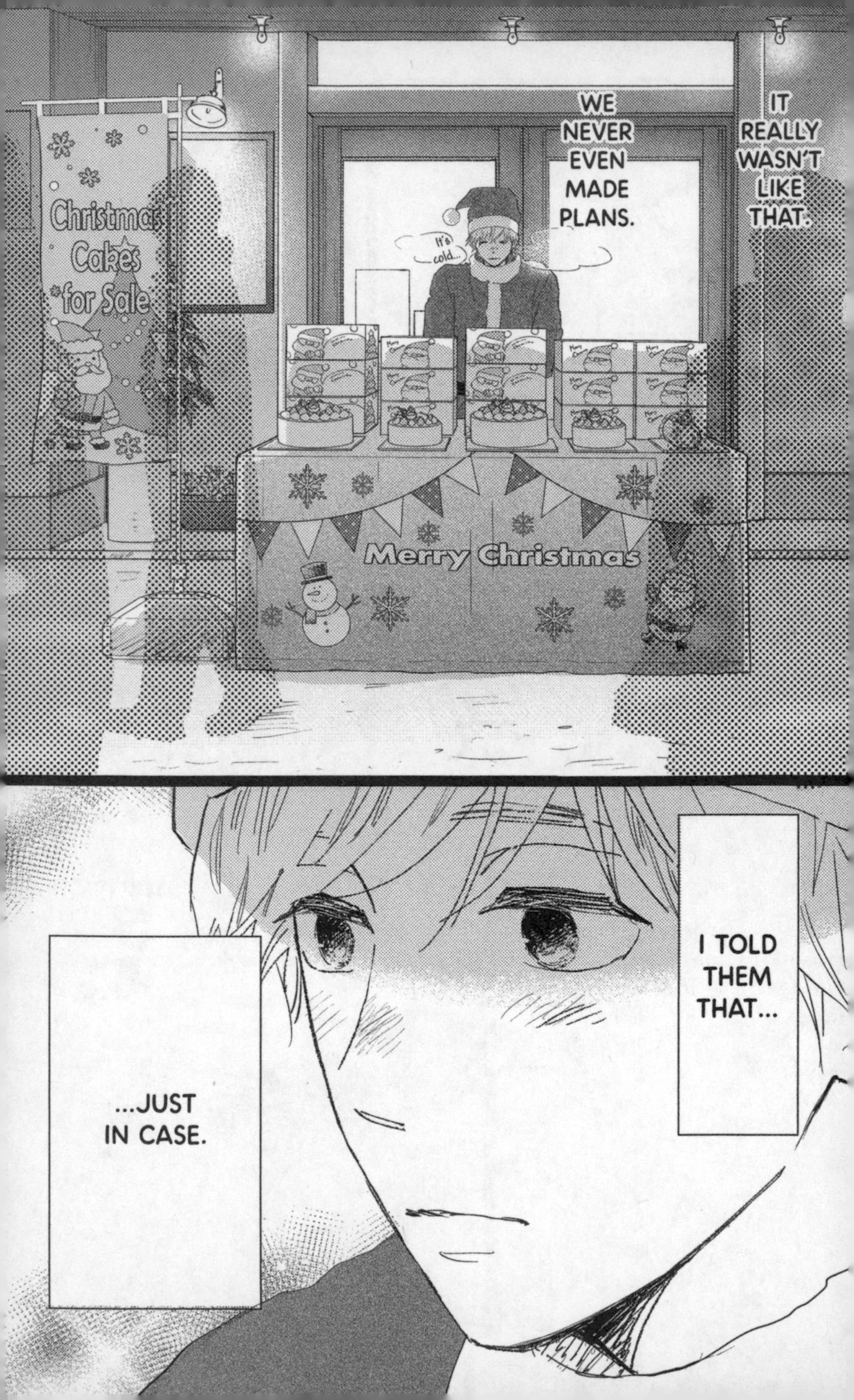
IT REALLY WASN'T LIKE THAT.
WE NEVER EVEN MADE PLANS.
It's cold...
Christmas Cakes for Sale
Merry Christmas
I TOLD THEM THAT...
...JUST IN CASE.

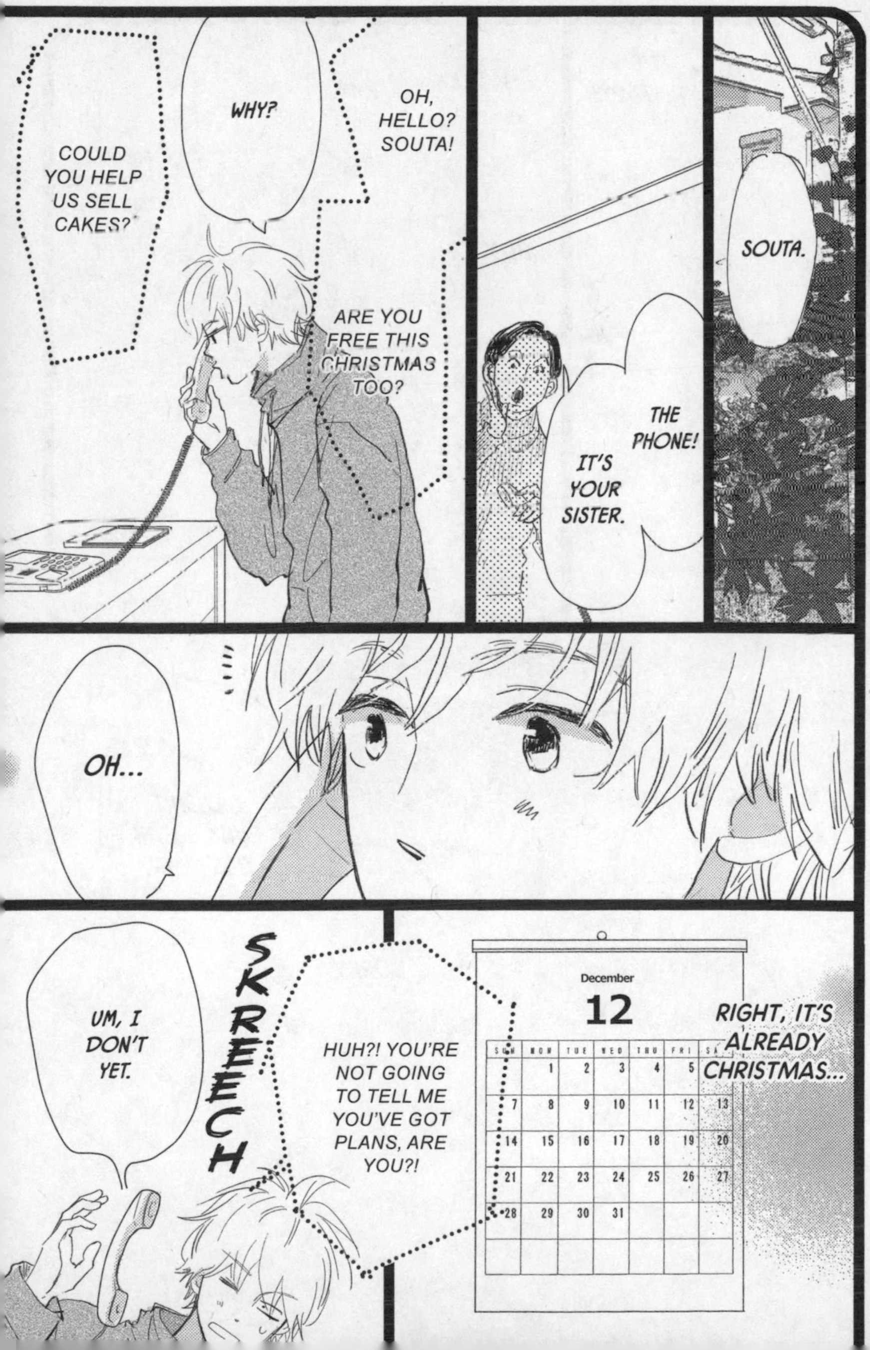
SOUTA.
THE PHONE!
IT'S YOUR SISTER.
OH, HELLO? SOUTA!
ARE YOU FREE THIS CHRISTMAS TOO?
WHY?
COULD YOU HELP US SELL CAKES?
OH...
RIGHT, IT'S ALREADY CHRISTMAS...
December
12
HUH?! YOU'RE NOT GOING TO TELL ME YOU'VE GOT PLANS, ARE YOU?!
SKREECH
UM, I DON'T YET.

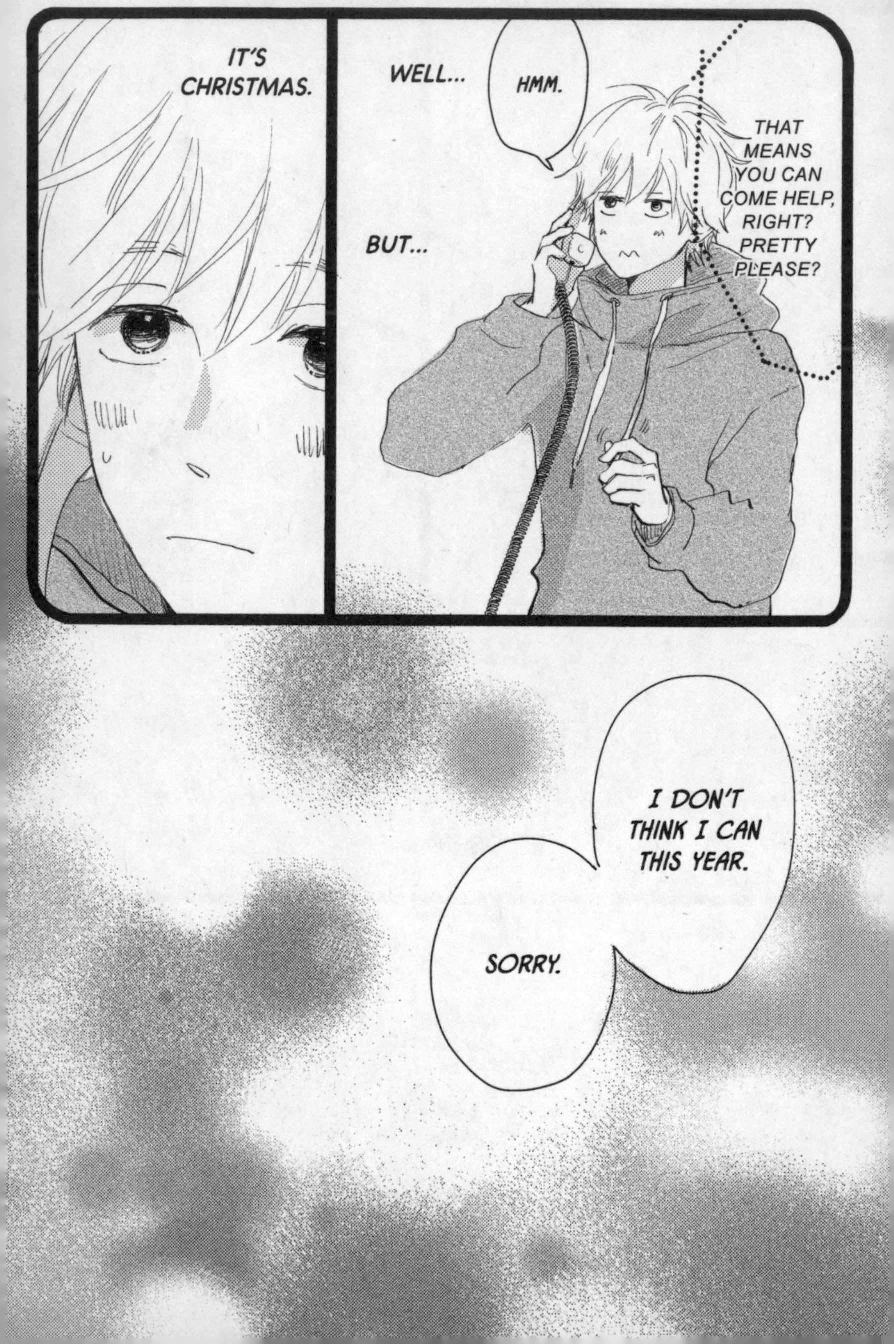
THAT MEANS YOU CAN COME HELP, RIGHT? PRETTY PLEASE?
HMM.
WELL...
BUT...
IT'S CHRISTMAS.
I DON'T THINK I CAN THIS YEAR.
SORRY.

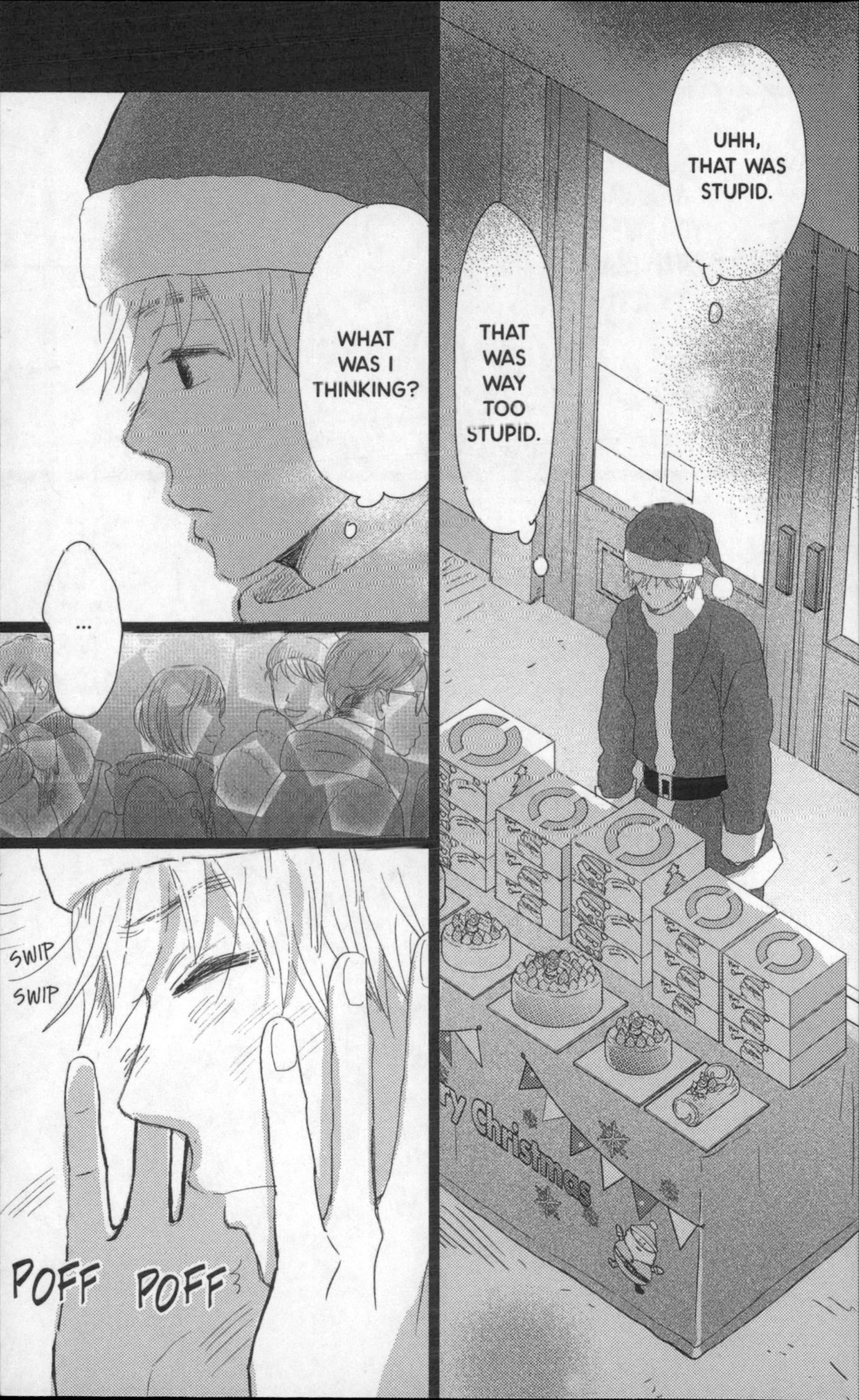
UHH, THAT WAS STUPID.
THAT WAS WAY TOO STUPID.
ry Christmas
WHAT WAS I THINKING?
...
SWIP
SWIP
POFF POFF

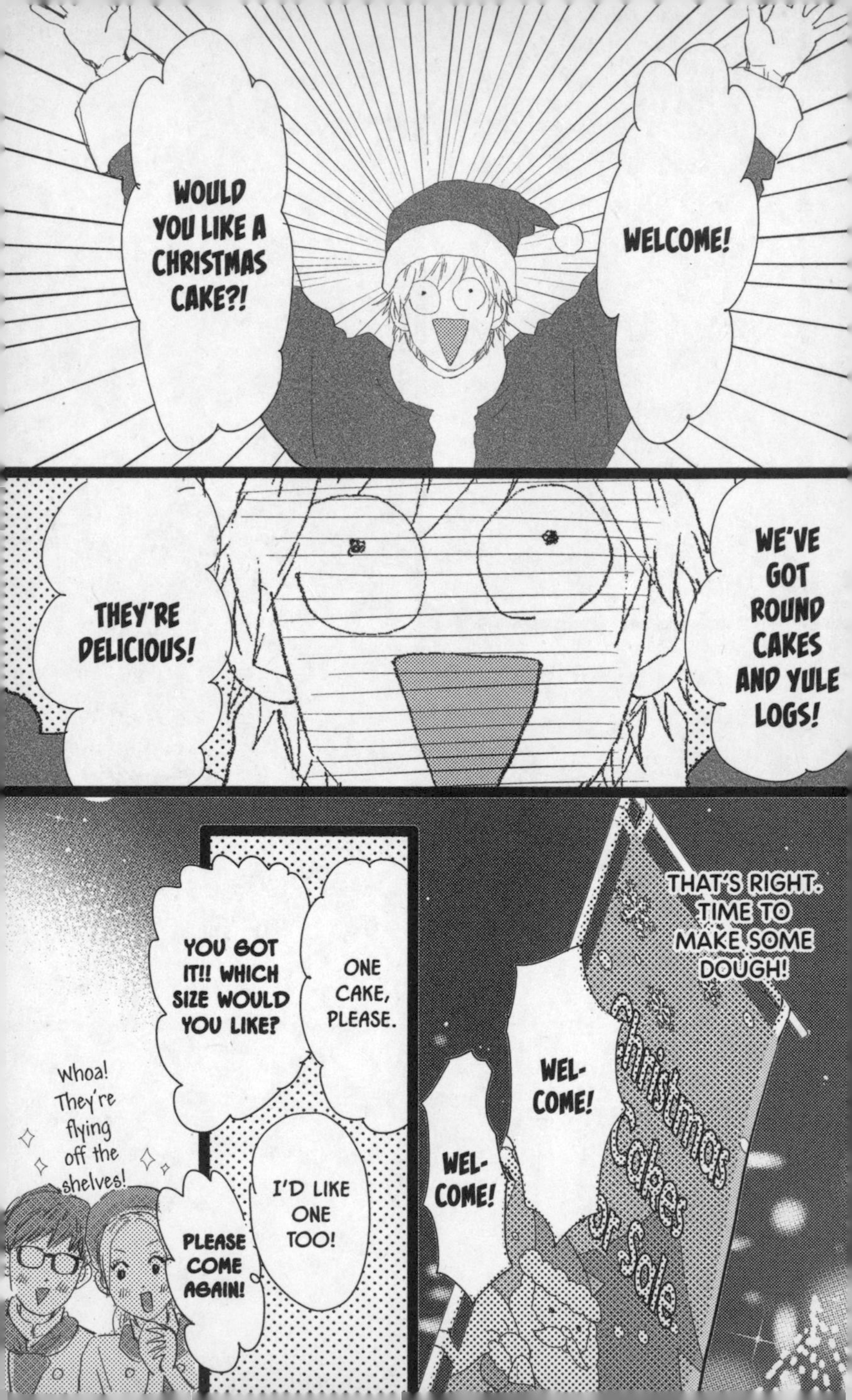
WELCOME!
WOULD YOU LIKE A CHRISTMAS CAKE?!
WE'VE GOT ROUND CAKES AND YULE LOGS!
THEY'RE DELICIOUS!
THAT'S RIGHT. TIME TO MAKE SOME DOUGH!
Christmas Cakes
r Sale
WEL-COME!
WEL-COME!
ONE CAKE, PLEASE.
YOU GOT IT!! WHICH SIZE WOULD YOU LIKE?
I'D LIKE ONE TOO!
PLEASE COME AGAIN!
Whoa! They're flying off the shelves!

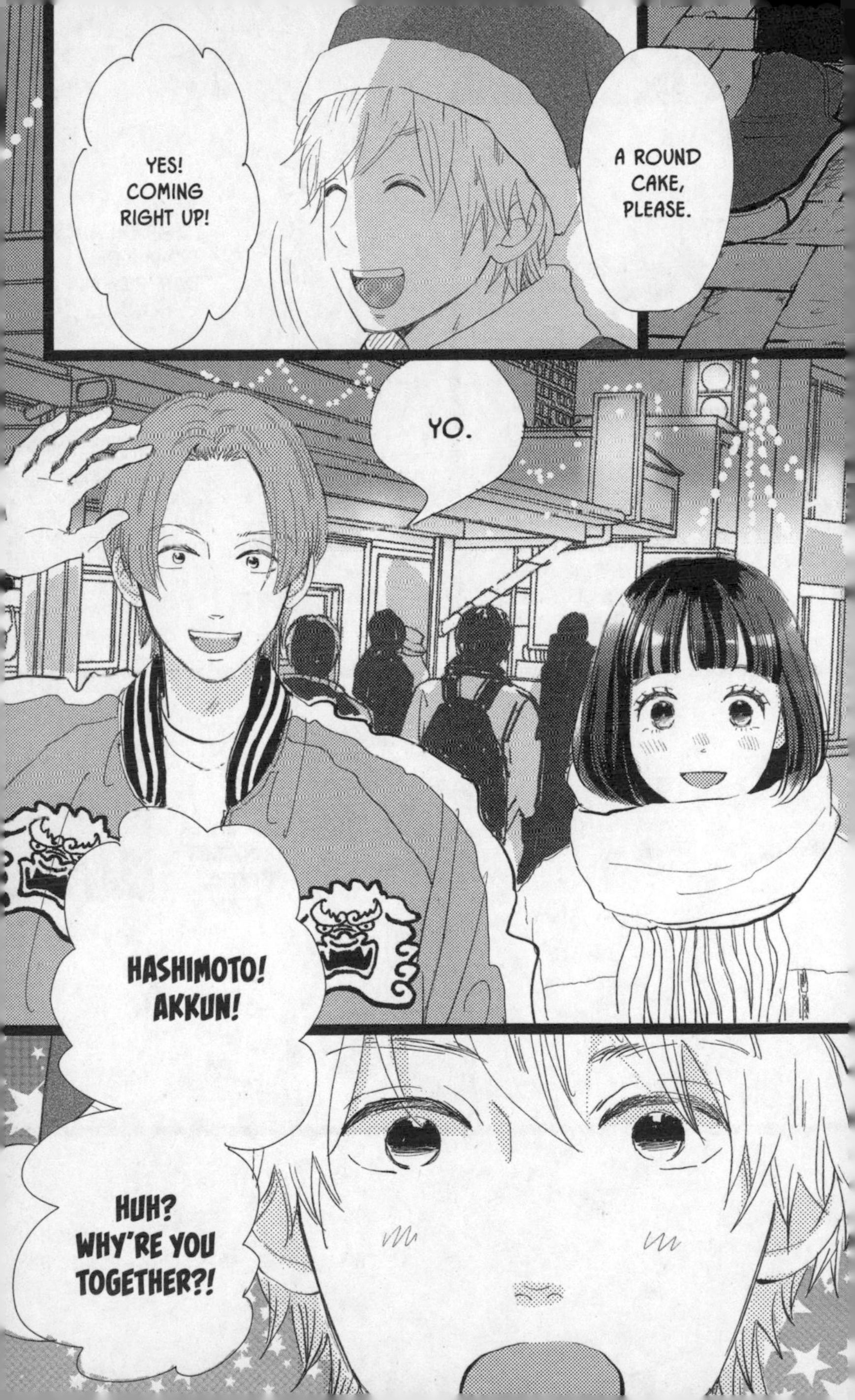
A ROUND CAKE, PLEASE.
YES! COMING RIGHT UP!
YO.
HASHIMOTO! AKKUN!
HUH? WHY'RE YOU TOGETHER?!

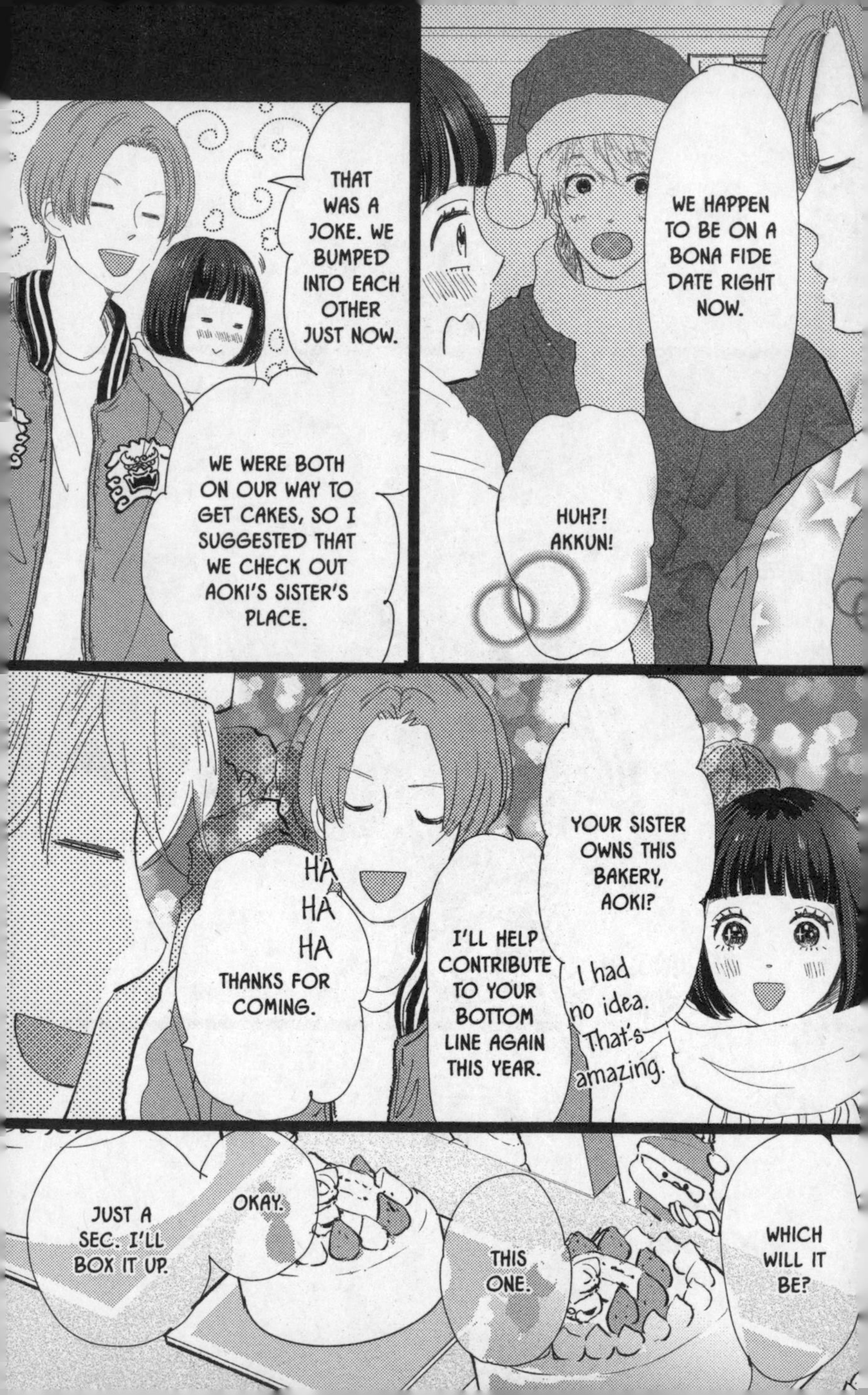
WE HAPPEN TO BE ON A BONA FIDE DATE RIGHT NOW.
HUH?! AKKUN!
THAT WAS A JOKE. WE BUMPED INTO EACH OTHER JUST NOW.
WE WERE BOTH ON OUR WAY TO GET CAKES, SO I SUGGESTED THAT WE CHECK OUT AOKI'S SISTER'S PLACE.
YOUR SISTER OWNS THIS BAKERY, AOKI?
I had no idea. That's amazing.
I'LL HELP CONTRIBUTE TO YOUR BOTTOM LINE AGAIN THIS YEAR.
HA HA HA
THANKS FOR COMING.
WHICH WILL IT BE?
THIS ONE.
OKAY.
JUST A SEC. I'LL BOX IT UP.

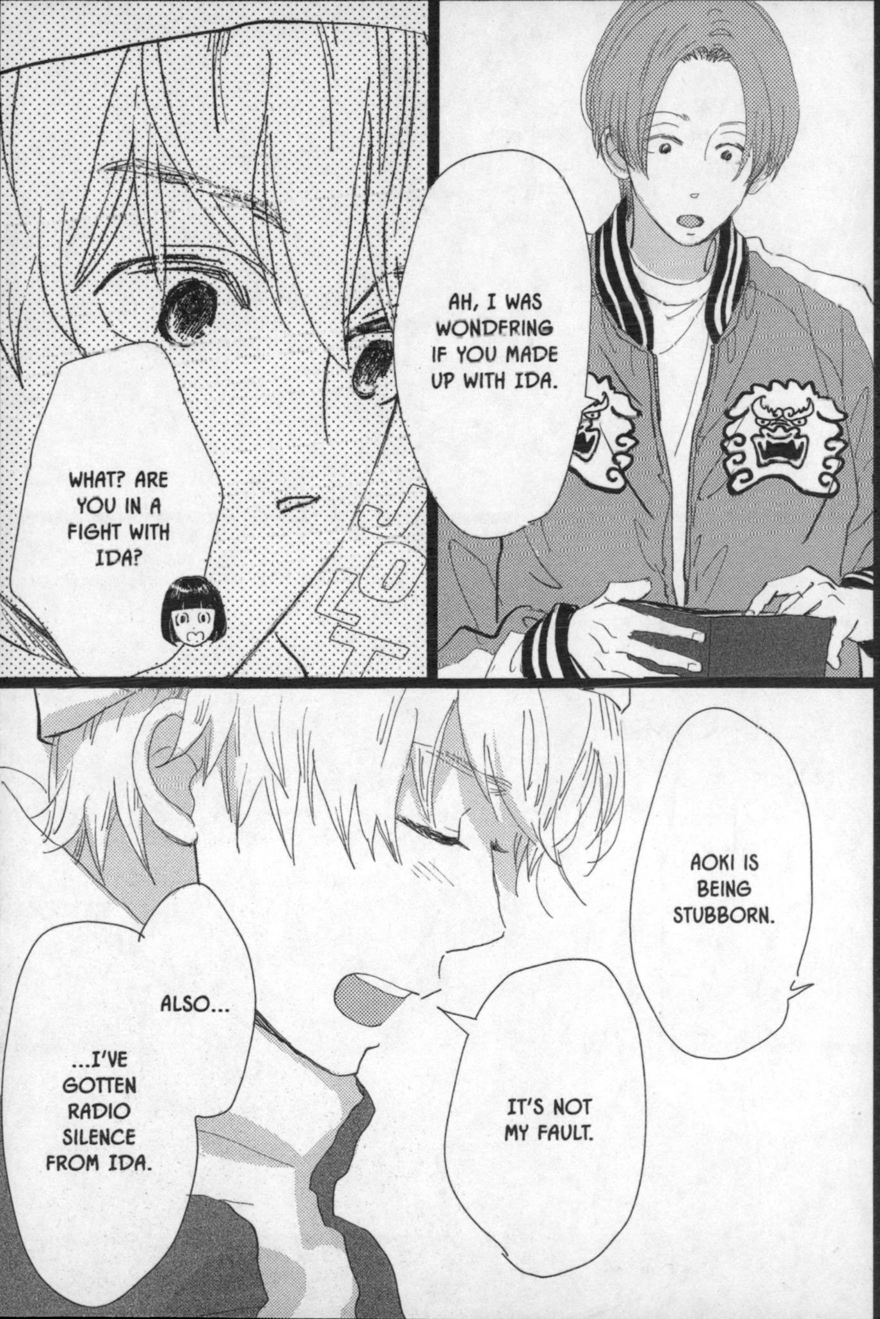
AH, I WAS WONDERING IF YOU MADE UP WITH IDA.
WHAT? ARE YOU IN A FIGHT WITH IDA?
AOKI IS BEING STUBBORN.
IT'S NOT MY FAULT.
ALSO...
...I'VE GOTTEN RADIO SILENCE FROM IDA.

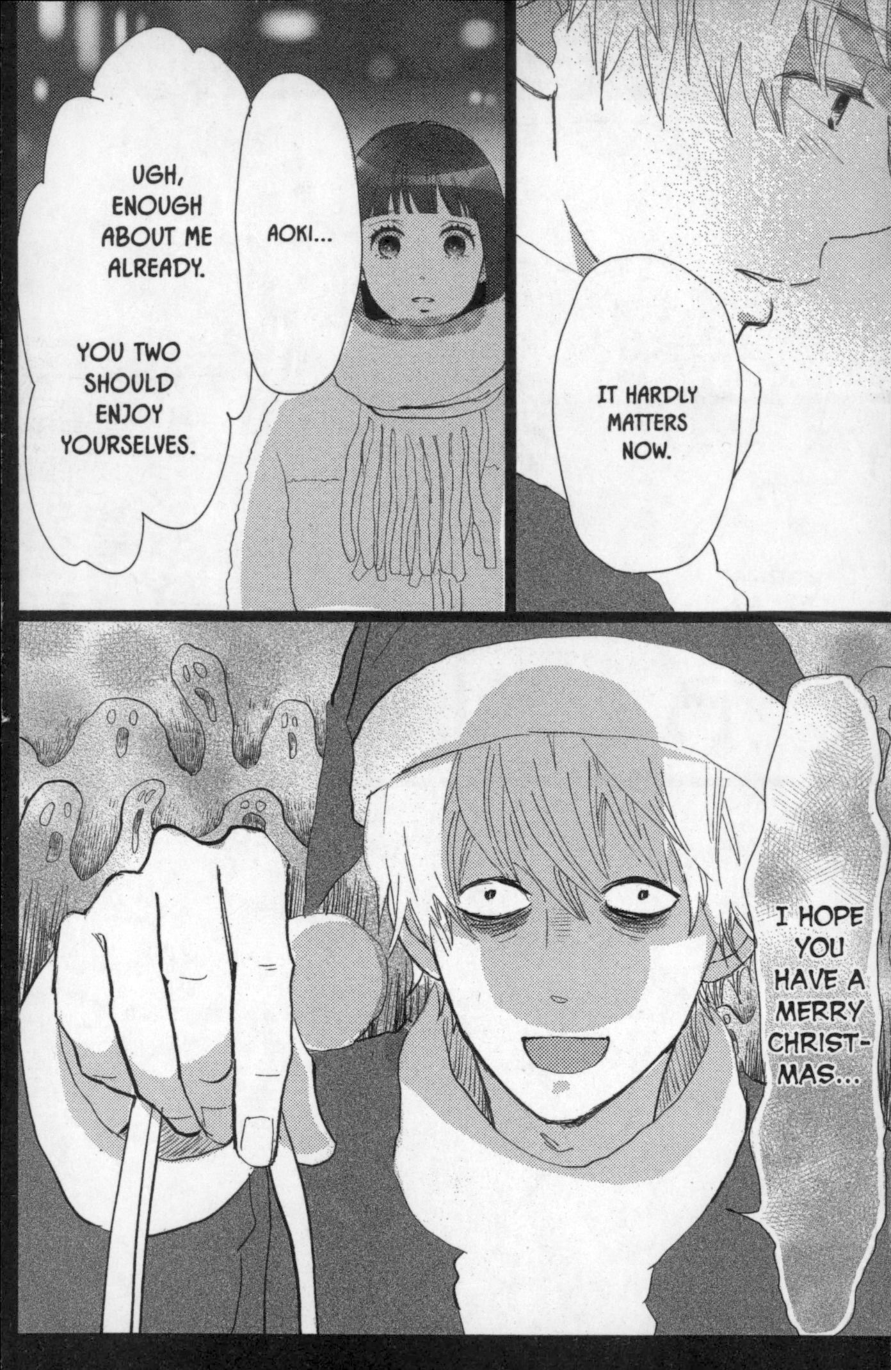
IT HARDLY MATTERS NOW.
AOKI...
UGH, ENOUGH ABOUT ME ALREADY.
YOU TWO SHOULD ENJOY YOURSELVES.
I HOPE YOU HAVE A MERRY CHRIST-MAS...

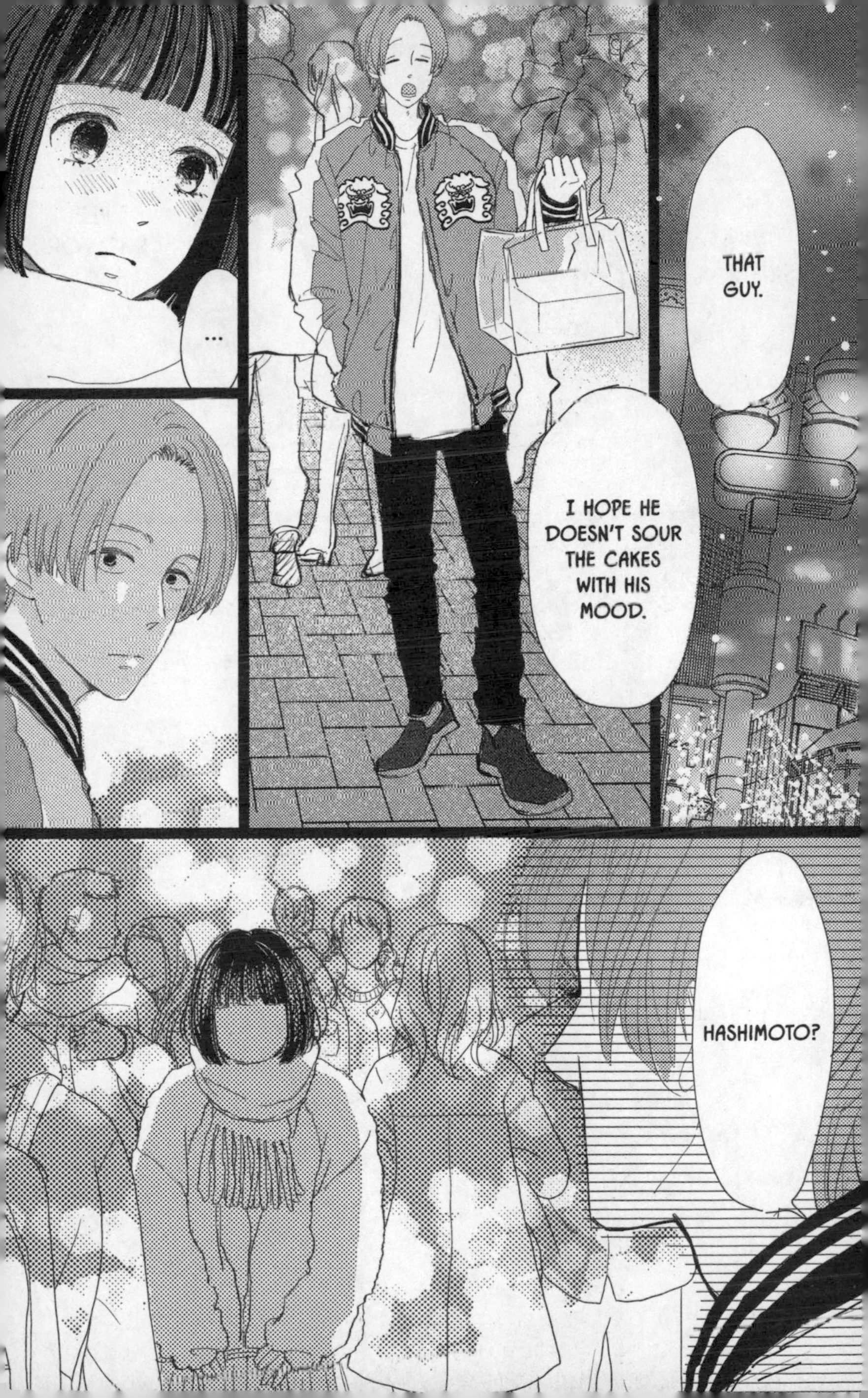
THAT GUY.
I HOPE HE DOESN'T SOUR THE CAKES WITH HIS MOOD.
...
HASHIMOTO?

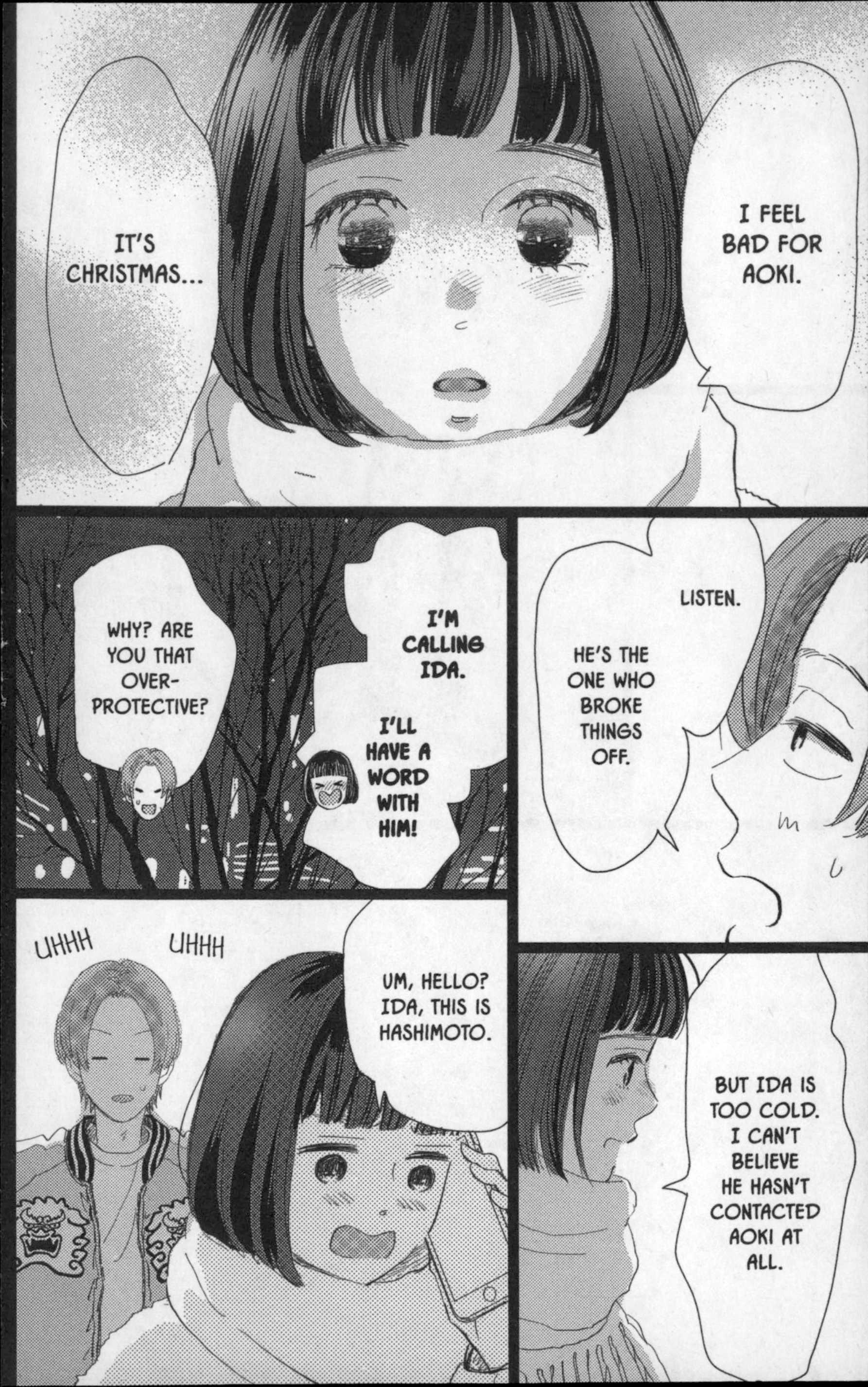
I FEEL BAD FOR AOKI.
IT'S CHRISTMAS...
LISTEN.
HE'S THE ONE WHO BROKE THINGS OFF.
BUT IDA IS TOO COLD. I CAN'T BELIEVE HE HASN'T CONTACTED AOKI AT ALL.
I'M CALLING IDA.
I'LL HAVE A WORD WITH HIM!
WHY? ARE YOU THAT OVER-PROTECTIVE?
UM, HELLO? IDA, THIS IS HASHIMOTO.
UHHH
UHHH

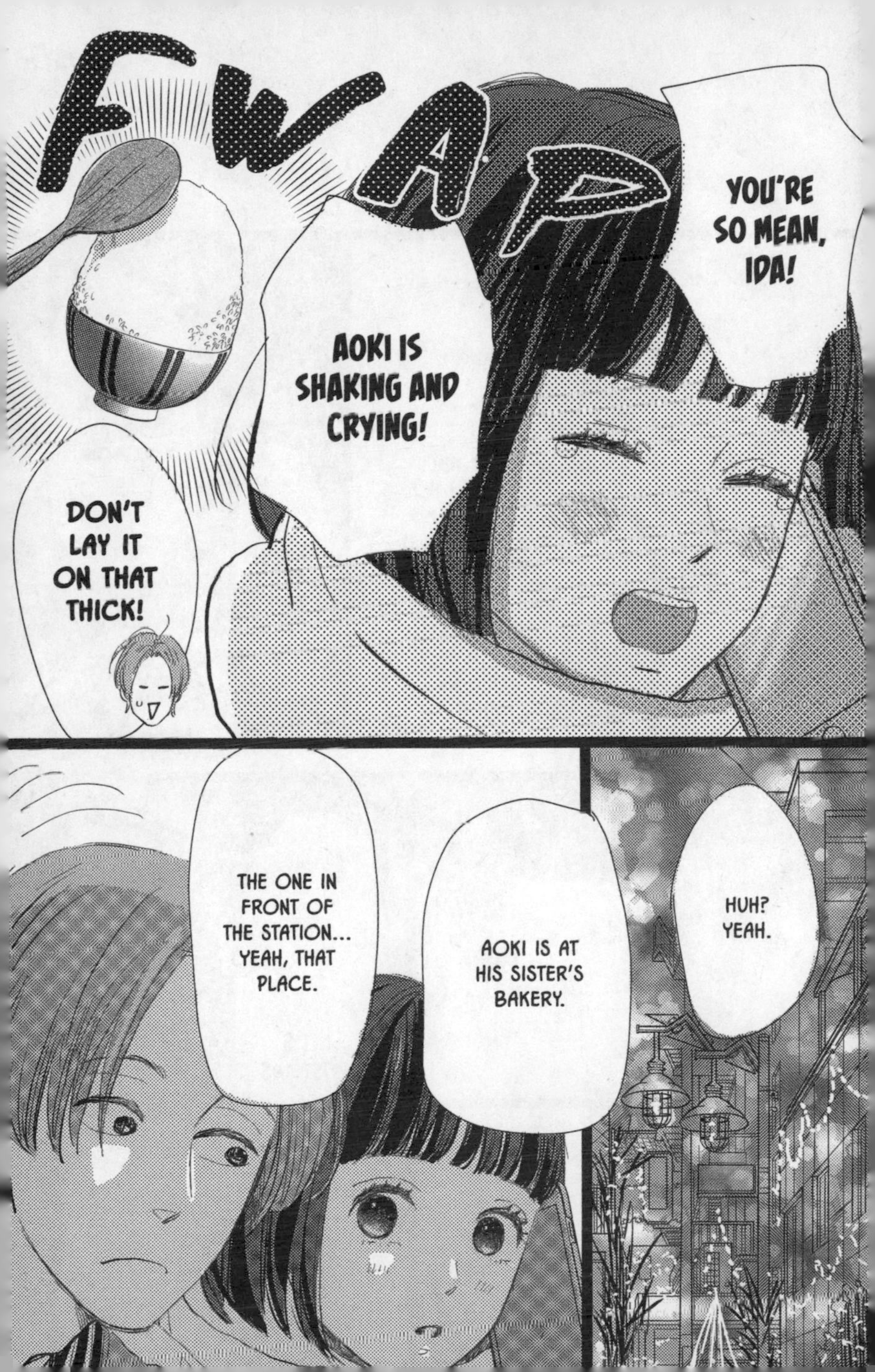
FWAP
YOU'RE SO MEAN, IDA!
AOKI IS SHAKING AND CRYING!
DON'T LAY IT ON THAT THICK!
HUH? YEAH.
AOKI IS AT HIS SISTER'S BAKERY.
THE ONE IN FRONT OF THE STATION... YEAH, THAT PLACE.

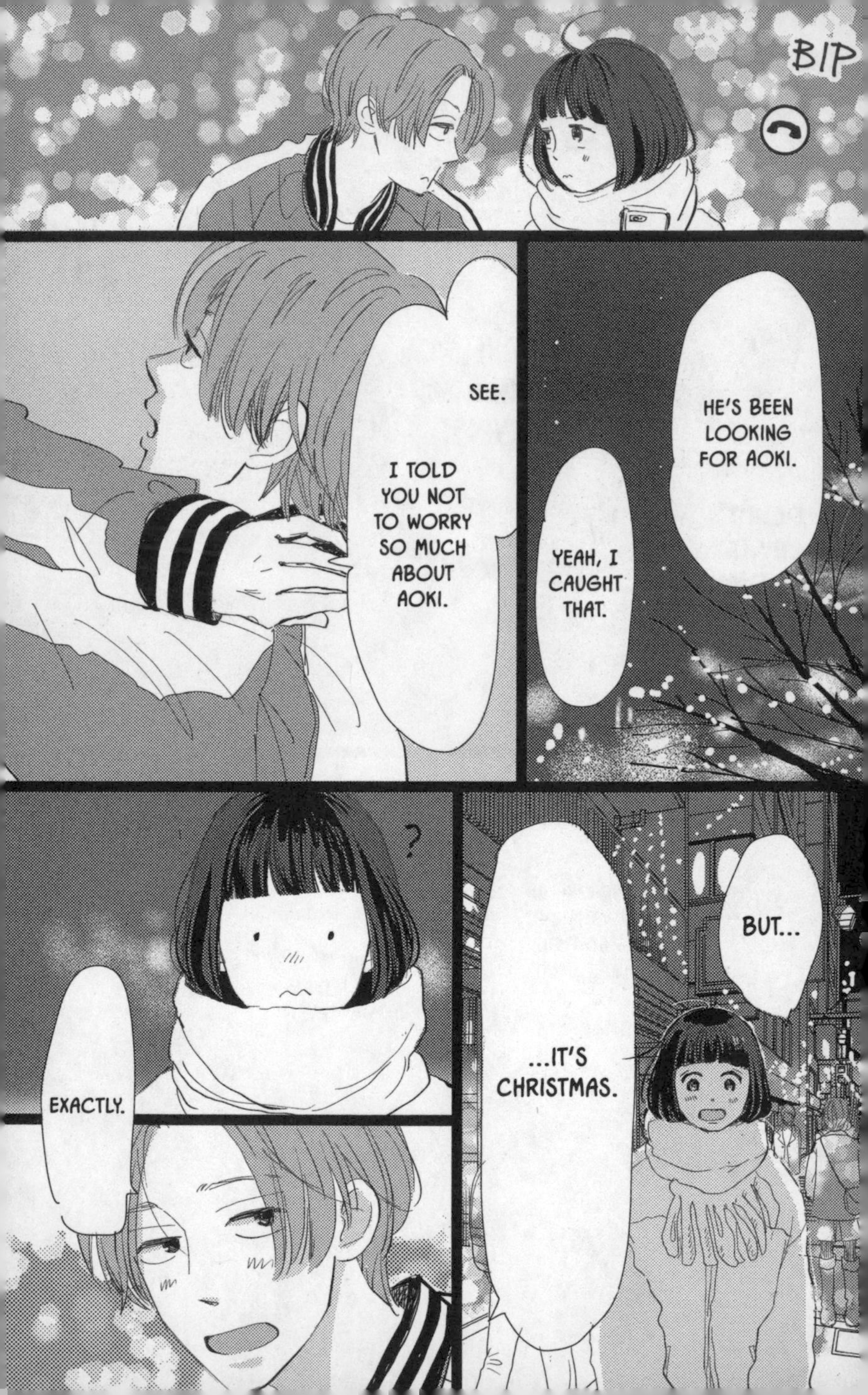
BIP
HE'S BEEN LOOKING FOR AOKI.
YEAH, I CAUGHT THAT.
SEE.
I TOLD YOU NOT TO WORRY SO MUCH ABOUT AOKI.
BUT...
...IT'S CHRISTMAS.
?
EXACTLY.

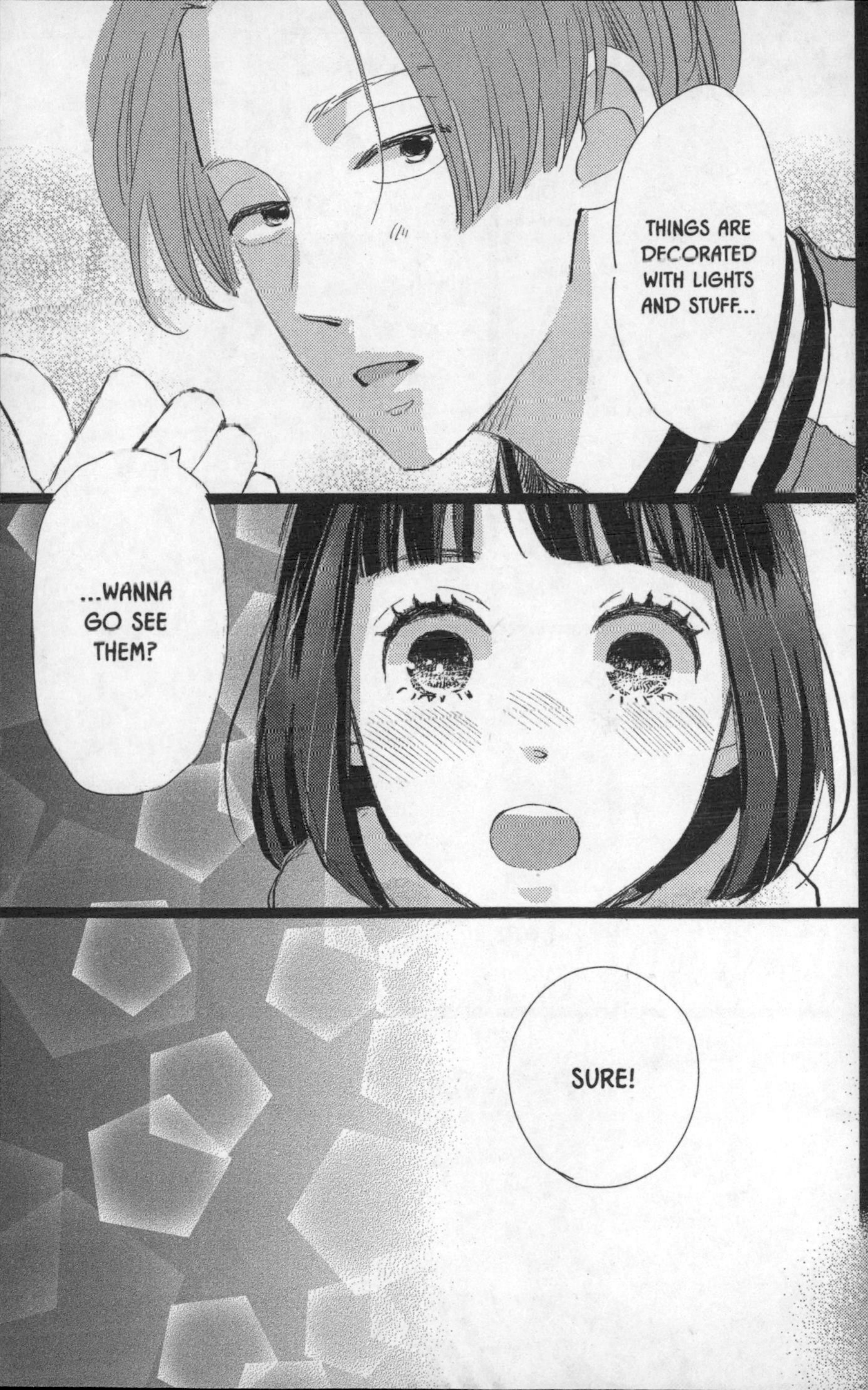
THINGS ARE DECORATED WITH LIGHTS AND STUFF...
...WANNA GO SEE THEM?
SURE!

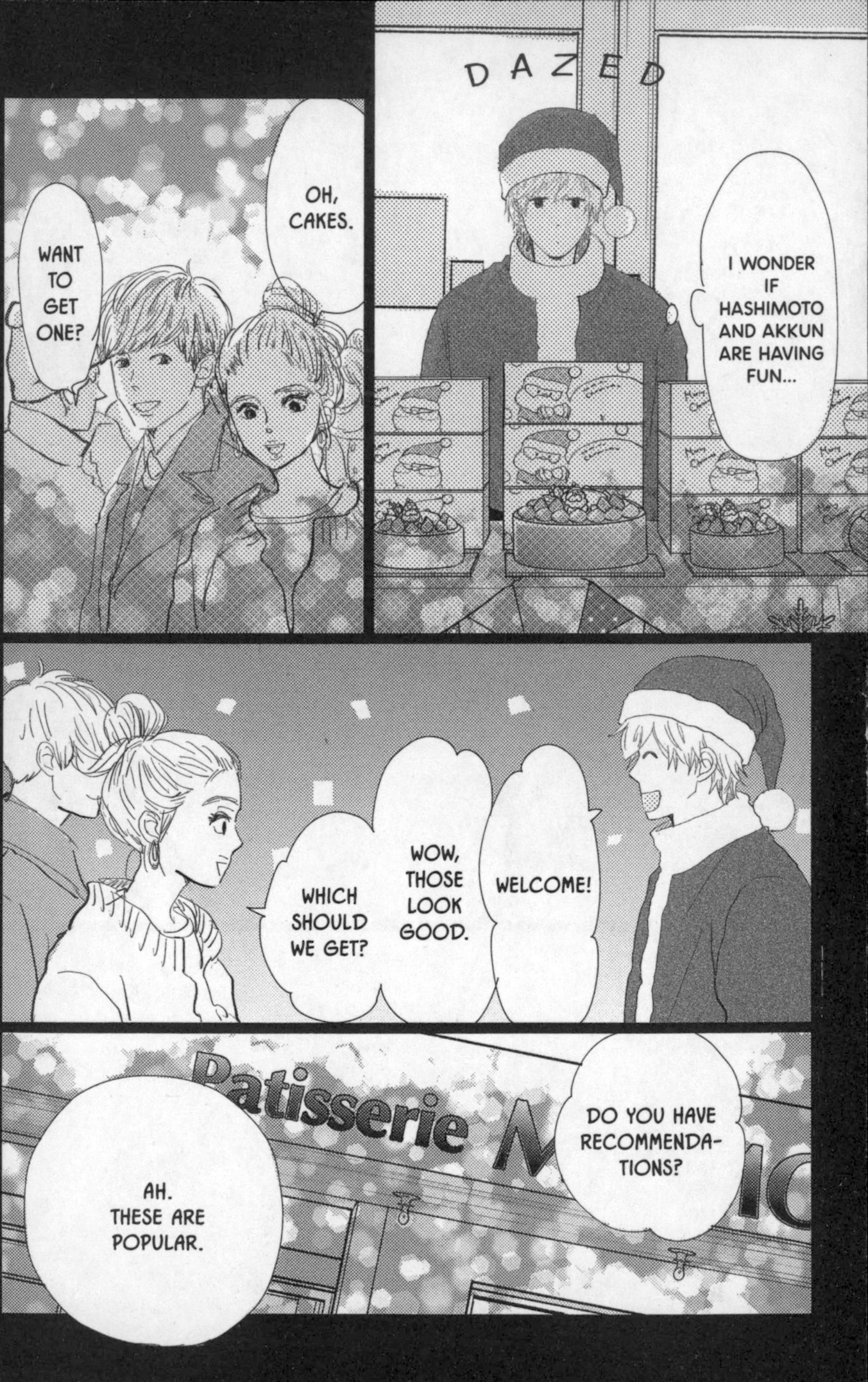
DAZED
I WONDER IF HASHIMOTO AND AKKUN ARE HAVING FUN...
OH, CAKES.
WANT TO GET ONE?
WELCOME!
WOW, THOSE LOOK GOOD.
WHICH SHOULD WE GET?
DO YOU HAVE RECOMMENDA-TIONS?
Patisserie
AH. THESE ARE POPULAR.

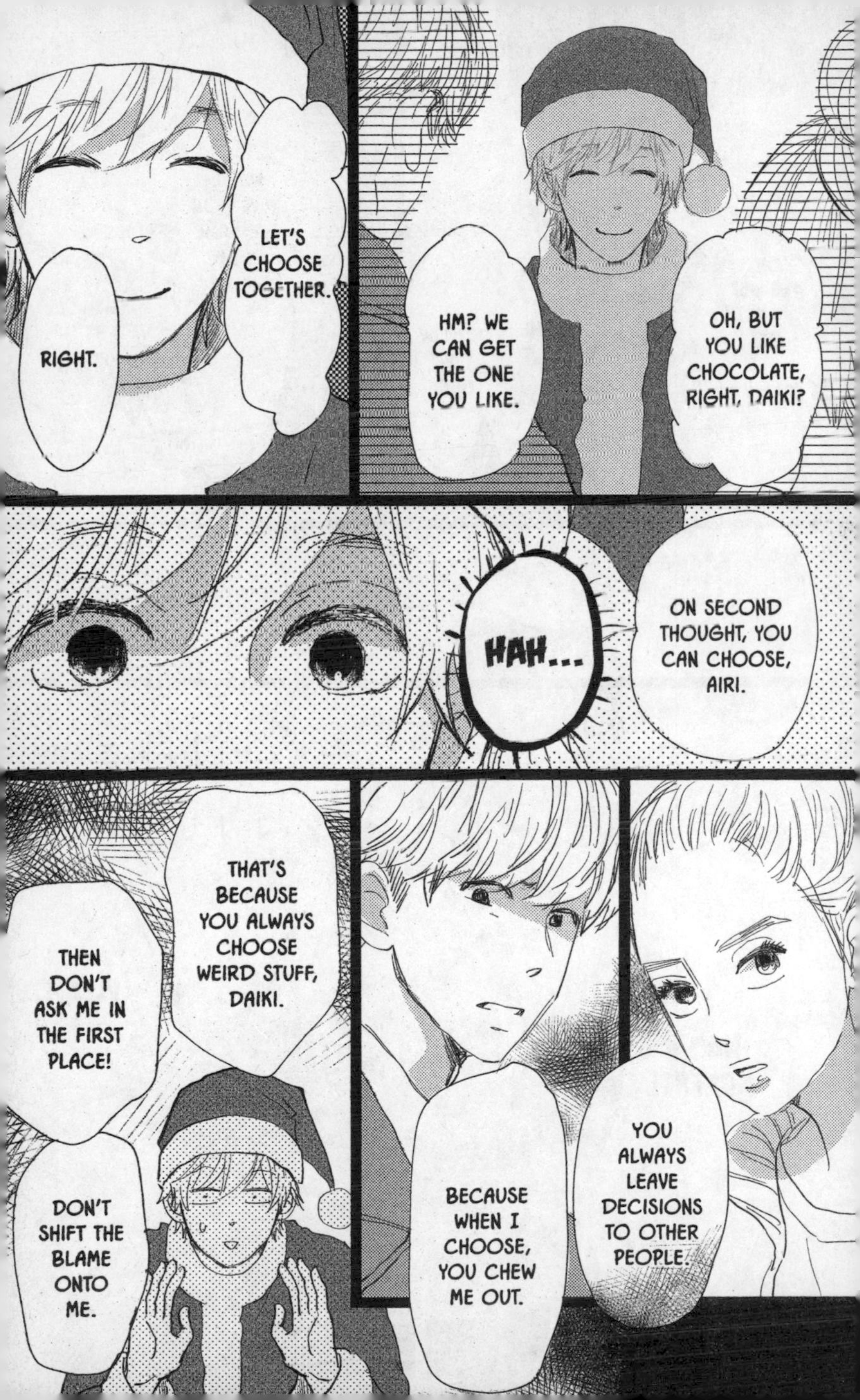
OH, BUT YOU LIKE CHOCOLATE, RIGHT, DAIKI?
HM? WE CAN GET THE ONE YOU LIKE.
LET'S CHOOSE TOGETHER.
RIGHT.
ON SECOND THOUGHT, YOU CAN CHOOSE, AIRI.
HAH...
YOU ALWAYS LEAVE DECISIONS TO OTHER PEOPLE.
BECAUSE WHEN I CHOOSE, YOU CHEW ME OUT.
THAT'S BECAUSE YOU ALWAYS CHOOSE WEIRD STUFF, DAIKI.
THEN DON'T ASK ME IN THE FIRST PLACE!
DON'T SHIFT THE BLAME ONTO ME.

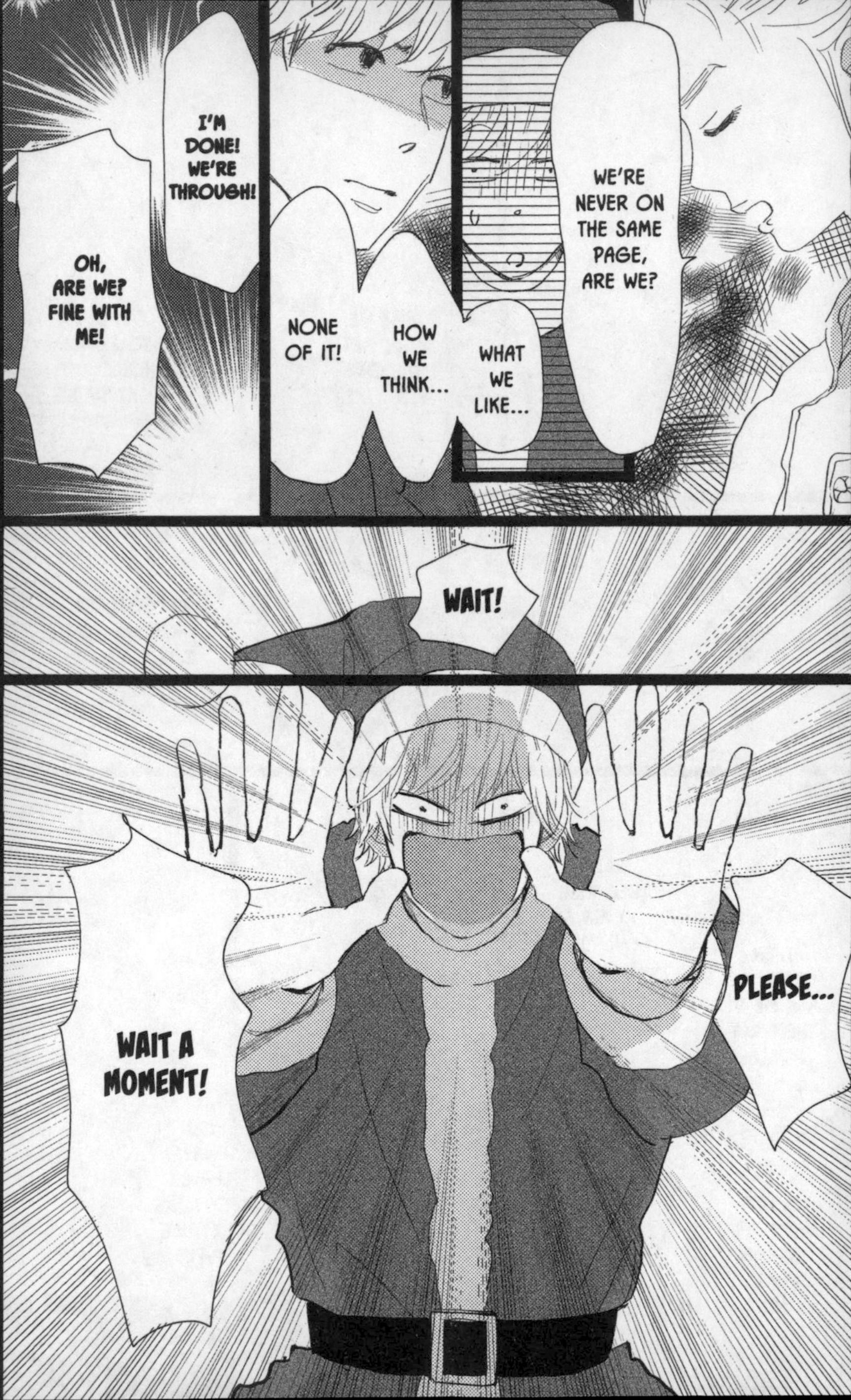
WE'RE NEVER ON THE SAME PAGE, ARE WE?
WHAT WE LIKE...
HOW WE THINK...
NONE OF IT!
I'M DONE! WE'RE THROUGH!
OH, ARE WE? FINE WITH ME!
WAIT!
PLEASE...
WAIT A MOMENT!

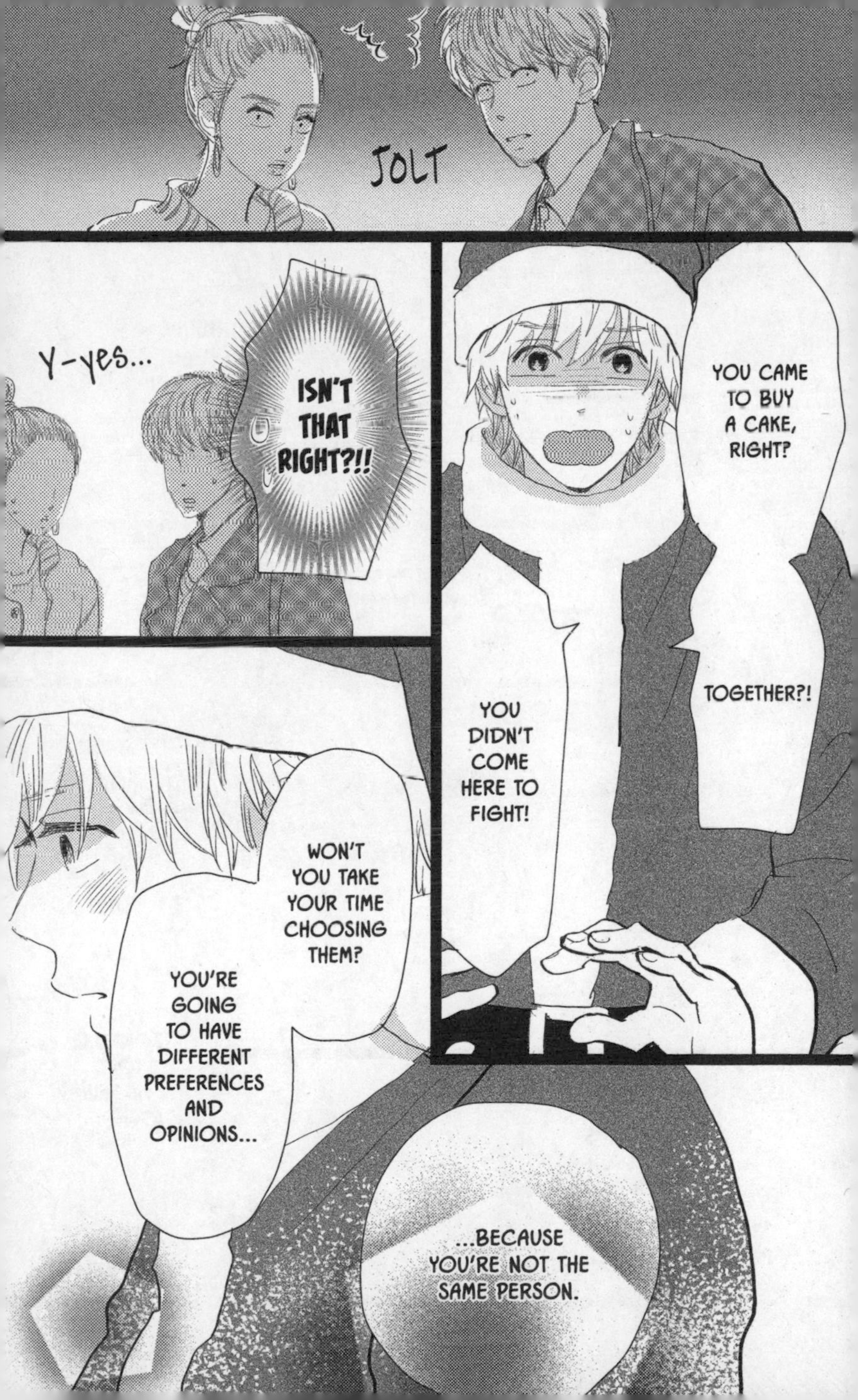
JOLT
YOU CAME TO BUY A CAKE, RIGHT?
TOGETHER?!
YOU DIDN'T COME HERE TO FIGHT!
ISN'T THAT RIGHT?!!
Y-yes...
WON'T YOU TAKE YOUR TIME CHOOSING THEM?
YOU'RE GOING TO HAVE DIFFERENT PREFERENCES AND OPINIONS...
...BECAUSE YOU'RE NOT THE SAME PERSON.

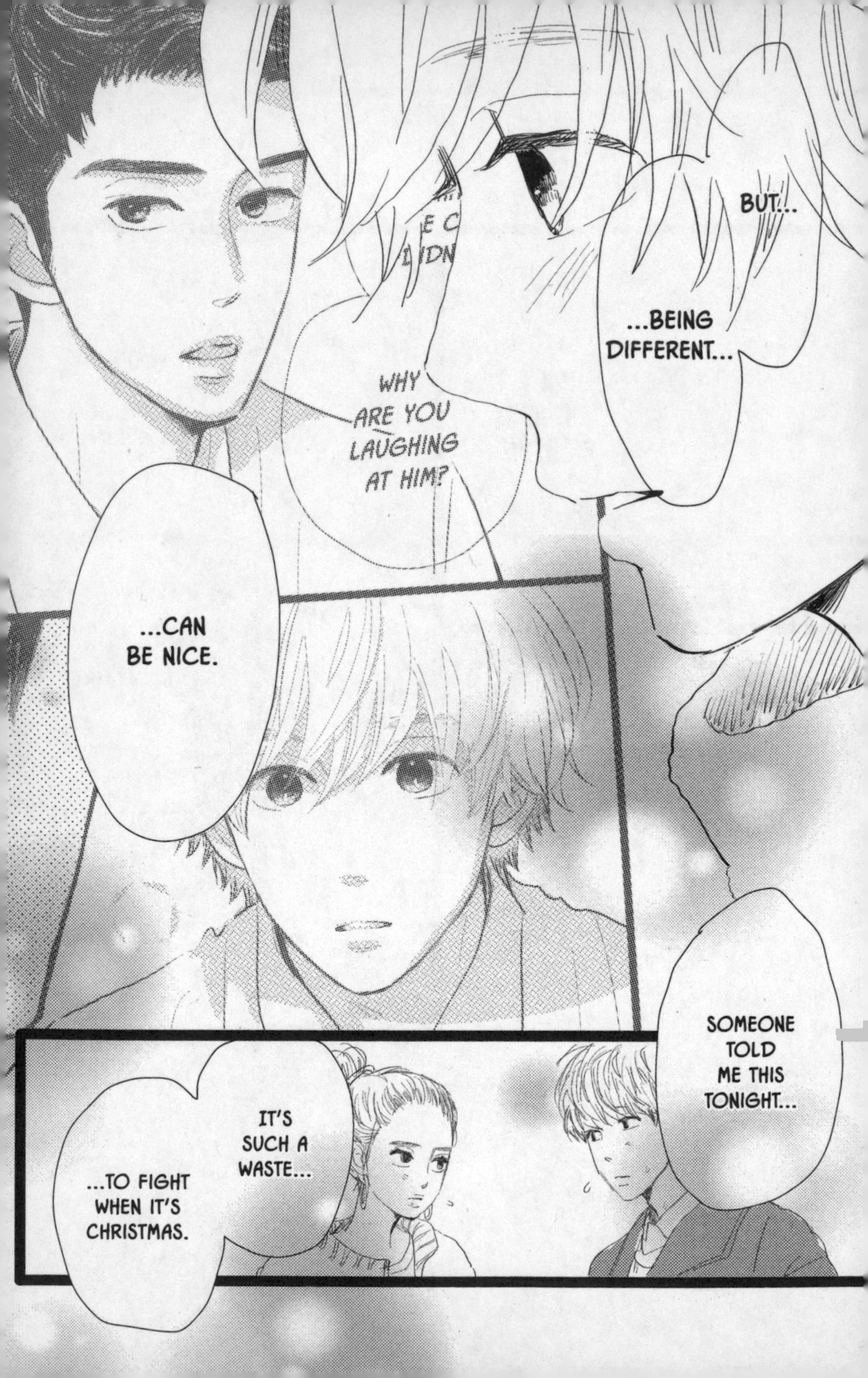
BUT...
...BEING DIFFERENT...
WHY ARE YOU LAUGHING AT HIM?
...CAN BE NICE.
SOMEONE TOLD ME THIS TONIGHT...
IT'S SUCH A WASTE...
...TO FIGHT WHEN IT'S CHRISTMAS.

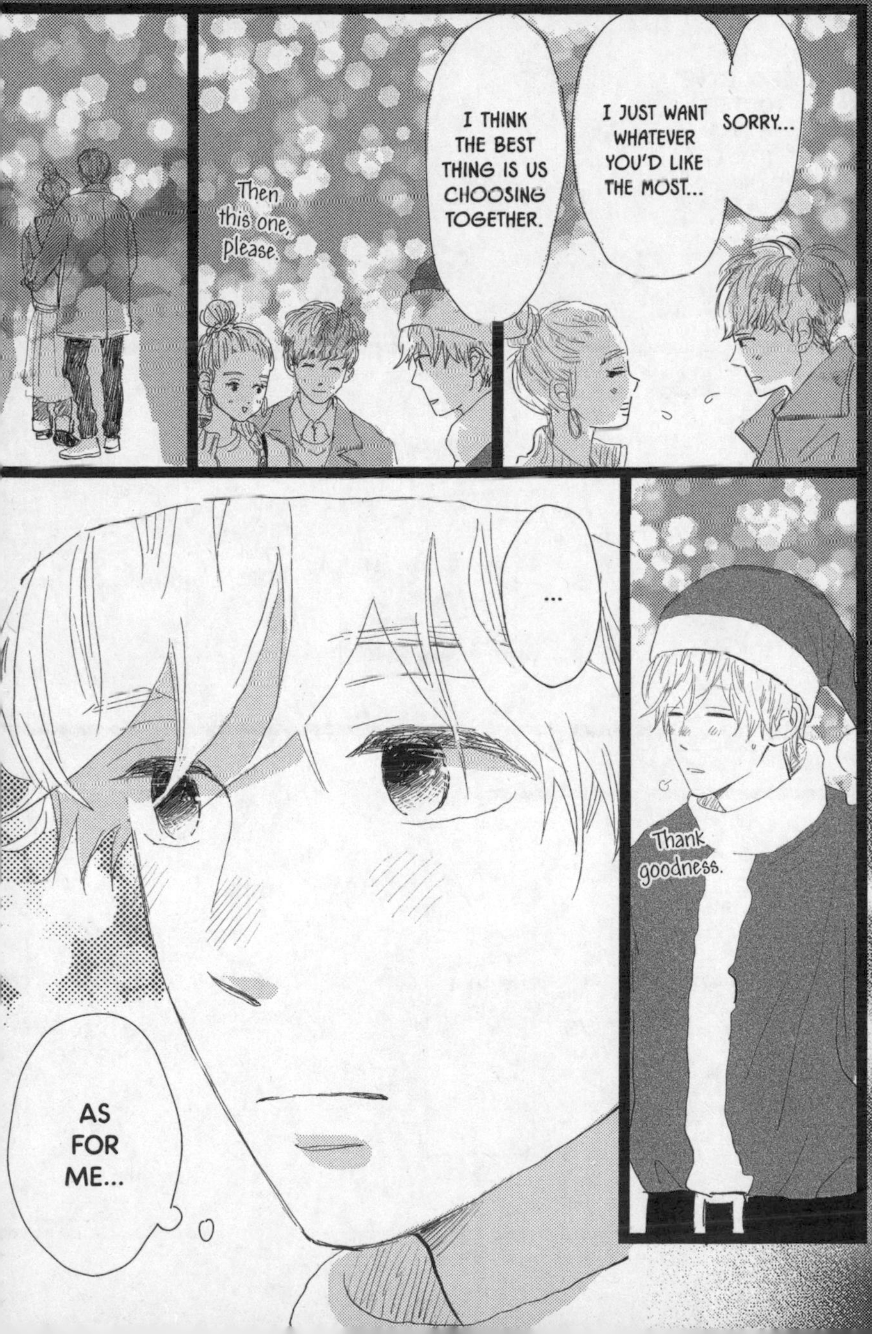
SORRY...
I JUST WANT WHATEVER YOU'D LIKE THE MOST...
I THINK THE BEST THING IS US CHOOSING TOGETHER.
Then this one, please.
Thank goodness.
...
AS FOR ME...

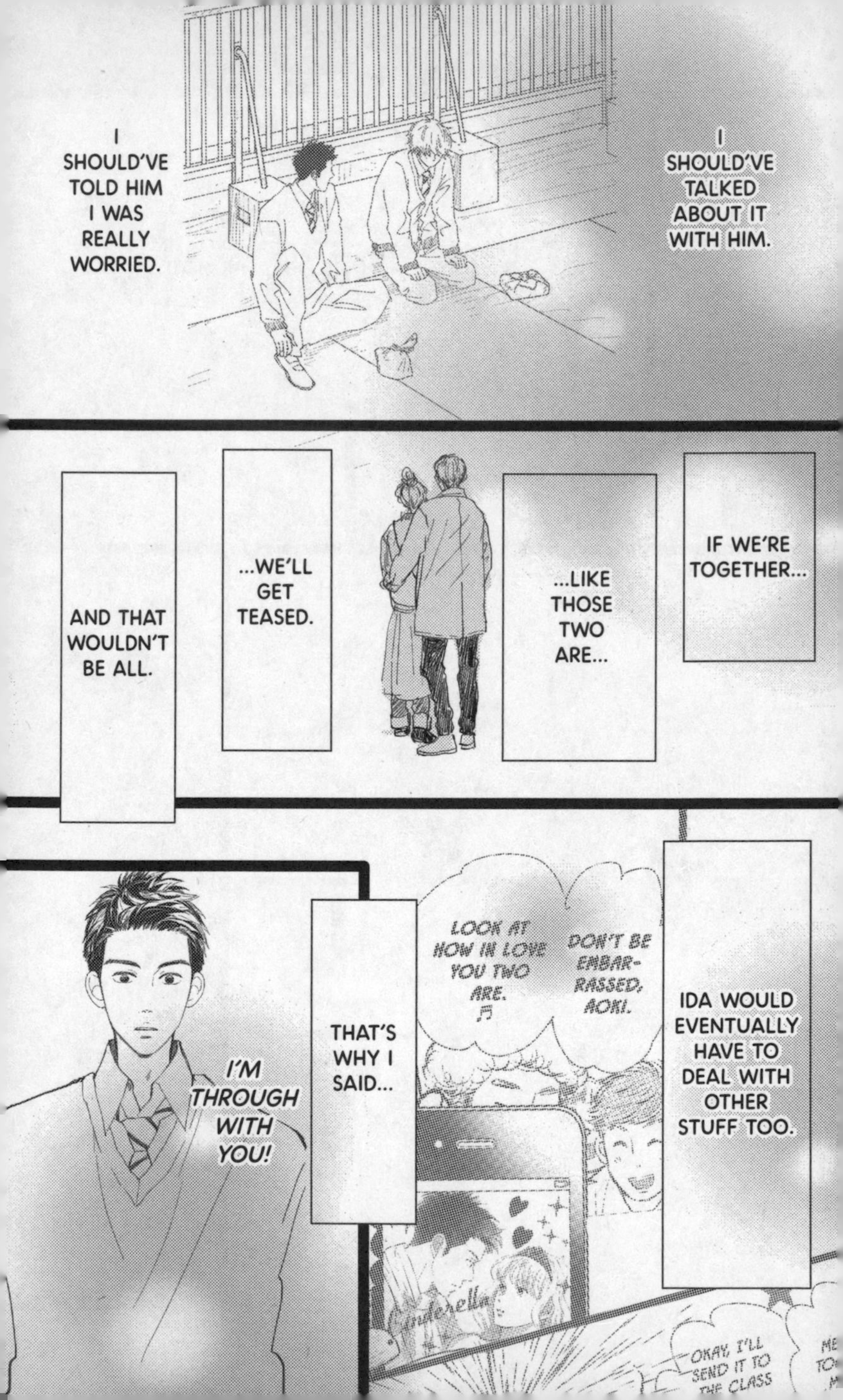
I SHOULD'VE TALKED ABOUT IT WITH HIM.
I SHOULD'VE TOLD HIM I WAS REALLY WORRIED.
IF WE'RE TOGETHER...
...LIKE THOSE TWO ARE...
...WE'LL GET TEASED.
AND THAT WOULDN'T BE ALL.
IDA WOULD EVENTUALLY HAVE TO DEAL WITH OTHER STUFF TOO.
DON'T BE EMBARRASSED, AOKI.
LOOK AT HOW IN LOVE YOU TWO ARE. ♫
OKAY, I'LL SEND IT TO THE CLASS
Cinderella
THAT'S WHY I SAID...
I'M THROUGH WITH YOU!

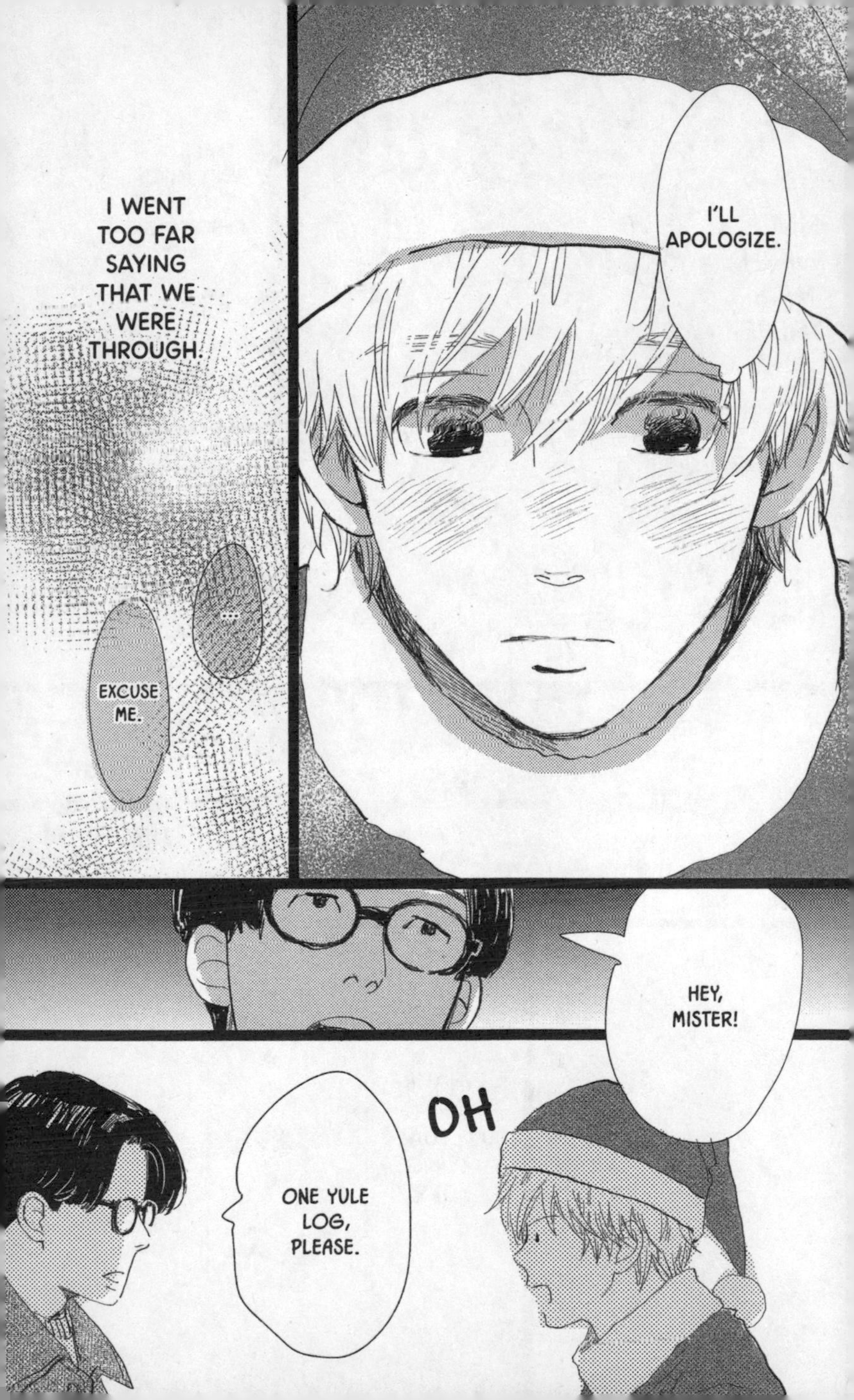
I'LL APOLOGIZE.
I WENT TOO FAR SAYING THAT WE WERE THROUGH.
...
EXCUSE ME.
HEY, MISTER!
OH
ONE YULE LOG, PLEASE.

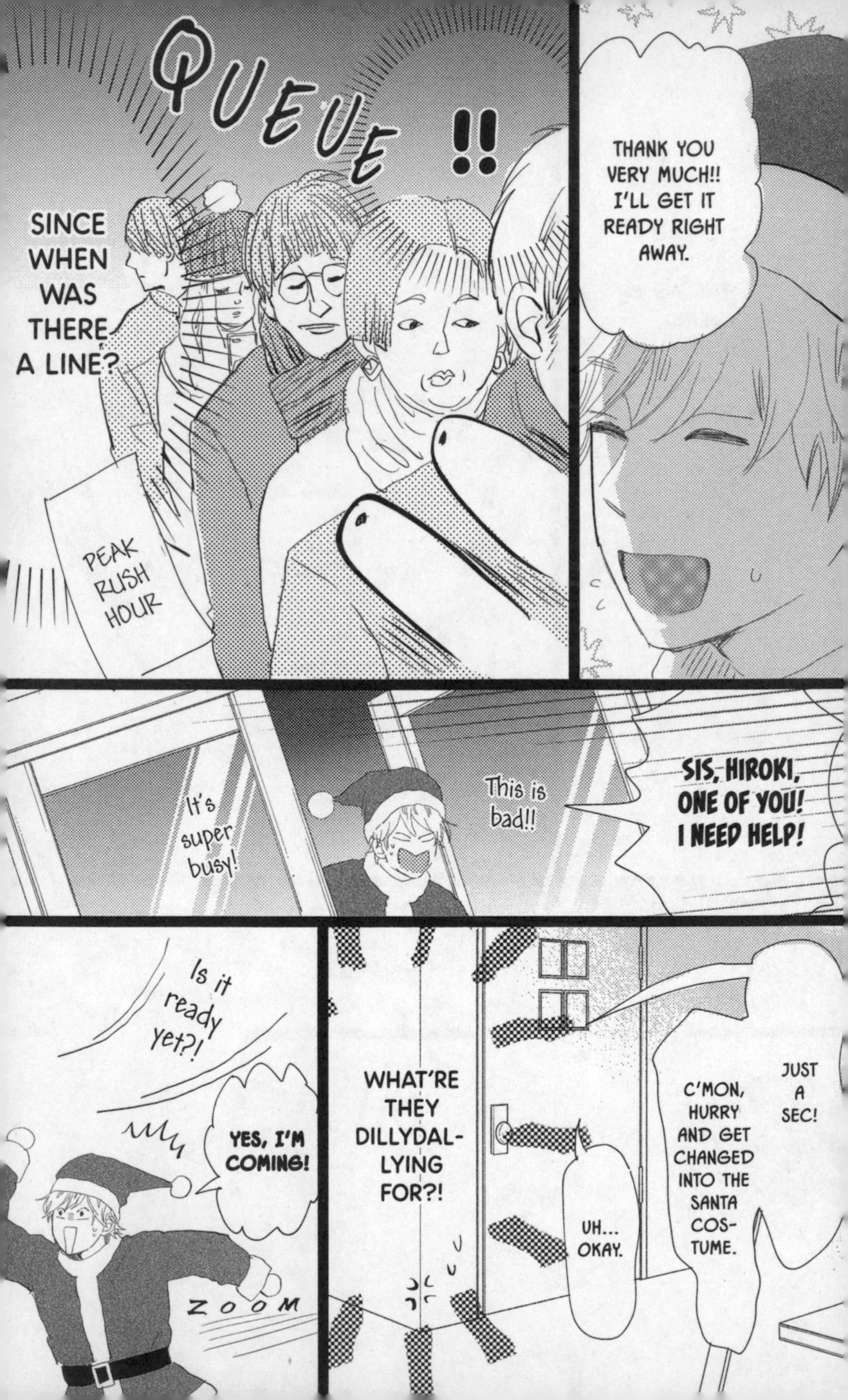
THANK YOU VERY MUCH!! I'LL GET IT READY RIGHT AWAY.
QUEUE!!
SINCE WHEN WAS THERE A LINE?
PEAK RUSH HOUR
SIS, HIROKI, ONE OF YOU! I NEED HELP!
This is bad!!
It's super busy!
JUST A SEC!
C'MON, HURRY AND GET CHANGED INTO THE SANTA COS-TUME.
WHAT'RE THEY DILLYDAL-LYING FOR?!
UH... OKAY.
Is it ready yet?!
YES, I'M COMING!
ZOOM

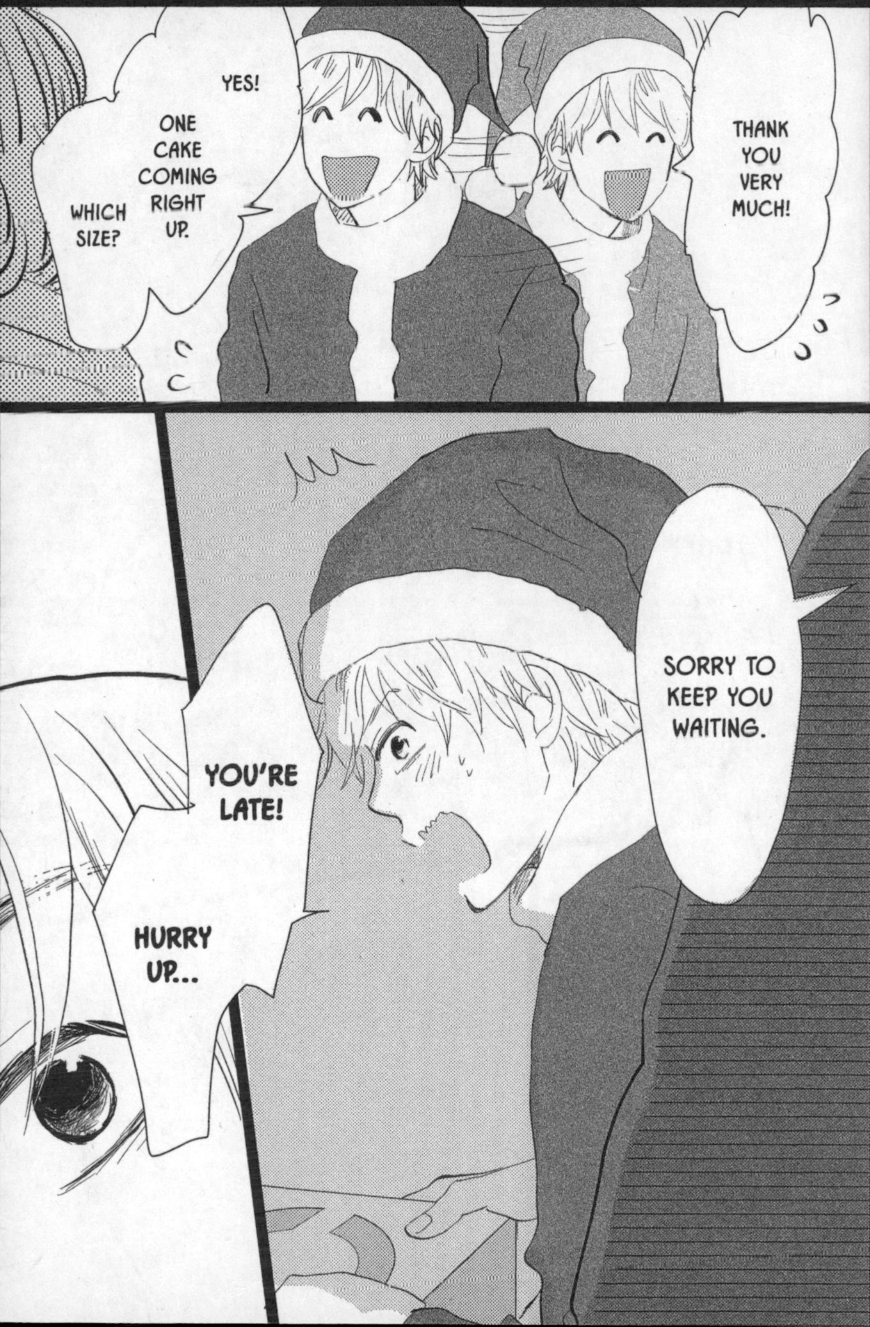
THANK YOU VERY MUCH!
YES!
ONE CAKE COMING RIGHT UP.
WHICH SIZE?
SORRY TO KEEP YOU WAITING.
YOU'RE LATE!
HURRY UP...

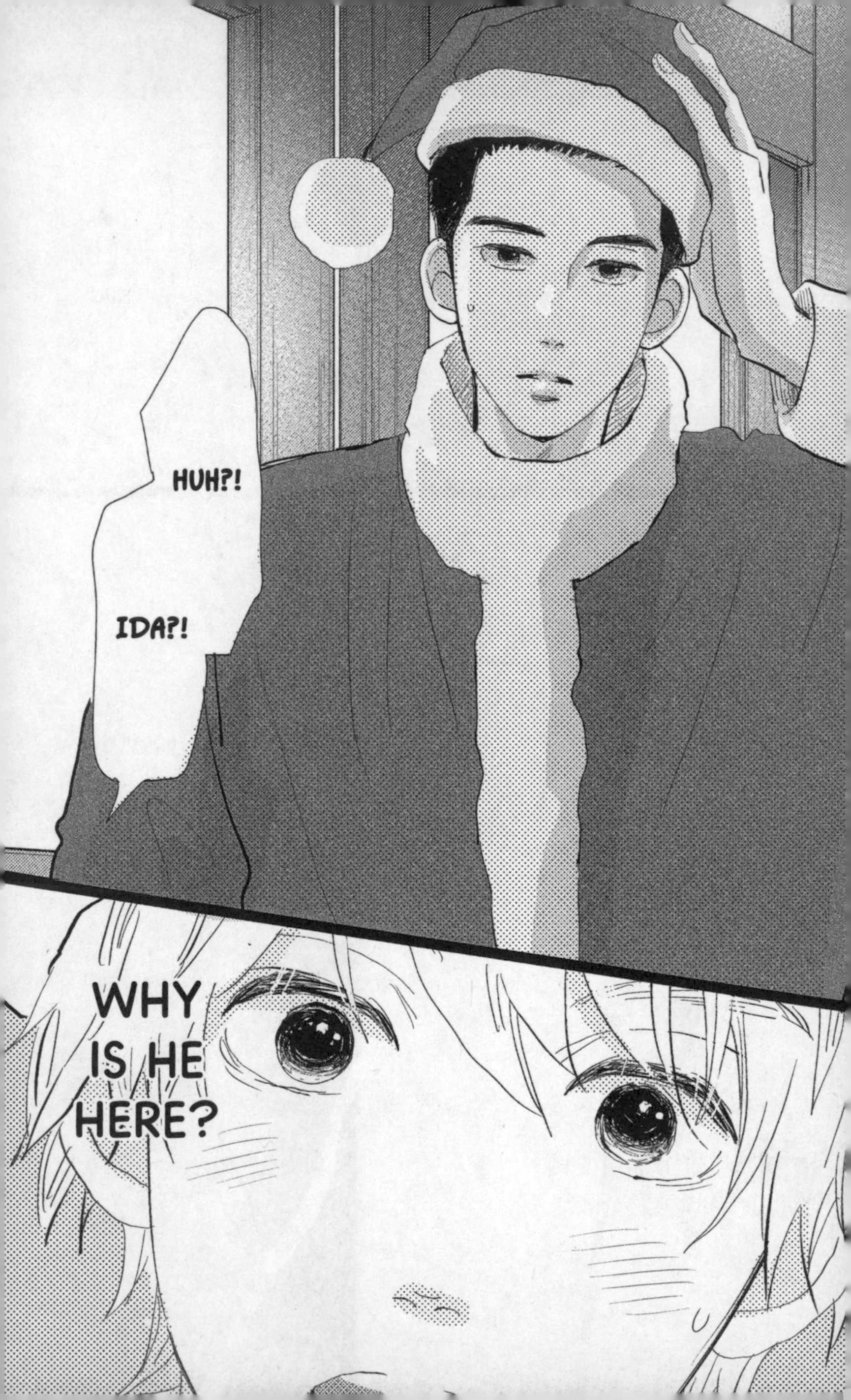
HUH?!
IDA?!
WHY IS HE HERE?

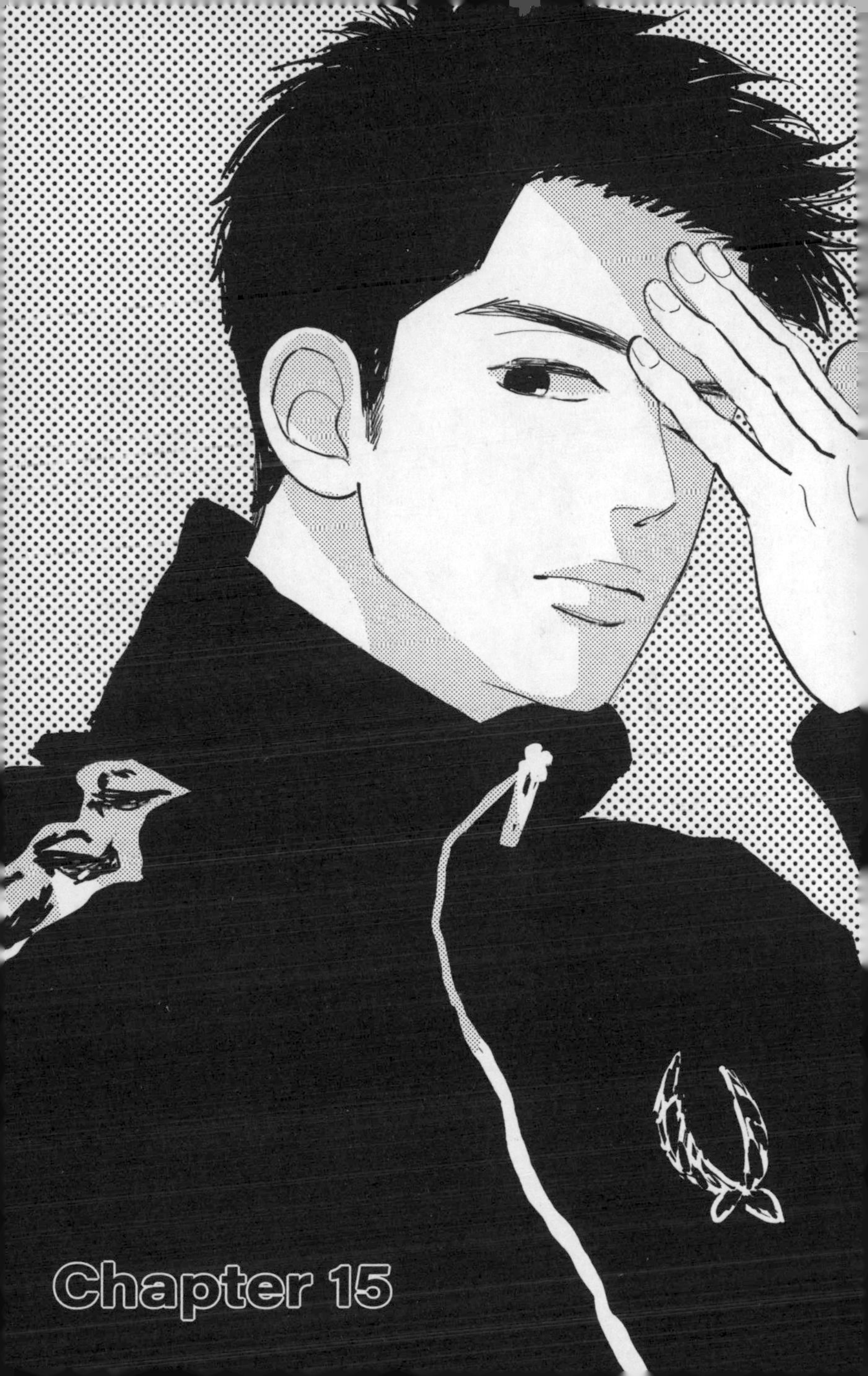
Chapter 15

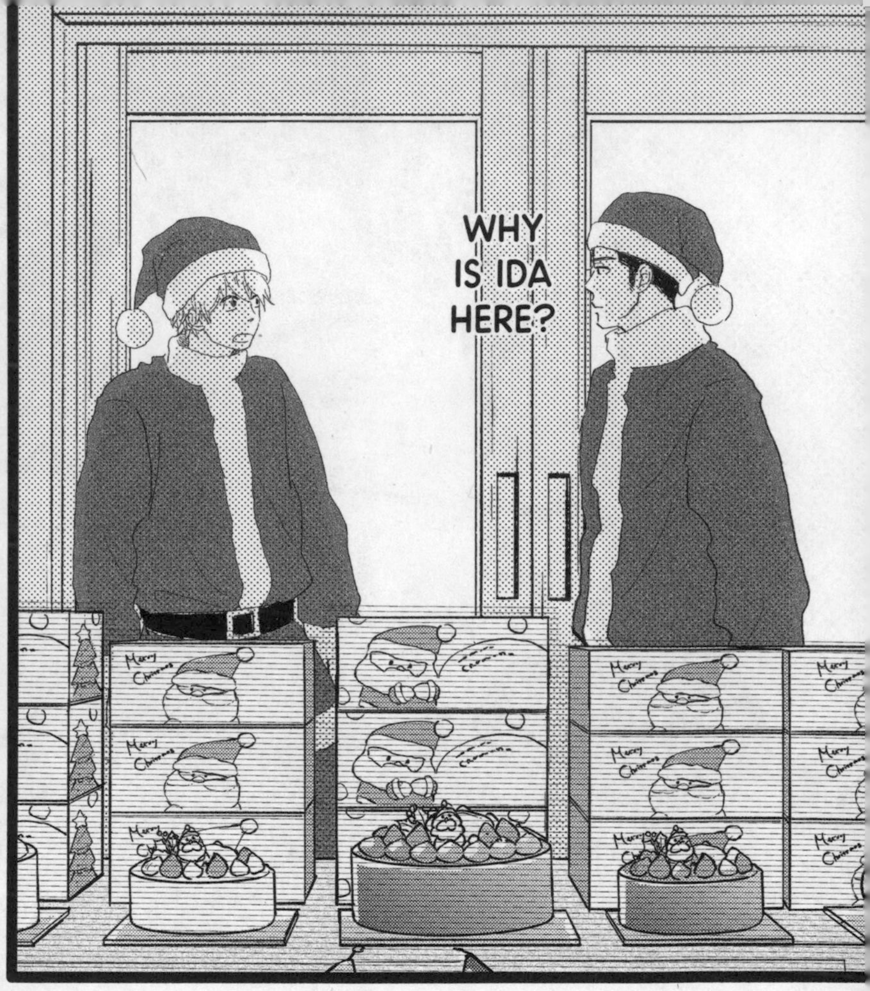
WHY IS IDA HERE?

My Love Mix-Up!

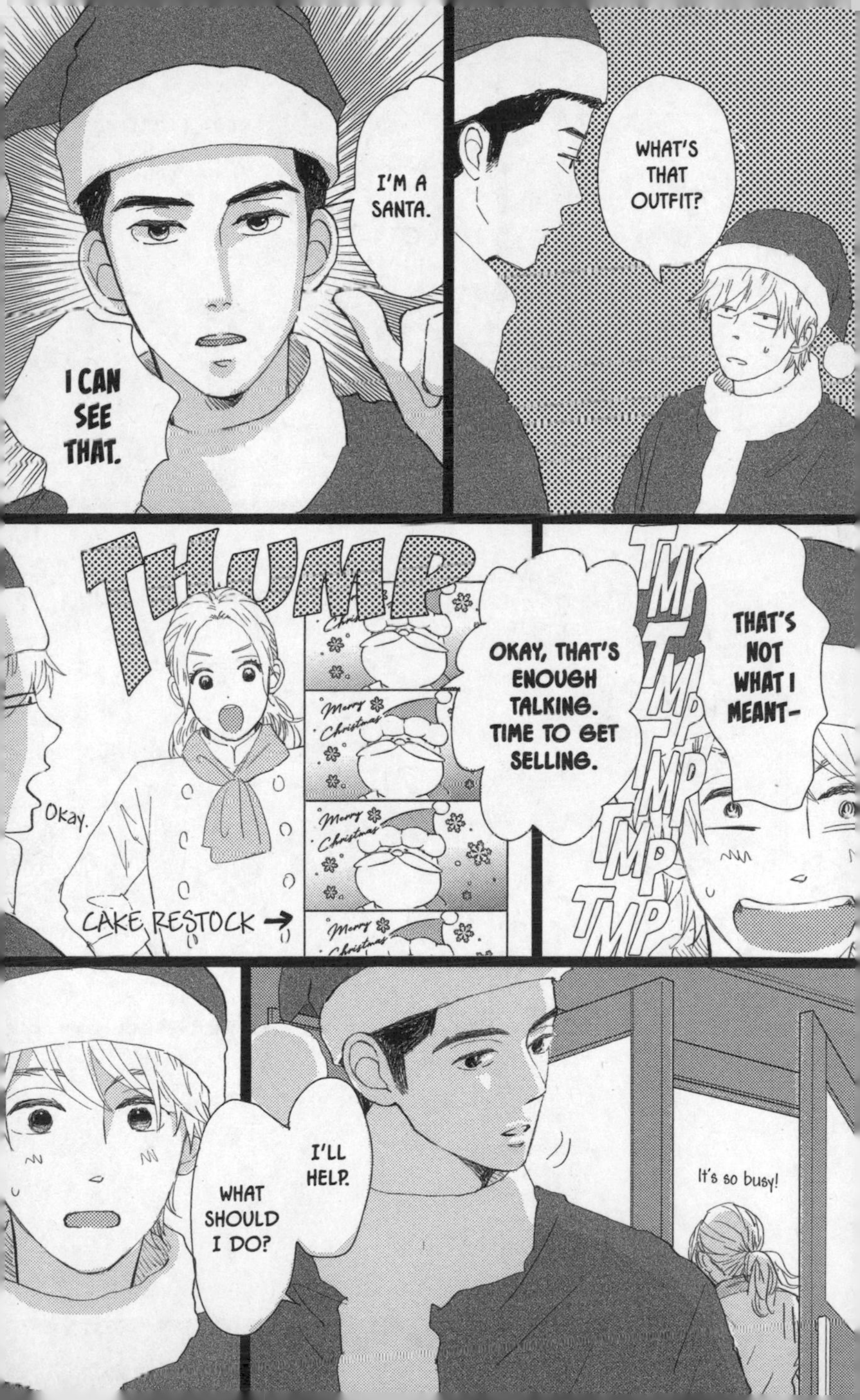
WHAT'S THAT OUTFIT?
I'M A SANTA.
I CAN SEE THAT.
THAT'S NOT WHAT I MEANT-
TMP TMP TMP TMP TMP TMP TMP
OKAY, THAT'S ENOUGH TALKING. TIME TO GET SELLING.
THUMP
Okay.
CAKE RESTOCK →
It's so busy!
I'LL HELP.
WHAT SHOULD I DO?

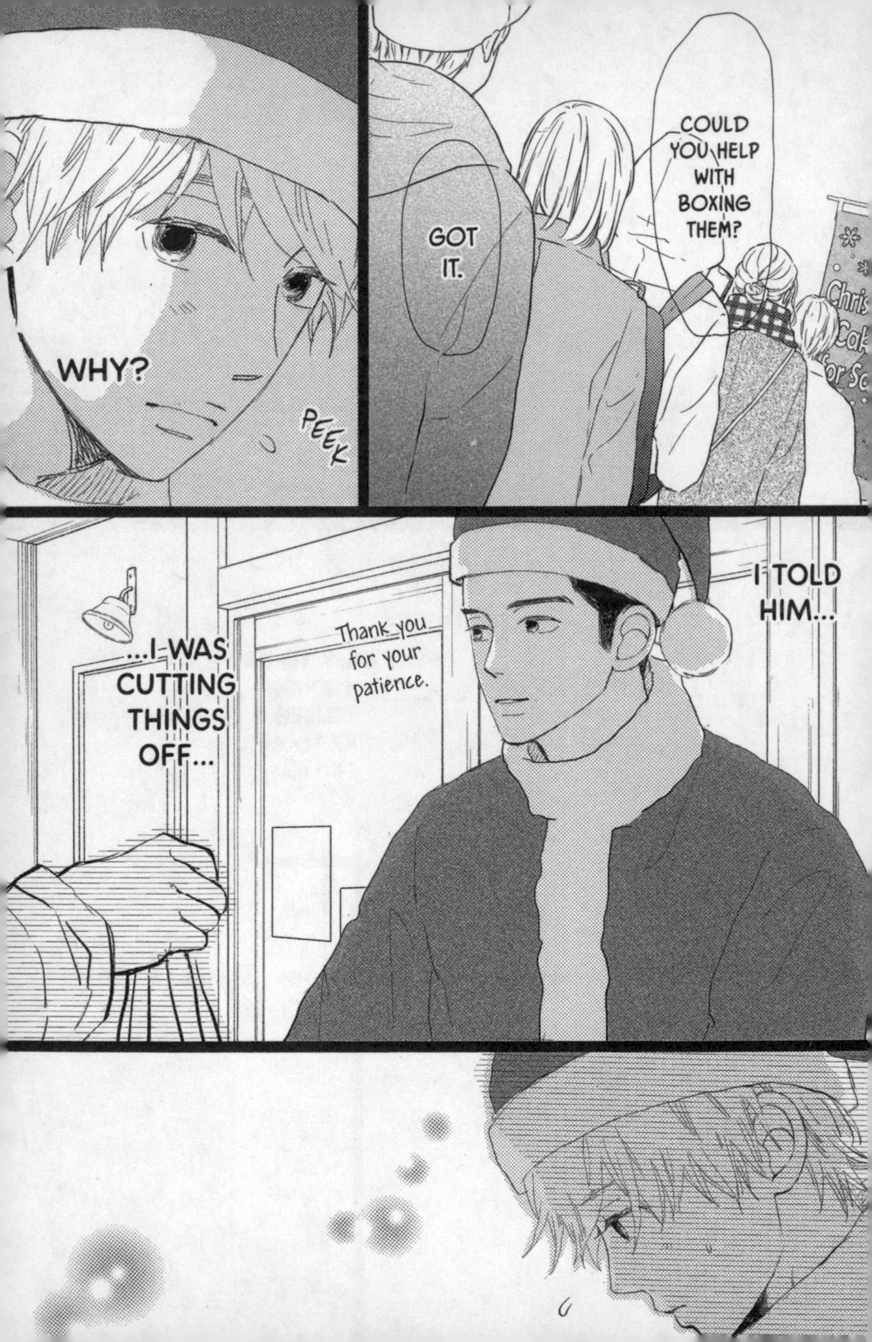
COULD YOU HELP WITH BOXING THEM?
GOT IT.
WHY?
PEEK
I TOLD HIM...
Thank you for your patience.
...I WAS CUTTING THINGS OFF...

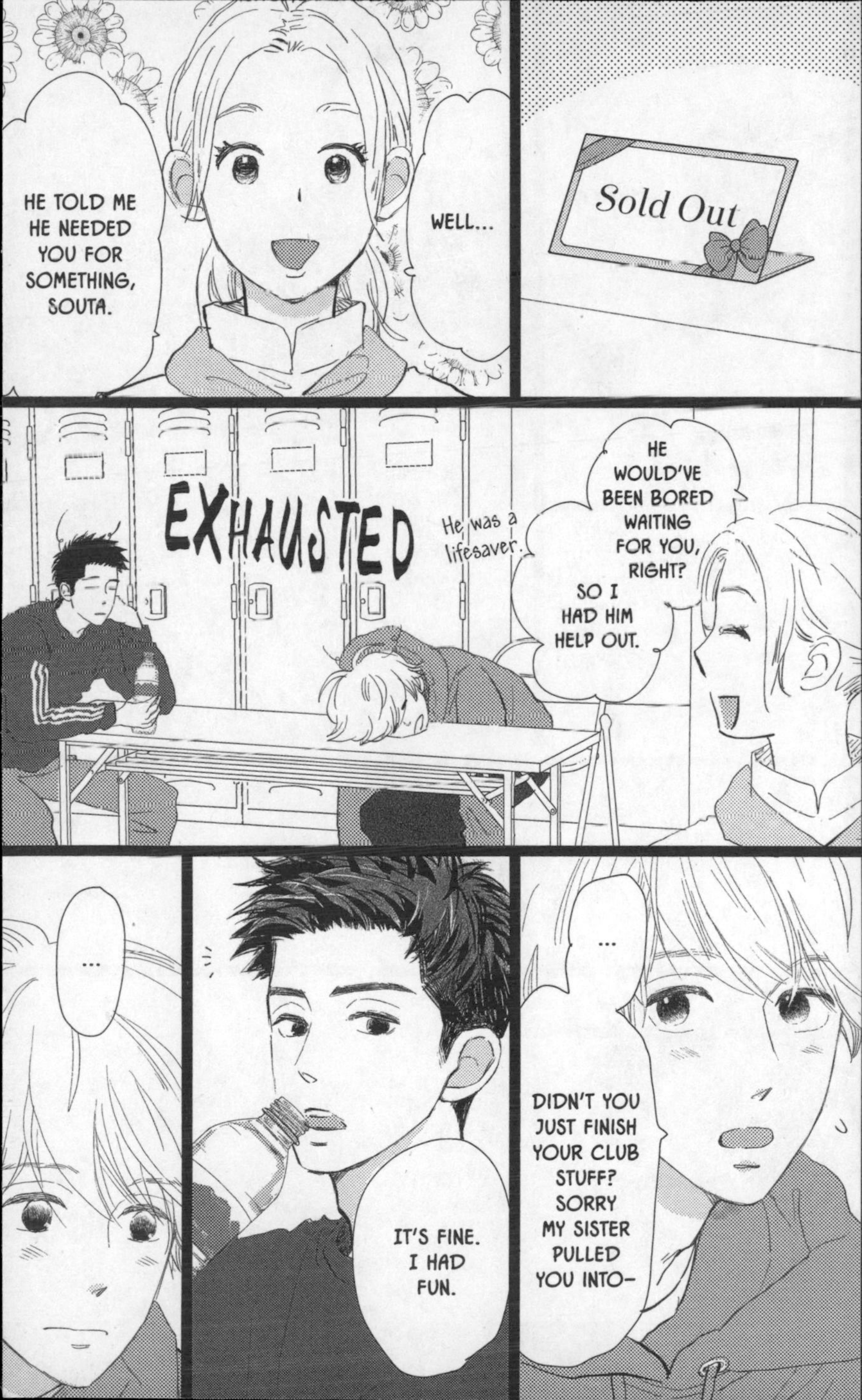
Sold Out
WELL...
HE TOLD ME HE NEEDED YOU FOR SOMETHING, SOUTA.
HE WOULD'VE BEEN BORED WAITING FOR YOU, RIGHT?
SO I HAD HIM HELP OUT.
He was a lifesaver.
EXHAUSTED
...
DIDN'T YOU JUST FINISH YOUR CLUB STUFF? SORRY MY SISTER PULLED YOU INTO-
IT'S FINE. I HAD FUN.
...

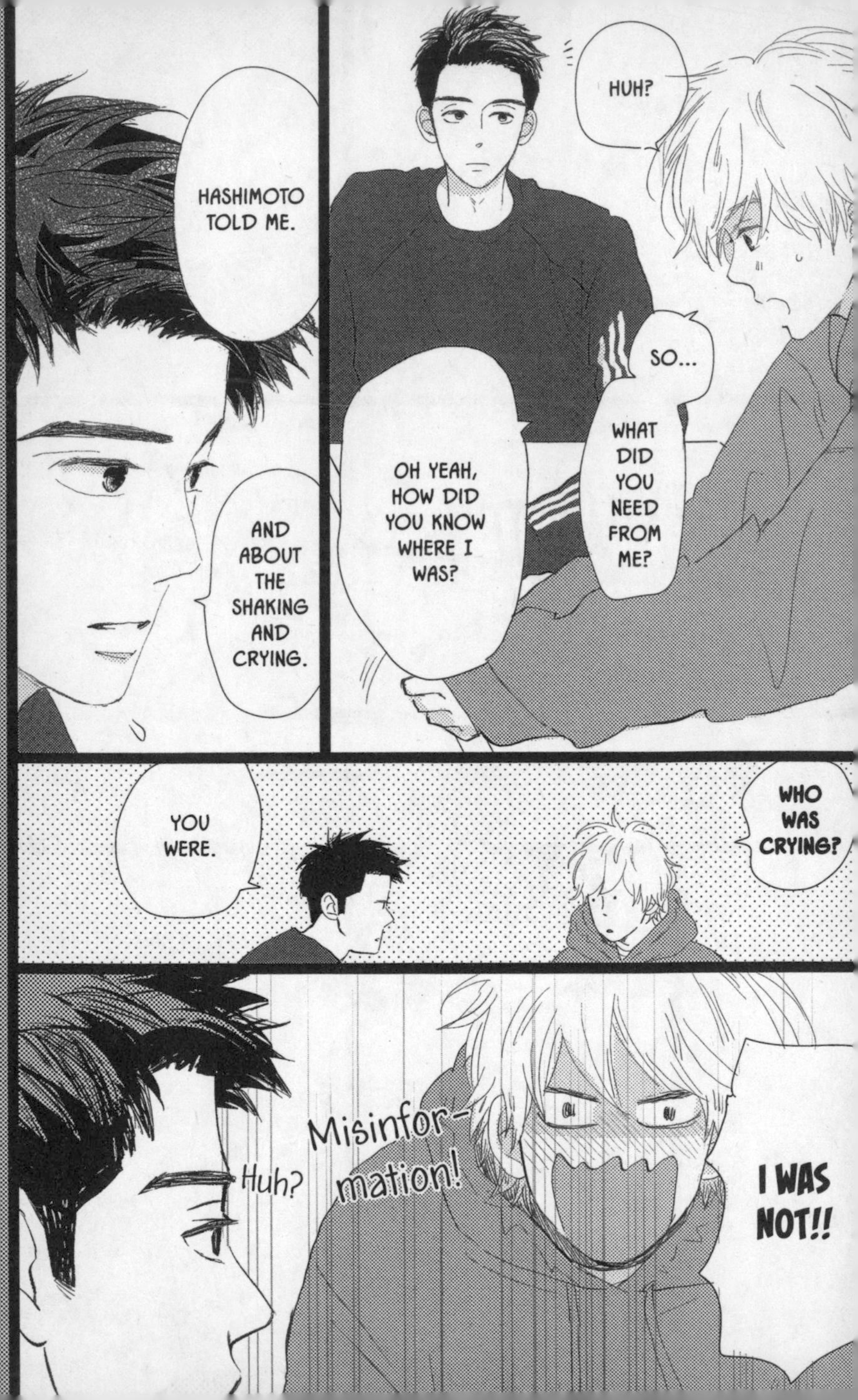
HUH?
SO...
WHAT DID YOU NEED FROM ME?
OH YEAH, HOW DID YOU KNOW WHERE I WAS?
HASHIMOTO TOLD ME.
AND ABOUT THE SHAKING AND CRYING.
WHO WAS CRYING?
YOU WERE.
I WAS NOT!!
Misinfor-mation!
Huh?

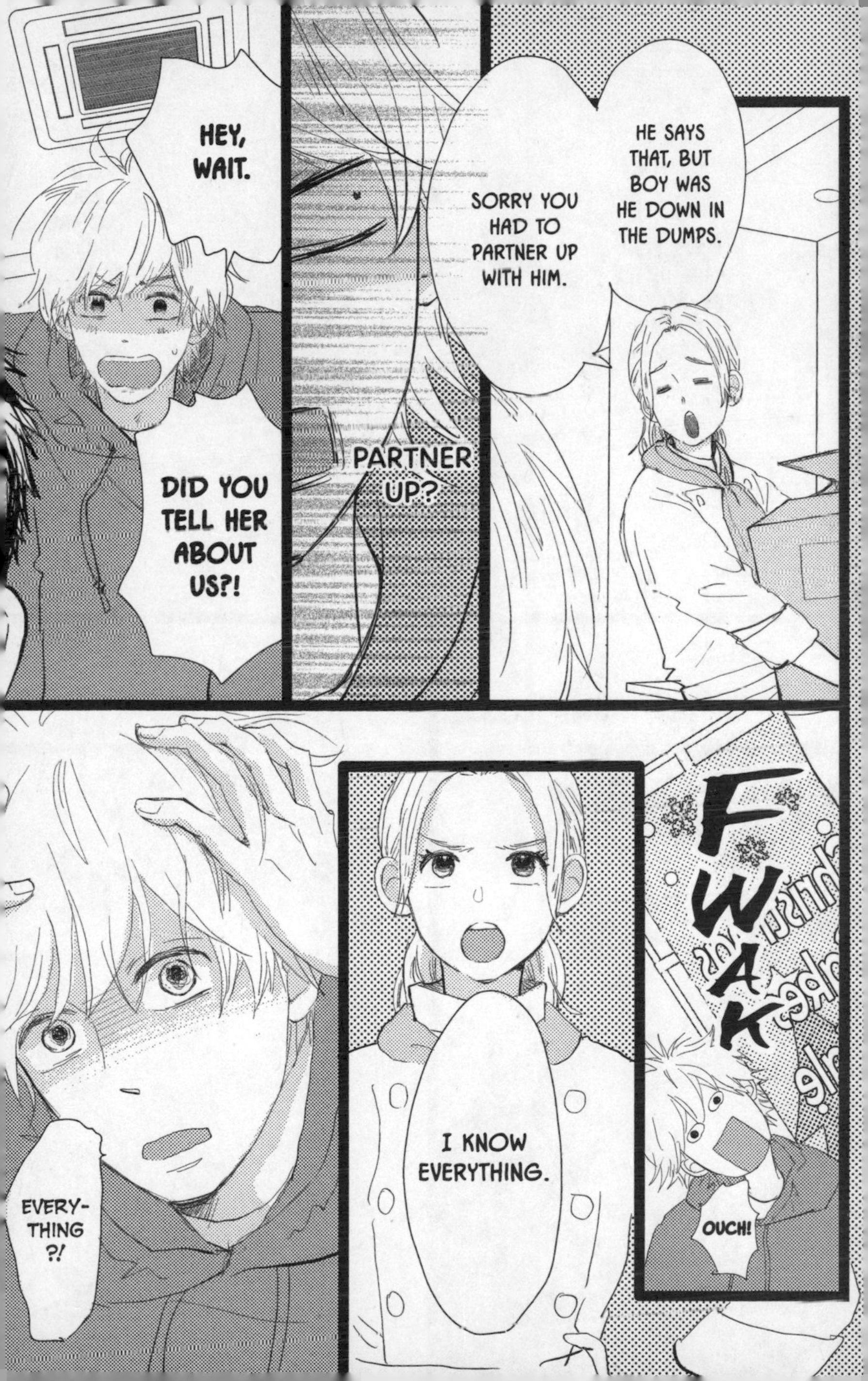
HE SAYS THAT, BUT BOY WAS HE DOWN IN THE DUMPS.
SORRY YOU HAD TO PARTNER UP WITH HIM.
PARTNER UP?
HEY, WAIT.
DID YOU TELL HER ABOUT US?!
FWAK
OUCH!
I KNOW EVERYTHING.
EVERY-THING ?!

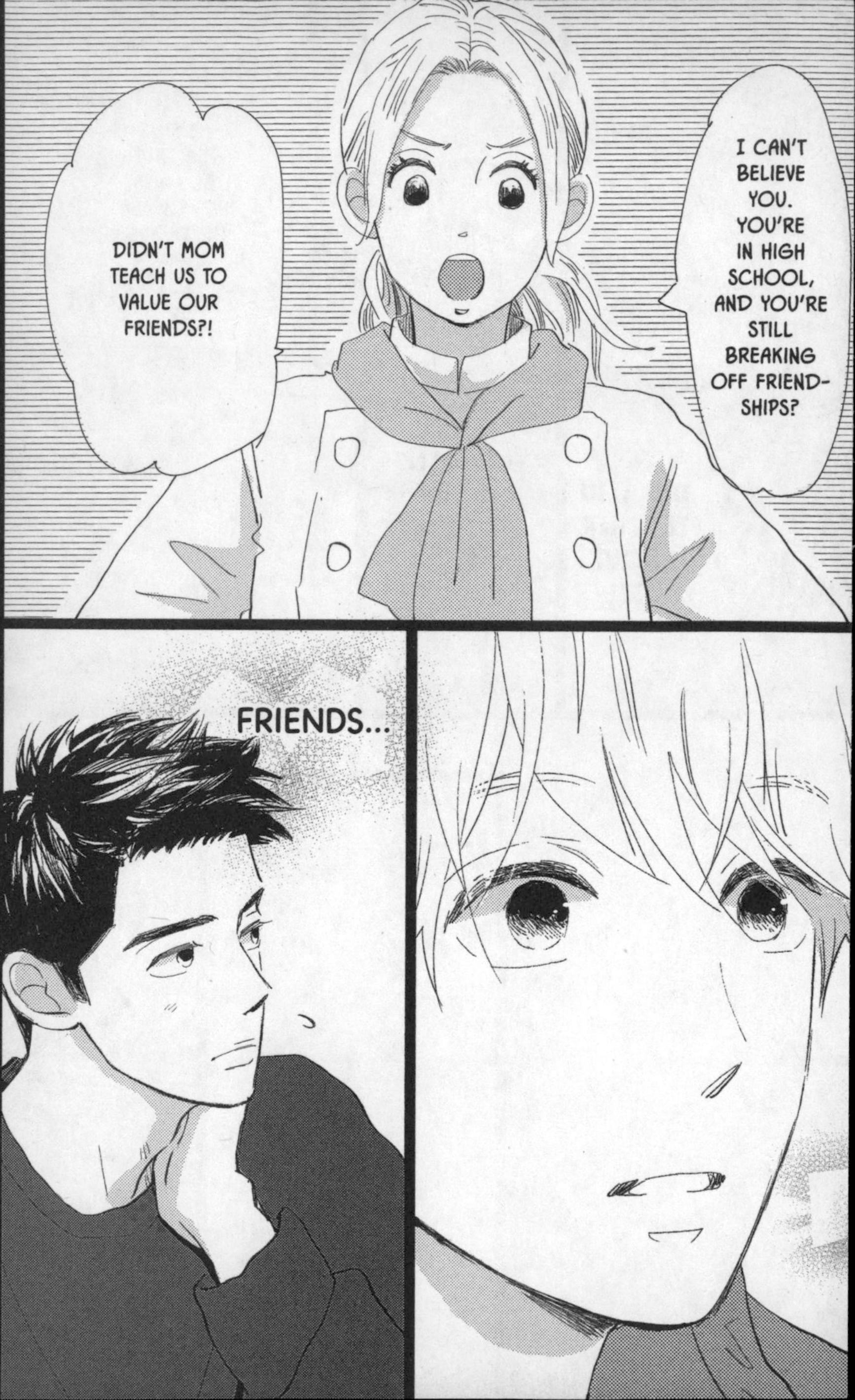
I CAN'T BELIEVE YOU. YOU'RE IN HIGH SCHOOL, AND YOU'RE STILL BREAKING OFF FRIEND-SHIPS?
DIDN'T MOM TEACH US TO VALUE OUR FRIENDS?!
FRIENDS...

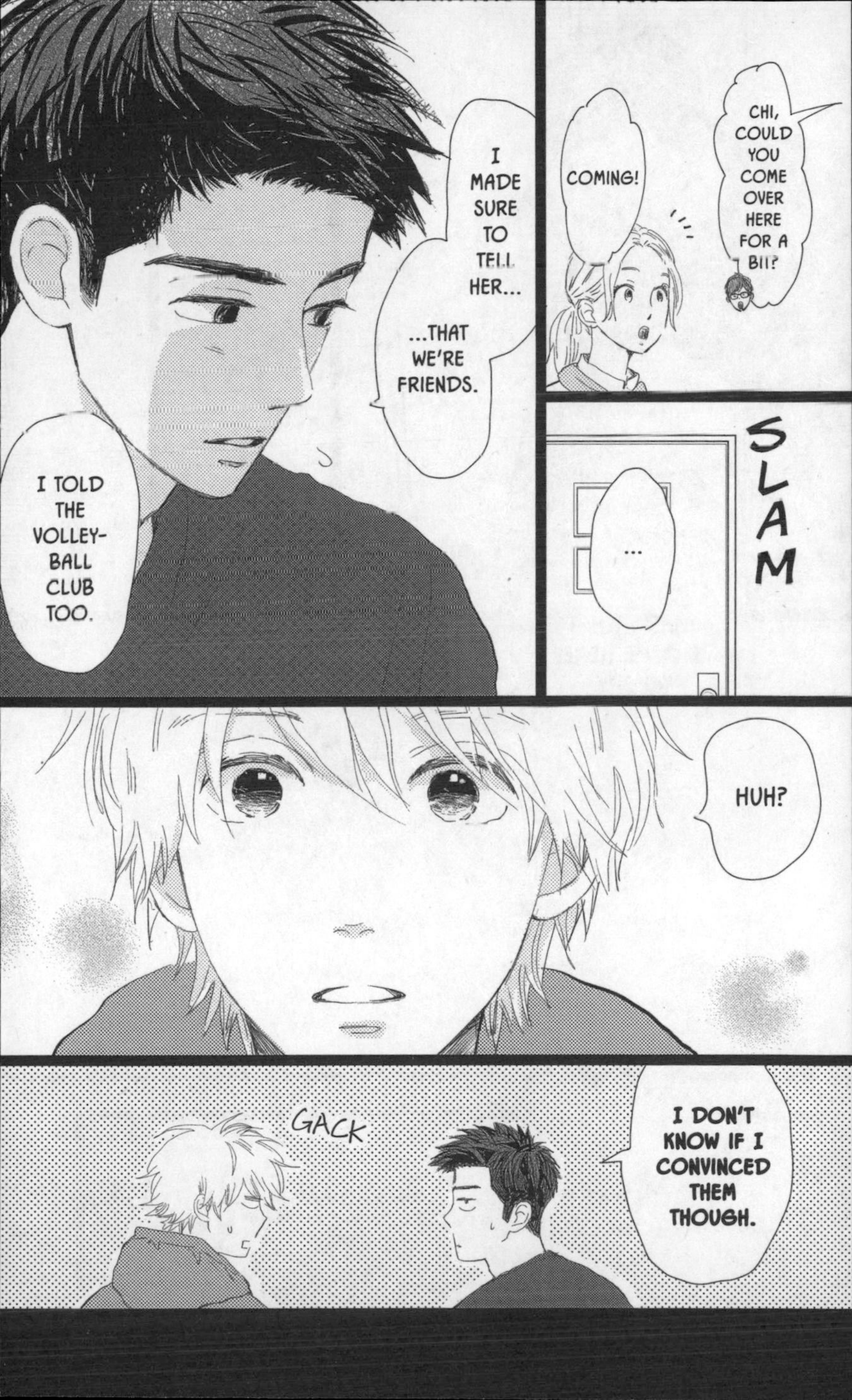
CHI, COULD YOU COME OVER HERE FOR A BIT?
COMING!
...
SLAM
I MADE SURE TO TELL HER...
...THAT WE'RE FRIENDS.
I TOLD THE VOLLEY-BALL CLUB TOO.
HUH?
I DON'T KNOW IF I CONVINCED THEM THOUGH.
GACK

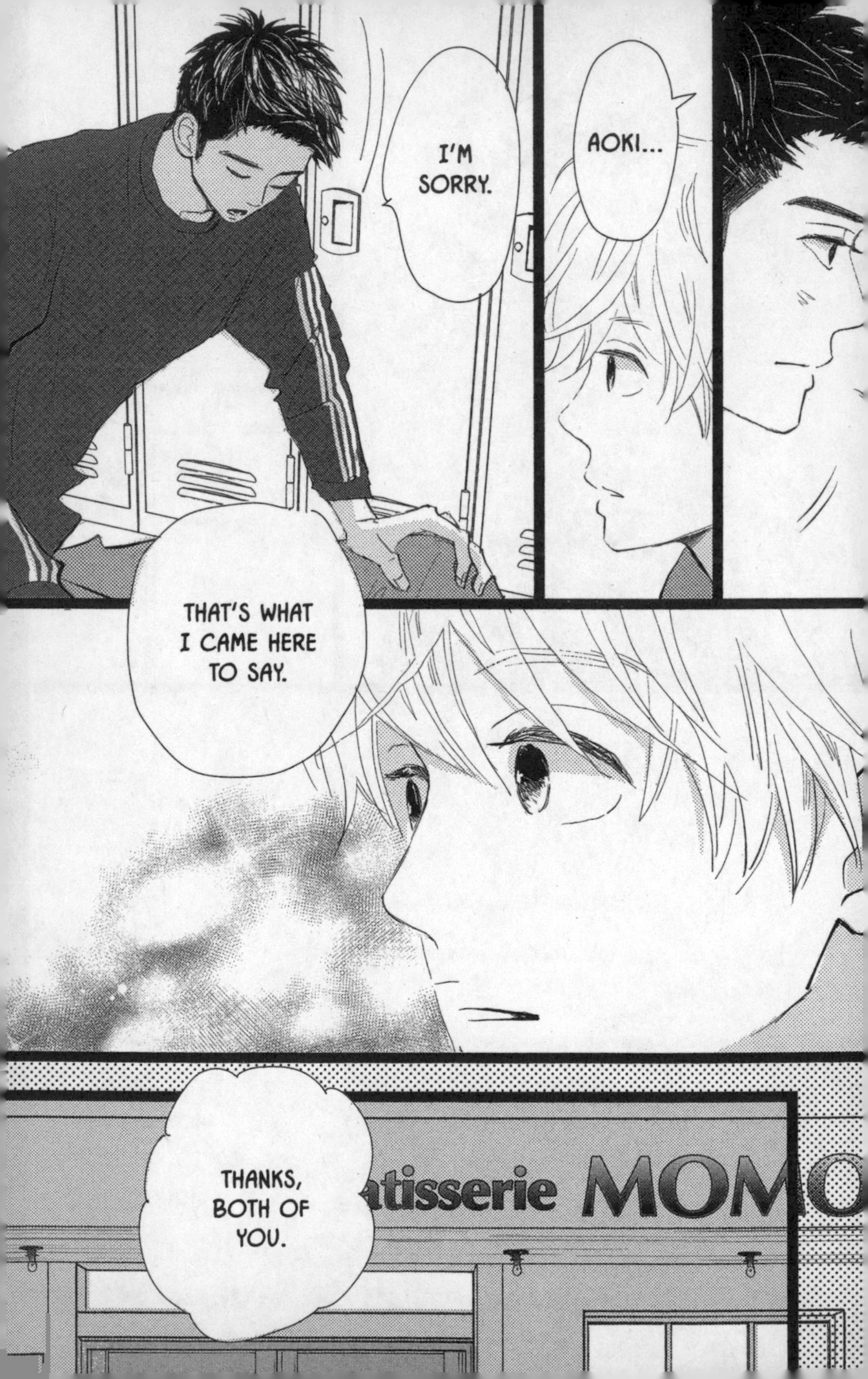
AOKI...
I'M SORRY.
THAT'S WHAT I CAME HERE TO SAY.
THANKS, BOTH OF YOU.

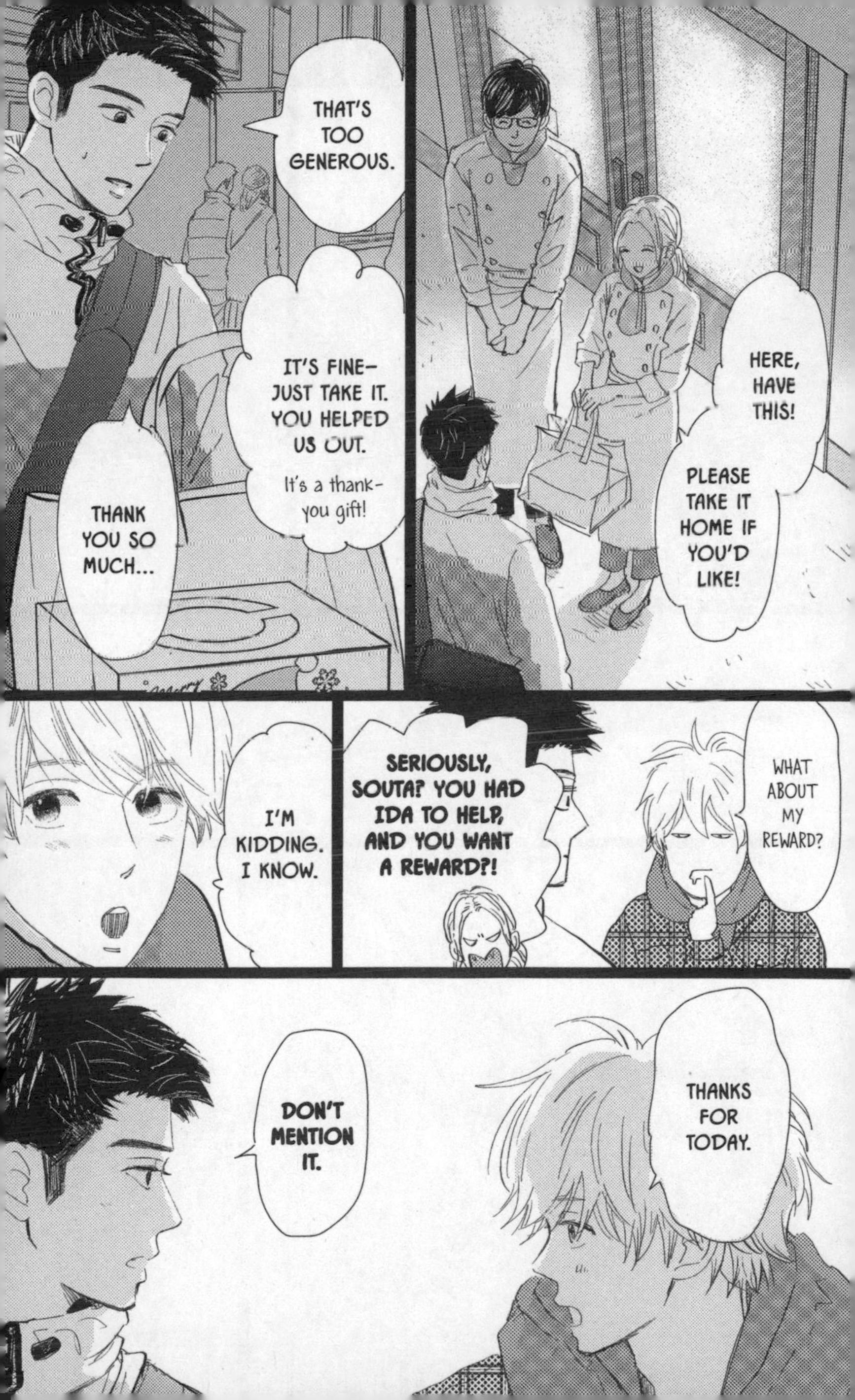
HERE, HAVE THIS!
PLEASE TAKE IT HOME IF YOU'D LIKE!
THAT'S TOO GENEROUS.
IT'S FINE— JUST TAKE IT. YOU HELPED US OUT.
It's a thank-you gift!
THANK YOU SO MUCH...
WHAT ABOUT MY REWARD?
SERIOUSLY, SOUTA? YOU HAD IDA TO HELP, AND YOU WANT A REWARD?!
I'M KIDDING. I KNOW.
THANKS FOR TODAY.
DON'T MENTION IT.

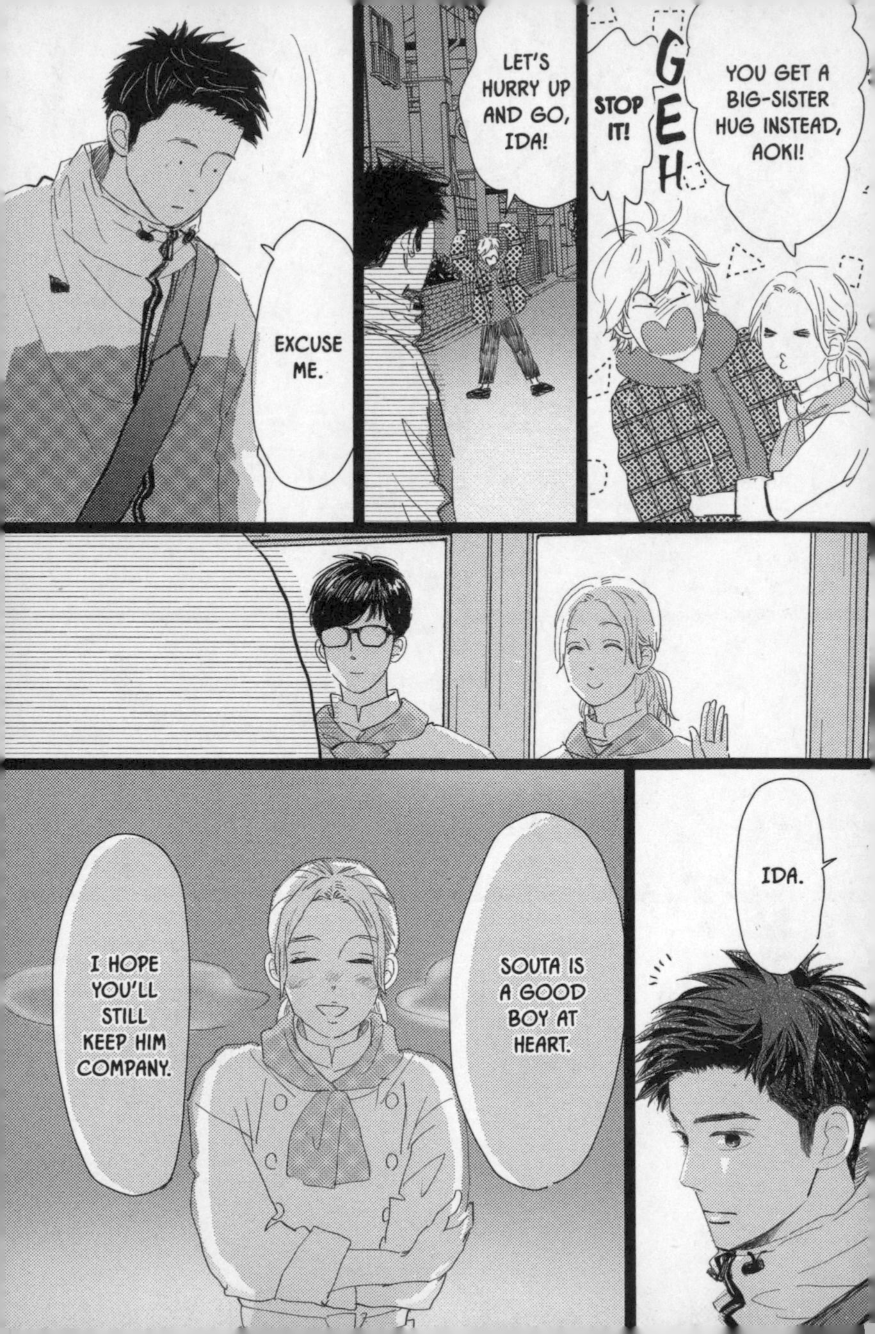
YOU GET A BIG-SISTER HUG INSTEAD, AOKI!
GEH
STOP IT!
LET'S HURRY UP AND GO, IDA!
EXCUSE ME.
IDA.
SOUTA IS A GOOD BOY AT HEART.
I HOPE YOU'LL STILL KEEP HIM COMPANY.

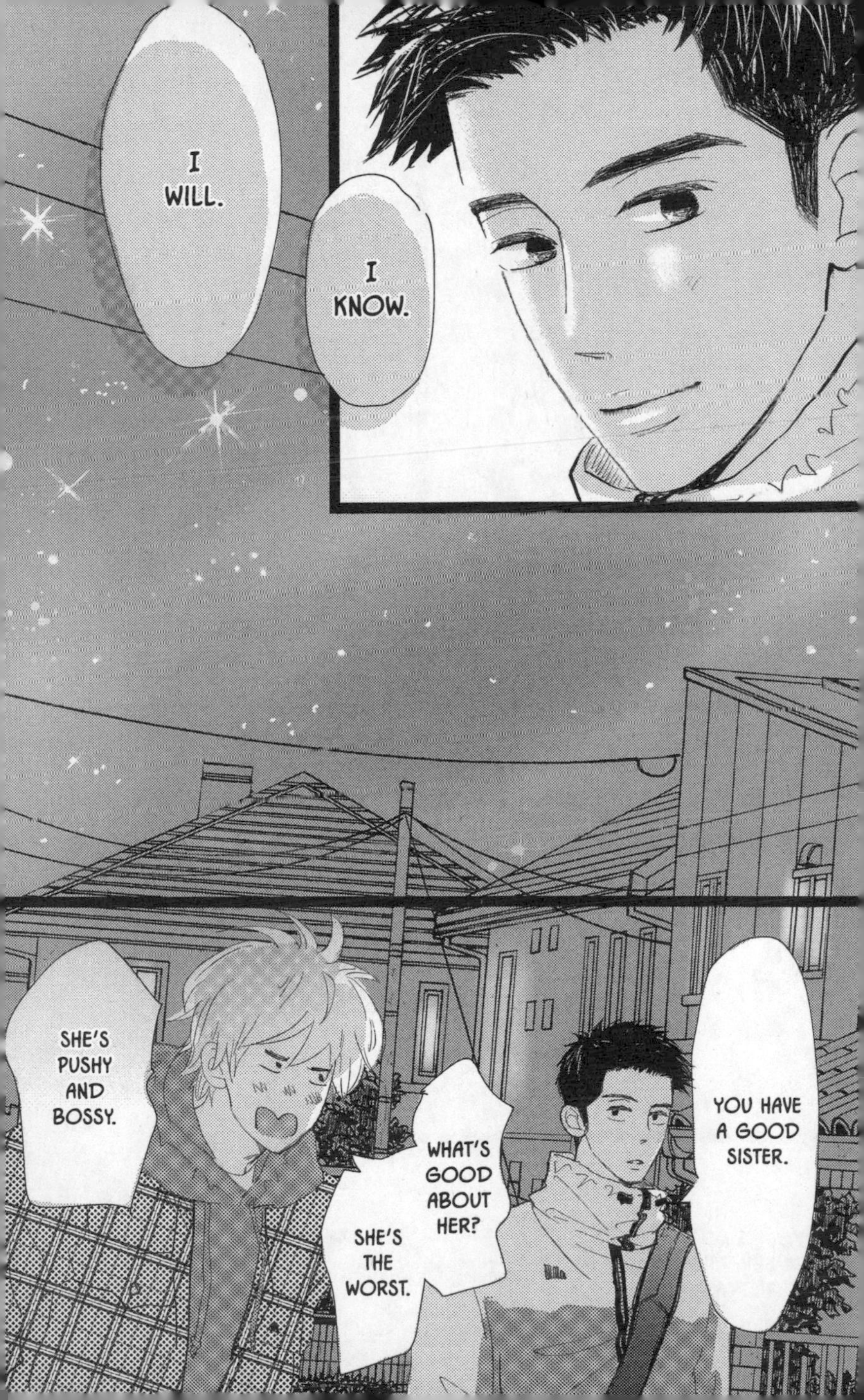
I KNOW.
I WILL.
YOU HAVE A GOOD SISTER.
WHAT'S GOOD ABOUT HER?
SHE'S THE WORST.
SHE'S PUSHY AND BOSSY.

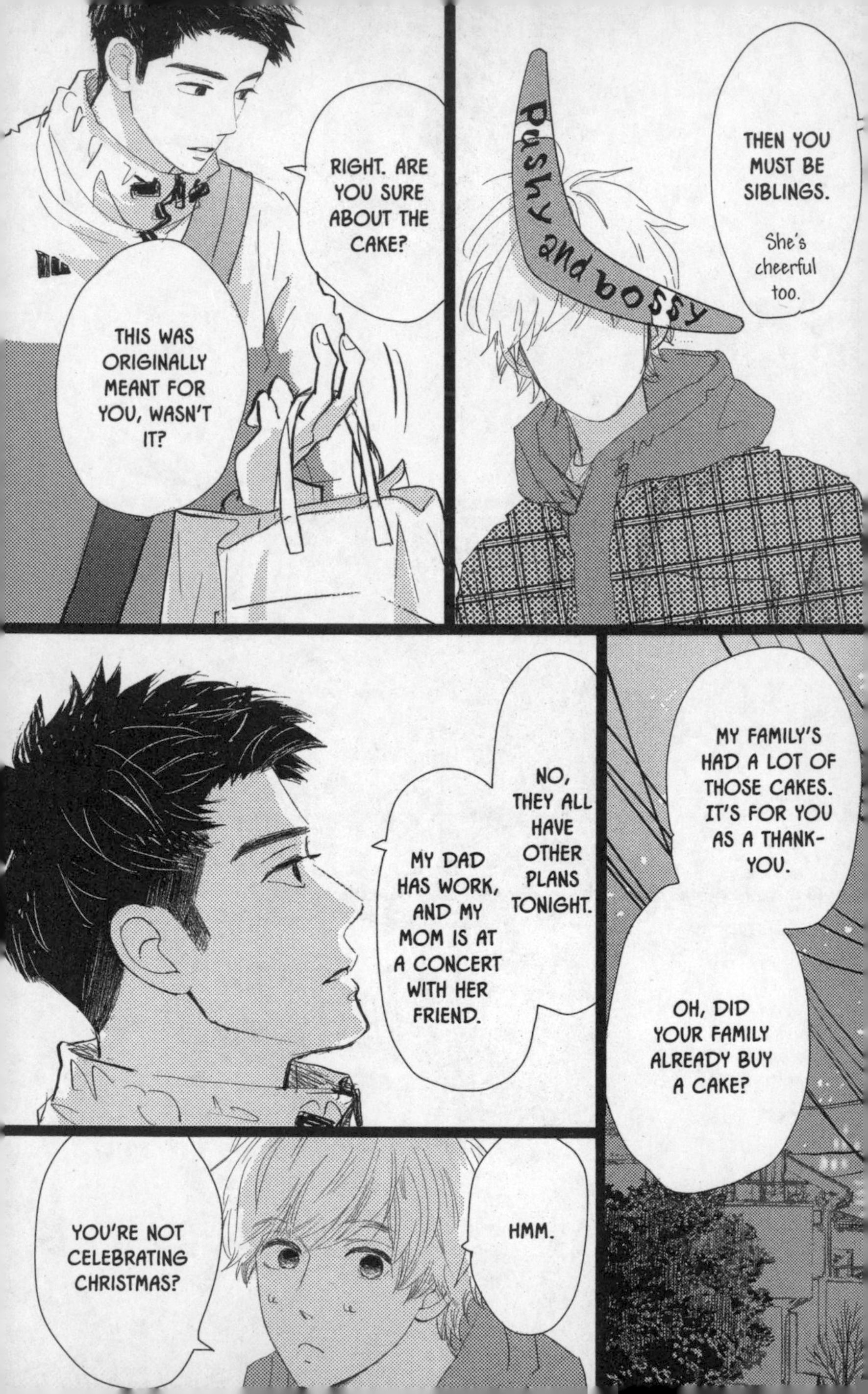
THEN YOU MUST BE SIBLINGS.
She's cheerful too.
Pushy and bossy
RIGHT. ARE YOU SURE ABOUT THE CAKE?
THIS WAS ORIGINALLY MEANT FOR YOU, WASN'T IT?
MY FAMILY'S HAD A LOT OF THOSE CAKES. IT'S FOR YOU AS A THANK-YOU.
OH, DID YOUR FAMILY ALREADY BUY A CAKE?
NO, THEY ALL HAVE OTHER PLANS TONIGHT.
MY DAD HAS WORK, AND MY MOM IS AT A CONCERT WITH HER FRIEND.
HMM.
YOU'RE NOT CELEBRATING CHRISTMAS?

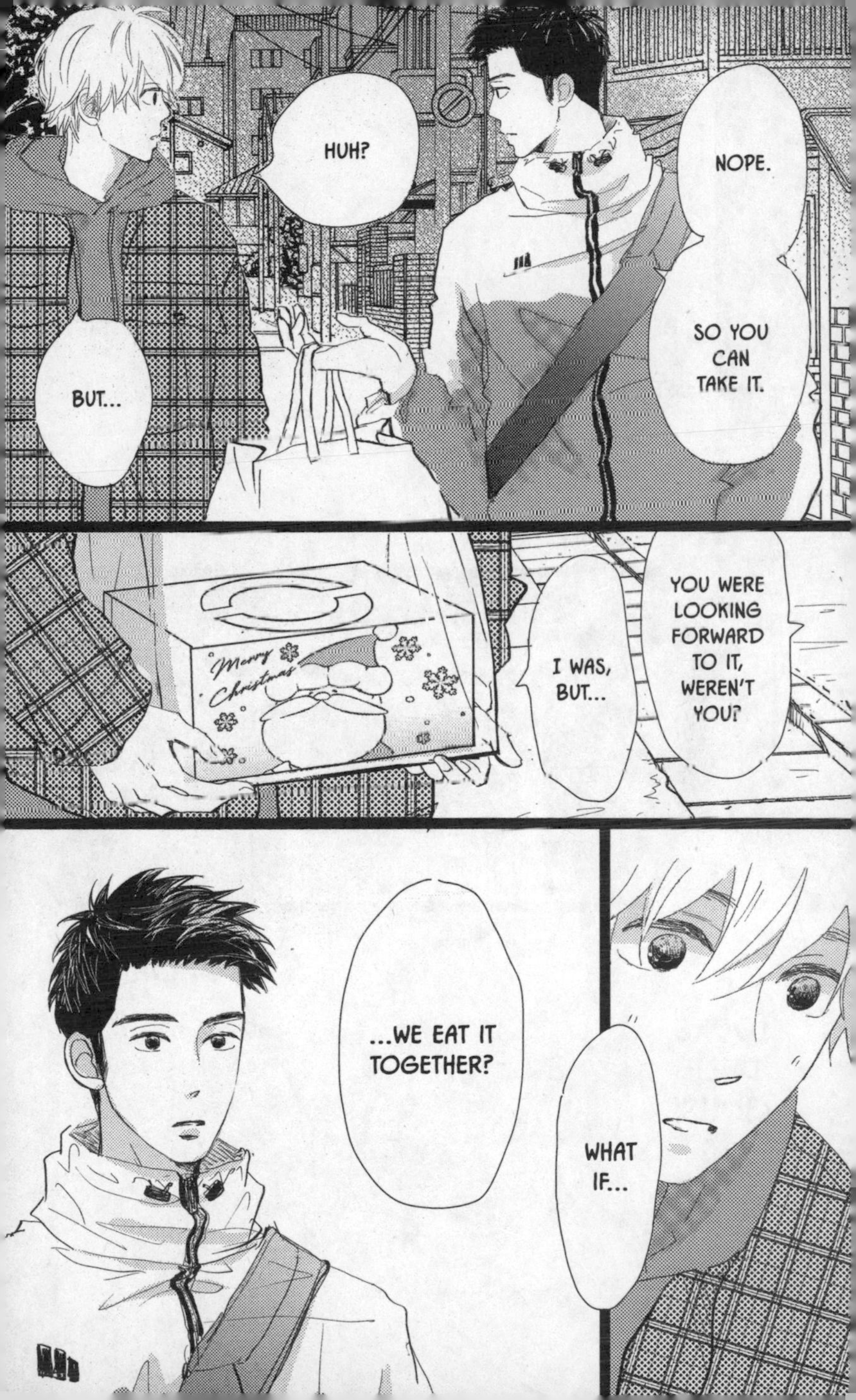
NOPE.
SO YOU CAN TAKE IT.
HUH?
BUT...
YOU WERE LOOKING FORWARD TO IT, WEREN'T YOU?
I WAS, BUT...
Merry Christmas
WHAT IF...
...WE EAT IT TOGETHER?

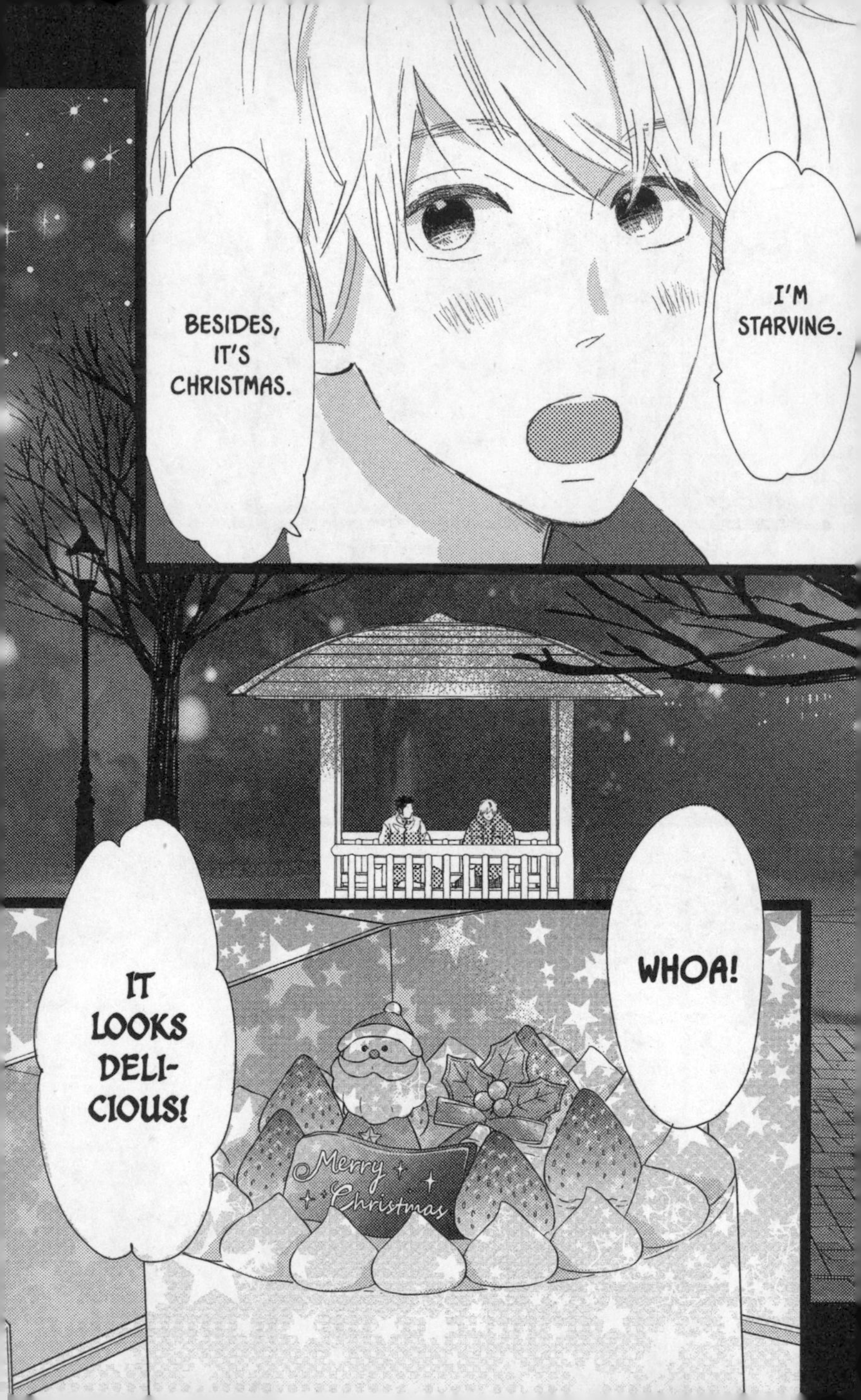
I'M STARVING.
BESIDES, IT'S CHRISTMAS.
WHOA!
IT LOOKS DELI- CIOUS!
Merry Christmas

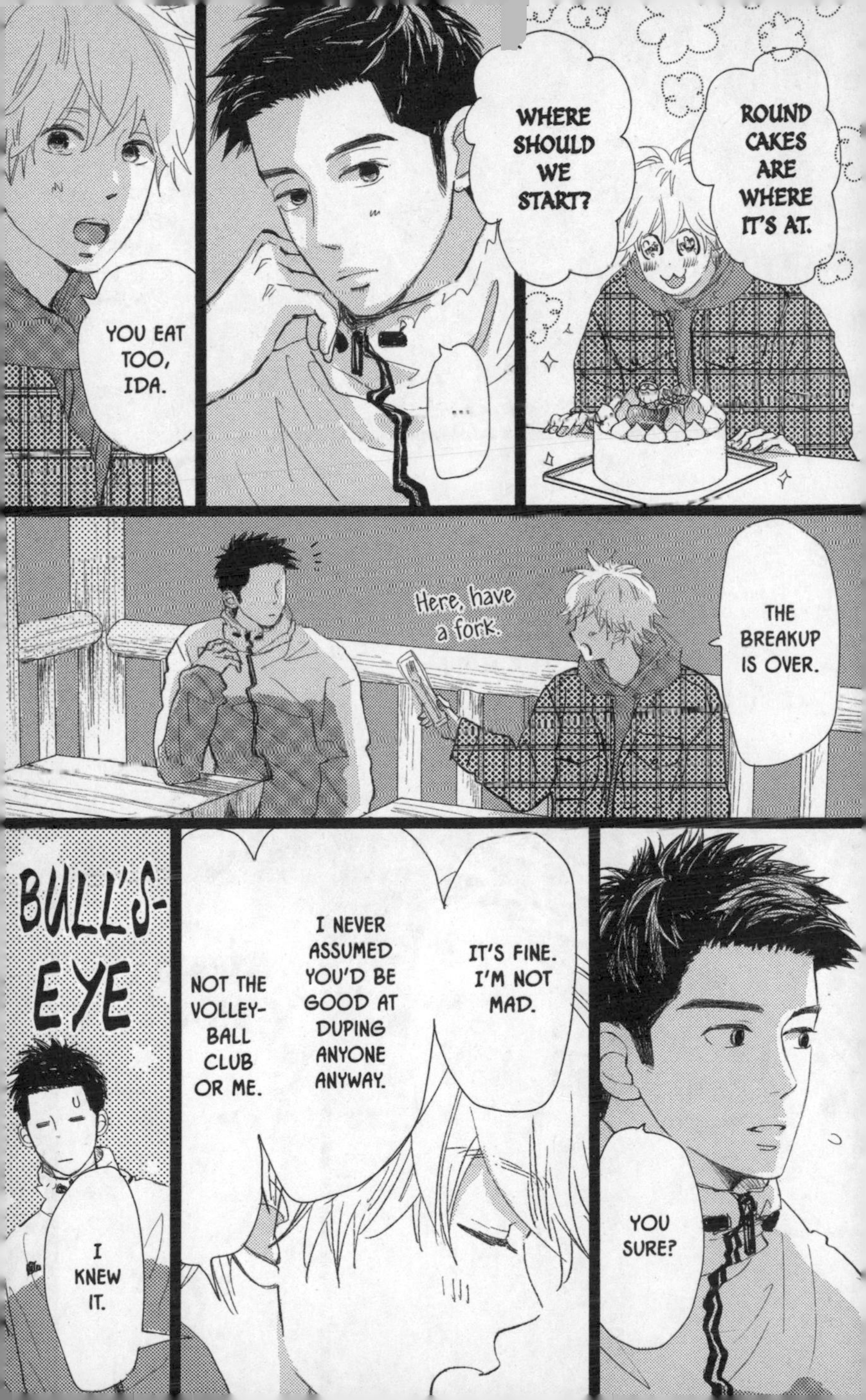
ROUND CAKES ARE WHERE IT'S AT.
WHERE SHOULD WE START?
...
YOU EAT TOO, IDA.
THE BREAKUP IS OVER.
Here, have a fork.
YOU SURE?
IT'S FINE. I'M NOT MAD.
I NEVER ASSUMED YOU'D BE GOOD AT DUPING ANYONE ANYWAY.
NOT THE VOLLEY-BALL CLUB OR ME.
BULL'S-EYE
I KNEW IT.

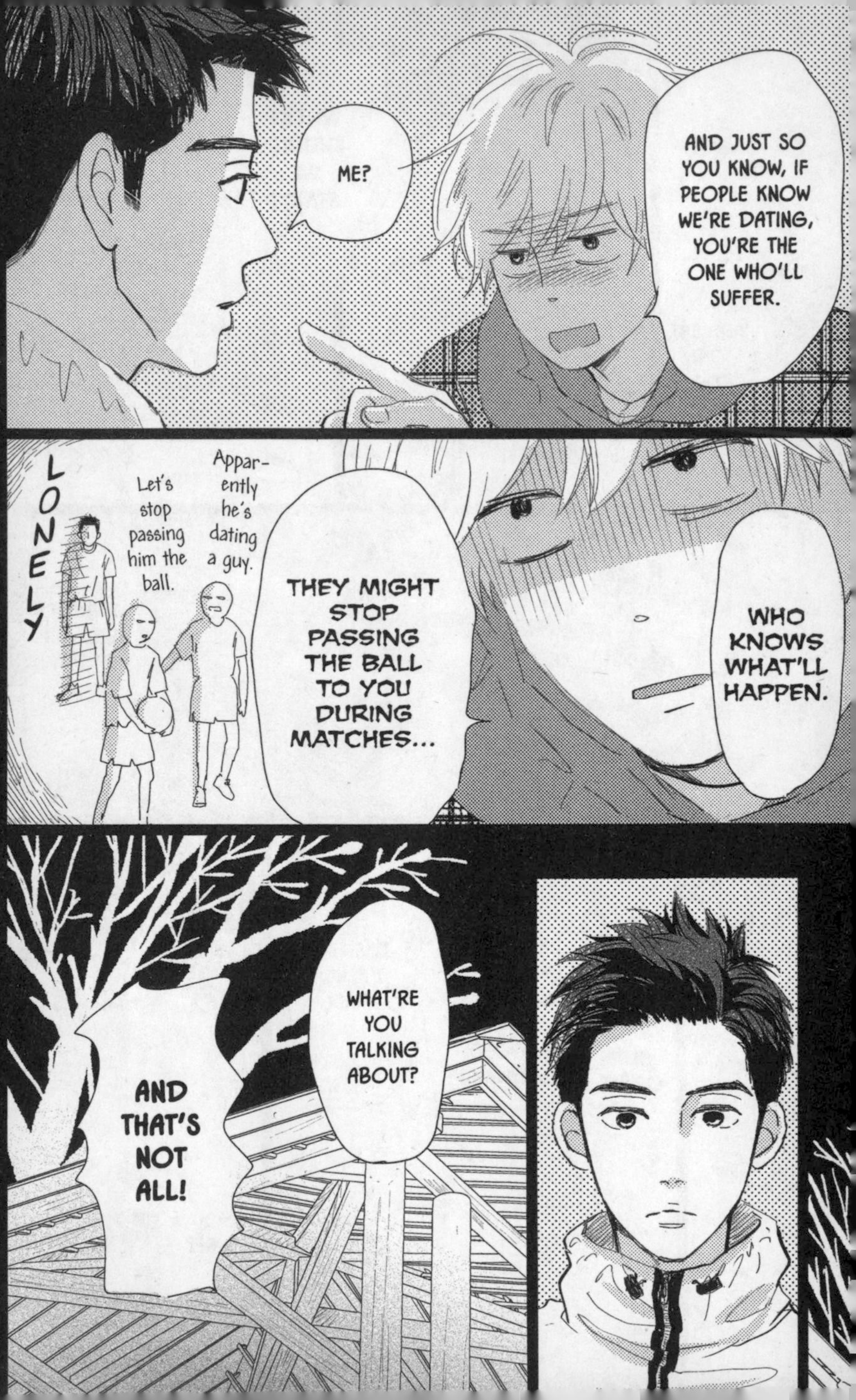
AND JUST SO YOU KNOW, IF PEOPLE KNOW WE'RE DATING, YOU'RE THE ONE WHO'LL SUFFER.
ME?
WHO KNOWS WHAT'LL HAPPEN.
THEY MIGHT STOP PASSING THE BALL TO YOU DURING MATCHES...
Apparently he's dating a guy.
Let's stop passing him the ball.
LONELY
WHAT'RE YOU TALKING ABOUT?
AND THAT'S NOT ALL!

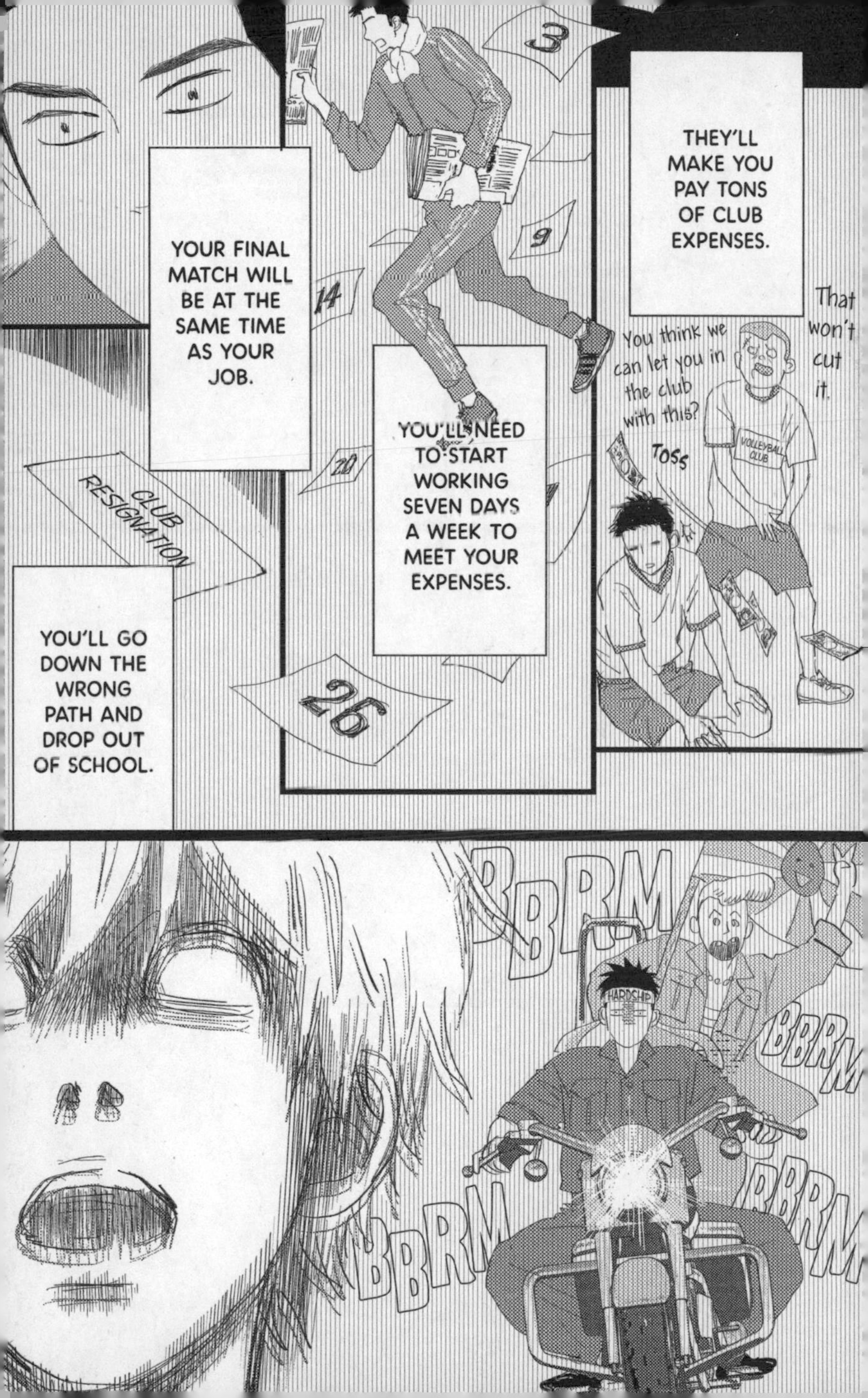
THEY'LL MAKE YOU PAY TONS OF CLUB EXPENSES.
That won't cut it.
You think we can let you in the club with this?
VOLLEYBALL CLUB
TOSS
3
9
14
20
26
YOU'LL NEED TO START WORKING SEVEN DAYS A WEEK TO MEET YOUR EXPENSES.
YOUR FINAL MATCH WILL BE AT THE SAME TIME AS YOUR JOB.
CLUB RESIGNATION
YOU'LL GO DOWN THE WRONG PATH AND DROP OUT OF SCHOOL.
BBRM
HARDSHIP
BBRM
BBRM
BBRM

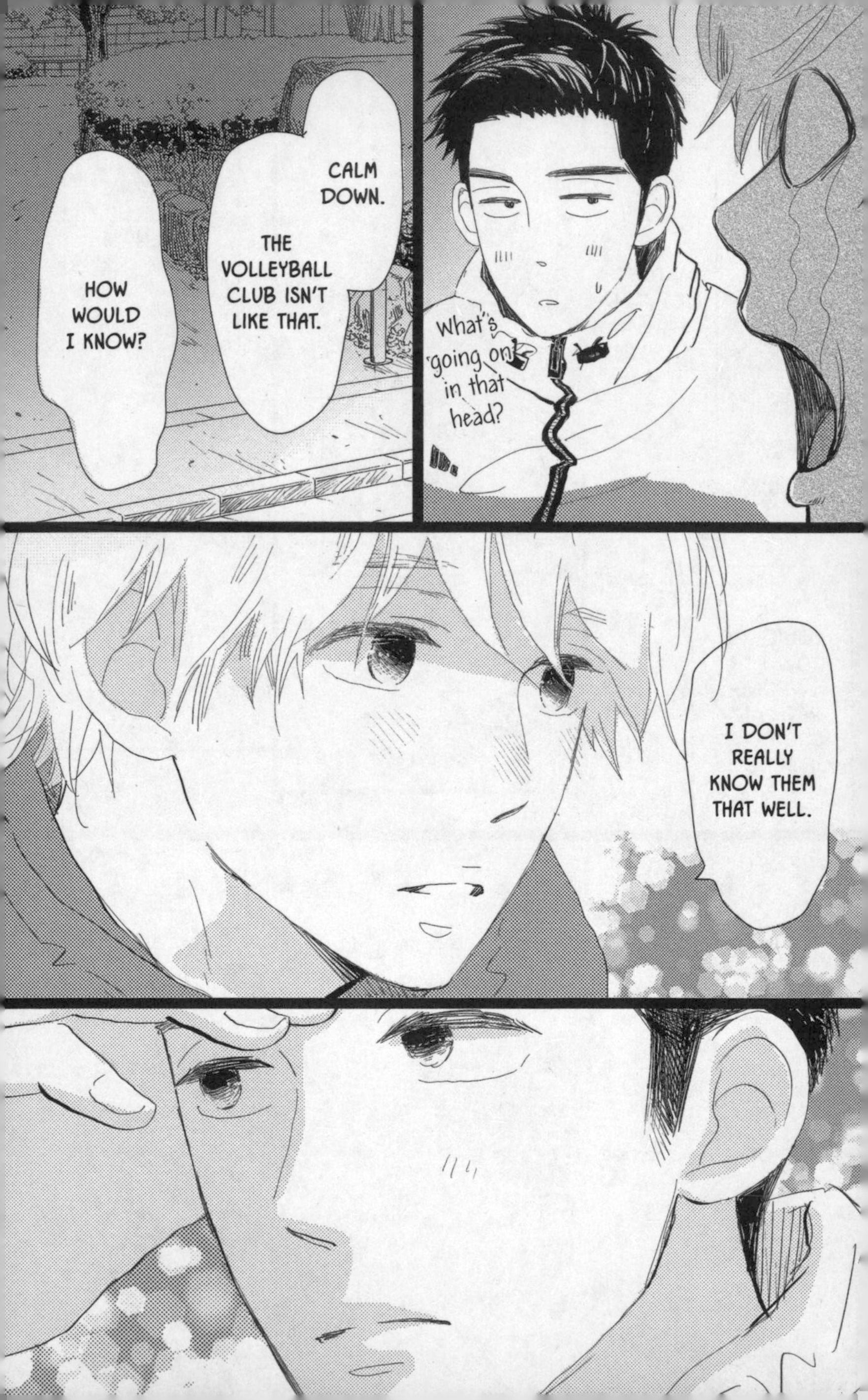
What's going on in that head?
CALM DOWN.
THE VOLLEYBALL CLUB ISN'T LIKE THAT.
HOW WOULD I KNOW?
I DON'T REALLY KNOW THEM THAT WELL.

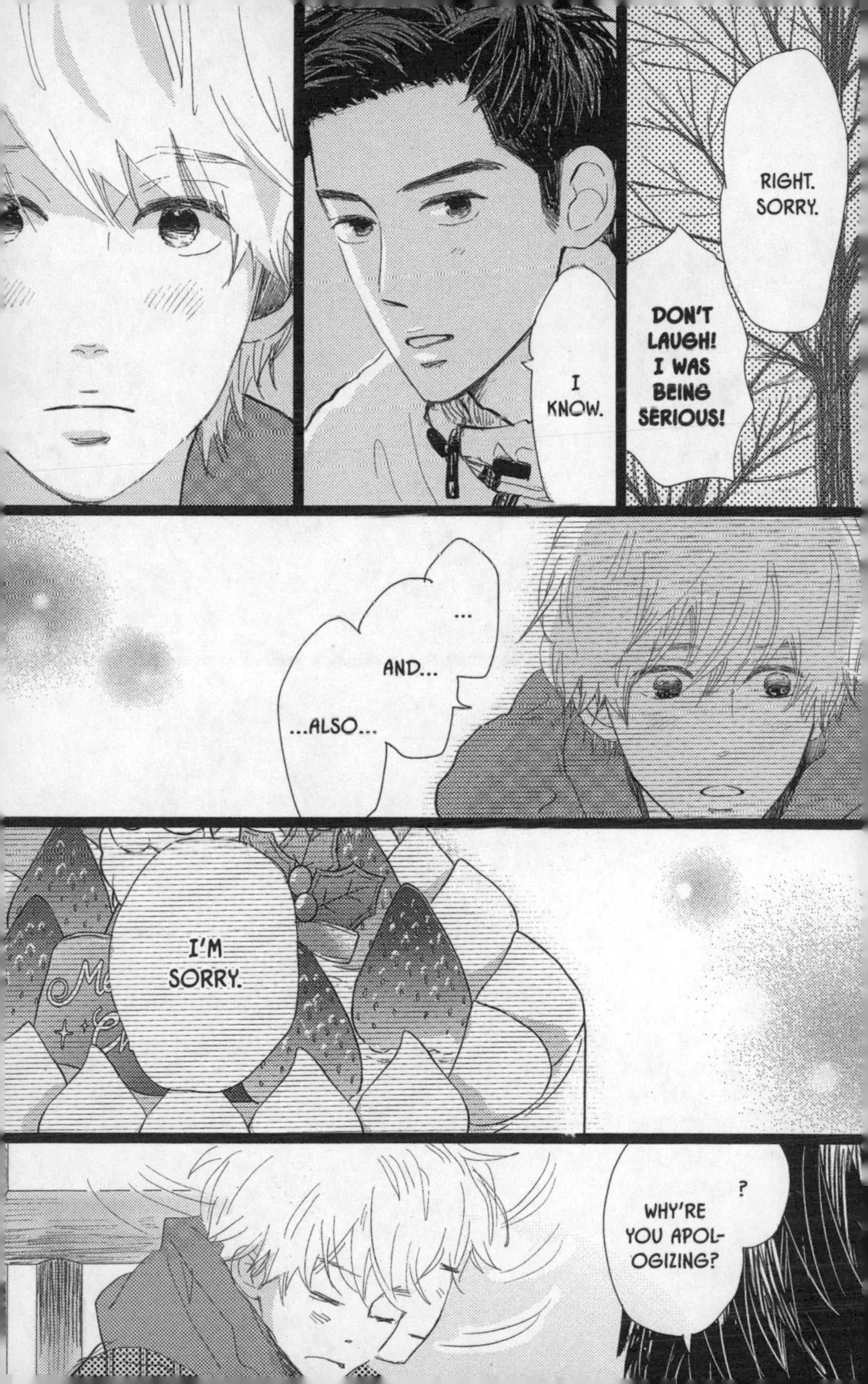
RIGHT. SORRY.
DON'T LAUGH! I WAS BEING SERIOUS!
I KNOW.
...
AND...
...ALSO...
I'M SORRY.
?
WHY'RE YOU APOL-OGIZING?

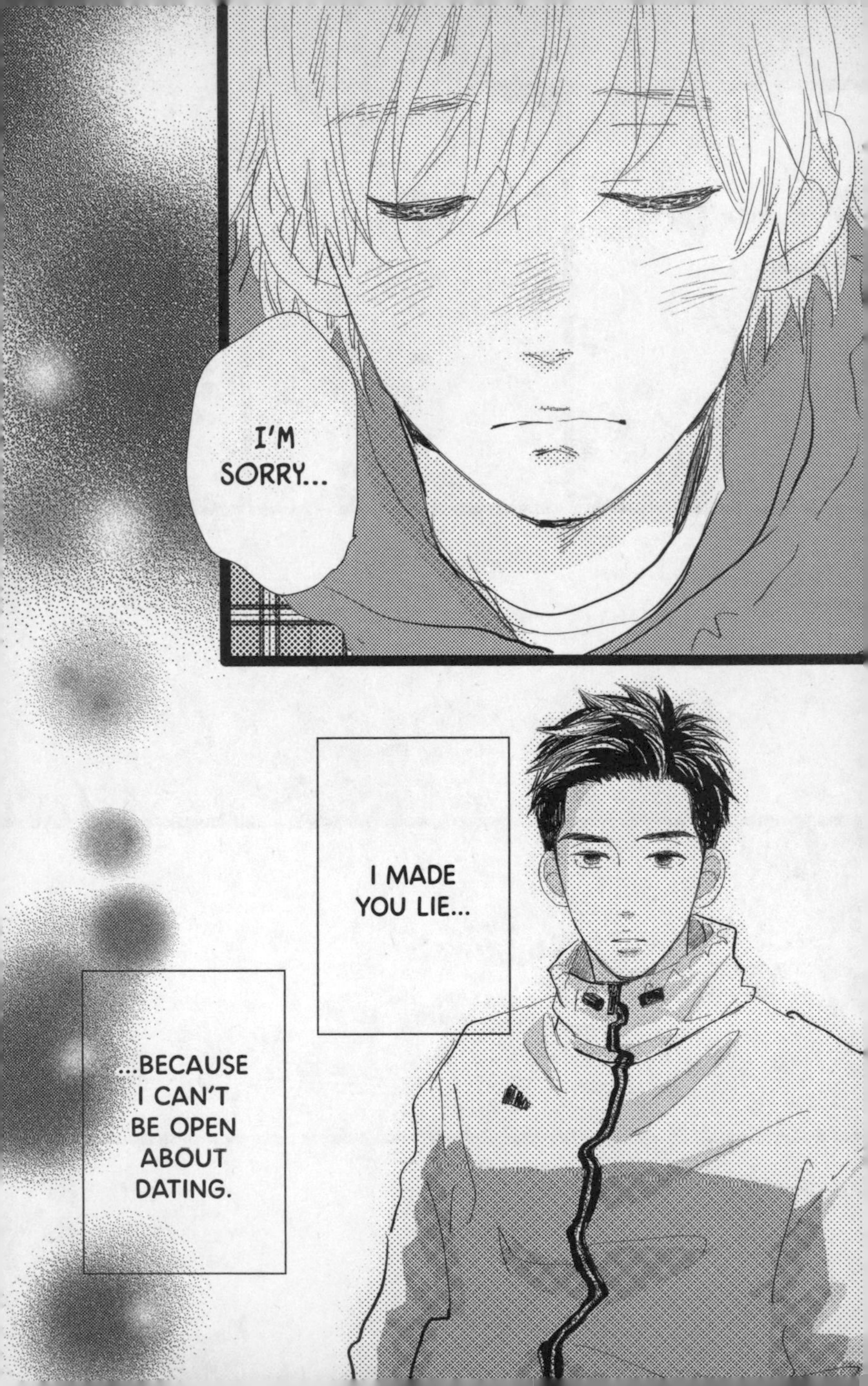
I'M SORRY...
I MADE YOU LIE...
...BECAUSE I CAN'T BE OPEN ABOUT DATING.

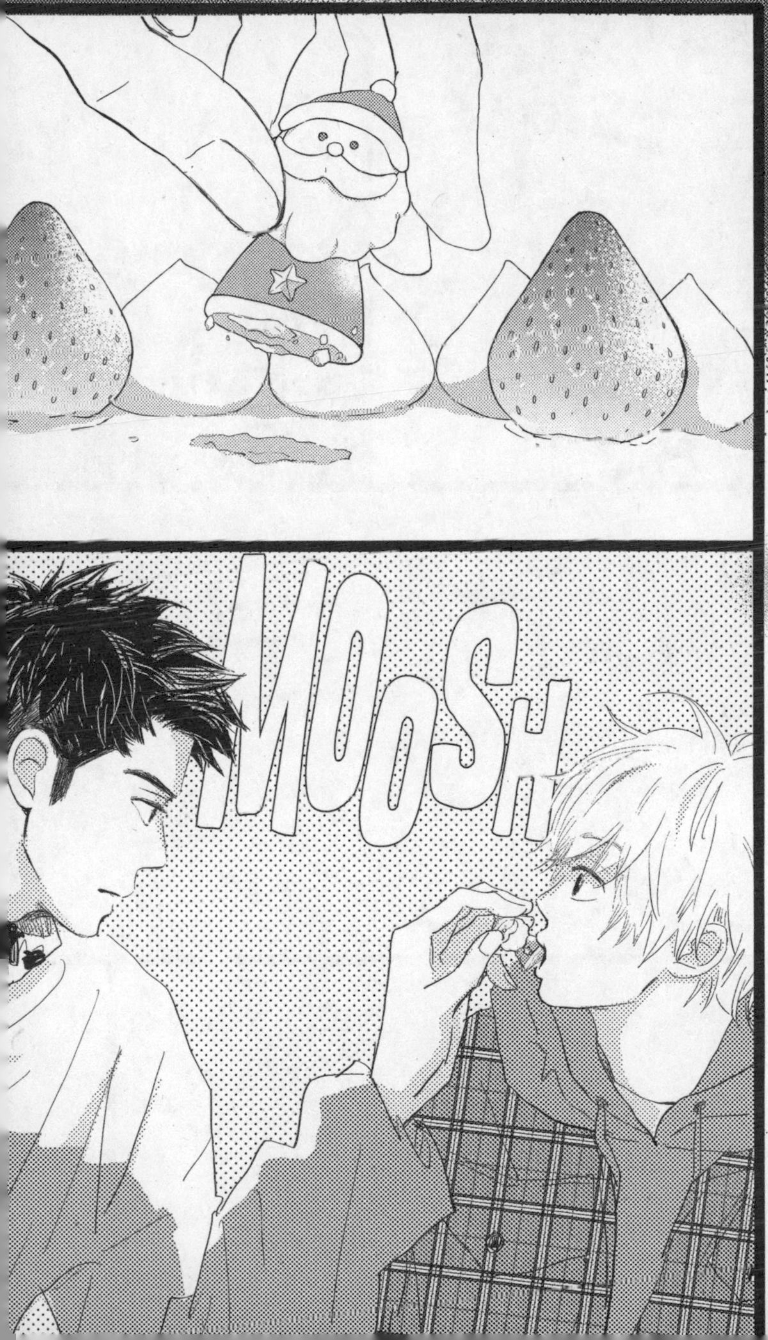
MOOSH

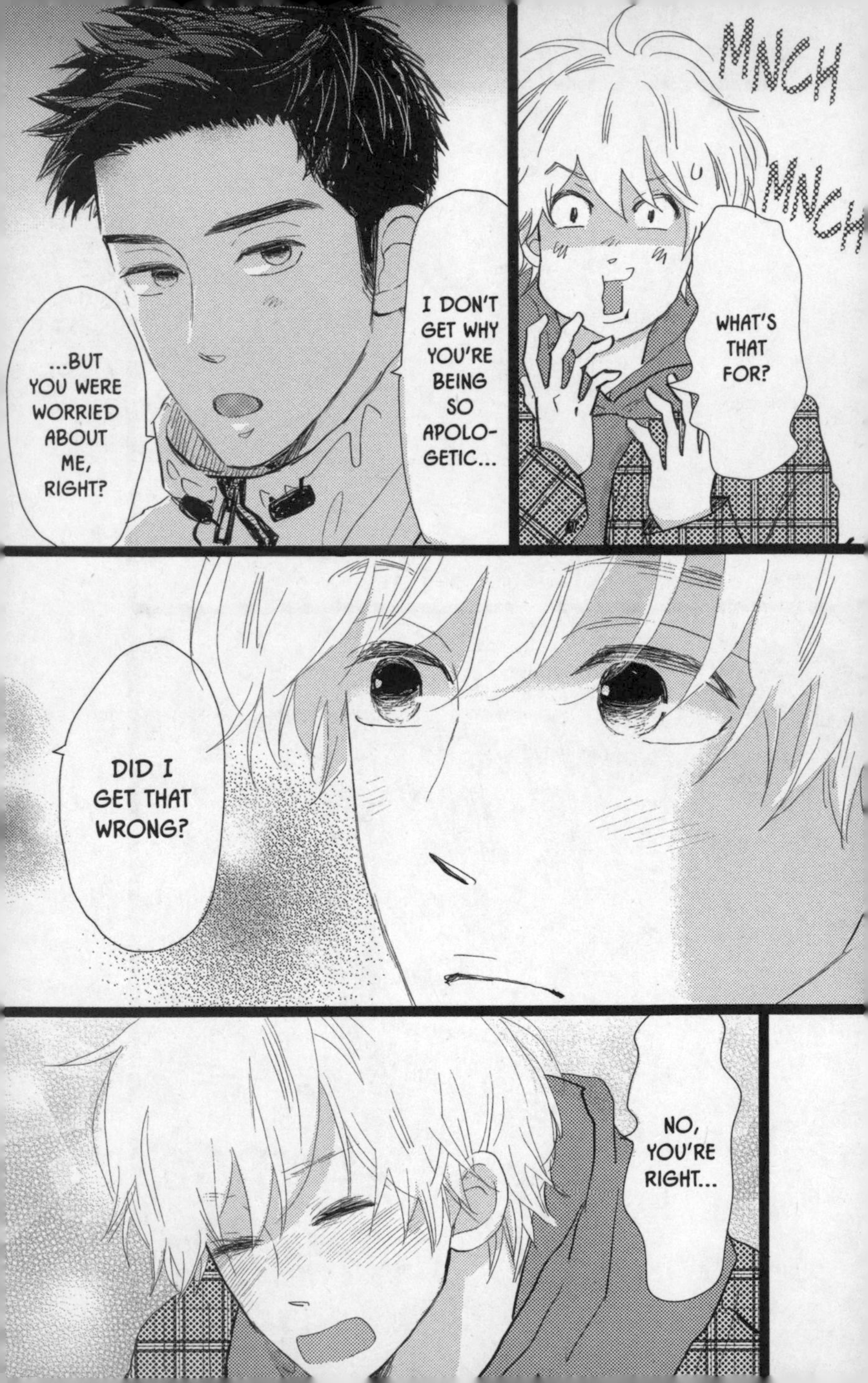
MNCH
MNCH
WHAT'S THAT FOR?
I DON'T GET WHY YOU'RE BEING SO APOLO-GETIC...
...BUT YOU WERE WORRIED ABOUT ME, RIGHT?
DID I GET THAT WRONG?
NO, YOU'RE RIGHT...

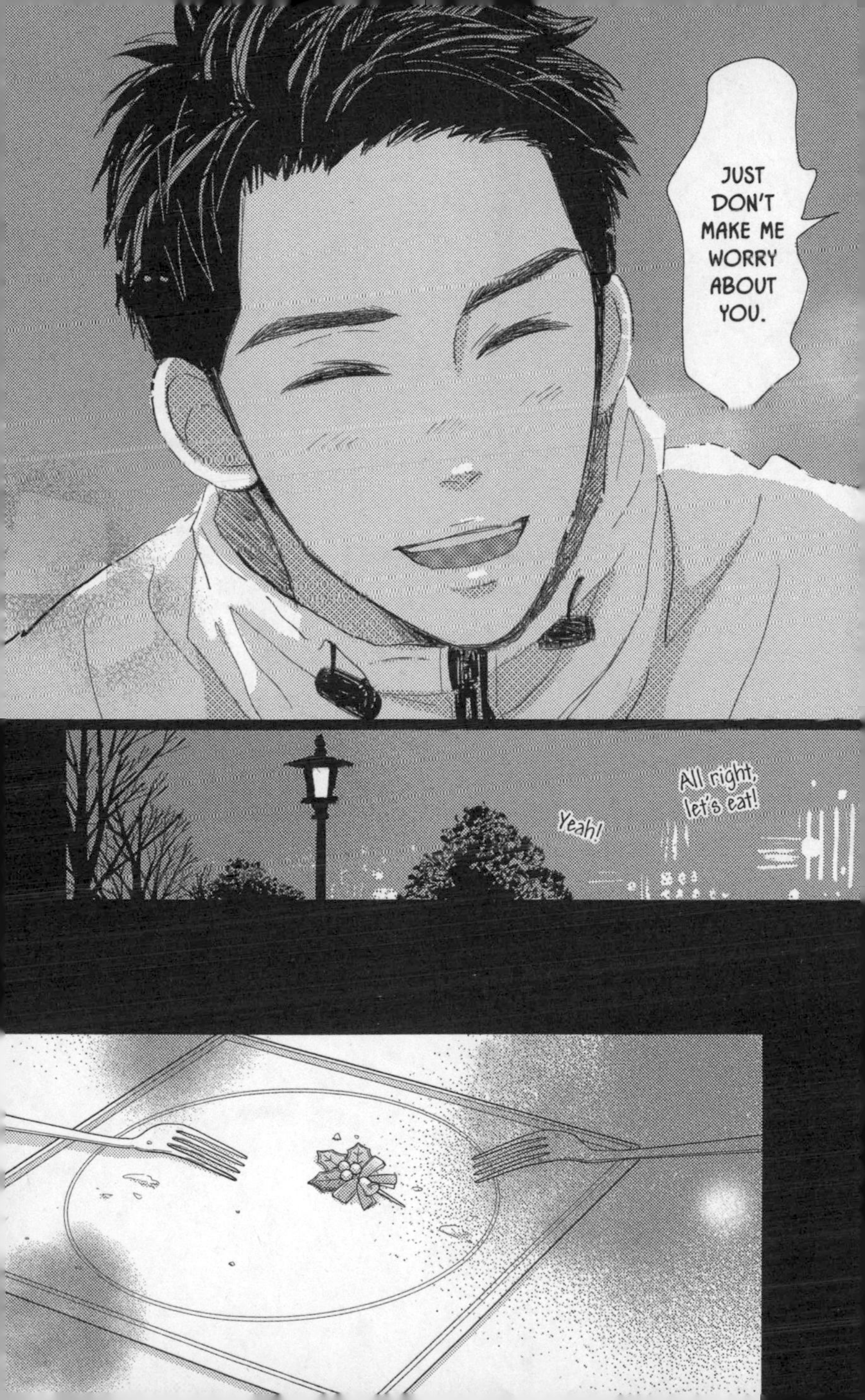
JUST DON'T MAKE ME WORRY ABOUT YOU.
All right, let's eat!
Yeah!

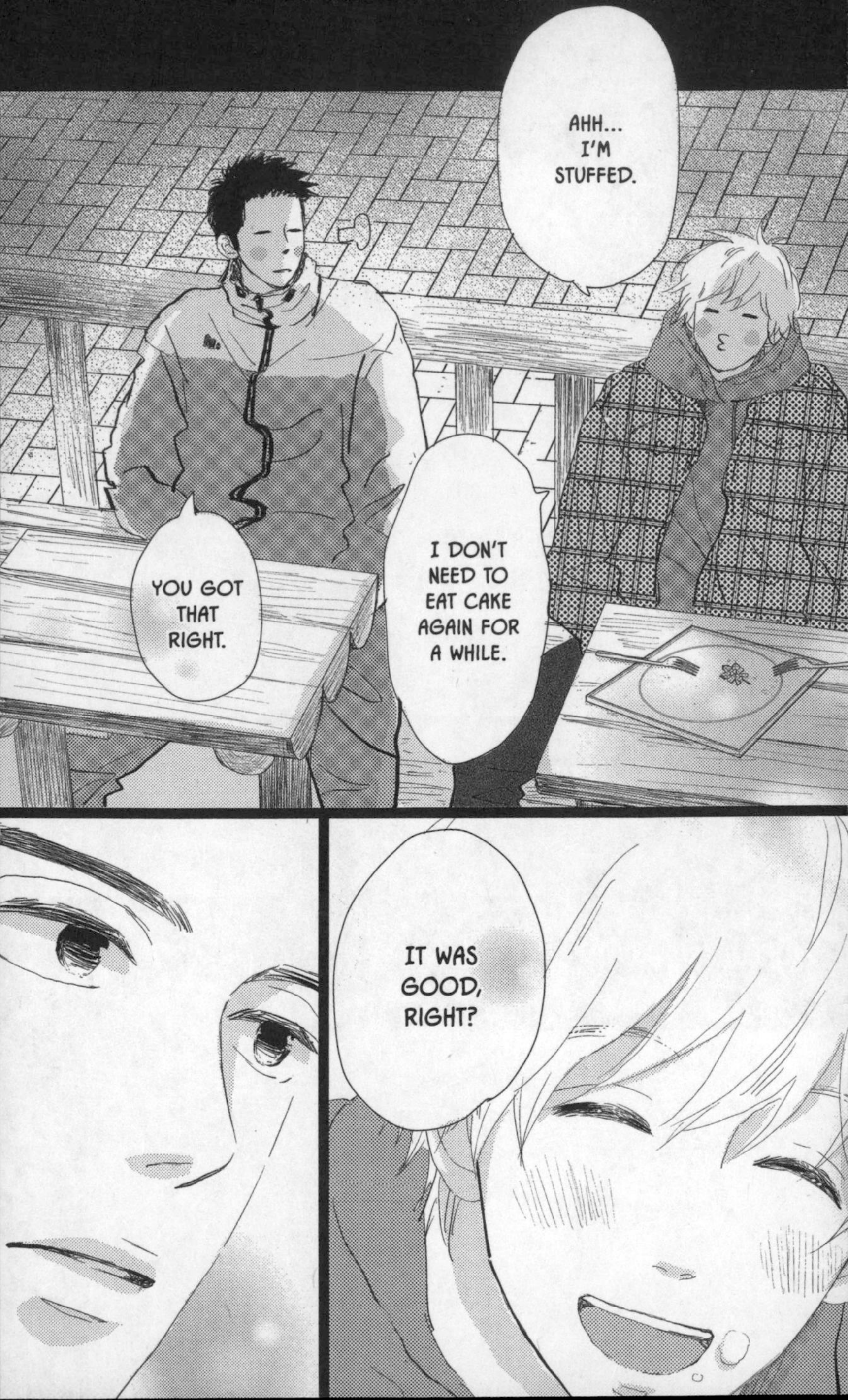
AHH... I'M STUFFED.
I DON'T NEED TO EAT CAKE AGAIN FOR A WHILE.
YOU GOT THAT RIGHT.
IT WAS GOOD, RIGHT?

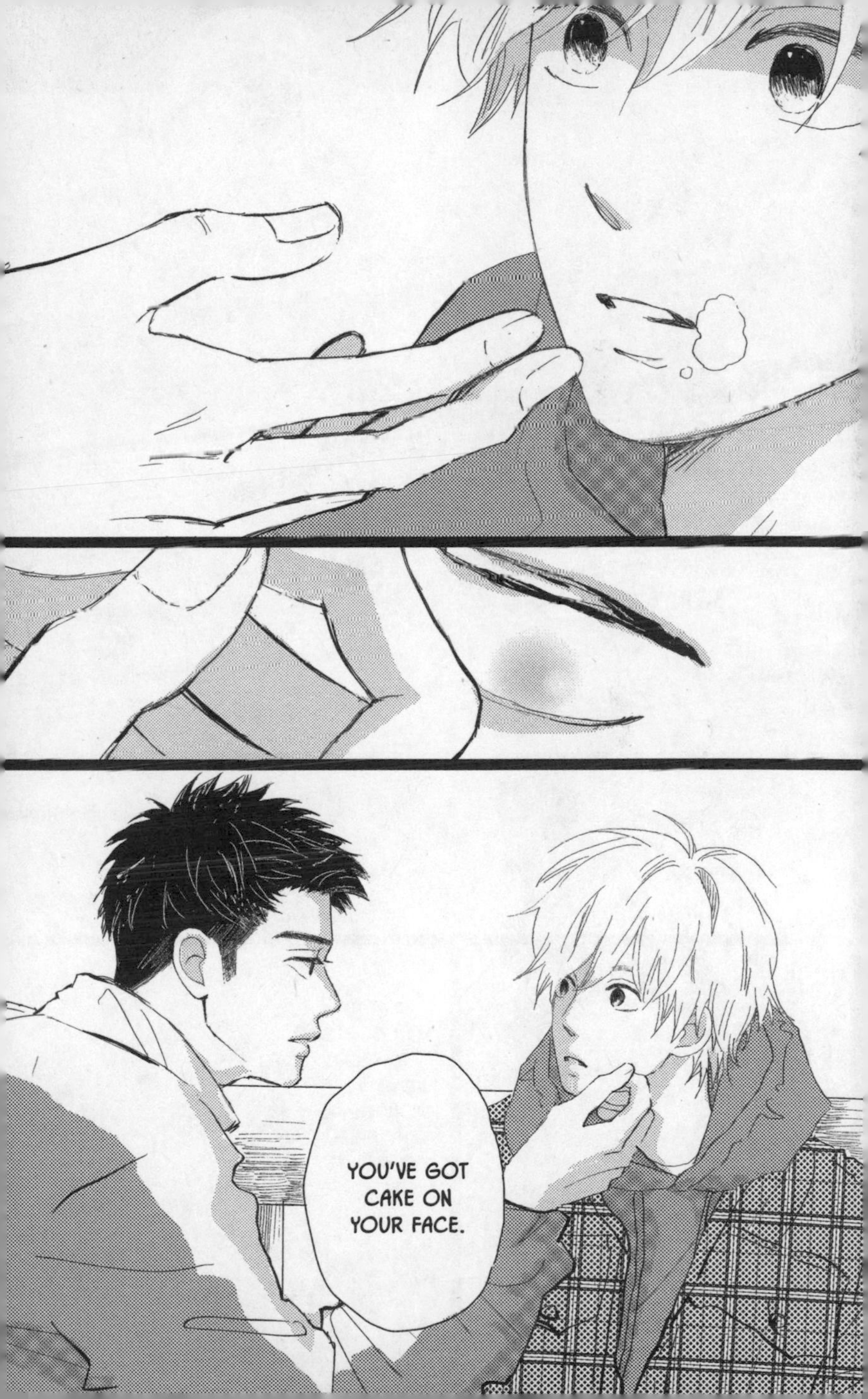
YOU'VE GOT CAKE ON YOUR FACE.

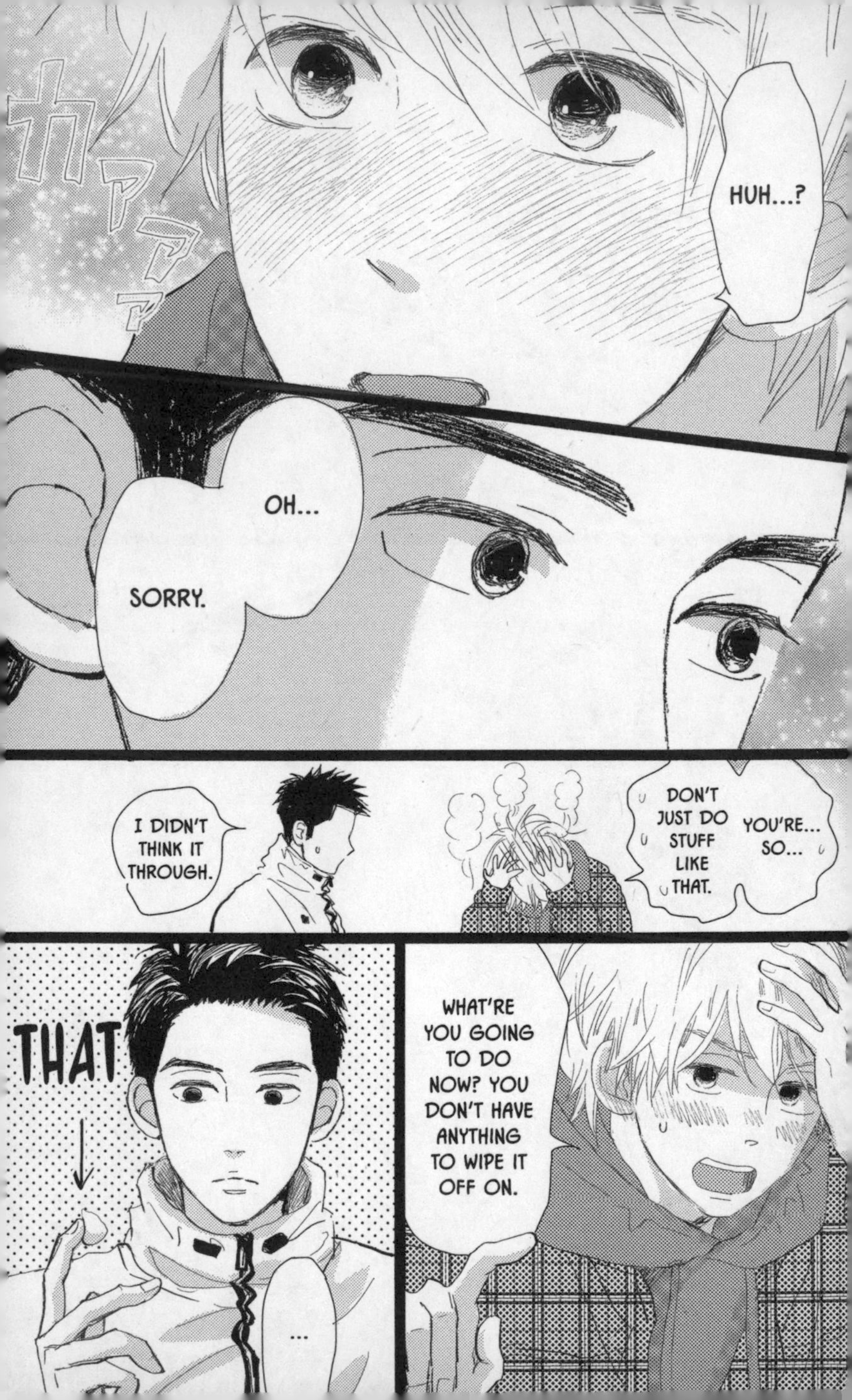

HUH...?
カァァァ
OH... SORRY.
YOU'RE... SO... DON'T JUST DO STUFF LIKE THAT.
I DIDN'T THINK IT THROUGH.
WHAT'RE YOU GOING TO DO NOW? YOU DON'T HAVE ANYTHING TO WIPE IT OFF ON.
THAT
...

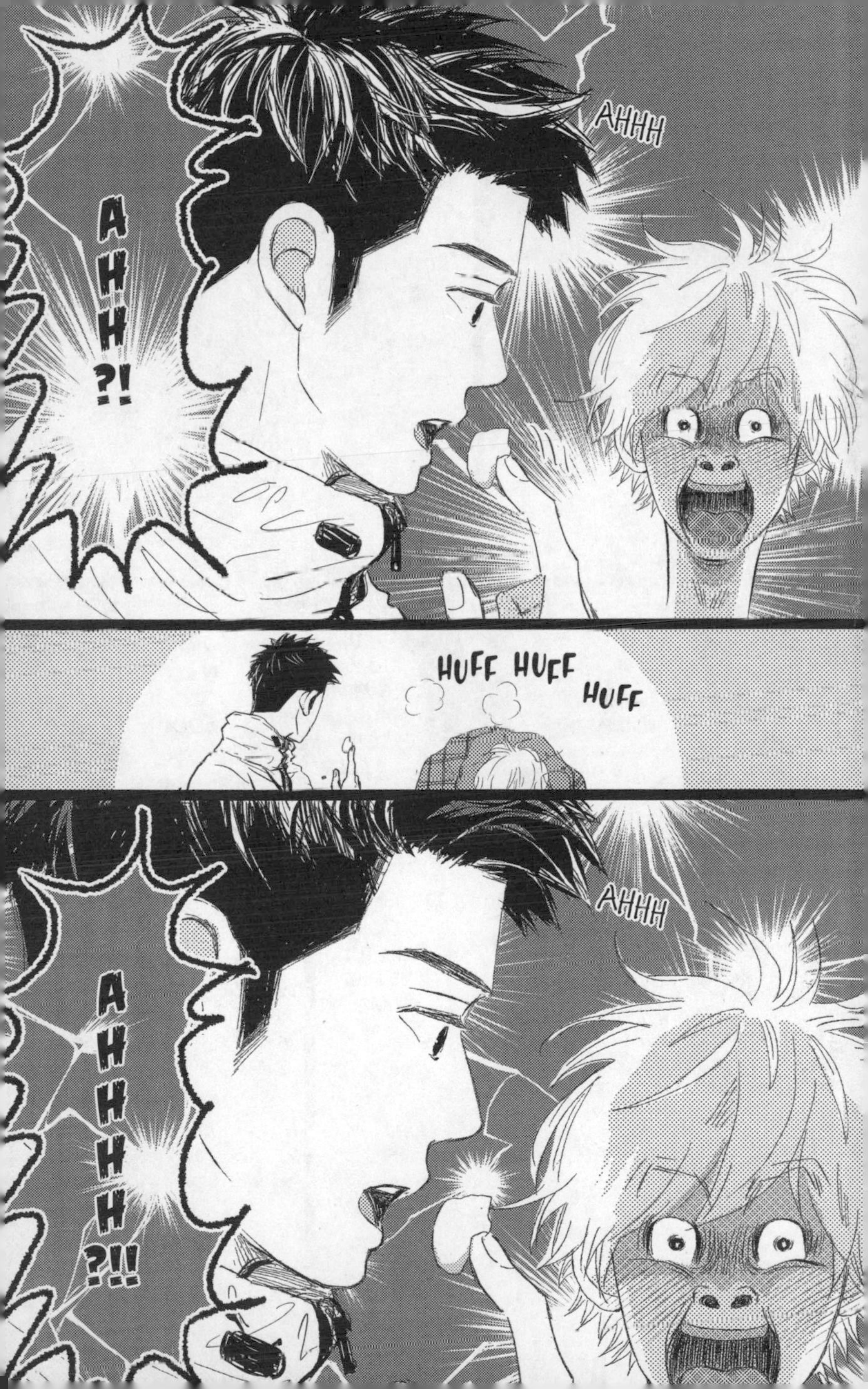
AHHH
AHHH?!
HUFF HUFF HUFF
AHHH
AHHHHH?!!

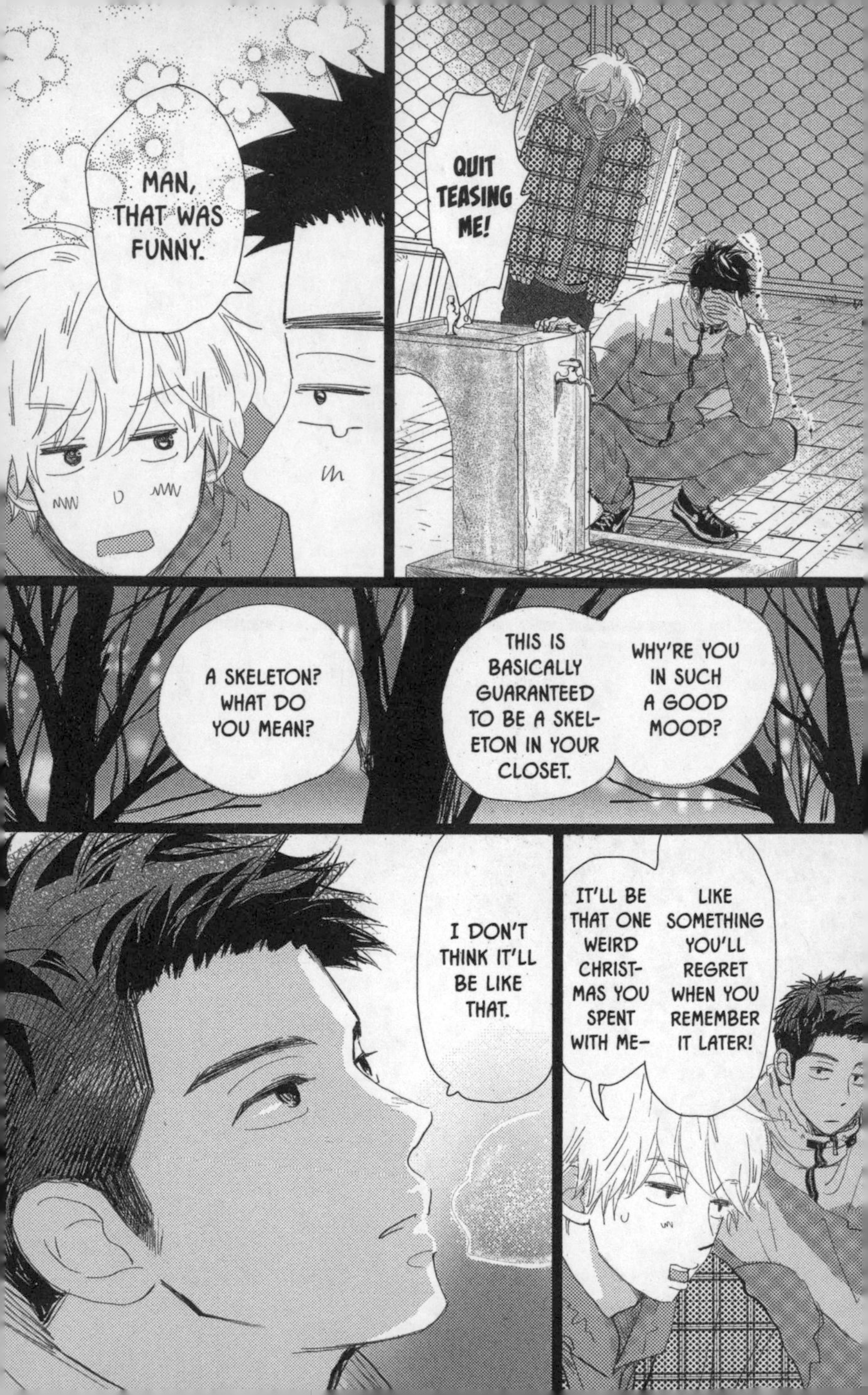
QUIT TEASING ME!
MAN, THAT WAS FUNNY.
WHY'RE YOU IN SUCH A GOOD MOOD?
THIS IS BASICALLY GUARANTEED TO BE A SKELETON IN YOUR CLOSET.
A SKELETON? WHAT DO YOU MEAN?
IT'LL BE THAT ONE WEIRD CHRISTMAS YOU SPENT WITH ME—
LIKE SOMETHING YOU'LL REGRET WHEN YOU REMEMBER IT LATER!
I DON'T THINK IT'LL BE LIKE THAT.

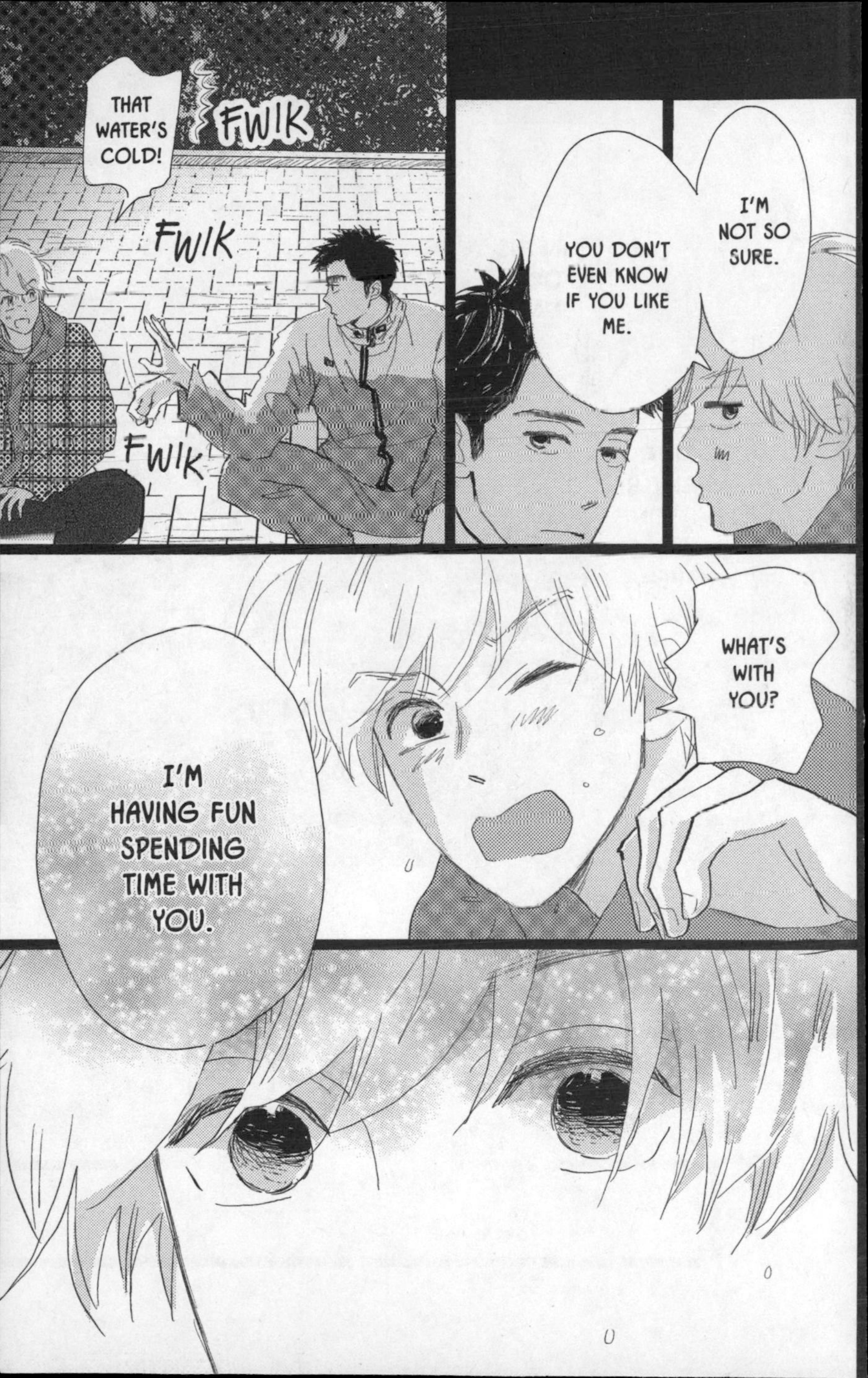
I'M NOT SO SURE.
YOU DON'T EVEN KNOW IF YOU LIKE ME.
FWIK
THAT WATER'S COLD!
FWIK
FWIK
WHAT'S WITH YOU?
I'M HAVING FUN SPENDING TIME WITH YOU.

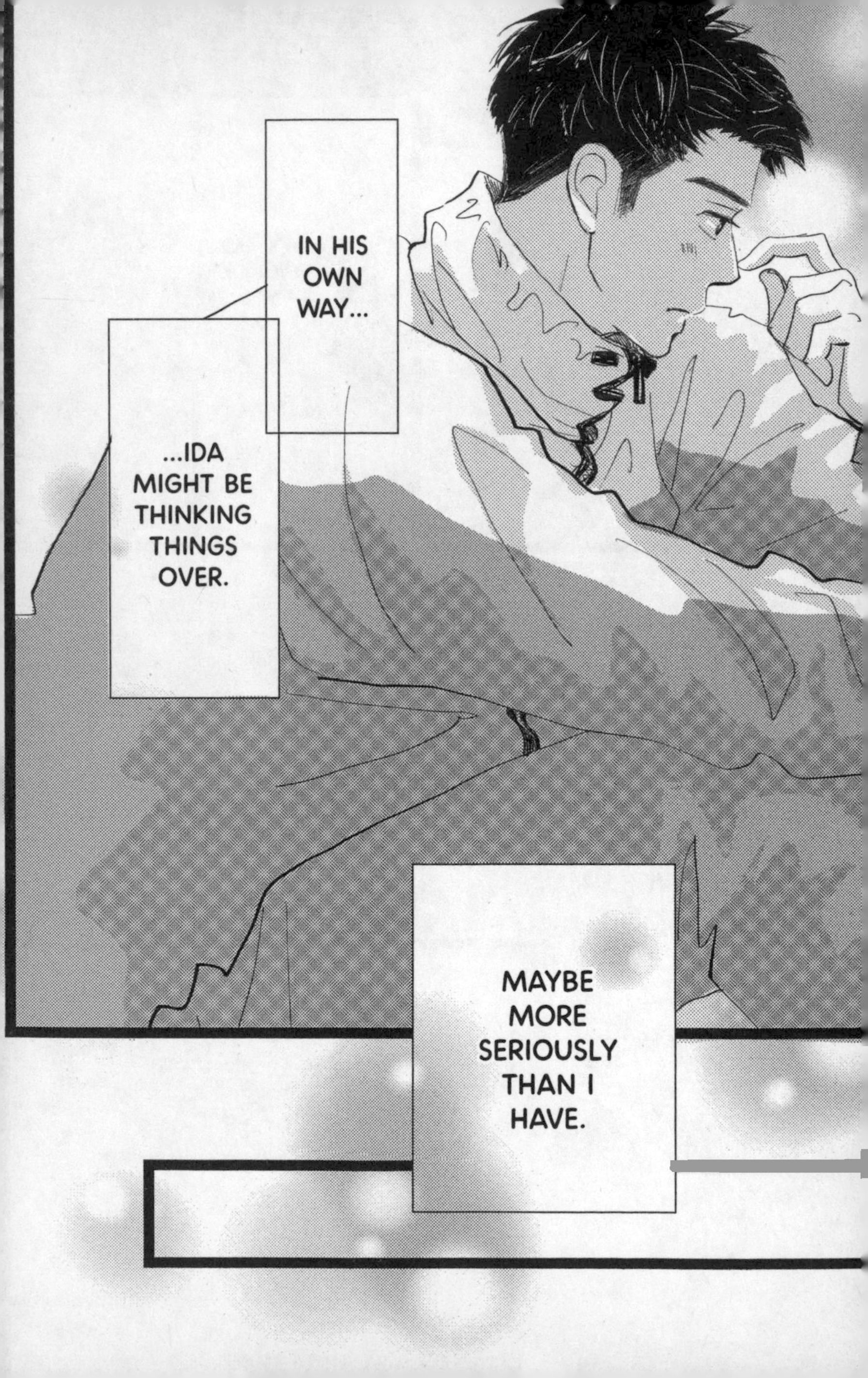
IN HIS OWN WAY...
...IDA MIGHT BE THINKING THINGS OVER.
MAYBE MORE SERIOUSLY THAN I HAVE.

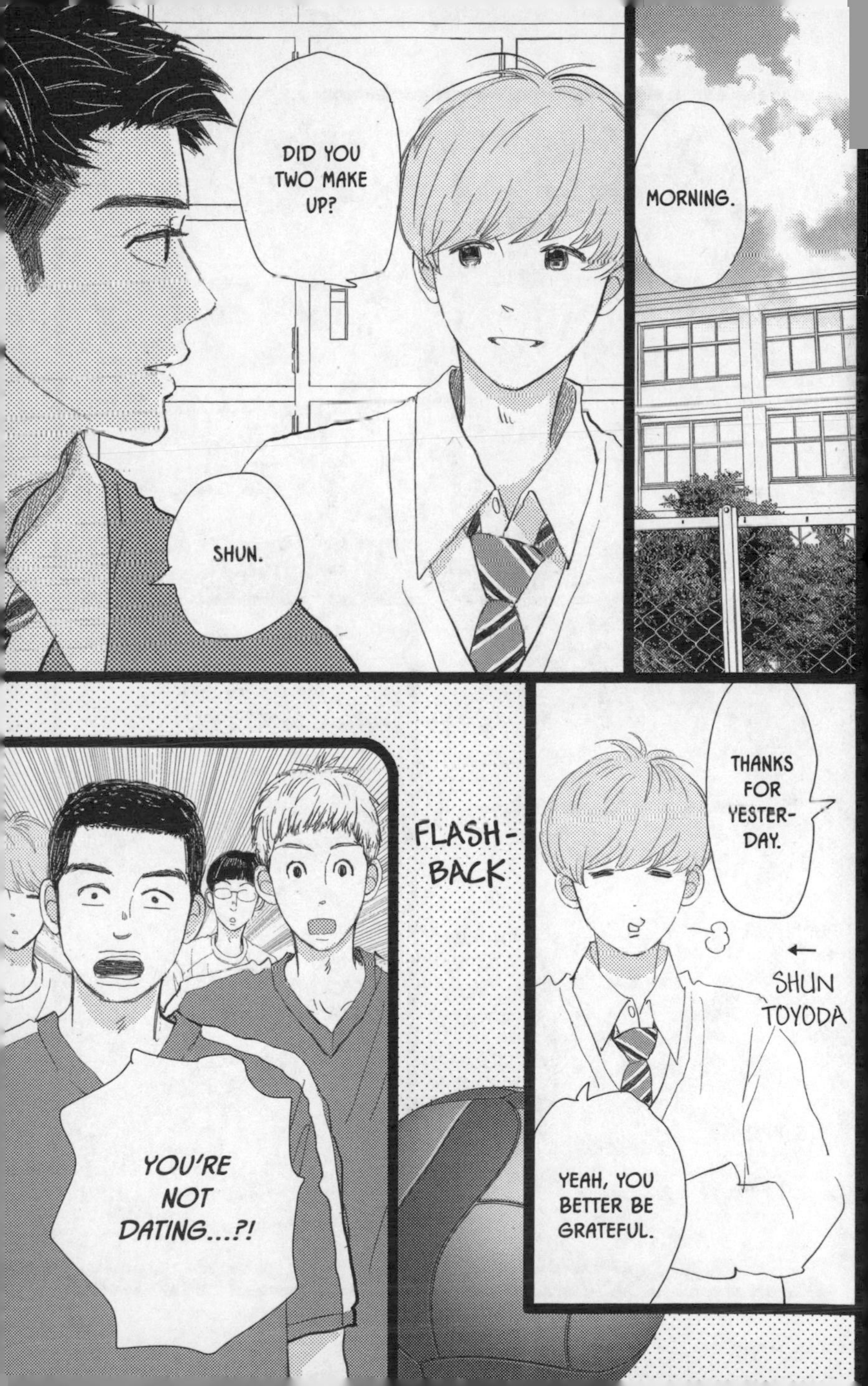
MORNING.
DID YOU TWO MAKE UP?
SHUN.
THANKS FOR YESTER-DAY.
← SHUN TOYODA
YEAH, YOU BETTER BE GRATEFUL.
FLASH-BACK
YOU'RE NOT DATING...?!

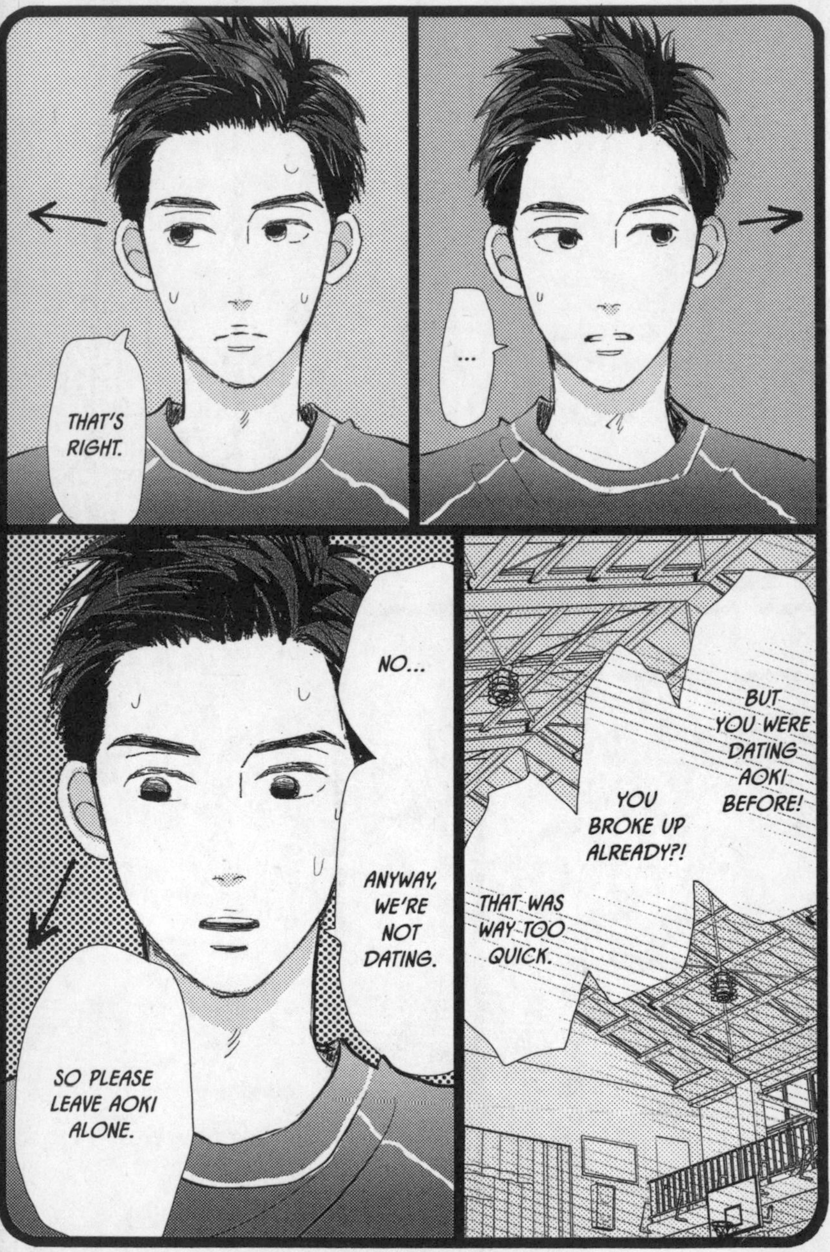
...
THAT'S RIGHT.
BUT YOU WERE DATING AOKI BEFORE!
YOU BROKE UP ALREADY?!
THAT WAS WAY TOO QUICK.
NO...
ANYWAY, WE'RE NOT DATING.
SO PLEASE LEAVE AOKI ALONE.

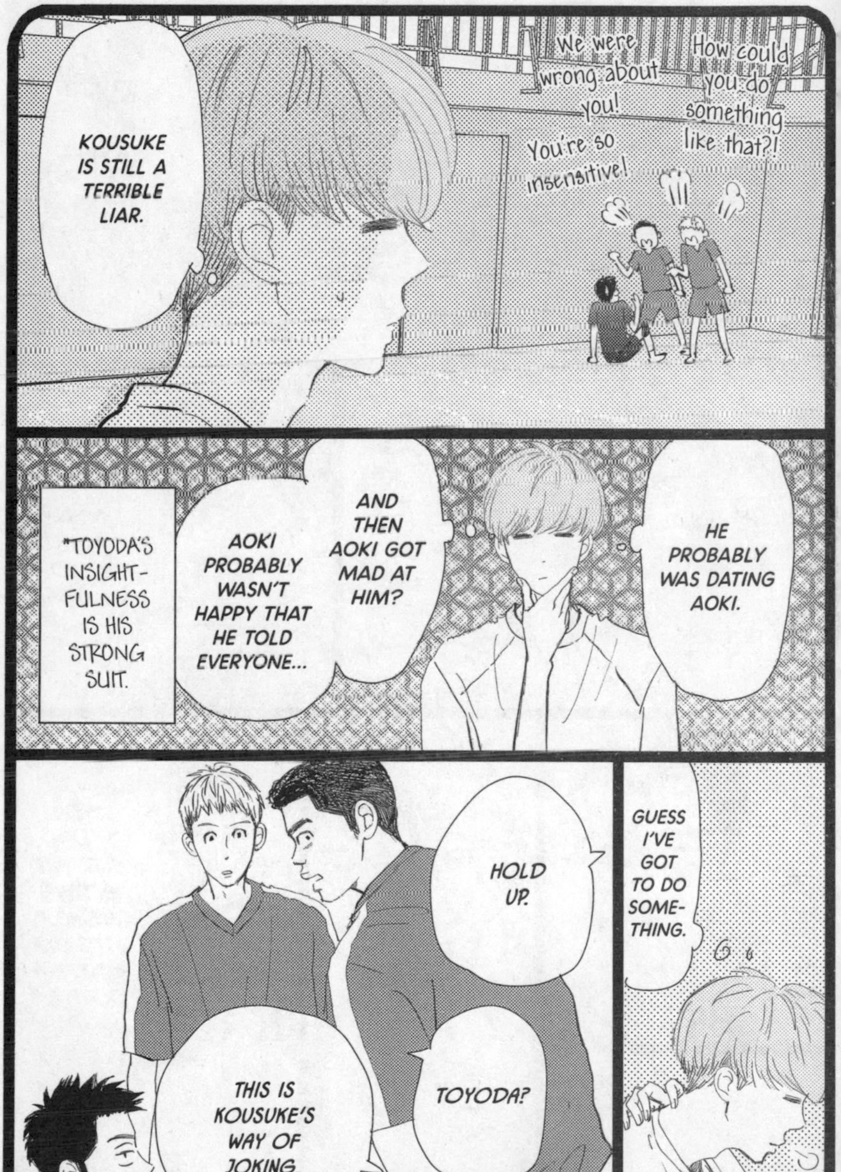
How could you do something like that?!
We were wrong about you!
You're so insensitive!
KOUSUKE IS STILL A TERRIBLE LIAR.
HE PROBABLY WAS DATING AOKI.
AND THEN AOKI GOT MAD AT HIM?
AOKI PROBABLY WASN'T HAPPY THAT HE TOLD EVERYONE...
*TOYODA'S INSIGHT-FULNESS IS HIS STRONG SUIT.
GUESS I'VE GOT TO DO SOME-THING.
HOLD UP.
TOYODA?
THIS IS KOUSUKE'S WAY OF JOKING.

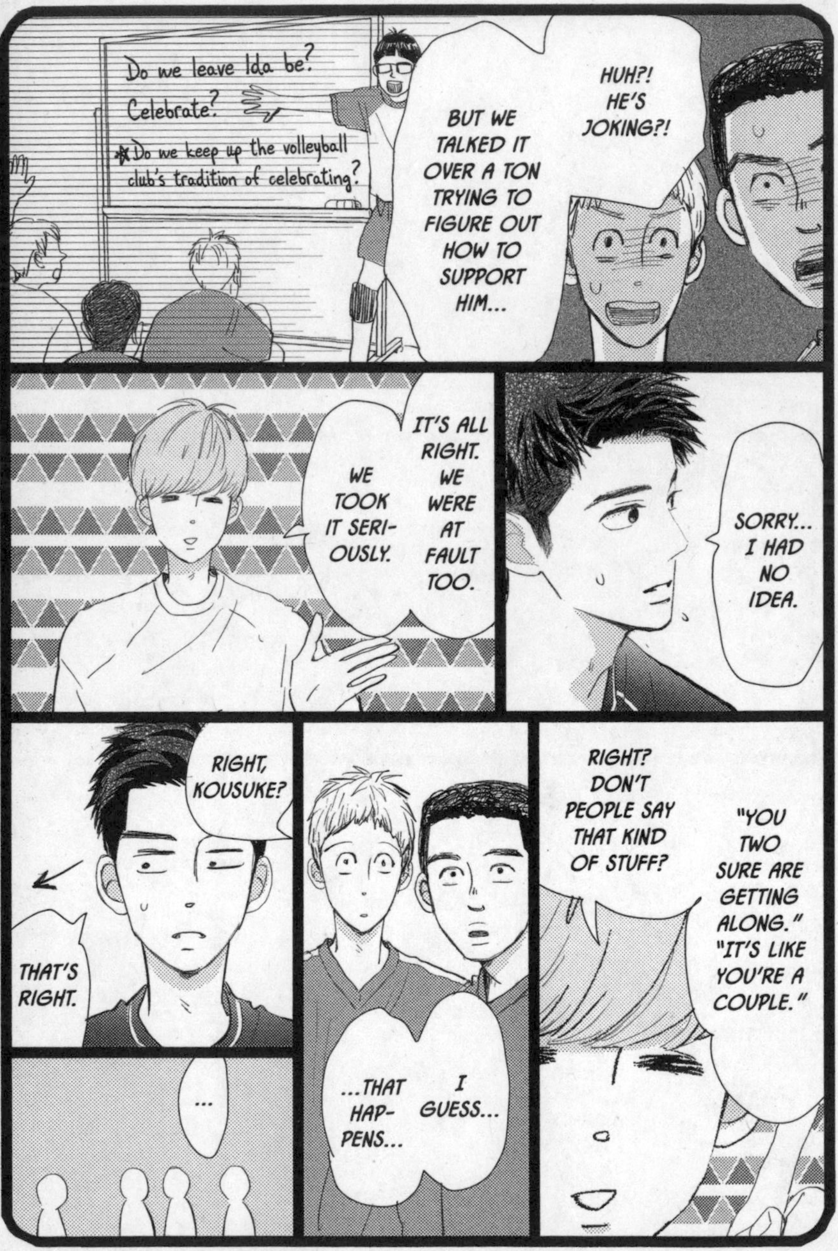
HUH?! HE'S JOKING?!
BUT WE TALKED IT OVER A TON TRYING TO FIGURE OUT HOW TO SUPPORT HIM...
Do we leave Ida be?
Celebrate?
Do we keep up the volleyball club's tradition of celebrating?
SORRY... I HAD NO IDEA.
IT'S ALL RIGHT. WE WERE AT FAULT TOO.
WE TOOK IT SERIOUSLY.
"YOU TWO SURE ARE GETTING ALONG." "IT'S LIKE YOU'RE A COUPLE."
RIGHT? DON'T PEOPLE SAY THAT KIND OF STUFF?
I GUESS...
...THAT HAPPENS...
RIGHT, KOUSUKE?
THAT'S RIGHT.
...

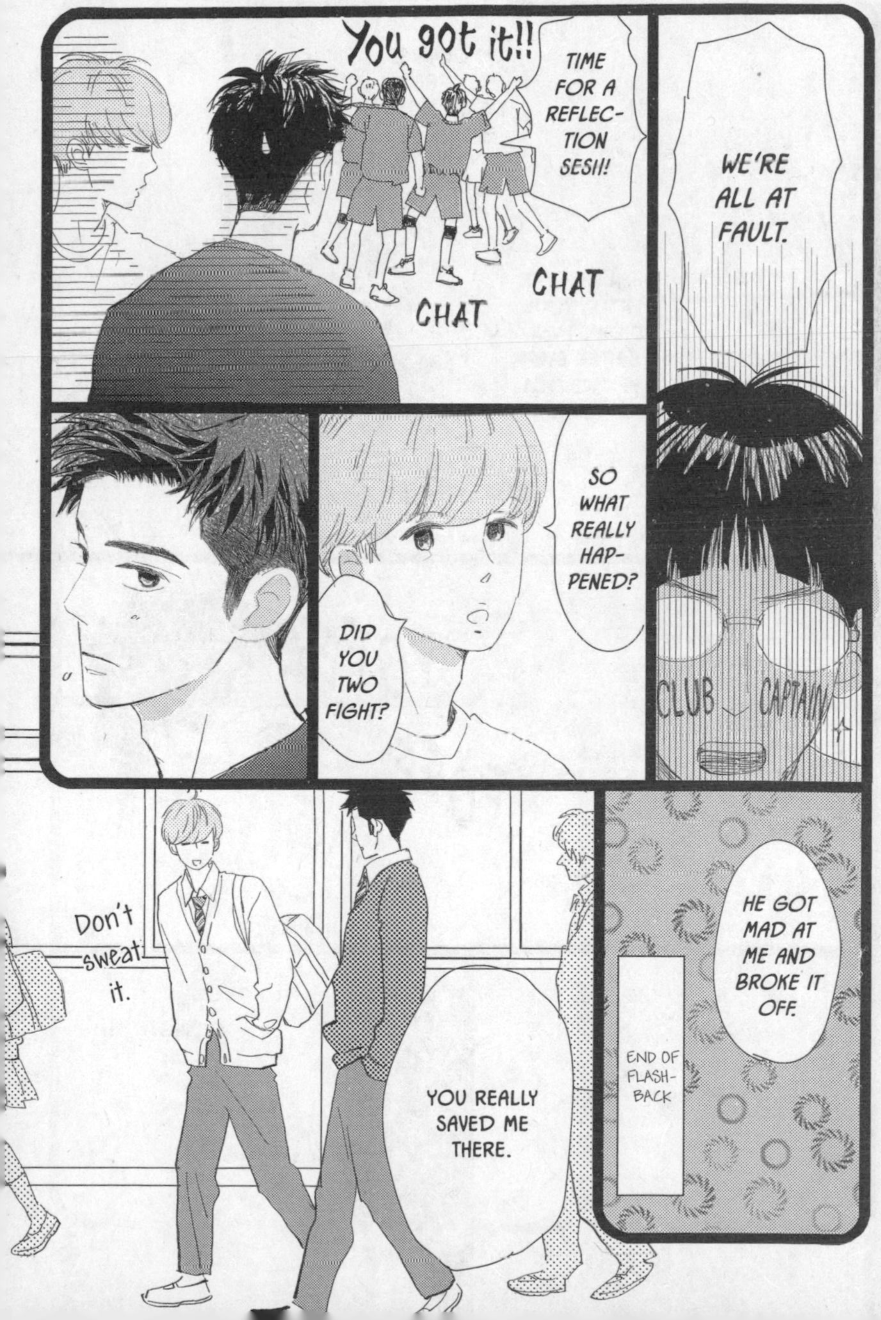
WE'RE ALL AT FAULT.
CLUB CAPTAIN
TIME FOR A REFLECTION SESH!
You got it!!
CHAT
CHAT
SO WHAT REALLY HAPPENED?
DID YOU TWO FIGHT?
HE GOT MAD AT ME AND BROKE IT OFF.
END OF FLASHBACK
YOU REALLY SAVED ME THERE.
Don't sweat it.

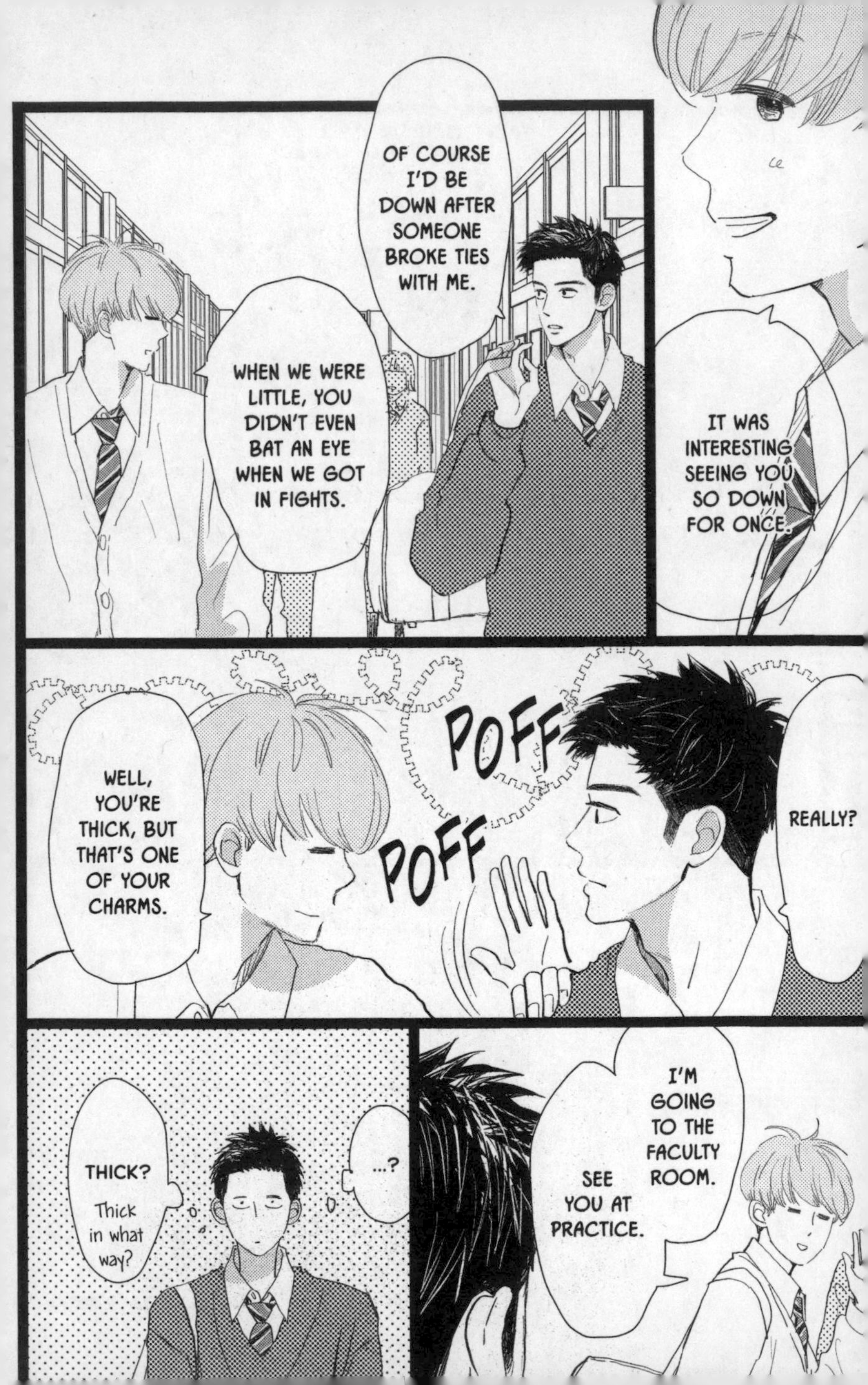
IT WAS INTERESTING SEEING YOU SO DOWN FOR ONCE.
OF COURSE I'D BE DOWN AFTER SOMEONE BROKE TIES WITH ME.
WHEN WE WERE LITTLE, YOU DIDN'T EVEN BAT AN EYE WHEN WE GOT IN FIGHTS.
REALLY?
POFF
POFF
WELL, YOU'RE THICK, BUT THAT'S ONE OF YOUR CHARMS.
I'M GOING TO THE FACULTY ROOM.
SEE YOU AT PRACTICE.
...?
THICK?
Thick in what way?

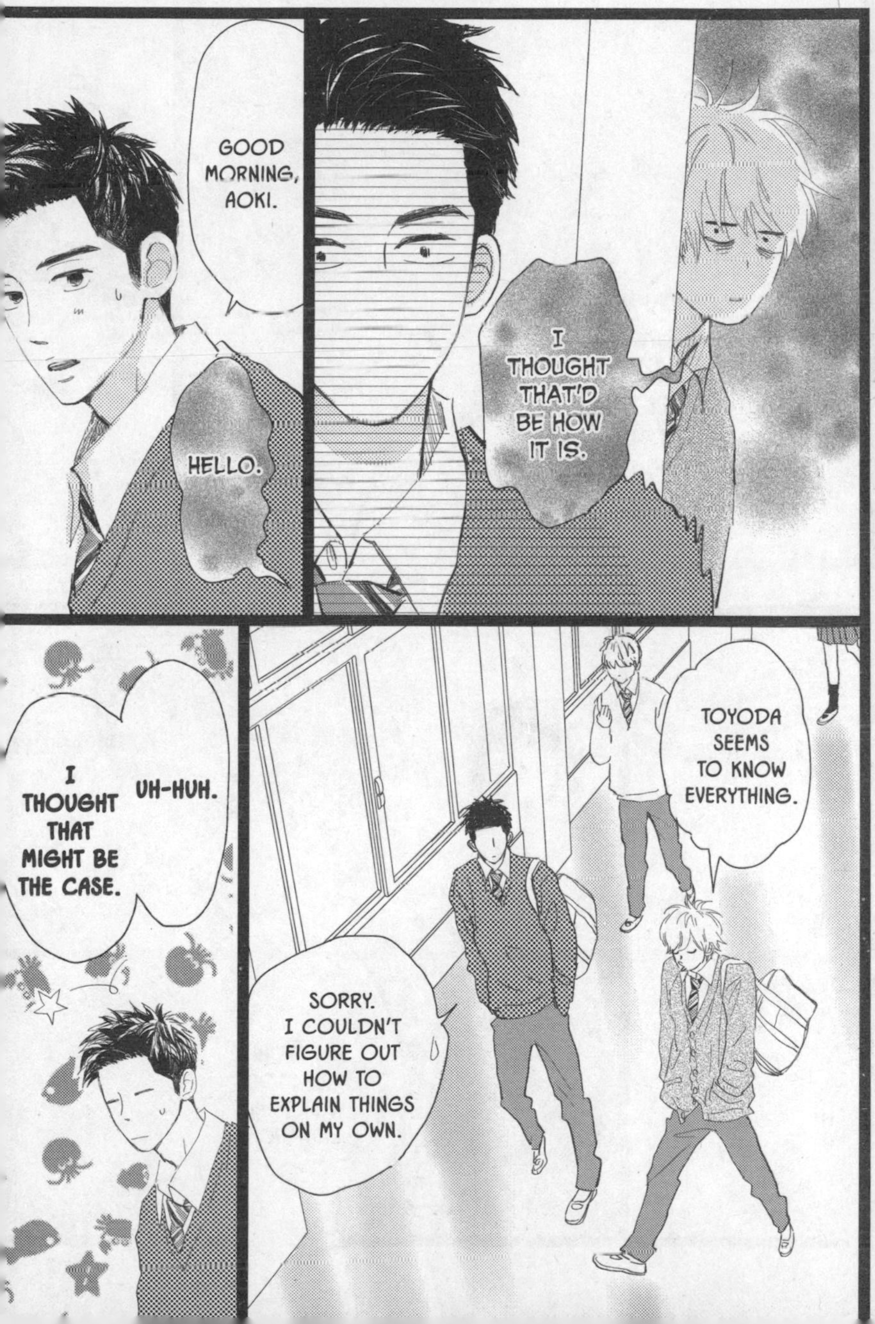
I THOUGHT THAT'D BE HOW IT IS.
GOOD MORNING, AOKI.
HELLO.
TOYODA SEEMS TO KNOW EVERYTHING.
SORRY. I COULDN'T FIGURE OUT HOW TO EXPLAIN THINGS ON MY OWN.
UH-HUH.
I THOUGHT THAT MIGHT BE THE CASE.

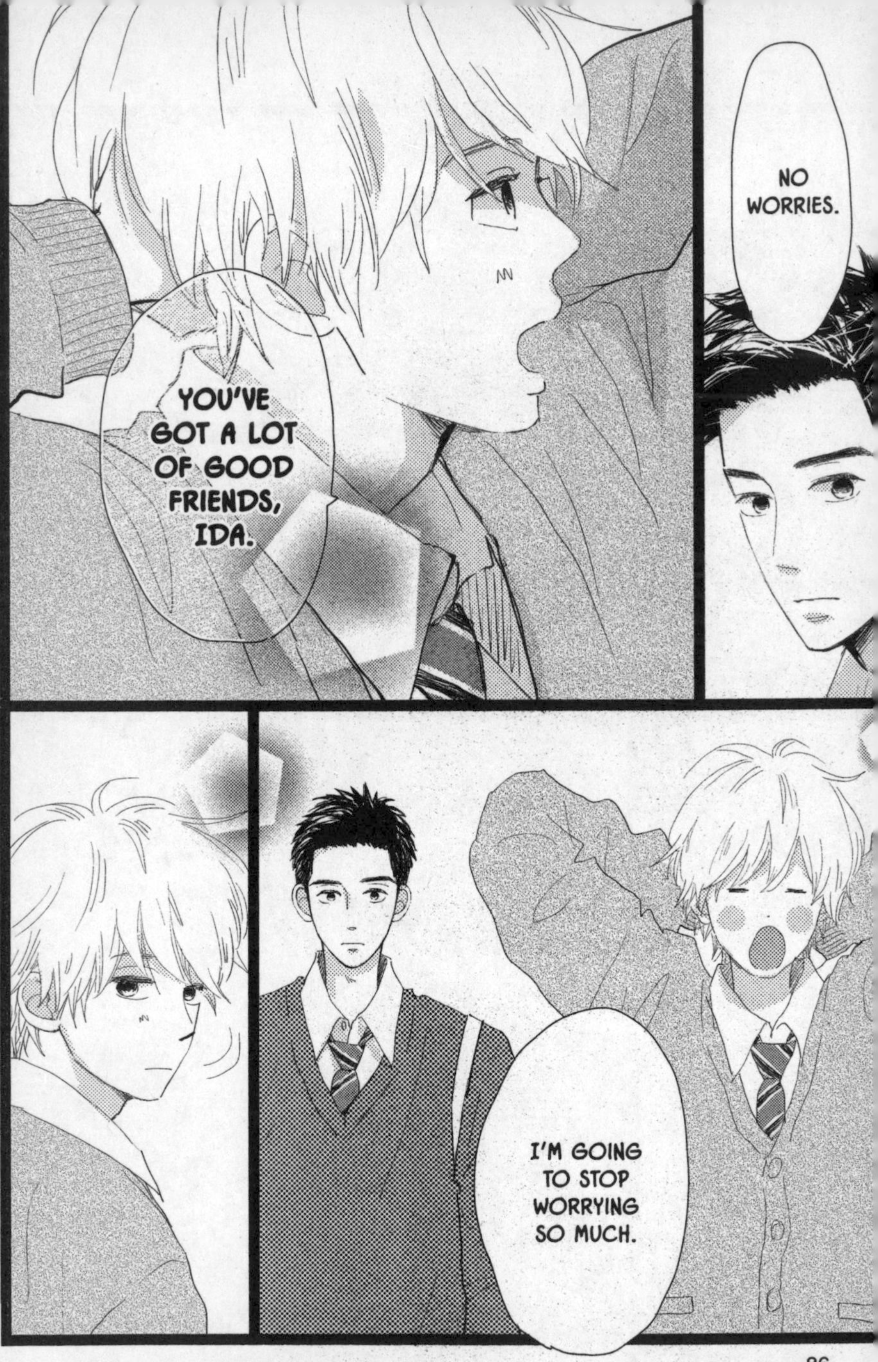
NO WORRIES.
YOU'VE GOT A LOT OF GOOD FRIENDS, IDA.
I'M GOING TO STOP WORRYING SO MUCH.

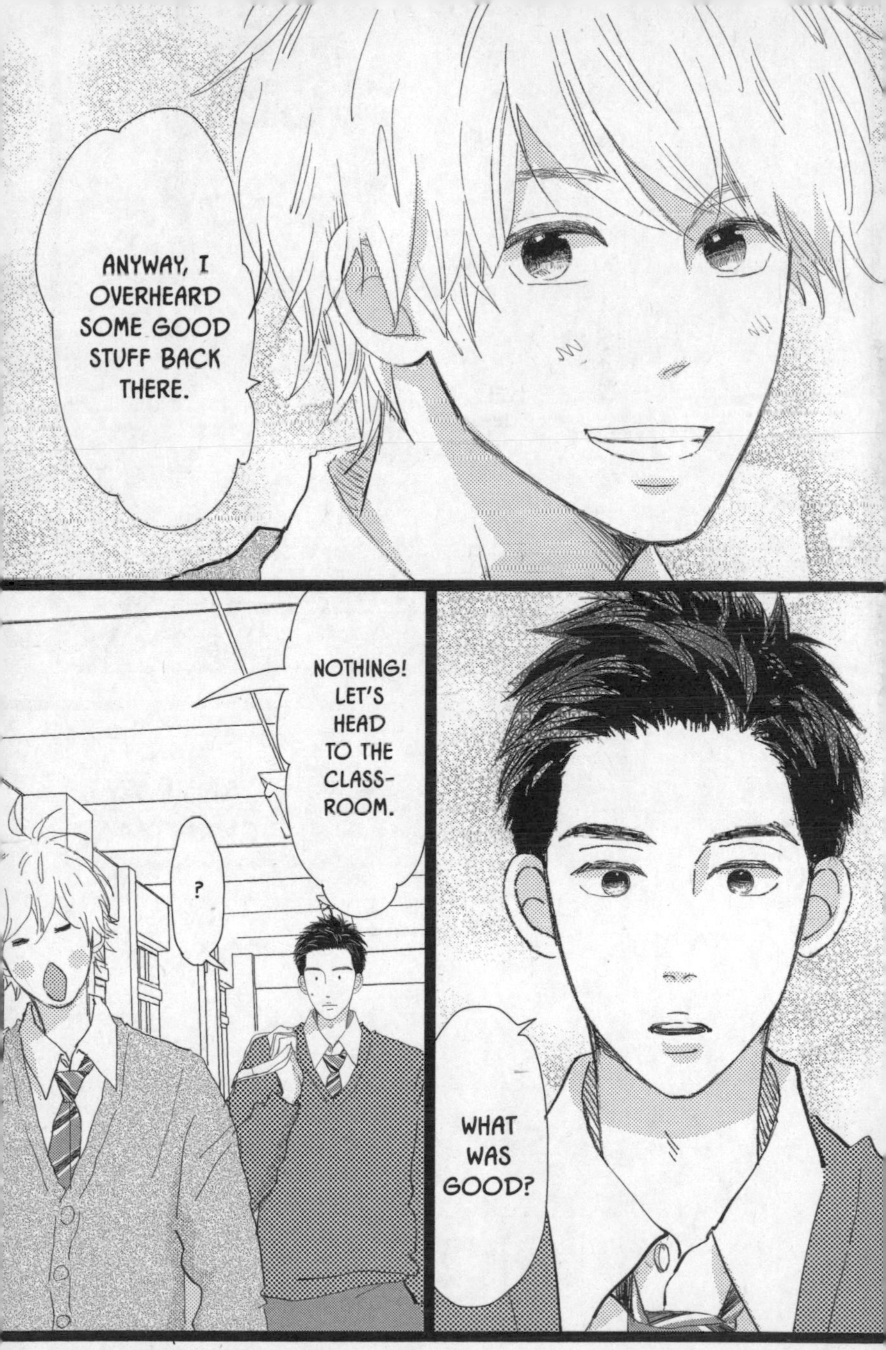
ANYWAY, I OVERHEARD SOME GOOD STUFF BACK THERE.
WHAT WAS GOOD?
NOTHING! LET'S HEAD TO THE CLASS-ROOM.
?

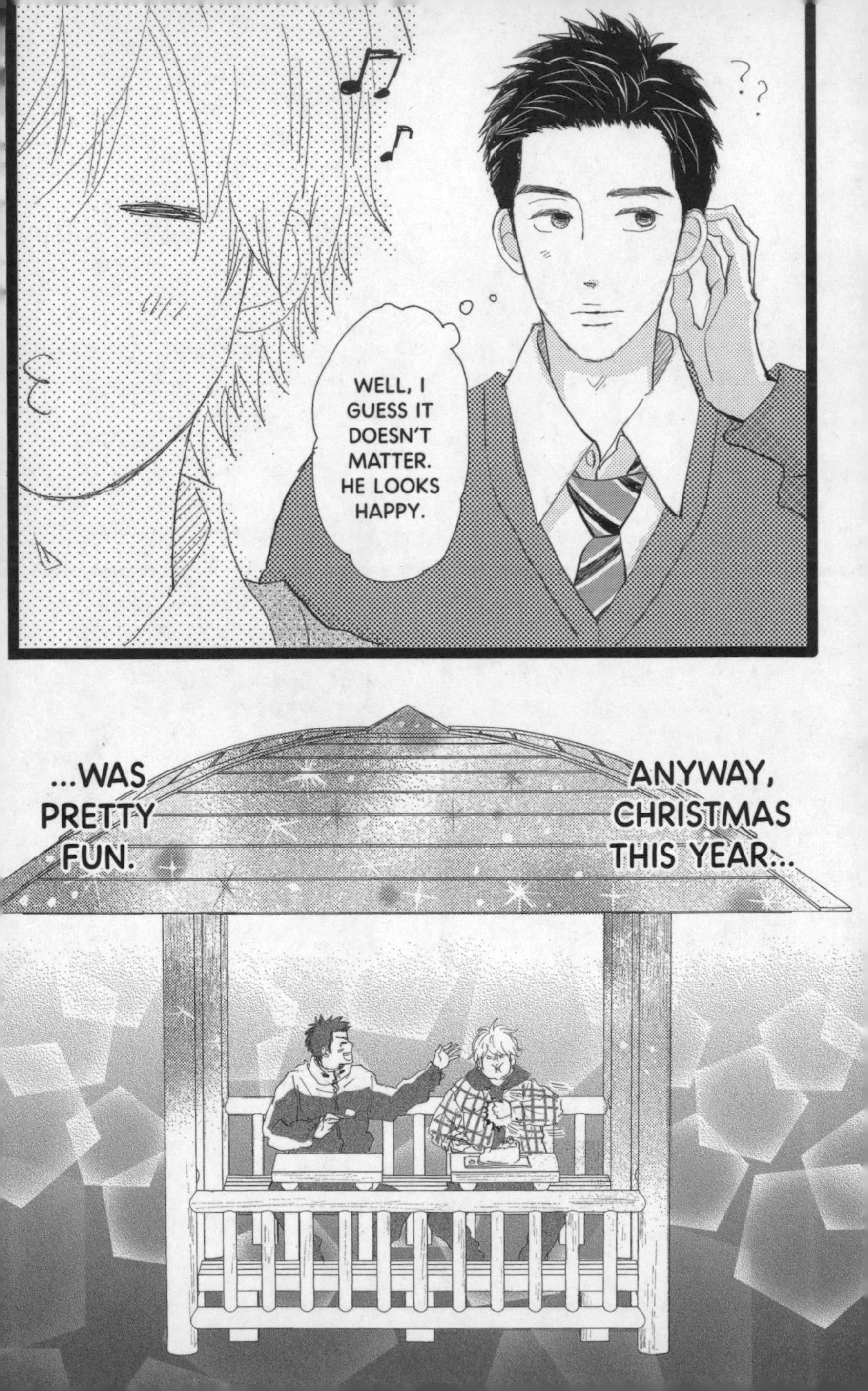
WELL, I GUESS IT DOESN'T MATTER. HE LOOKS HAPPY.
ANYWAY, CHRISTMAS THIS YEAR...
...WAS PRETTY FUN.

Chapter 16

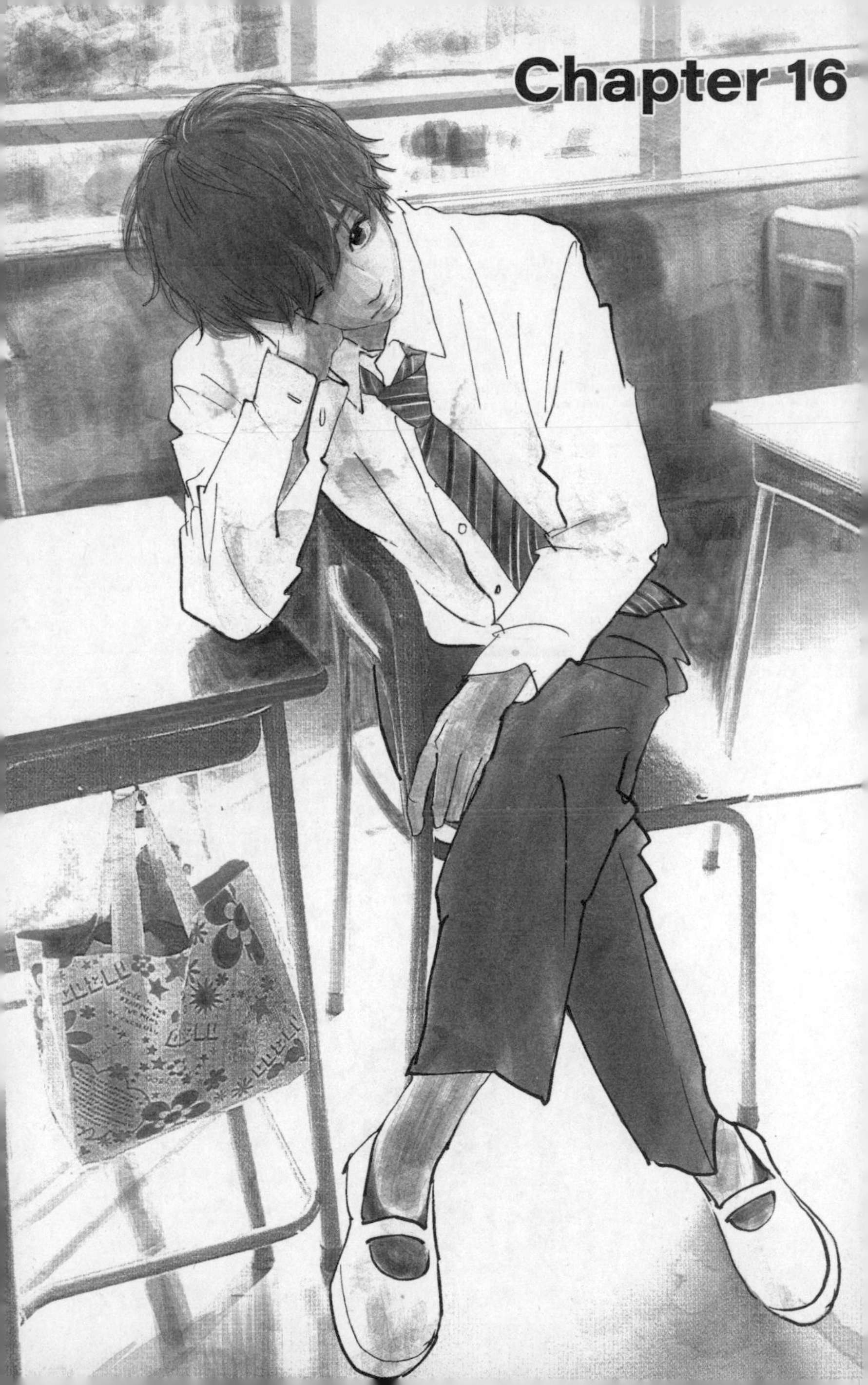

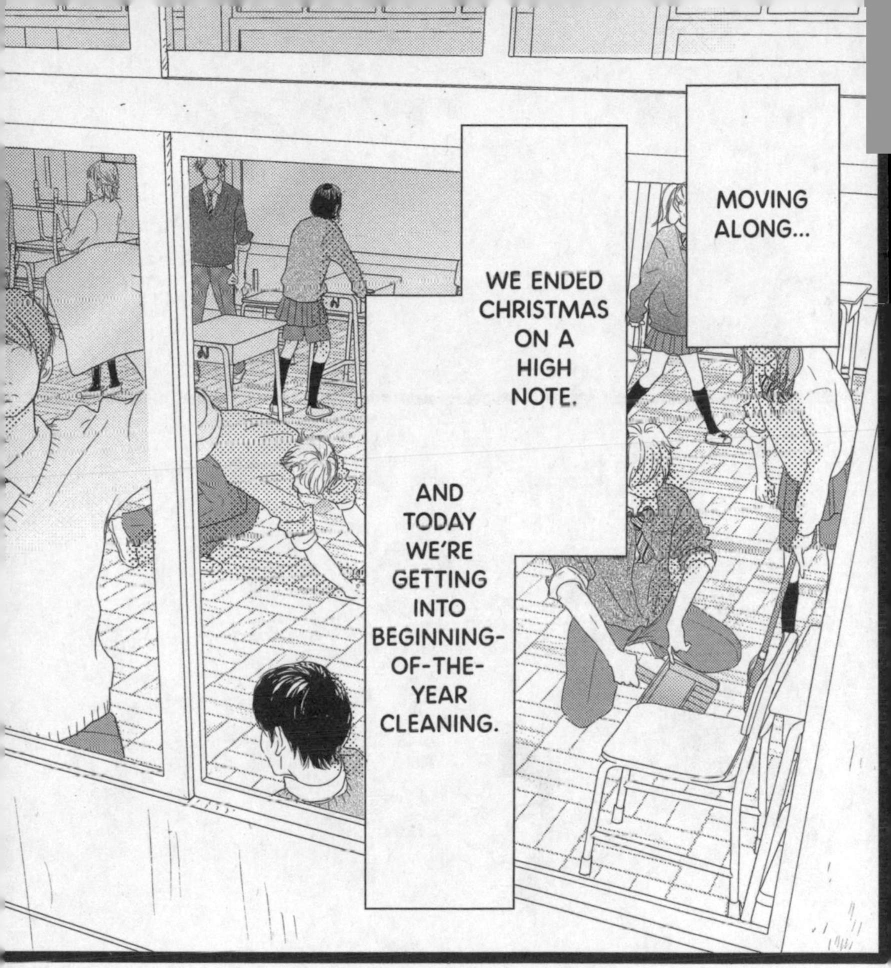
MOVING ALONG...
WE ENDED CHRISTMAS ON A HIGH NOTE.
AND TODAY WE'RE GETTING INTO BEGINNING-OF-THE-YEAR CLEANING.

My Love Mix-Up!

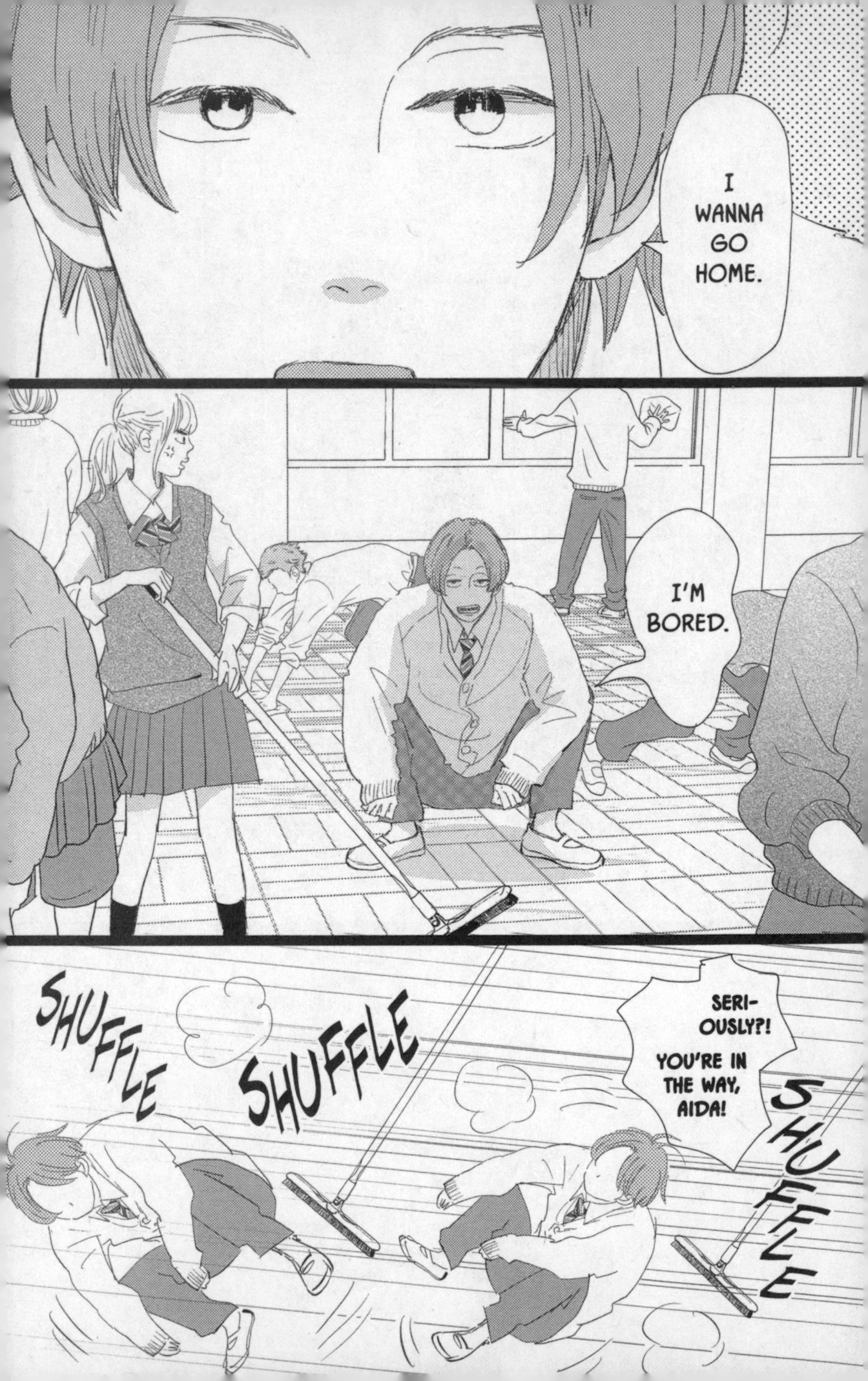
I WANNA GO HOME.
I'M BORED.
SHUFFLE
SERI-OUSLY?! YOU'RE IN THE WAY, AIDA!
SHUFFLE
SHUFFLE

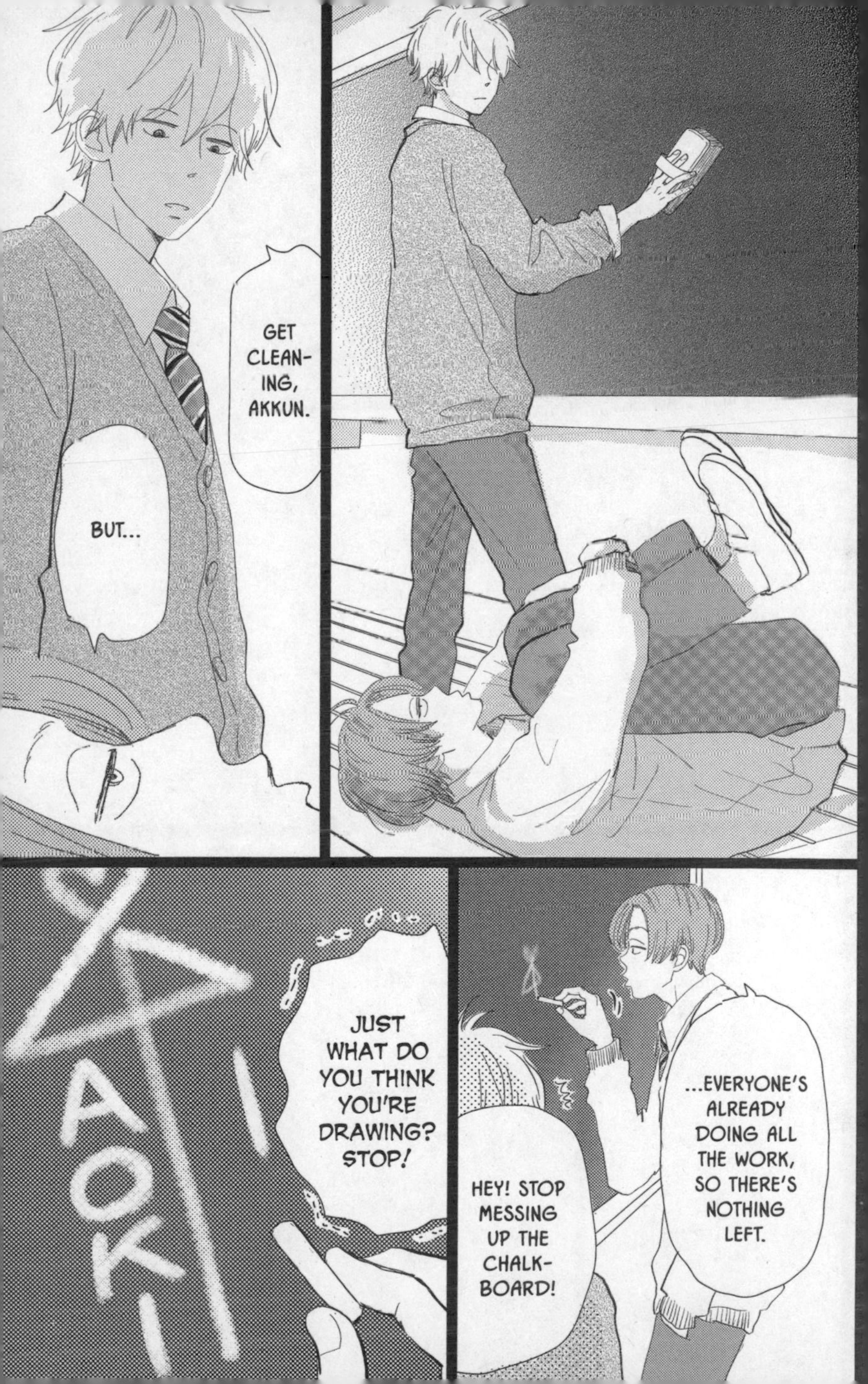
GET CLEANING, AKKUN.
BUT...
...EVERYONE'S ALREADY DOING ALL THE WORK, SO THERE'S NOTHING LEFT.
HEY! STOP MESSING UP THE CHALKBOARD!
JUST WHAT DO YOU THINK YOU'RE DRAWING? STOP!
AOKI

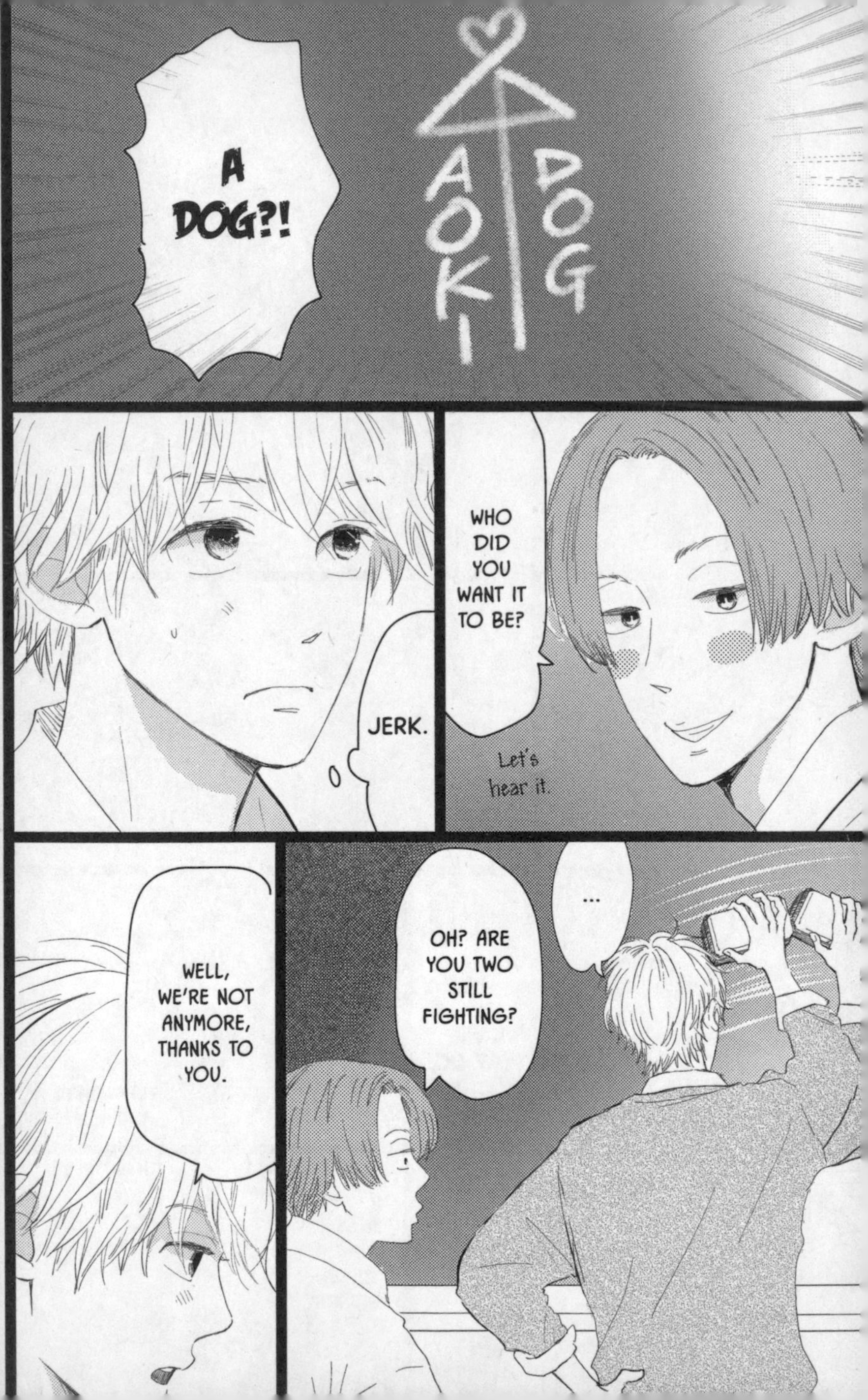
DOG
AOKI
A DOG?!
WHO DID YOU WANT IT TO BE?
Let's hear it.
JERK.
...
OH? ARE YOU TWO STILL FIGHTING?
WELL, WE'RE NOT ANYMORE, THANKS TO YOU.

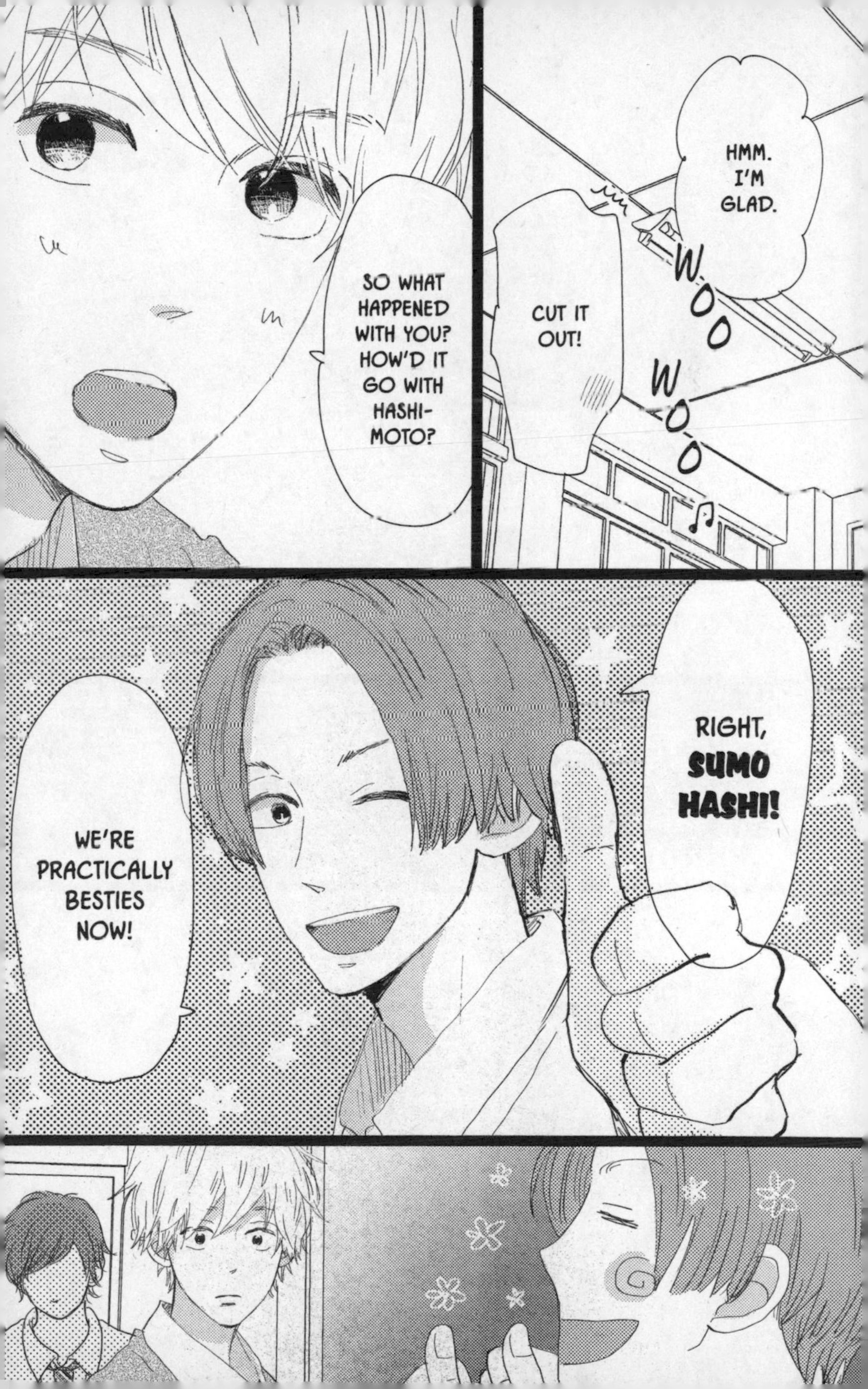
HMM. I'M GLAD.
CUT IT OUT!
WOO WOO ♪
SO WHAT HAPPENED WITH YOU? HOW'D IT GO WITH HASHI-MOTO?
RIGHT, **SUMO HASHI!**
WE'RE PRACTICALLY BESTIES NOW!

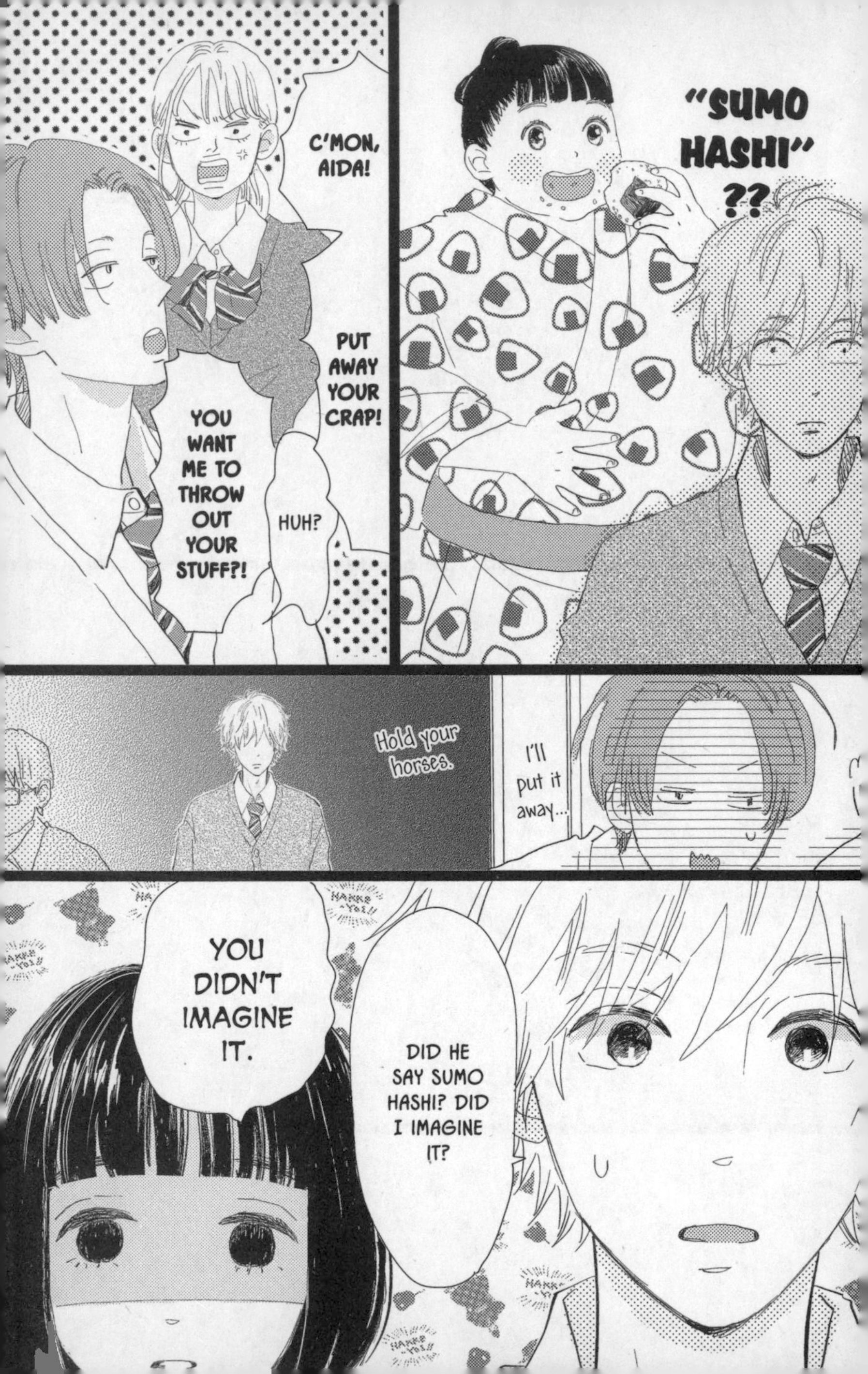
"SUMO HASHI"??
C'MON, AIDA!
PUT AWAY YOUR CRAP!
HUH?
YOU WANT ME TO THROW OUT YOUR STUFF?!
I'll put it away...
Hold your horses.
DID HE SAY SUMO HASHI? DID I IMAGINE IT?
YOU DIDN'T IMAGINE IT.

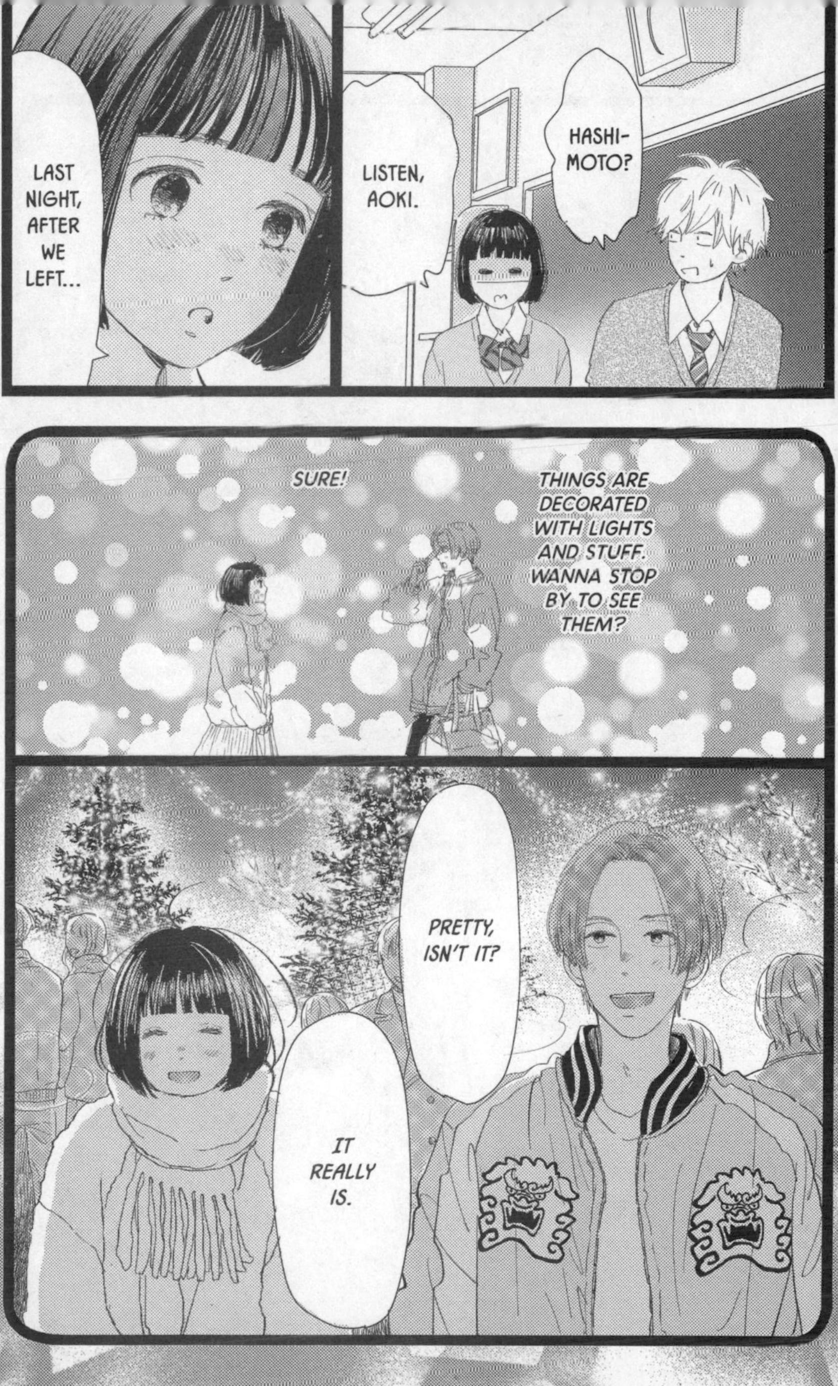
HASHI-MOTO?
LISTEN, AOKI.
LAST NIGHT, AFTER WE LEFT...
THINGS ARE DECORATED WITH LIGHTS AND STUFF. WANNA STOP BY TO SEE THEM?
SURE!
PRETTY, ISN'T IT?
IT REALLY IS.

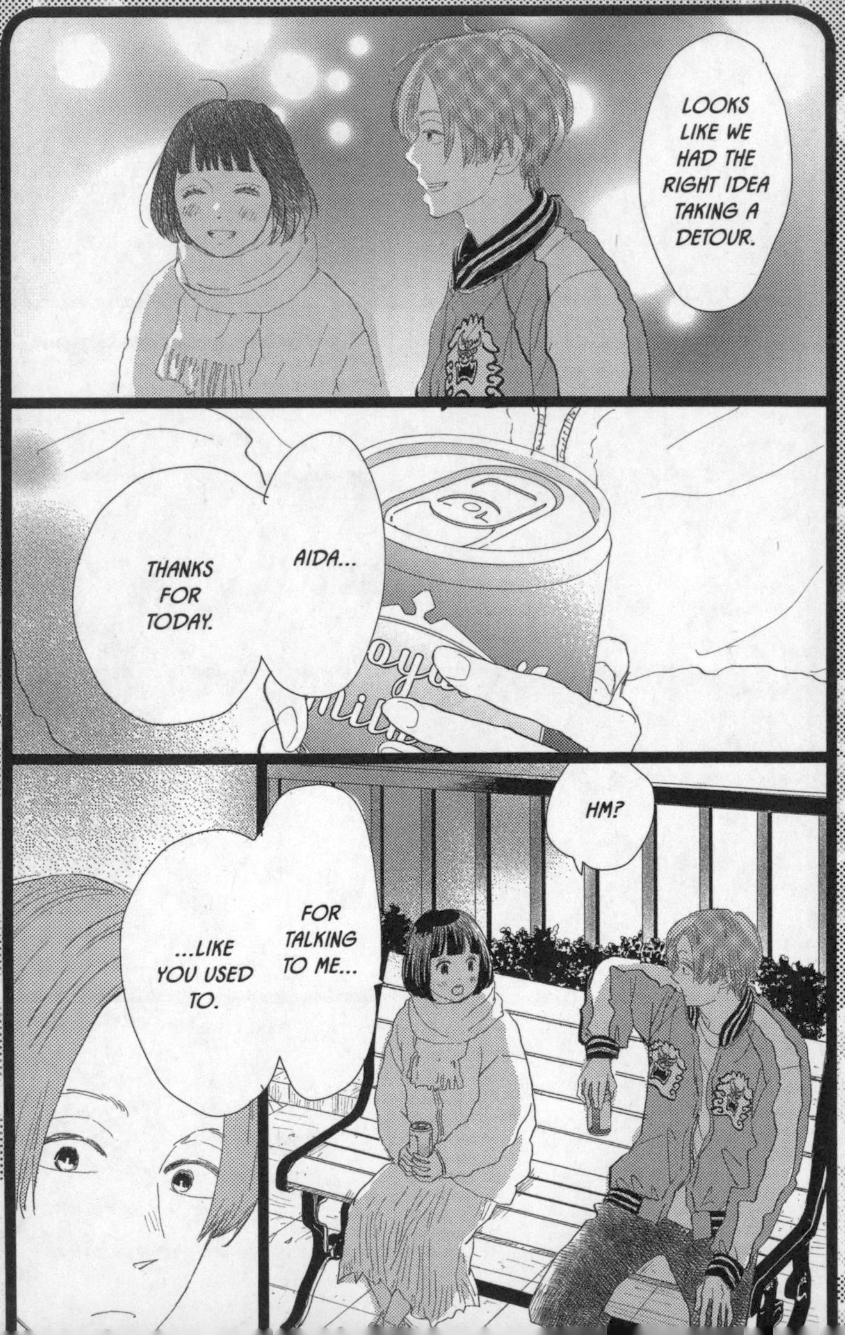
LOOKS LIKE WE HAD THE RIGHT IDEA TAKING A DETOUR.
AIDA...
THANKS FOR TODAY.
HM?
FOR TALKING TO ME...
...LIKE YOU USED TO.

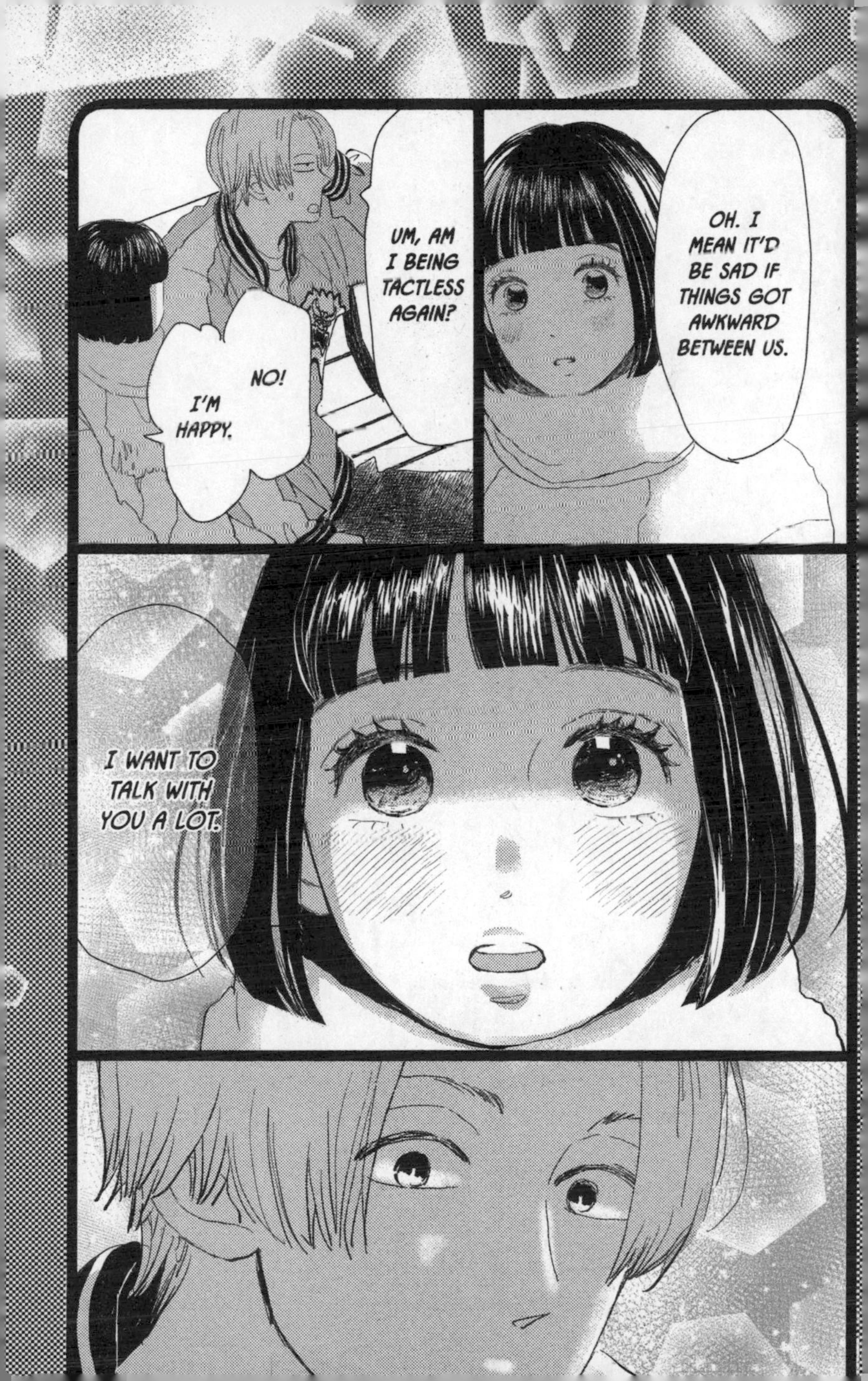
OH. I MEAN IT'D BE SAD IF THINGS GOT AWKWARD BETWEEN US.
UM, AM I BEING TACTLESS AGAIN?
NO!
I'M HAPPY.
I WANT TO TALK WITH YOU A LOT.

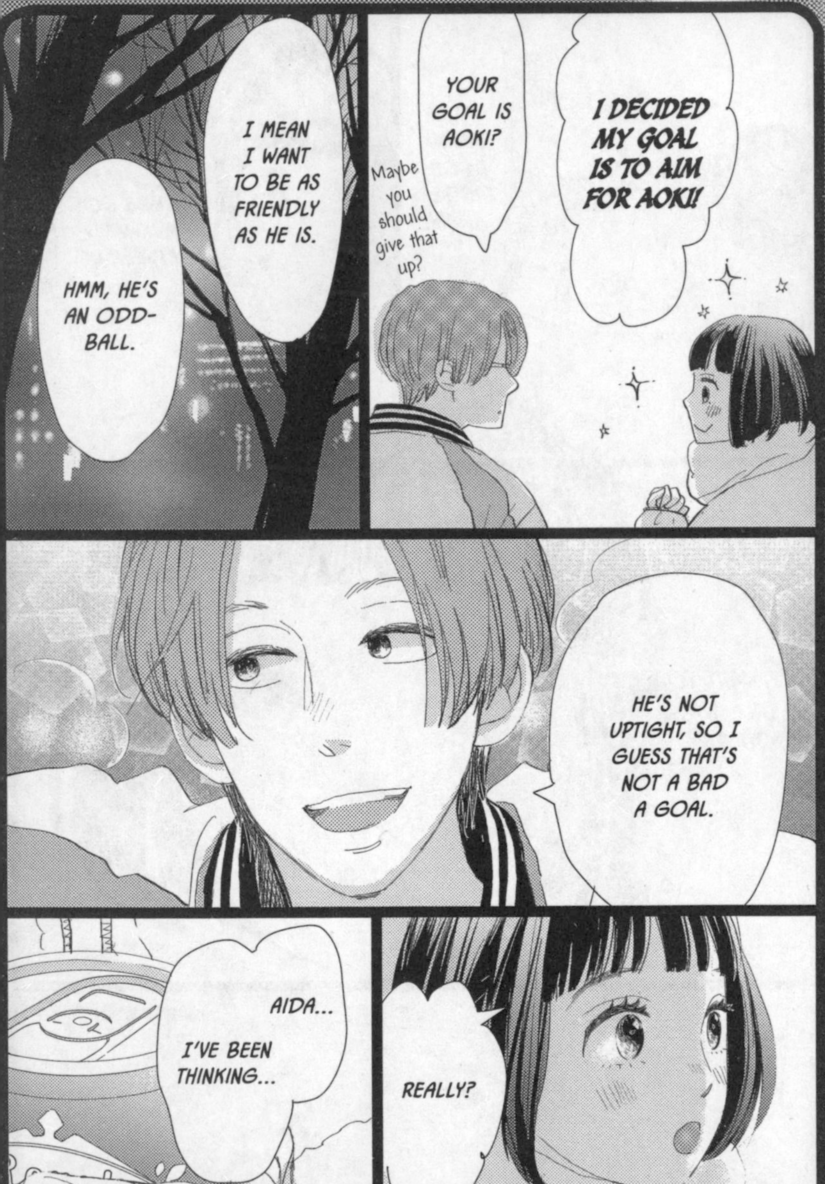
I DECIDED MY GOAL IS TO AIM FOR AOKI!
YOUR GOAL IS AOKI?
Maybe you should give that up?
I MEAN I WANT TO BE AS FRIENDLY AS HE IS.
HMM, HE'S AN ODD-BALL.
HE'S NOT UPTIGHT, SO I GUESS THAT'S NOT A BAD A GOAL.
REALLY?
AIDA...
I'VE BEEN THINKING...

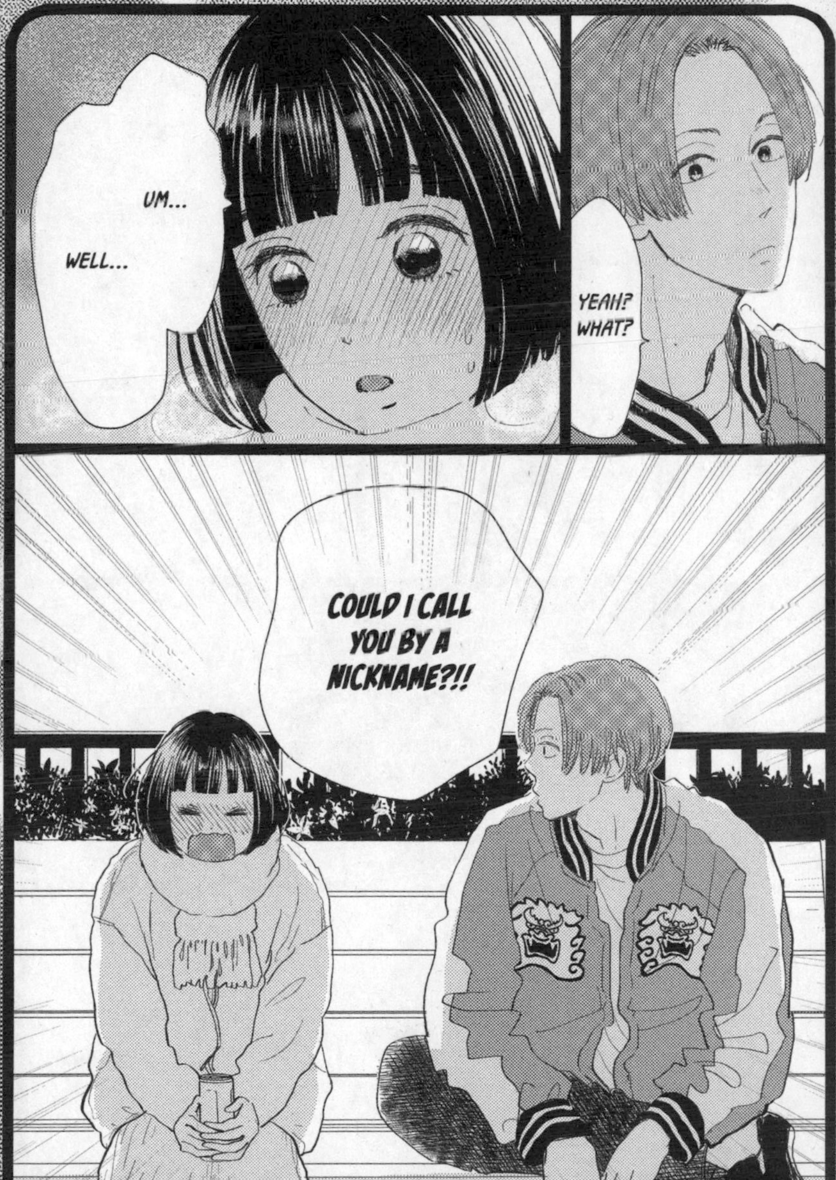
YEAH? WHAT?
UM... WELL...
COULD I CALL YOU BY A NICKNAME?!!

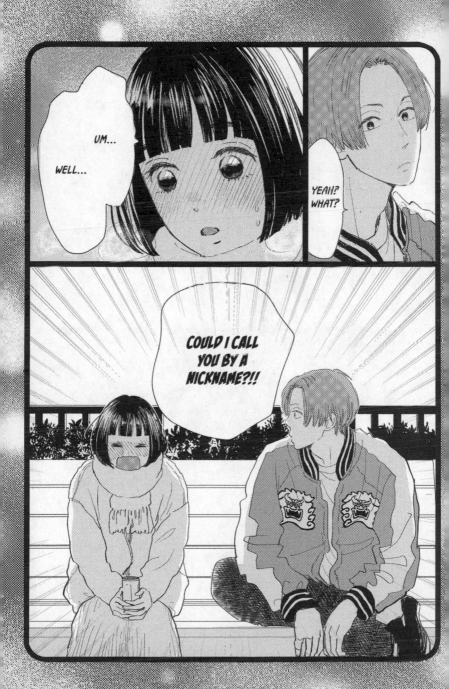

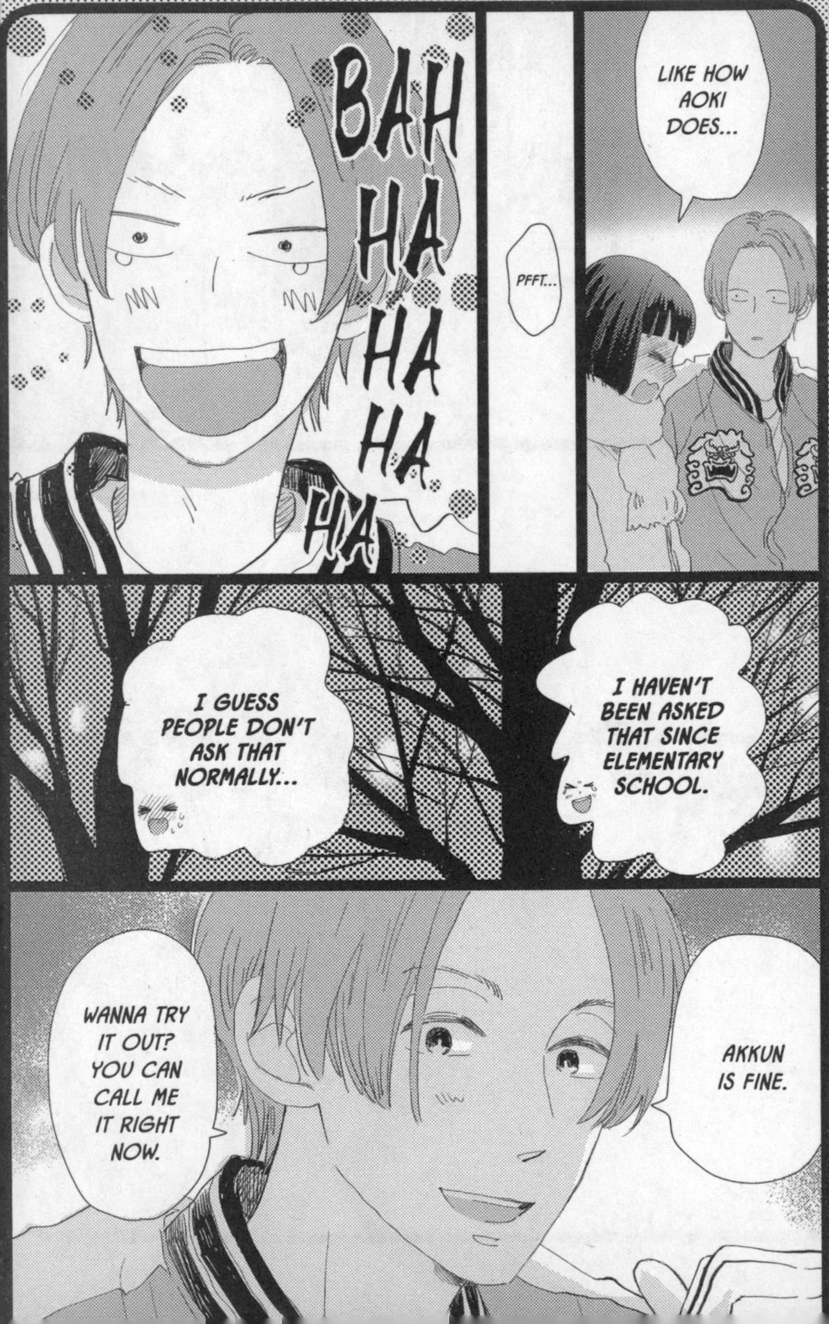
LIKE HOW AOKI DOES...
PFFT...
BAH HA HA HA HA HA
I HAVEN'T BEEN ASKED THAT SINCE ELEMENTARY SCHOOL.
I GUESS PEOPLE DON'T ASK THAT NORMALLY...
AKKUN IS FINE.
WANNA TRY IT OUT? YOU CAN CALL ME IT RIGHT NOW.

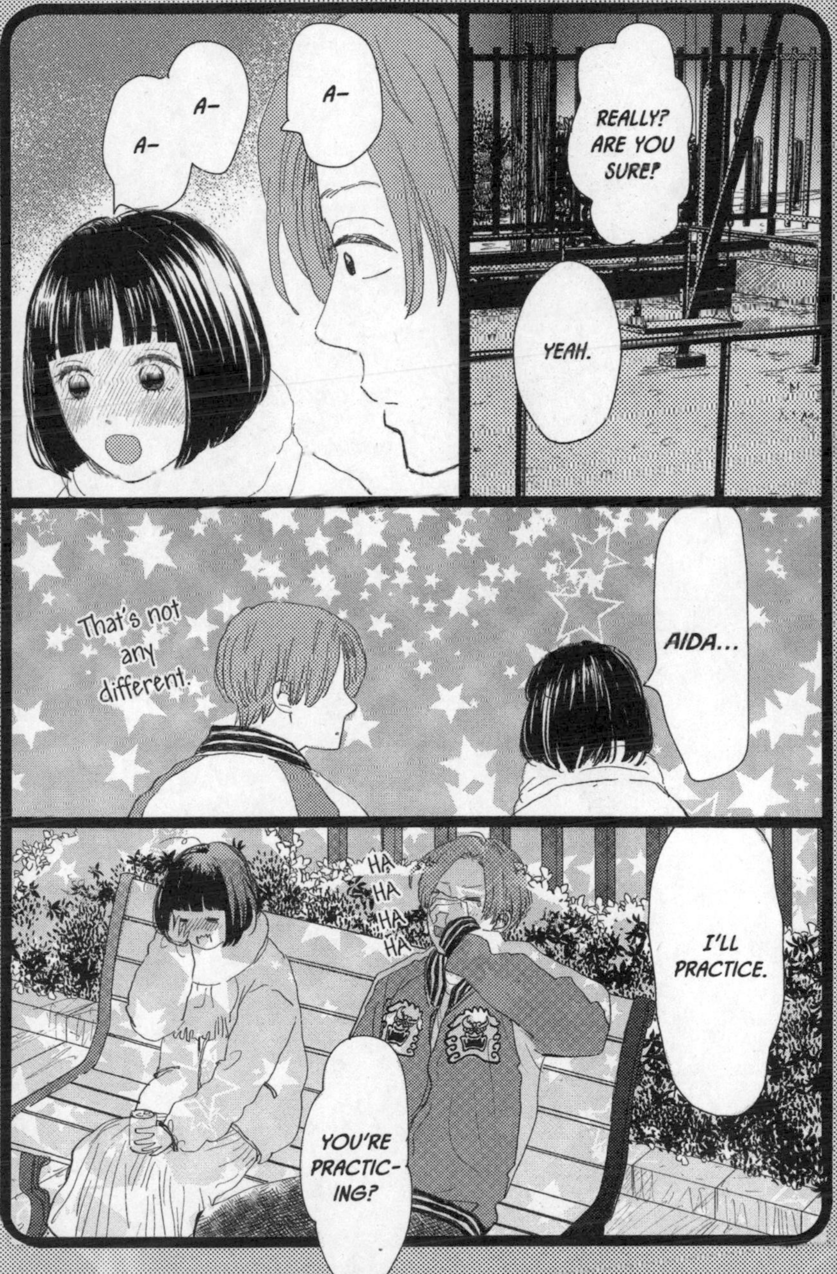
REALLY? ARE YOU SURE?
YEAH.
A-
A-
A-
AIDA...
That's not any different.
I'LL PRACTICE.
HA HA HA HA
YOU'RE PRACTIC-ING?

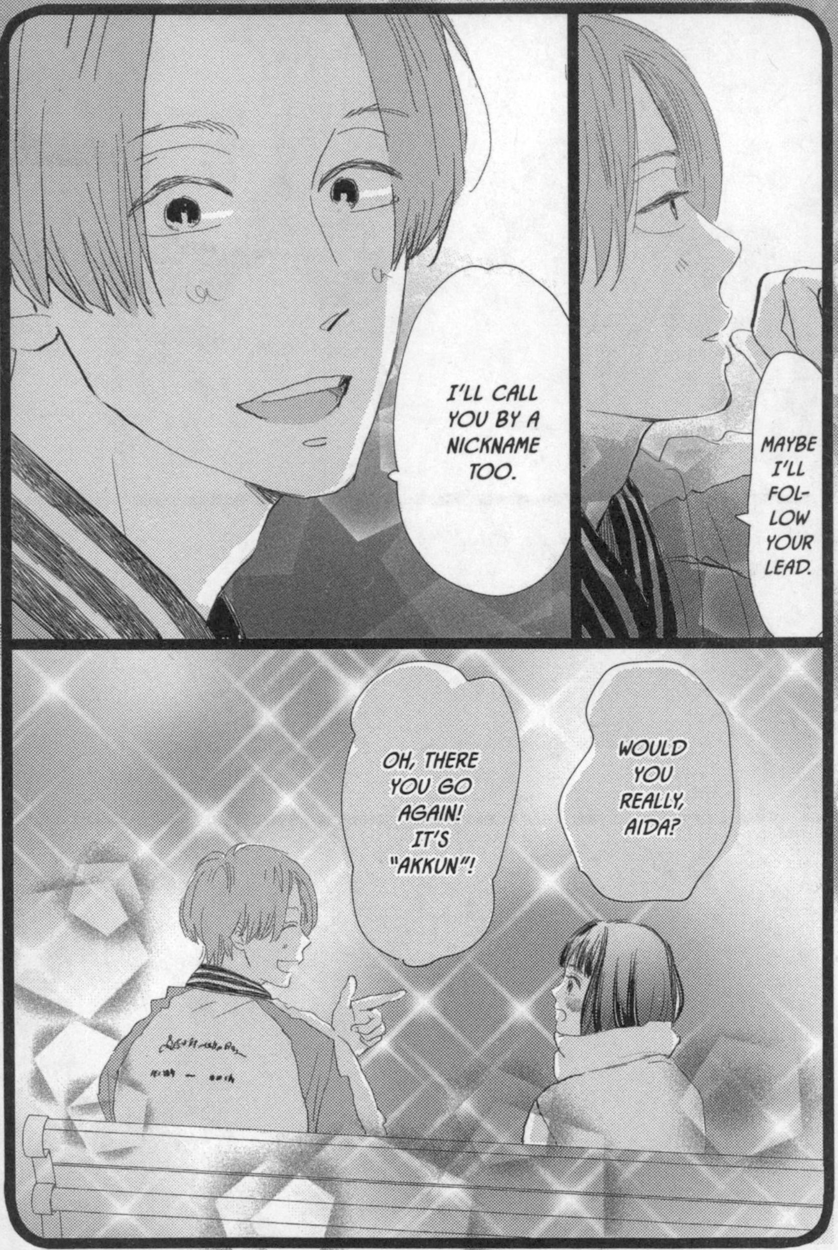
MAYBE I'LL FOL-LOW YOUR LEAD.
I'LL CALL YOU BY A NICKNAME TOO.
WOULD YOU REALLY, AIDA?
OH, THERE YOU GO AGAIN! IT'S "AKKUN"!

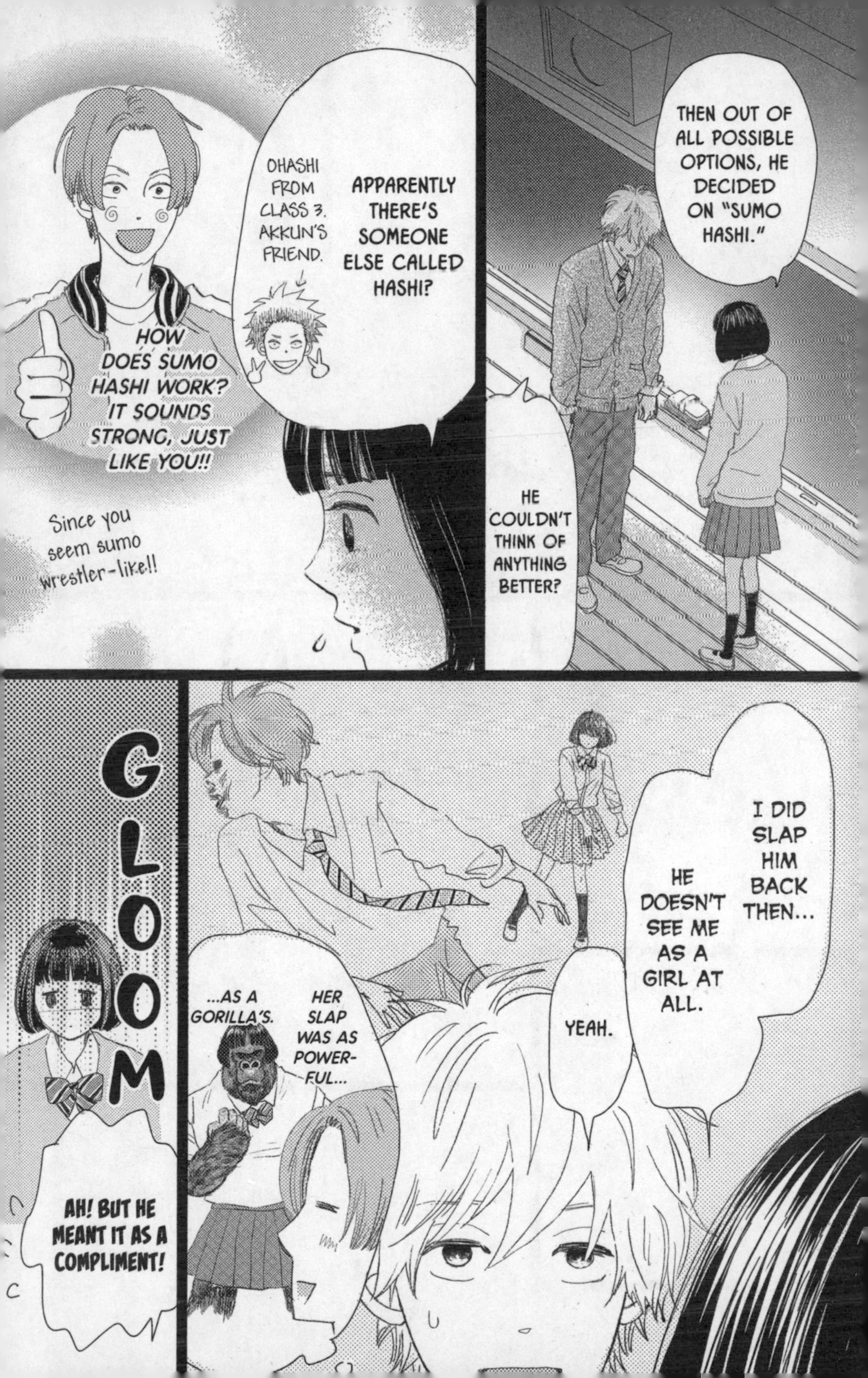
THEN OUT OF ALL POSSIBLE OPTIONS, HE DECIDED ON "SUMO HASHI."
HE COULDN'T THINK OF ANYTHING BETTER?
APPARENTLY THERE'S SOMEONE ELSE CALLED HASHI?
OHASHI FROM CLASS 3. AKKUN'S FRIEND.
HOW DOES SUMO HASHI WORK? IT SOUNDS STRONG, JUST LIKE YOU!!
Since you seem sumo wrestler-like!!
I DID SLAP HIM BACK THEN...
HE DOESN'T SEE ME AS A GIRL AT ALL.
YEAH.
HER SLAP WAS AS POWERFUL...
...AS A GORILLA'S.
GLOOM
AH! BUT HE MEANT IT AS A COMPLIMENT!

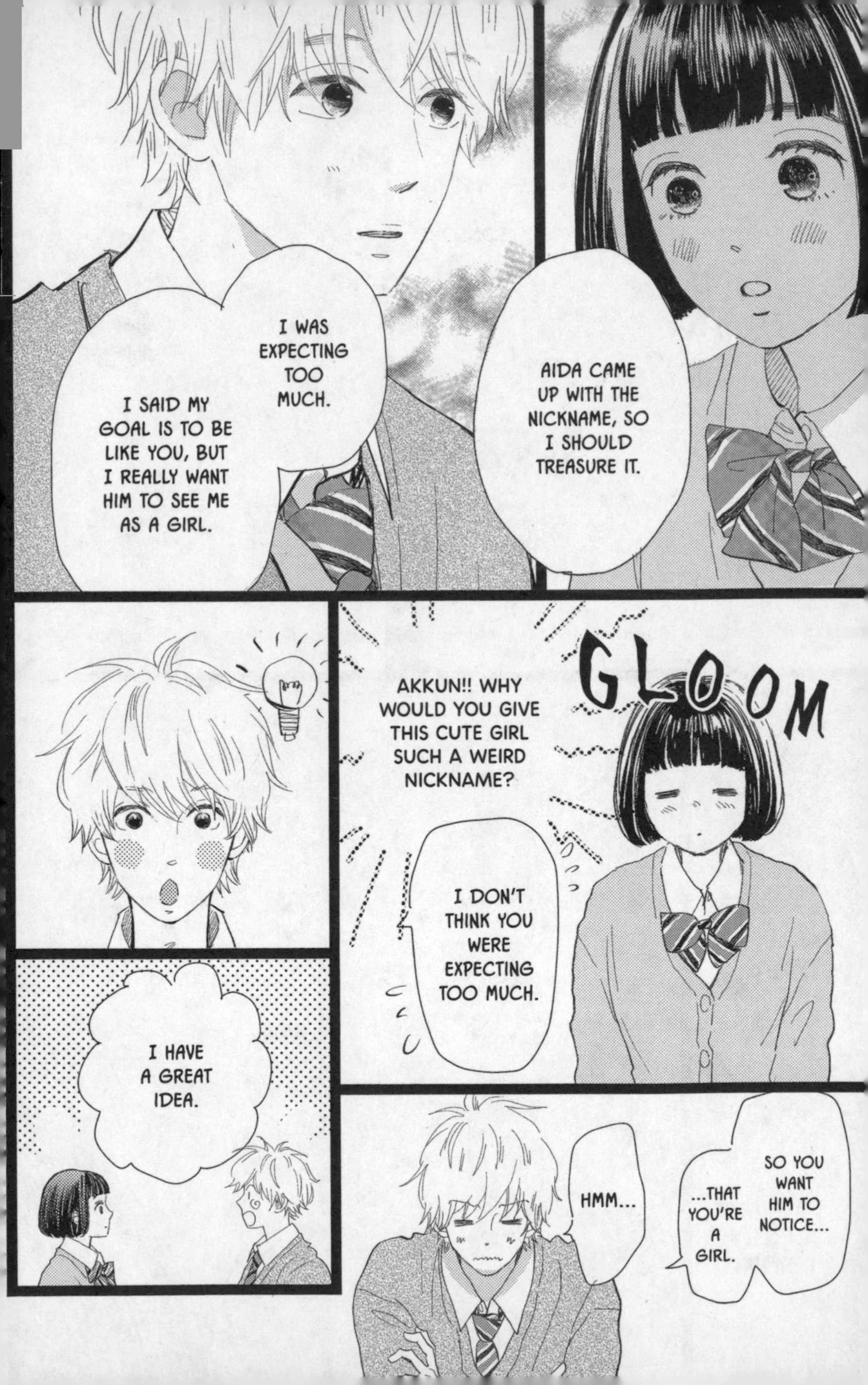
AIDA CAME UP WITH THE NICKNAME, SO I SHOULD TREASURE IT.
I WAS EXPECTING TOO MUCH.
I SAID MY GOAL IS TO BE LIKE YOU, BUT I REALLY WANT HIM TO SEE ME AS A GIRL.
GLOOM
AKKUN!! WHY WOULD YOU GIVE THIS CUTE GIRL SUCH A WEIRD NICKNAME?
I DON'T THINK YOU WERE EXPECTING TOO MUCH.
SO YOU WANT HIM TO NOTICE...
...THAT YOU'RE A GIRL.
HMM...
I HAVE A GREAT IDEA.

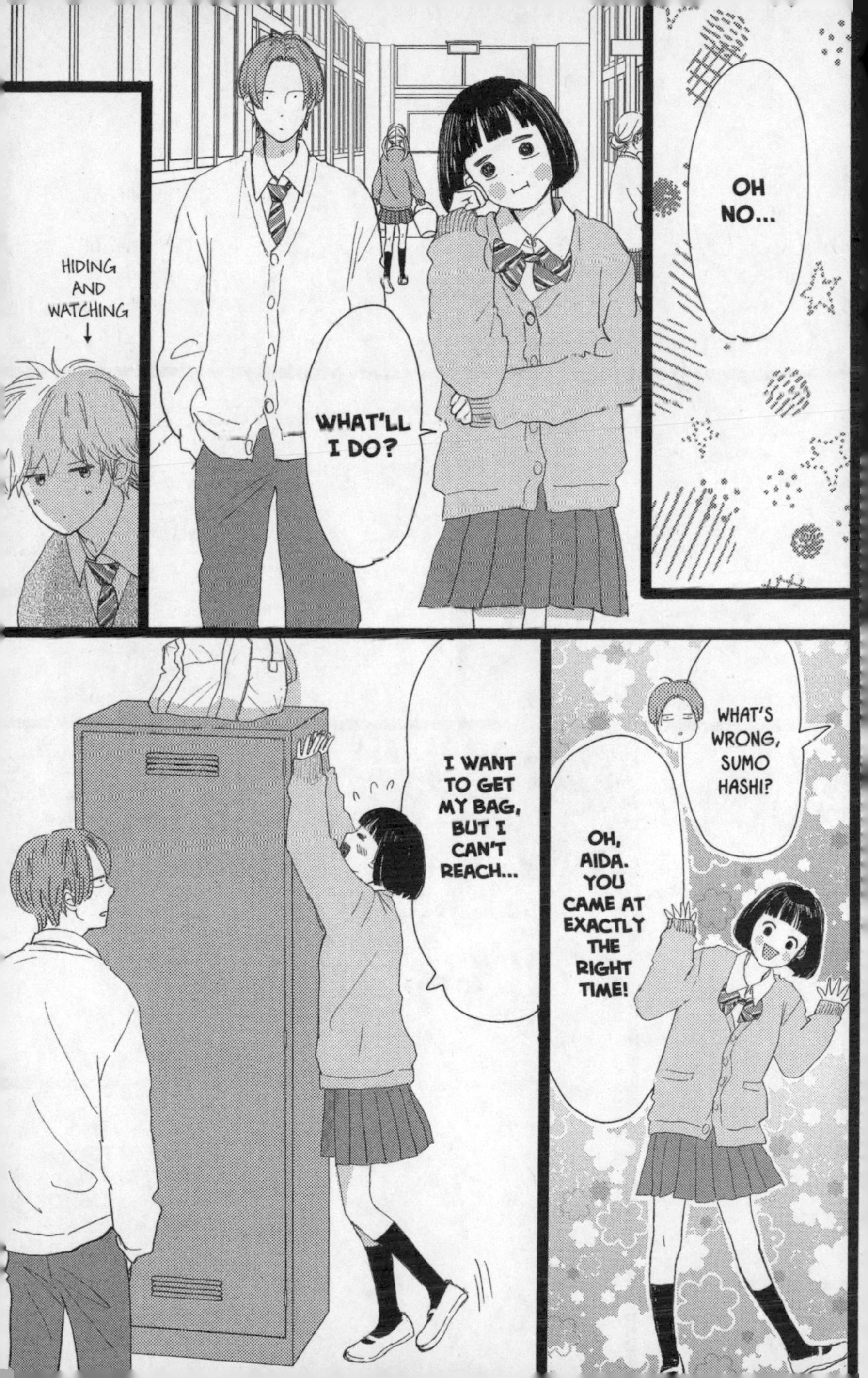
OH NO...
WHAT'LL I DO?
HIDING AND WATCHING ↓
WHAT'S WRONG, SUMO HASHI?
OH, AIDA. YOU CAME AT EXACTLY THE RIGHT TIME!
I WANT TO GET MY BAG, BUT I CAN'T REACH...

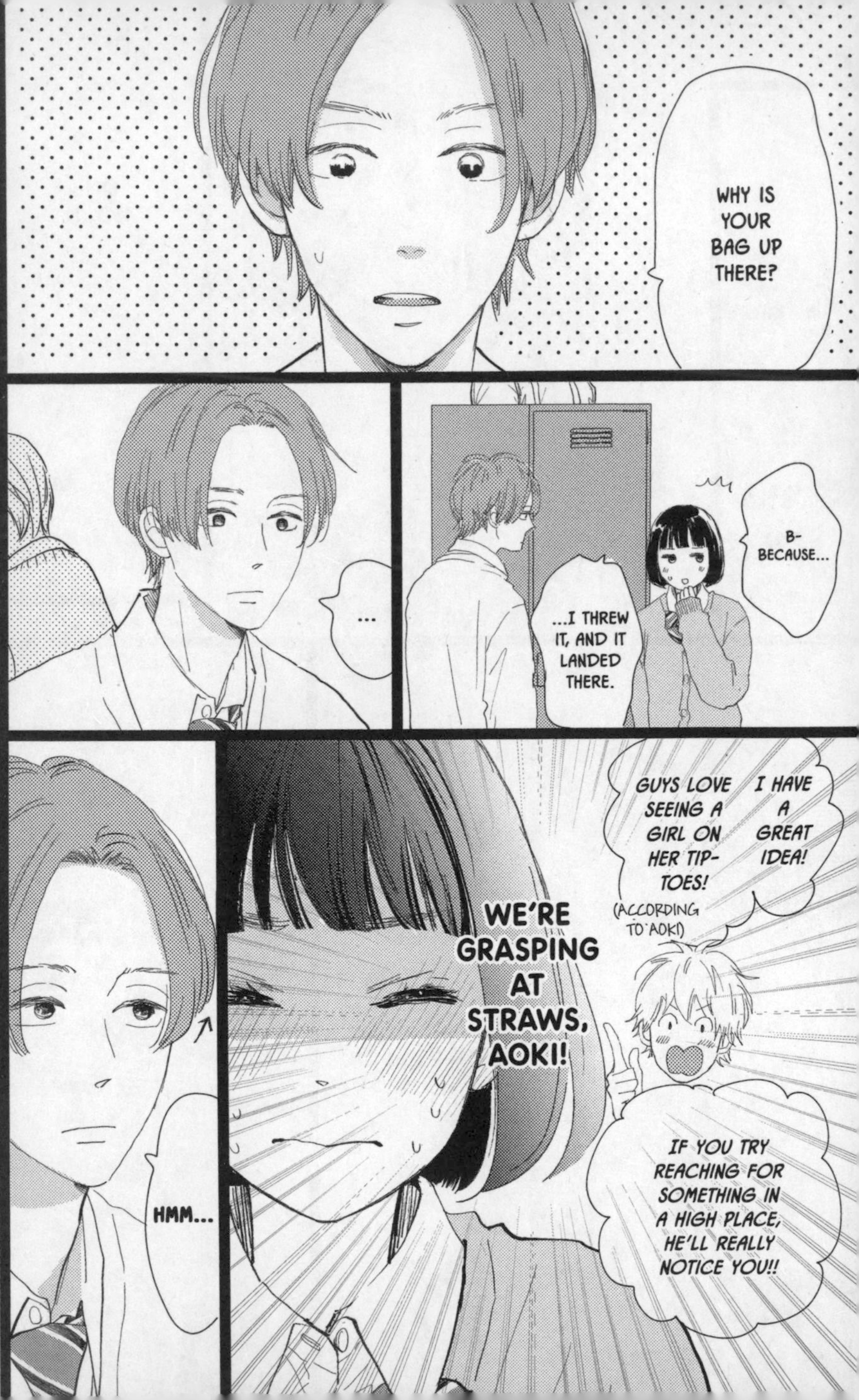
WHY IS YOUR BAG UP THERE?
B-BECAUSE...
...I THREW IT, AND IT LANDED THERE.
...
I HAVE A GREAT IDEA!
GUYS LOVE SEEING A GIRL ON HER TIP-TOES!
(ACCORDING TO AOKI)
IF YOU TRY REACHING FOR SOMETHING IN A HIGH PLACE, HE'LL REALLY NOTICE YOU!!
WE'RE GRASPING AT STRAWS, AOKI!
HMM...

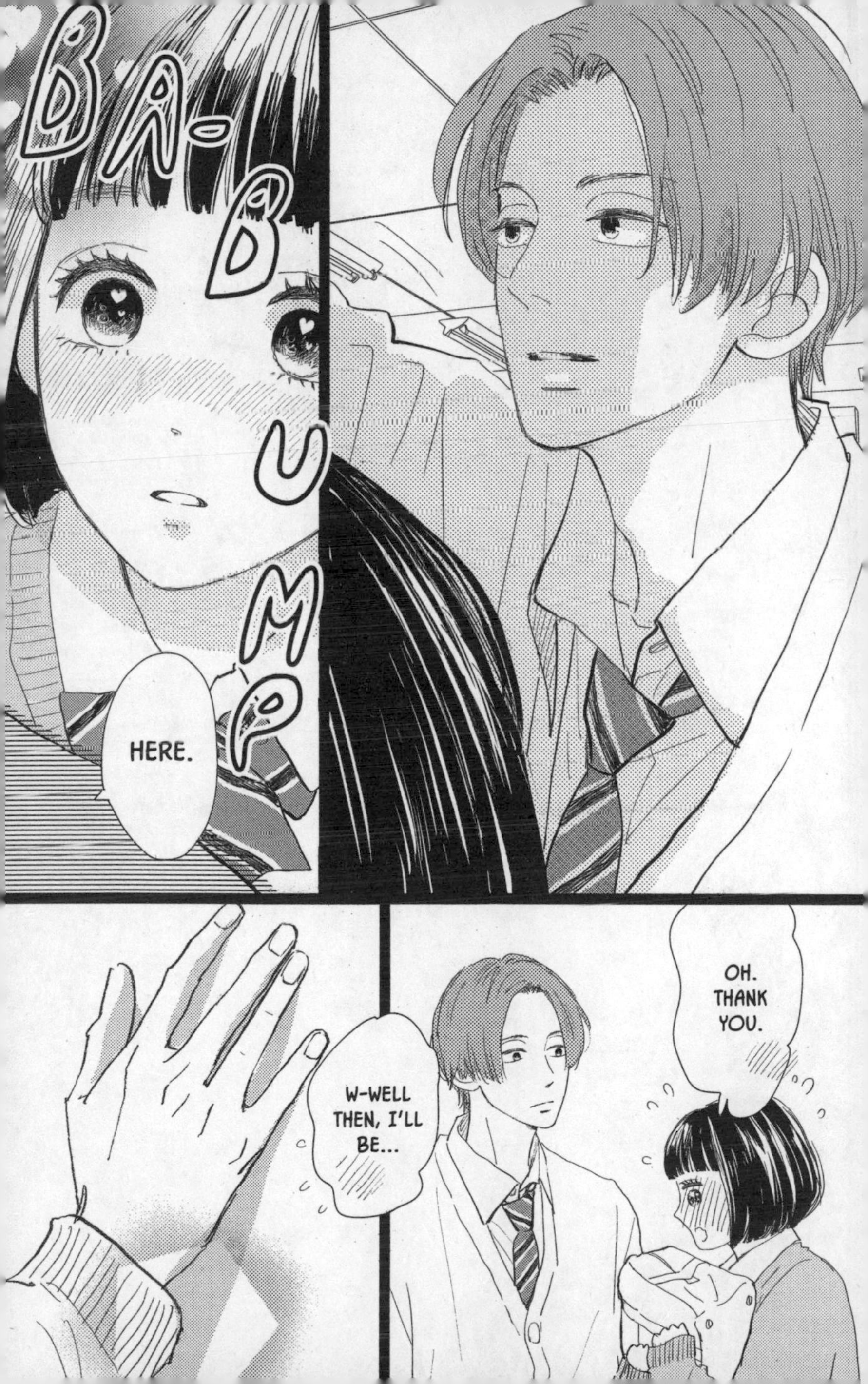
BA-BUMP
HERE.
OH. THANK YOU.
W-WELL THEN, I'LL BE...

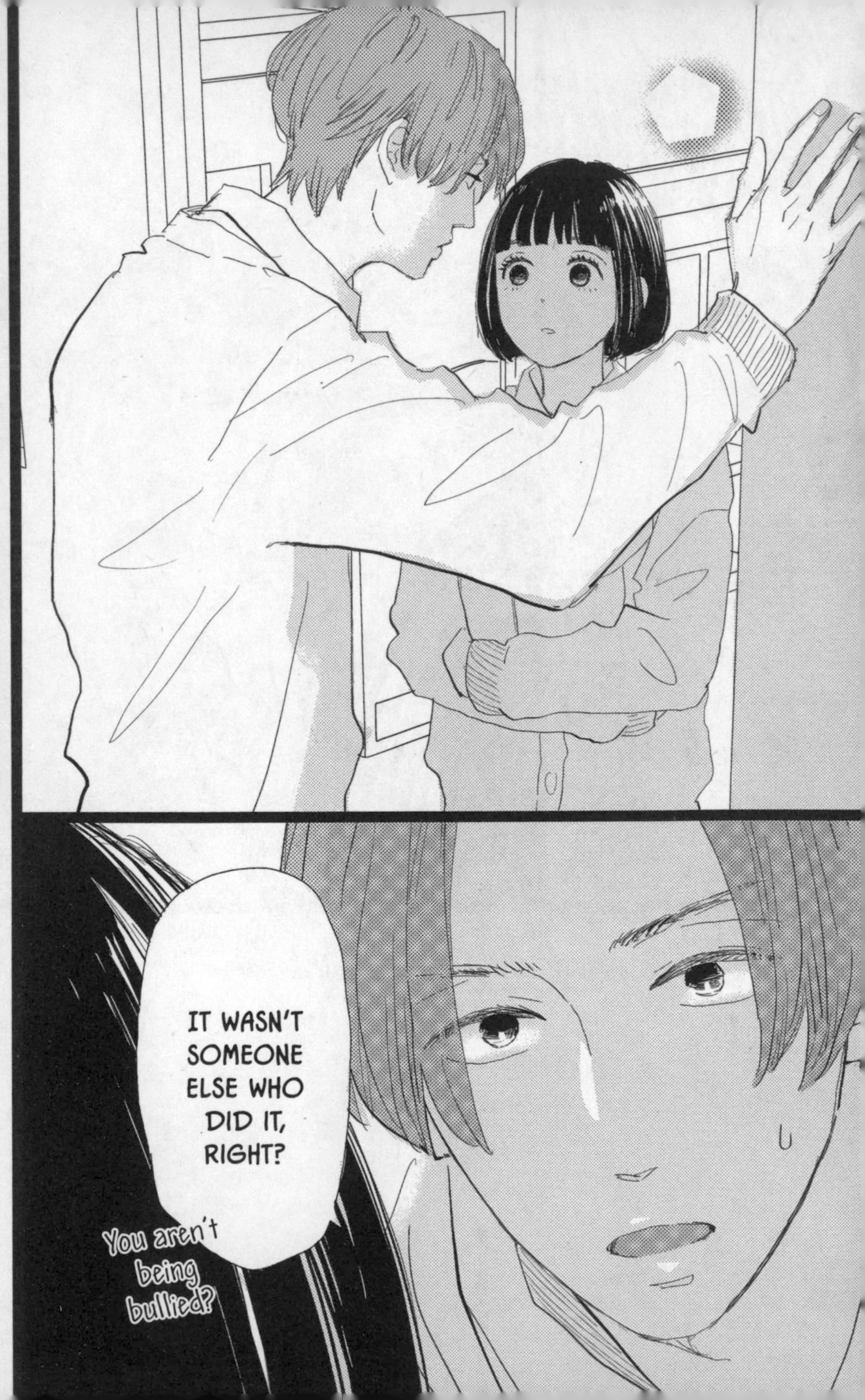
IT WASN'T SOMEONE ELSE WHO DID IT, RIGHT?
You aren't being bullied?

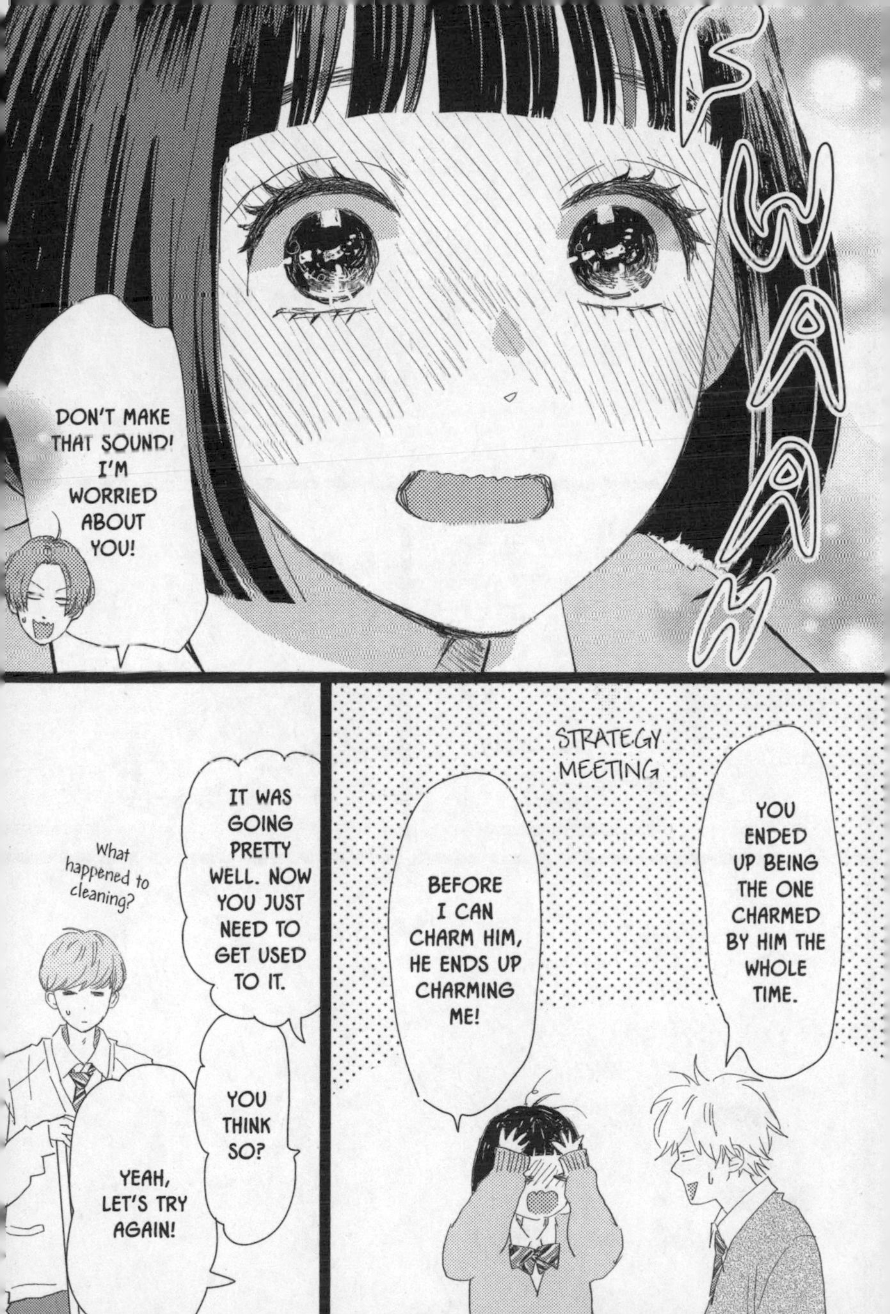
SWAAM
DON'T MAKE THAT SOUND! I'M WORRIED ABOUT YOU!
STRATEGY MEETING
YOU ENDED UP BEING THE ONE CHARMED BY HIM THE WHOLE TIME.
BEFORE I CAN CHARM HIM, HE ENDS UP CHARMING ME!
IT WAS GOING PRETTY WELL. NOW YOU JUST NEED TO GET USED TO IT.
What happened to cleaning?
YOU THINK SO?
YEAH, LET'S TRY AGAIN!

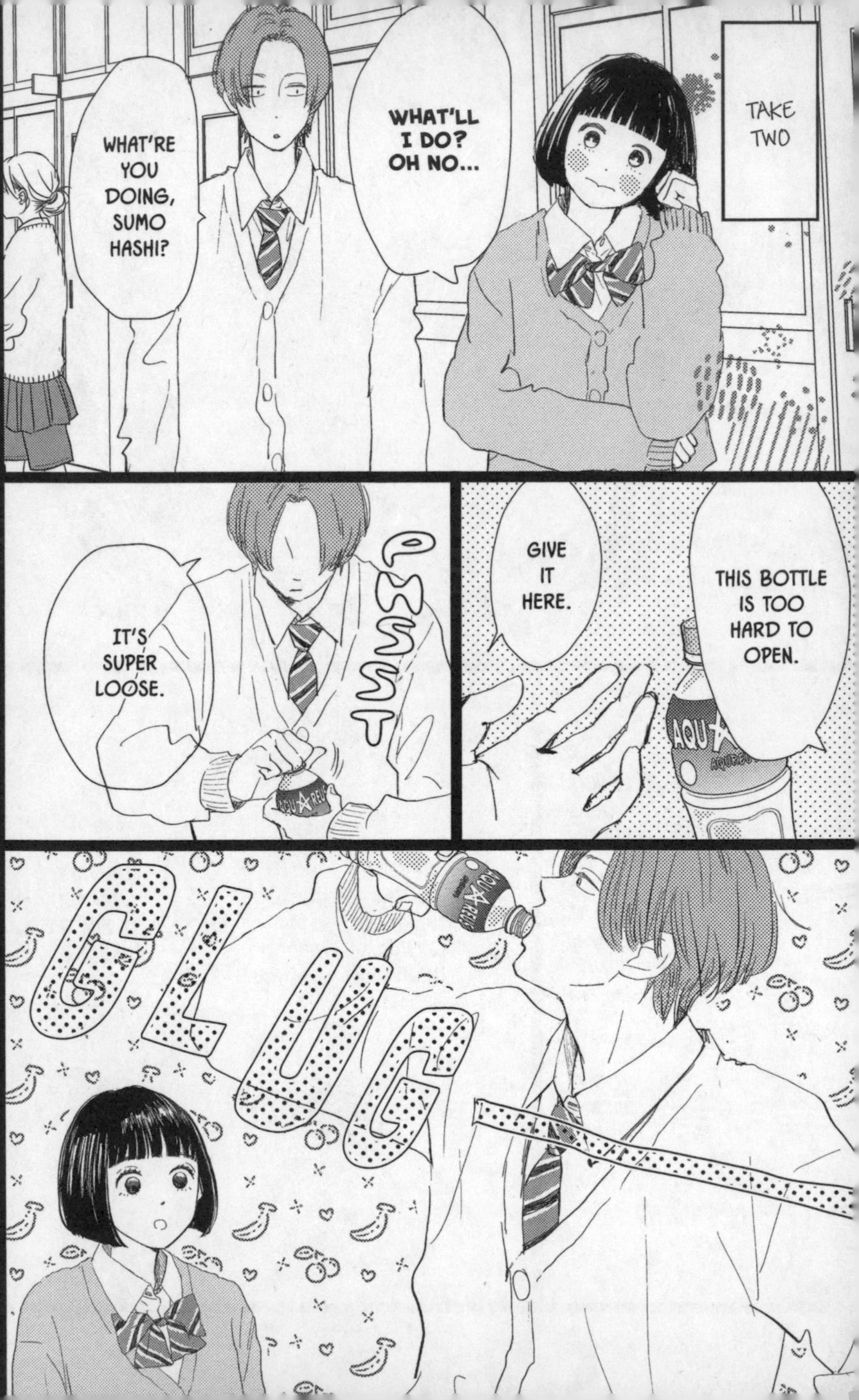
TAKE TWO
WHAT'LL I DO? OH NO...
WHAT'RE YOU DOING, SUMO HASHI?
THIS BOTTLE IS TOO HARD TO OPEN.
GIVE IT HERE.
PHSST
IT'S SUPER LOOSE.
GLUG

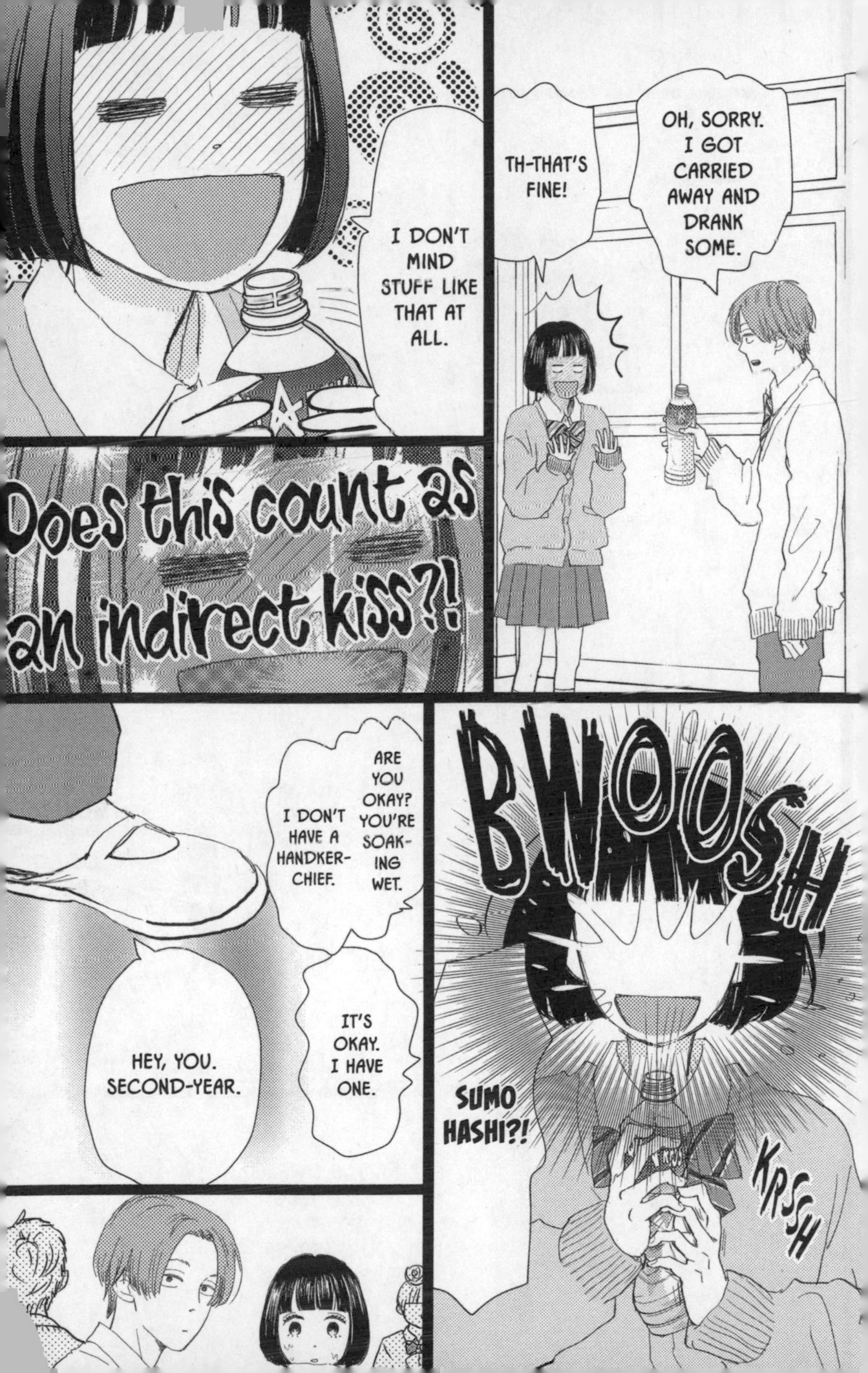
OH, SORRY. I GOT CARRIED AWAY AND DRANK SOME.
TH-THAT'S FINE!
I DON'T MIND STUFF LIKE THAT AT ALL.
Does this count as an indirect kiss?!
BWOOSH
KRSSH
SUMO HASHI?!
ARE YOU OKAY? YOU'RE SOAK-ING WET.
I DON'T HAVE A HANDKER-CHIEF.
IT'S OKAY. I HAVE ONE.
HEY, YOU. SECOND-YEAR.

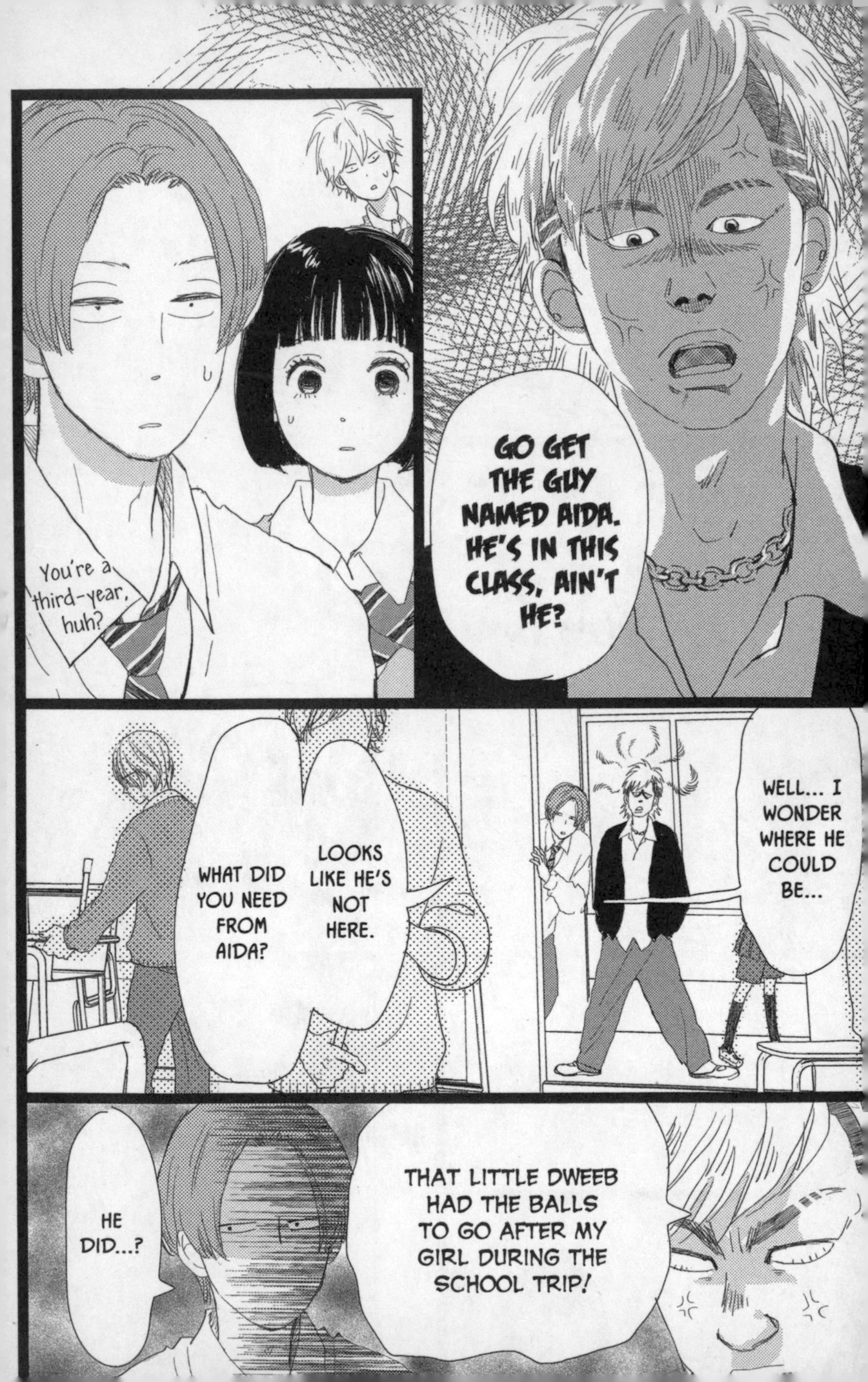
GO GET THE GUY NAMED AIDA. HE'S IN THIS CLASS, AIN'T HE?
You're a third-year, huh?
WELL... I WONDER WHERE HE COULD BE...
LOOKS LIKE HE'S NOT HERE.
WHAT DID YOU NEED FROM AIDA?
THAT LITTLE DWEEB HAD THE BALLS TO GO AFTER MY GIRL DURING THE SCHOOL TRIP!
HE DID...?

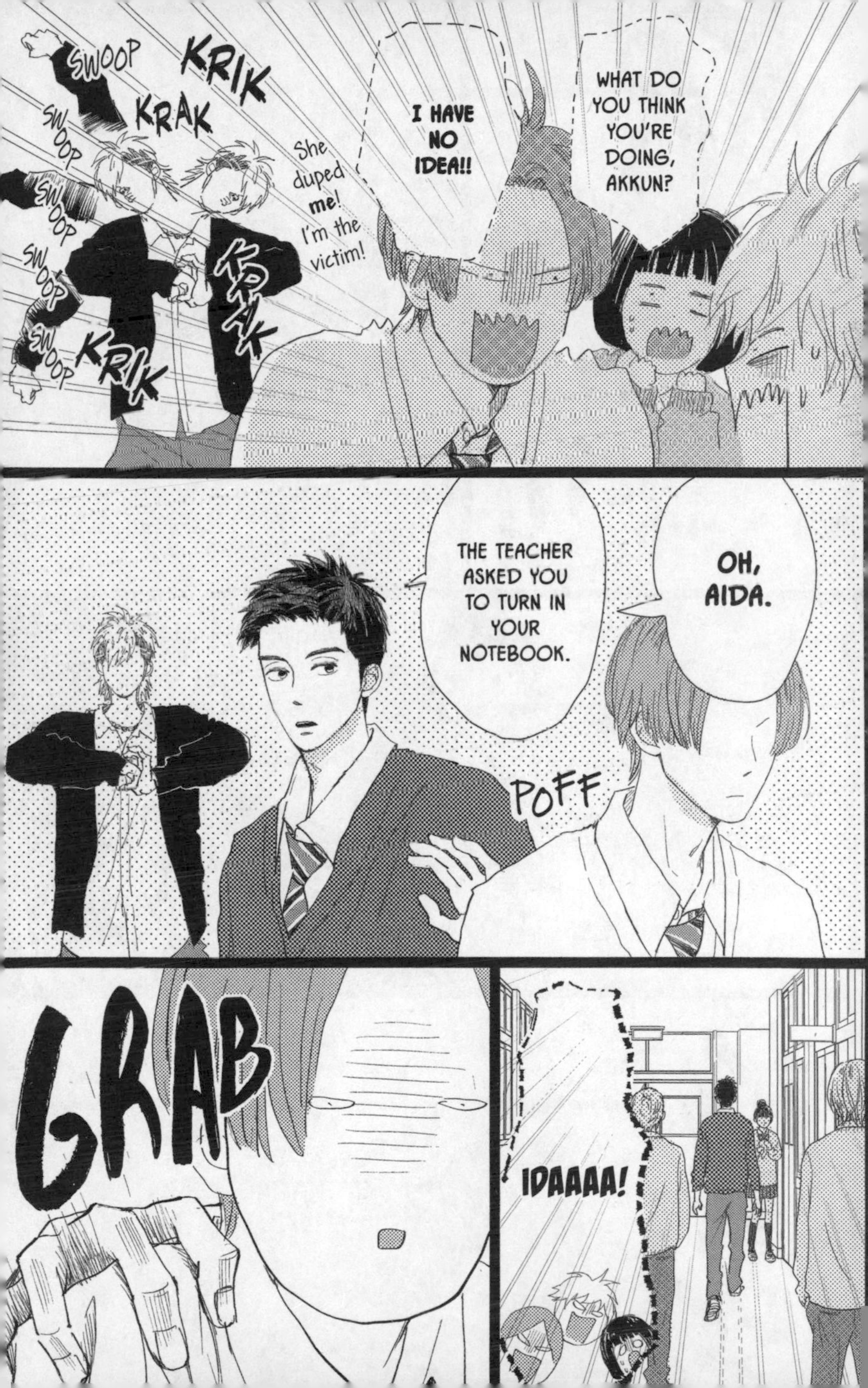
WHAT DO YOU THINK YOU'RE DOING, AKKUN?
I HAVE NO IDEA!!
She duped me! I'm the victim!
KRIK
SWOOP
KRAK
KRAK
SWOOP
SWOOP
SWOOP
SWOOP
KRIK
OH, AIDA.
THE TEACHER ASKED YOU TO TURN IN YOUR NOTEBOOK.
POFF
IDAAAA!
GRAB

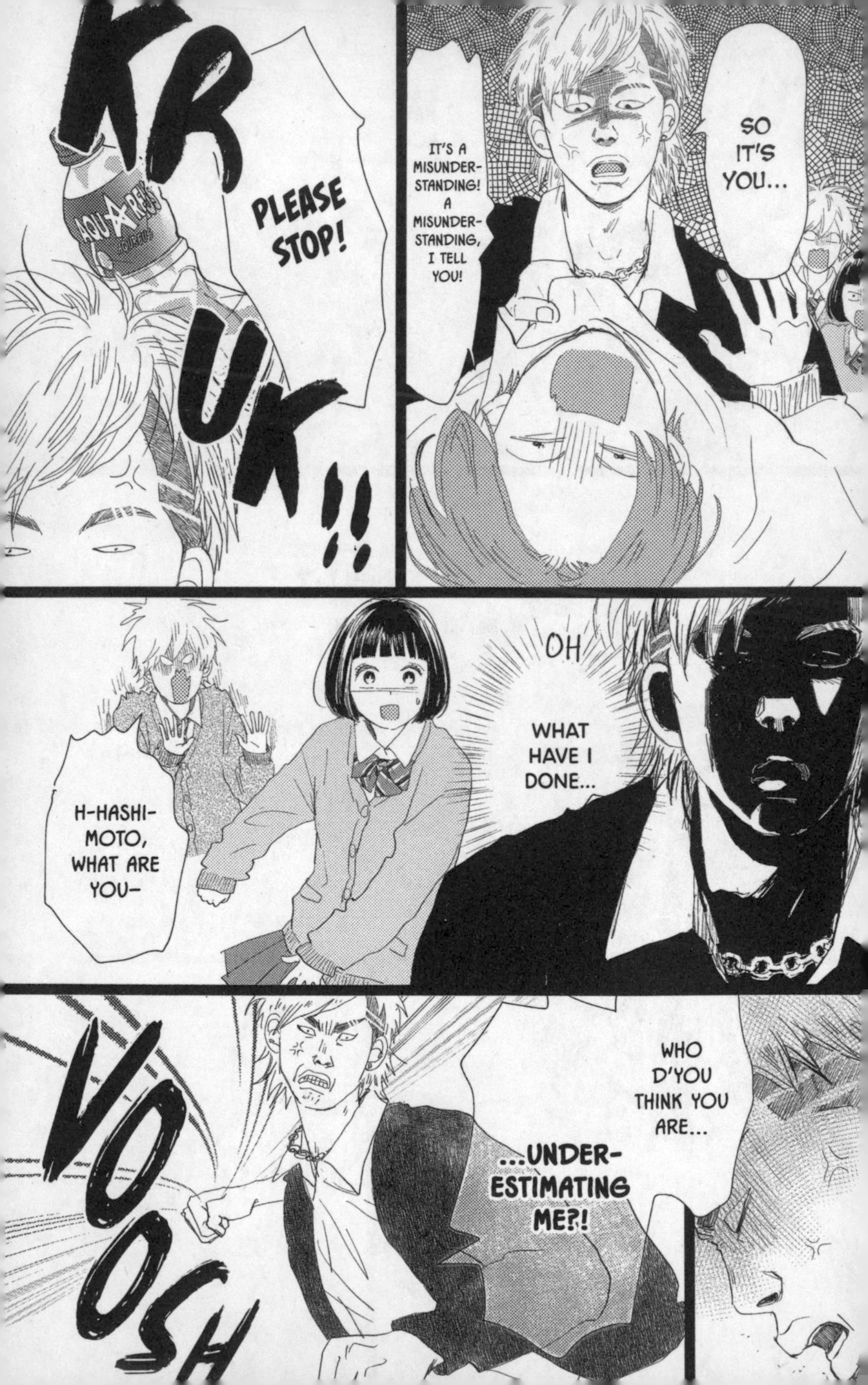
SO IT'S YOU...
IT'S A MISUNDERSTANDING! A MISUNDERSTANDING, I TELL YOU!
KRUK!!
PLEASE STOP!
OH
WHAT HAVE I DONE...
H-HASHIMOTO, WHAT ARE YOU–
WHO D'YOU THINK YOU ARE...
...UNDERESTIMATING ME?!
VOOSH

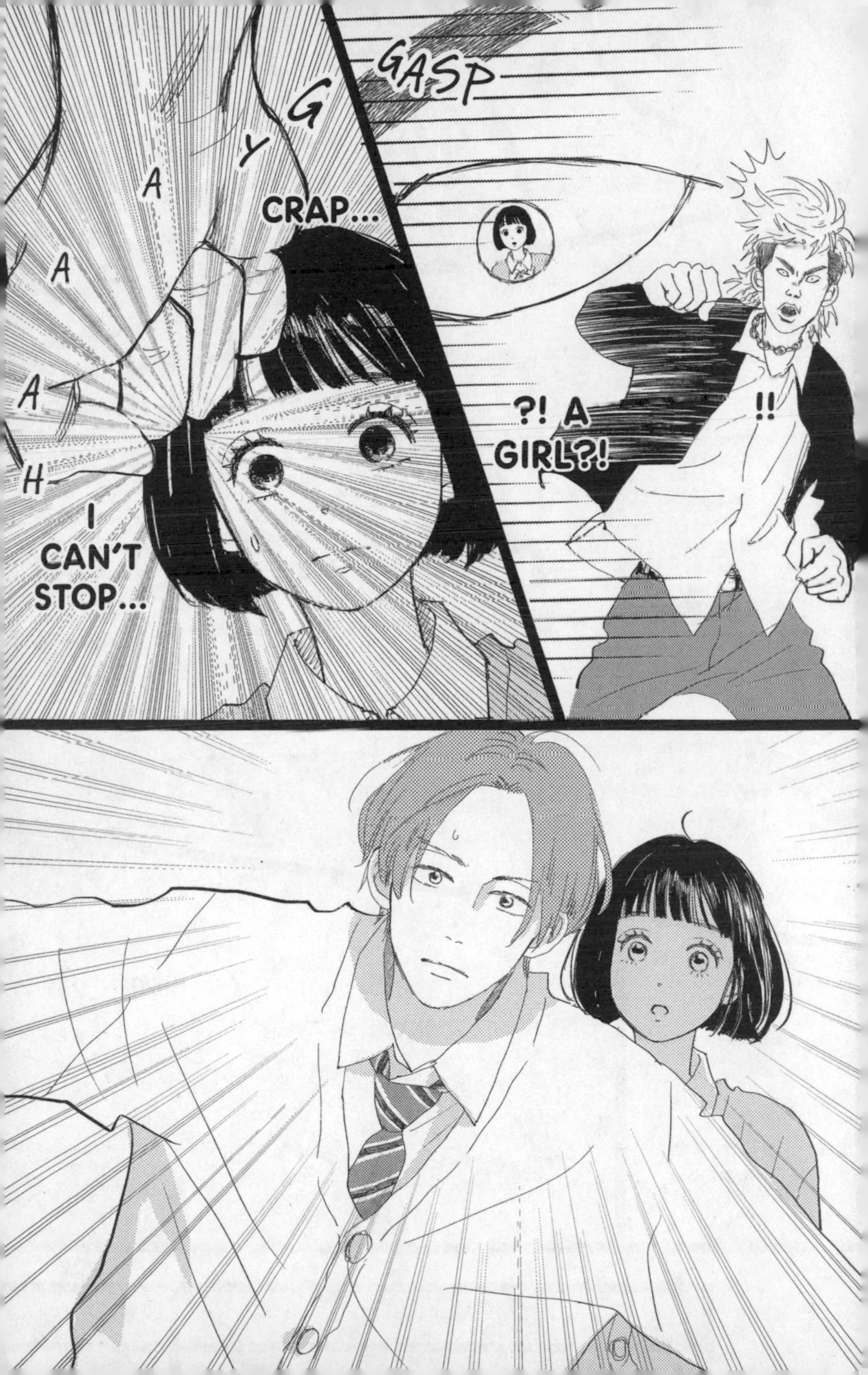
GASP
!!
?! A GIRL?!
GYAAAH
CRAP...
I CAN'T STOP...

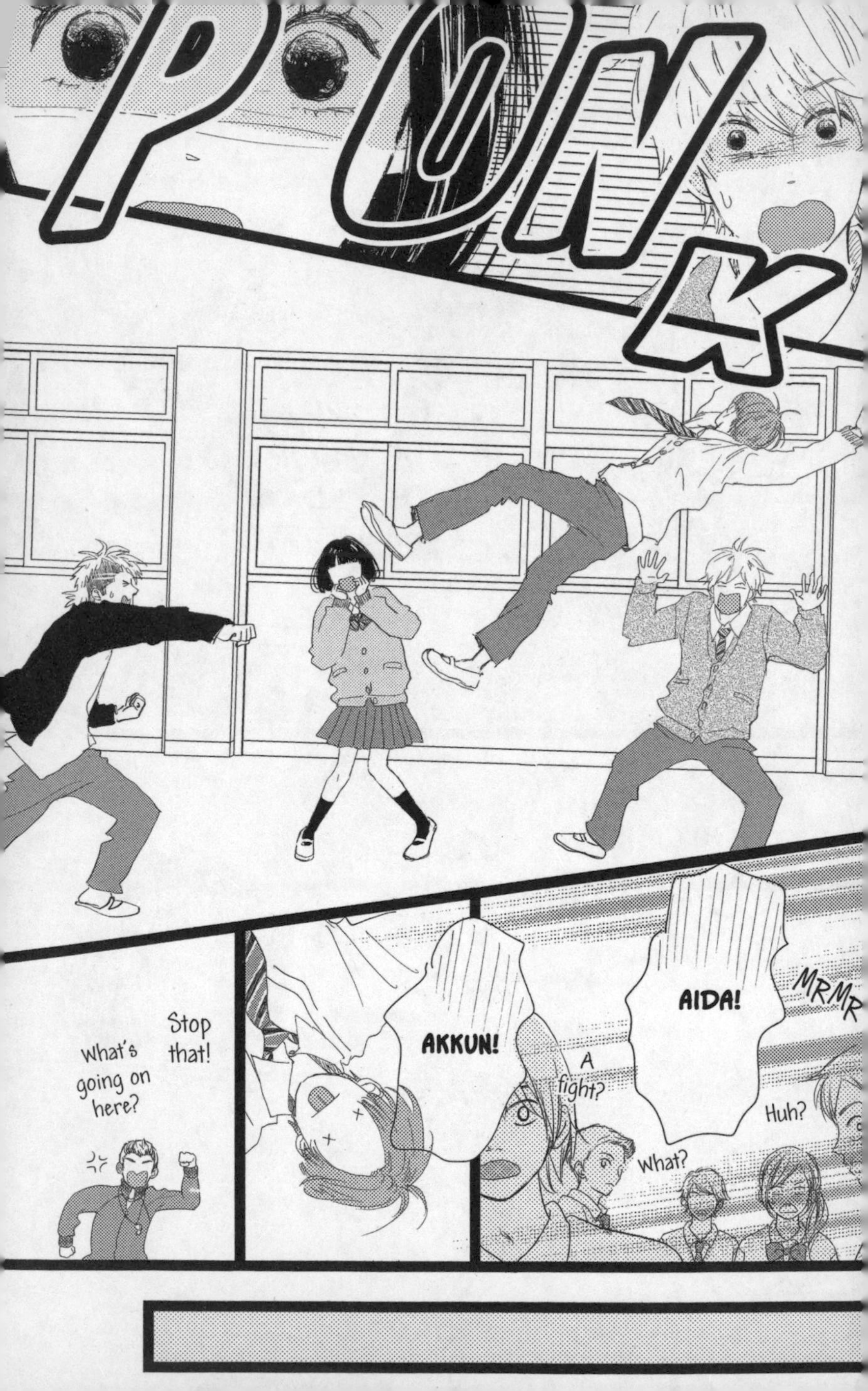
PONK
MRMR
AIDA!
Huh?
A fight?
What?
AKKUN!
Stop that!
What's going on here?

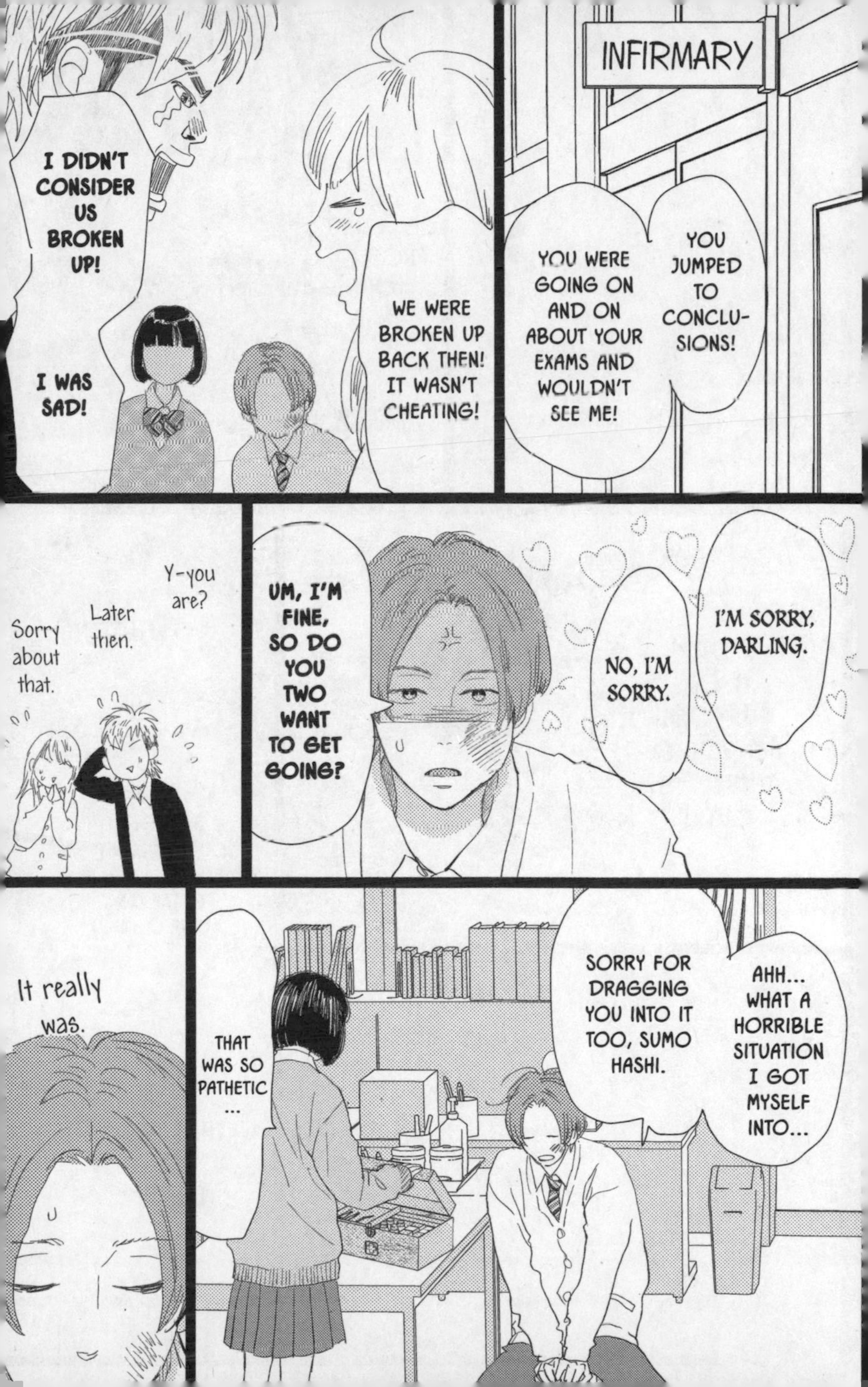
INFIRMARY
YOU JUMPED TO CONCLUSIONS!
YOU WERE GOING ON AND ON ABOUT YOUR EXAMS AND WOULDN'T SEE ME!
WE WERE BROKEN UP BACK THEN! IT WASN'T CHEATING!
I DIDN'T CONSIDER US BROKEN UP!
I WAS SAD!
I'M SORRY, DARLING.
NO, I'M SORRY.
UM, I'M FINE, SO DO YOU TWO WANT TO GET GOING?
Y-you are?
Later then.
Sorry about that.
AHH... WHAT A HORRIBLE SITUATION I GOT MYSELF INTO...
SORRY FOR DRAGGING YOU INTO IT TOO, SUMOHASHI.
THAT WAS SO PATHETIC...
It really was.

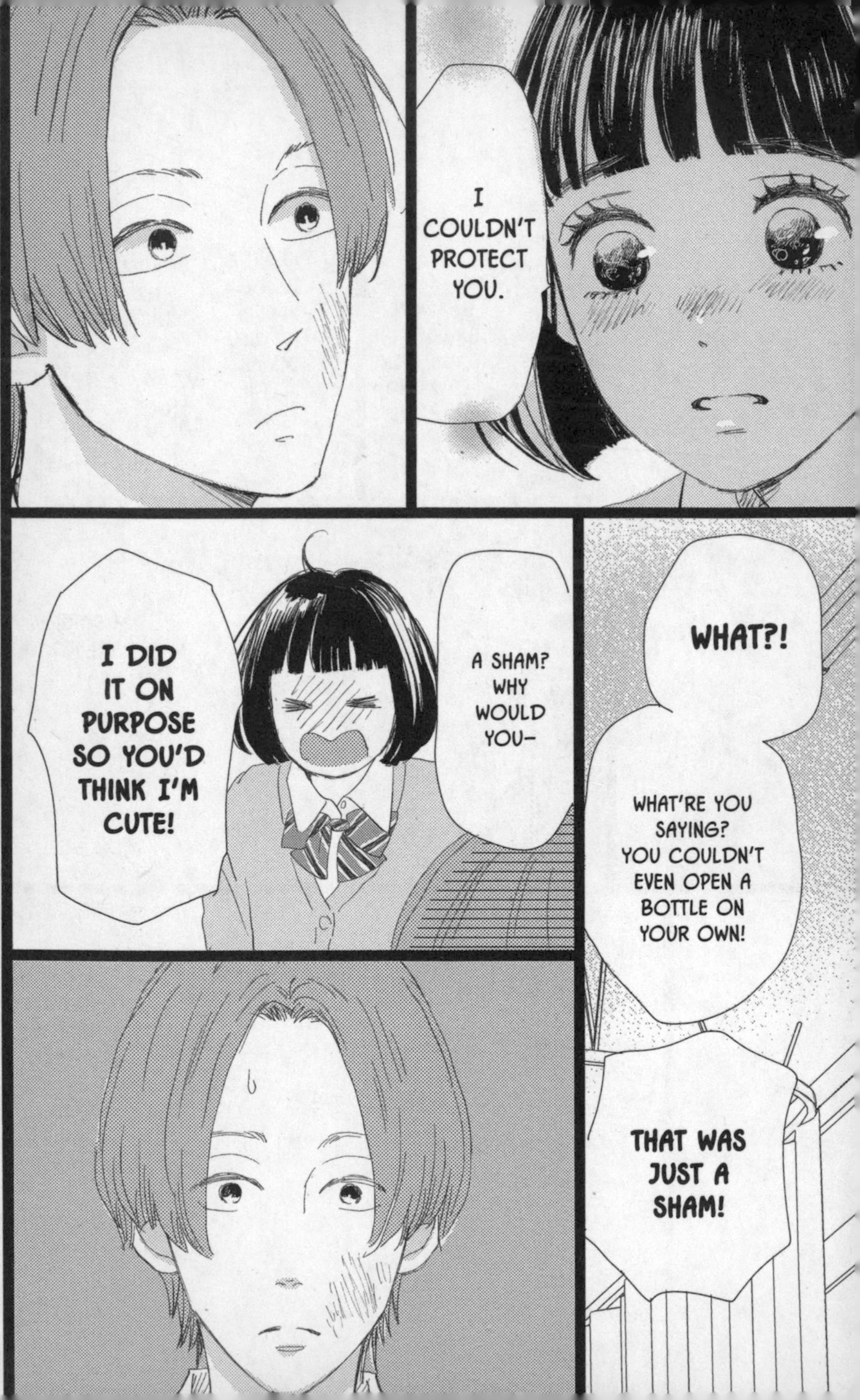
I COULDN'T PROTECT YOU.
WHAT?!
WHAT'RE YOU SAYING? YOU COULDN'T EVEN OPEN A BOTTLE ON YOUR OWN!
THAT WAS JUST A SHAM!
A SHAM? WHY WOULD YOU–
I DID IT ON PURPOSE SO YOU'D THINK I'M CUTE!

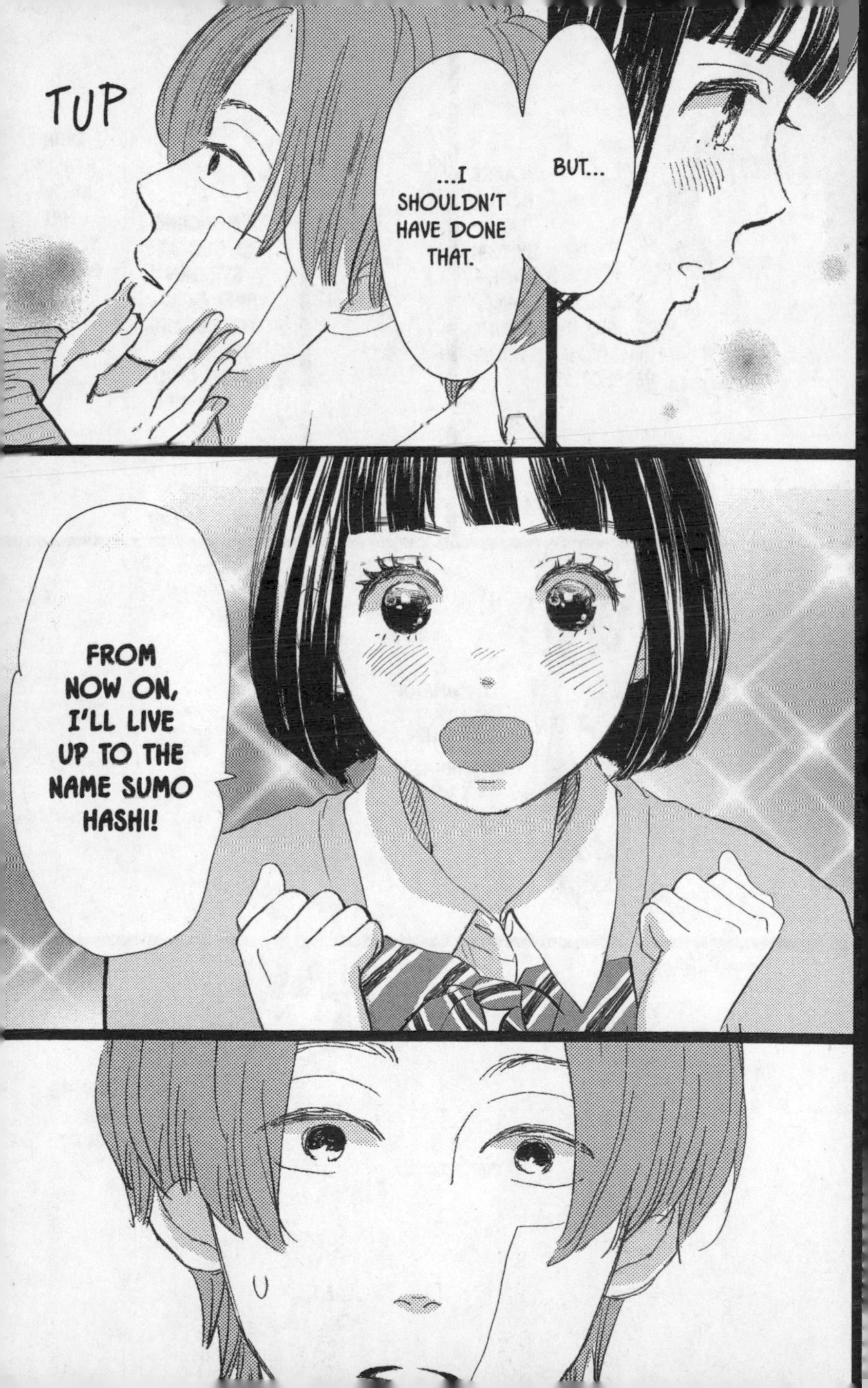
BUT...
...I SHOULDN'T HAVE DONE THAT.
TUP
FROM NOW ON, I'LL LIVE UP TO THE NAME SUMO HASHI!

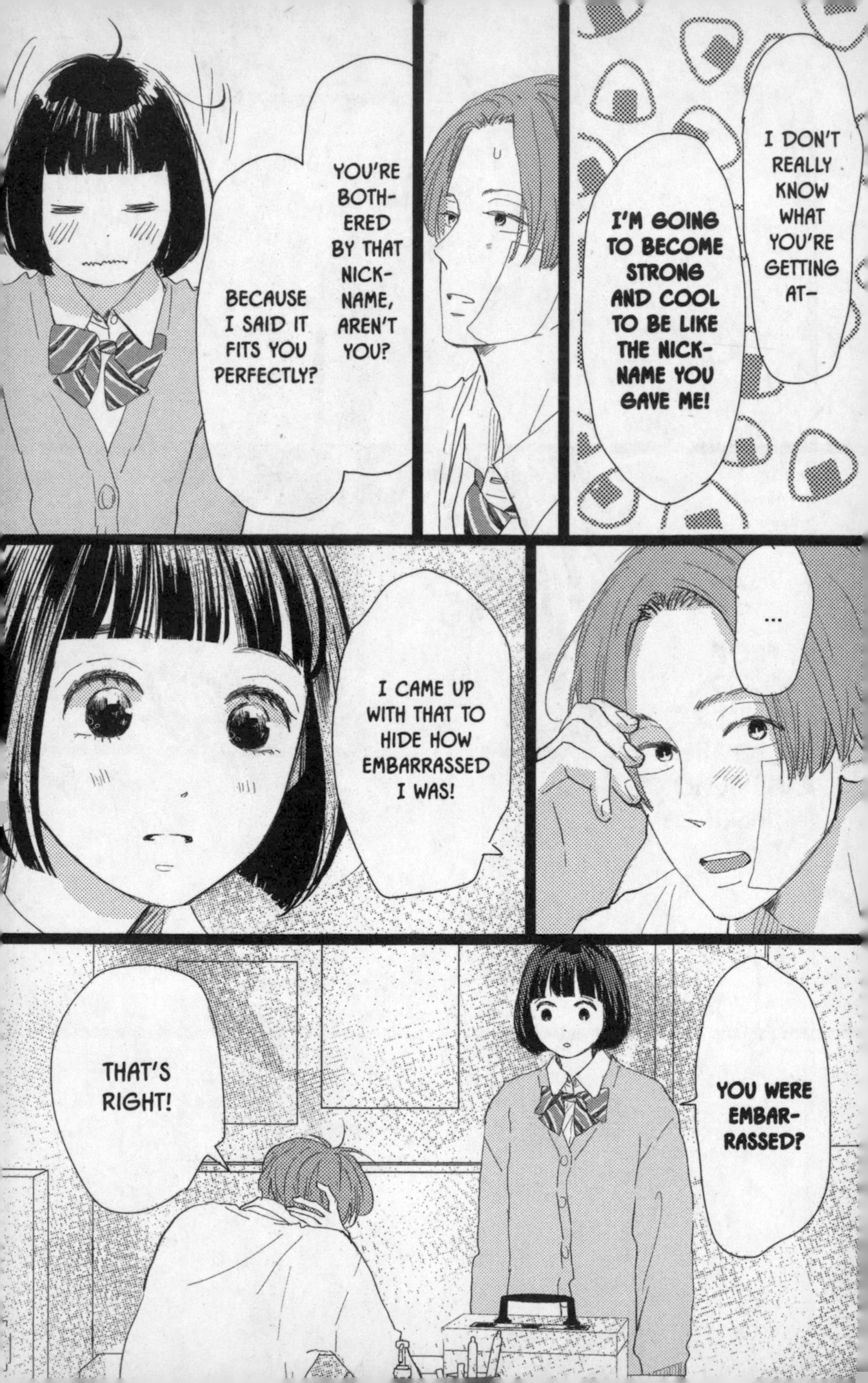
I DON'T REALLY KNOW WHAT YOU'RE GETTING AT-
I'M GOING TO BECOME STRONG AND COOL TO BE LIKE THE NICKNAME YOU GAVE ME!
YOU'RE BOTHERED BY THAT NICKNAME, AREN'T YOU?
BECAUSE I SAID IT FITS YOU PERFECTLY?
...
I CAME UP WITH THAT TO HIDE HOW EMBARRASSED I WAS!
YOU WERE EMBARRASSED?
THAT'S RIGHT!

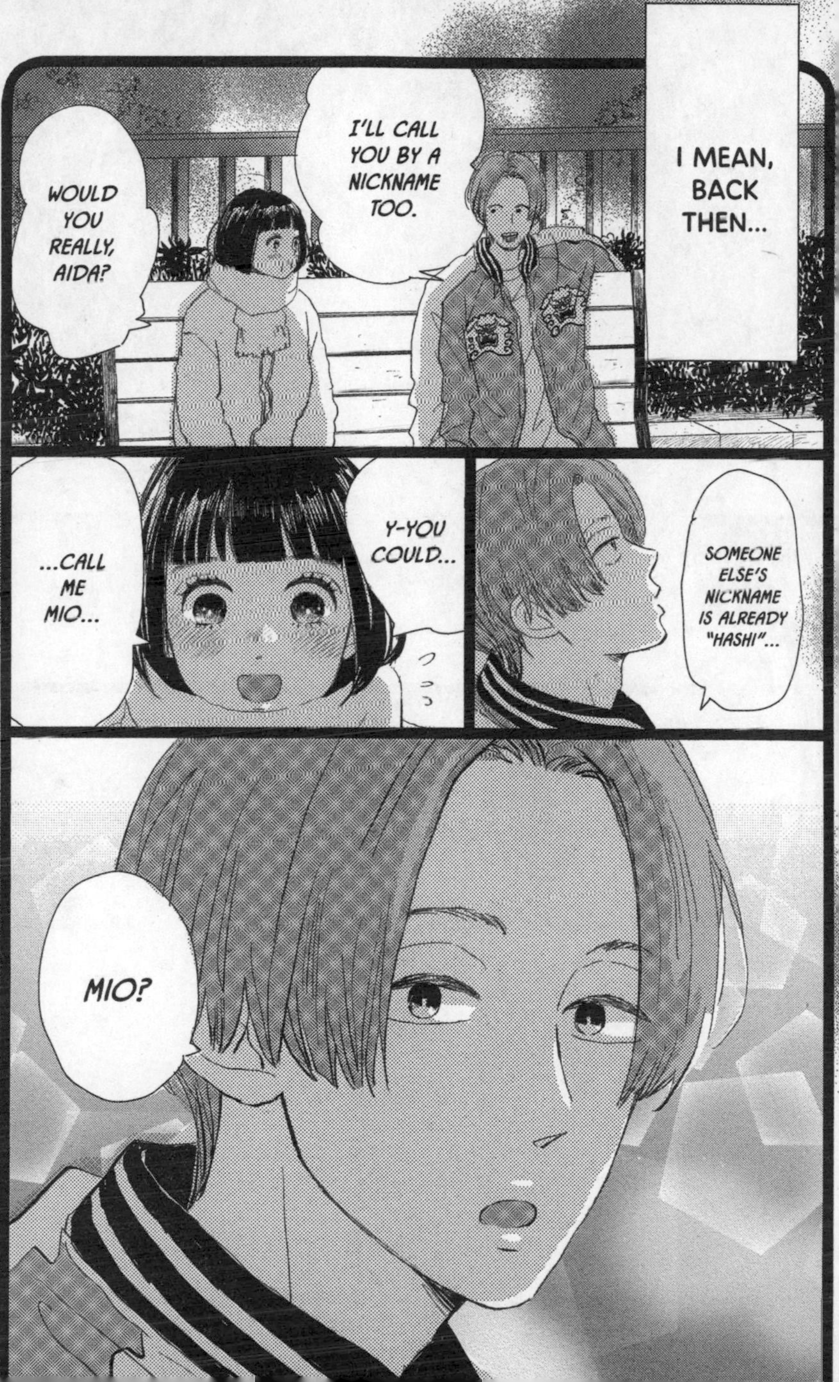
I MEAN, BACK THEN...
I'LL CALL YOU BY A NICKNAME TOO.
WOULD YOU REALLY, AIDA?
SOMEONE ELSE'S NICKNAME IS ALREADY "HASHI"...
Y-YOU COULD...
...CALL ME MIO...
MIO?

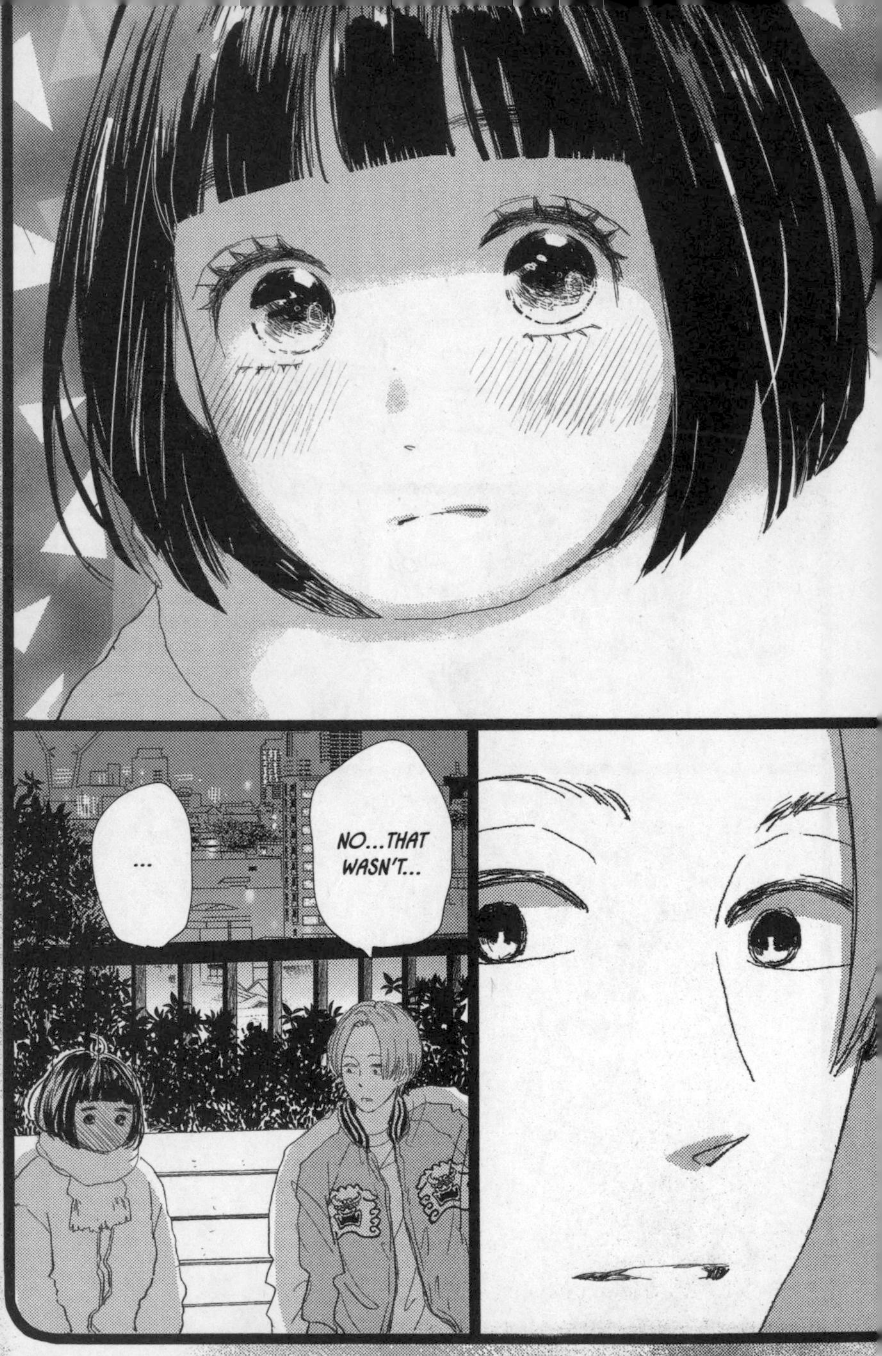
NO...THAT WASN'T...
...

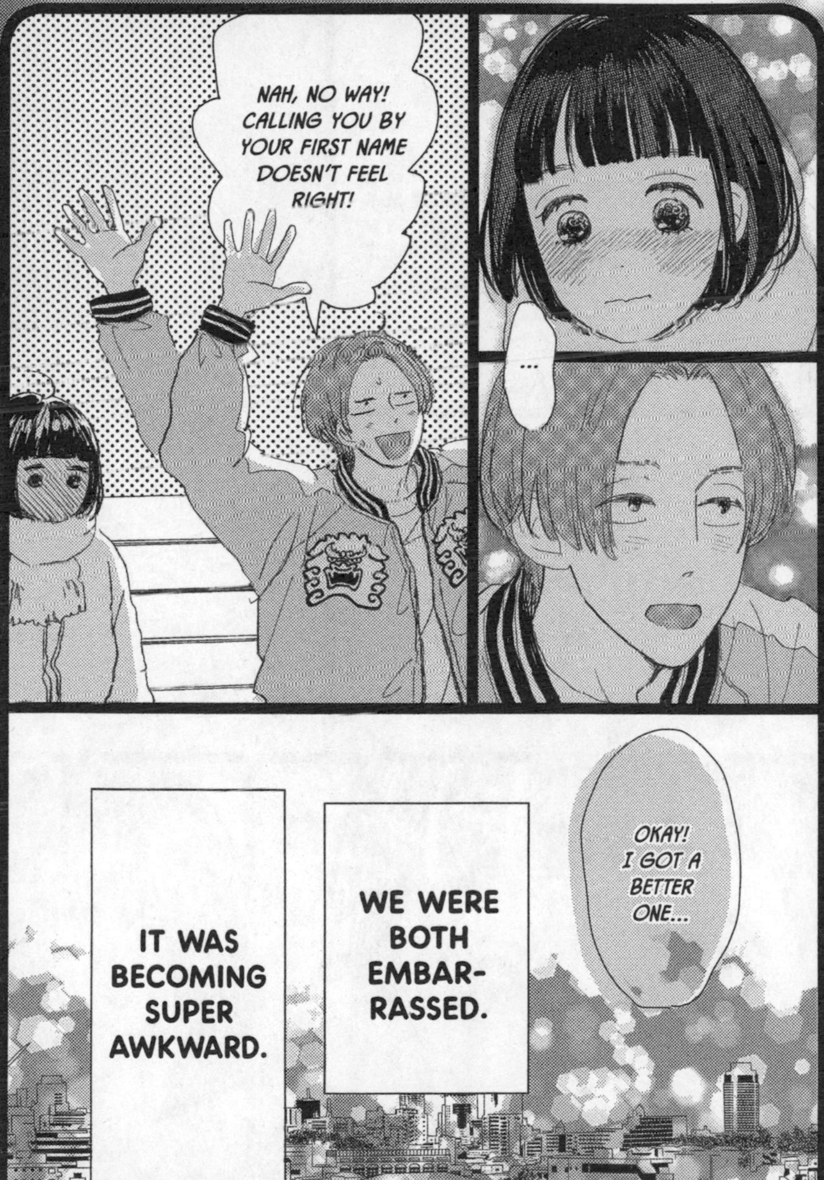
...
NAH, NO WAY! CALLING YOU BY YOUR FIRST NAME DOESN'T FEEL RIGHT!
OKAY! I GOT A BETTER ONE...
WE WERE BOTH EMBARRASSED.
IT WAS BECOMING SUPER AWKWARD.

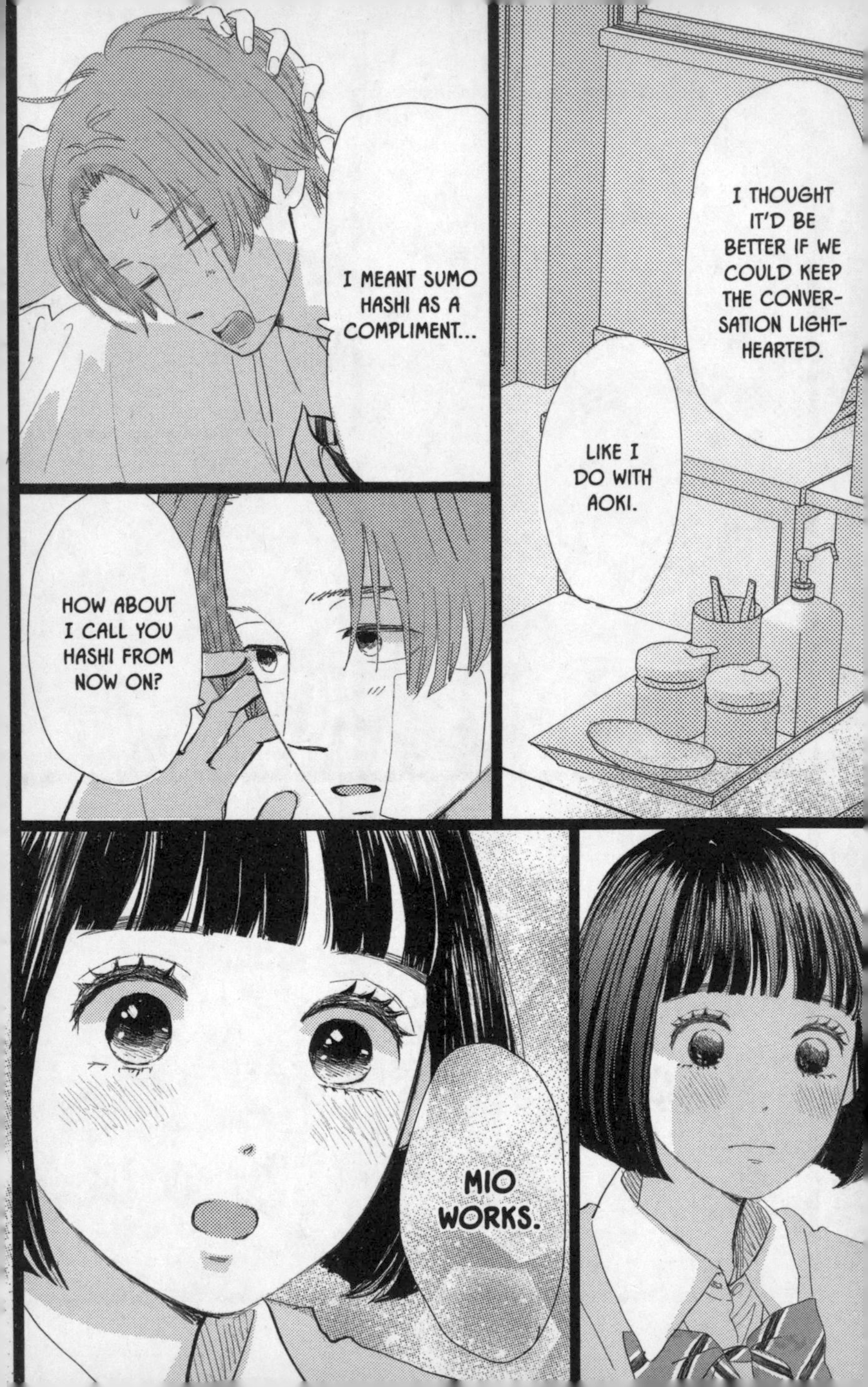
I THOUGHT IT'D BE BETTER IF WE COULD KEEP THE CONVER-SATION LIGHT-HEARTED.
LIKE I DO WITH AOKI.
I MEANT SUMO HASHI AS A COMPLIMENT...
HOW ABOUT I CALL YOU HASHI FROM NOW ON?
MIO WORKS.

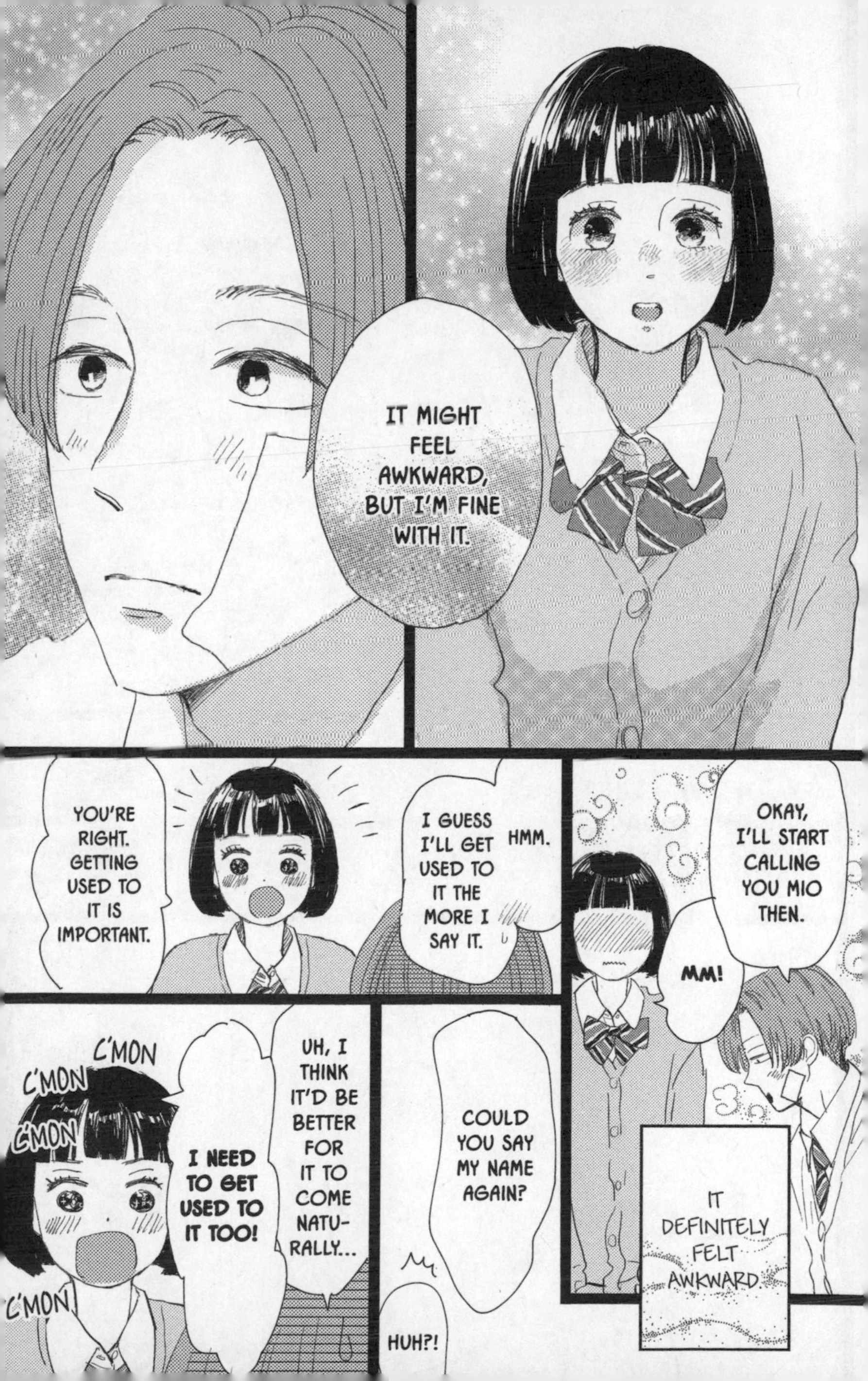
IT MIGHT FEEL AWKWARD, BUT I'M FINE WITH IT.
OKAY, I'LL START CALLING YOU MIO THEN.
MM!
IT DEFINITELY FELT AWKWARD.
HMM.
I GUESS I'LL GET USED TO IT THE MORE I SAY IT.
YOU'RE RIGHT. GETTING USED TO IT IS IMPORTANT.
COULD YOU SAY MY NAME AGAIN?
HUH?!
UH, I THINK IT'D BE BETTER FOR IT TO COME NATURALLY...
I NEED TO GET USED TO IT TOO!
C'MON
C'MON
C'MON
C'MON

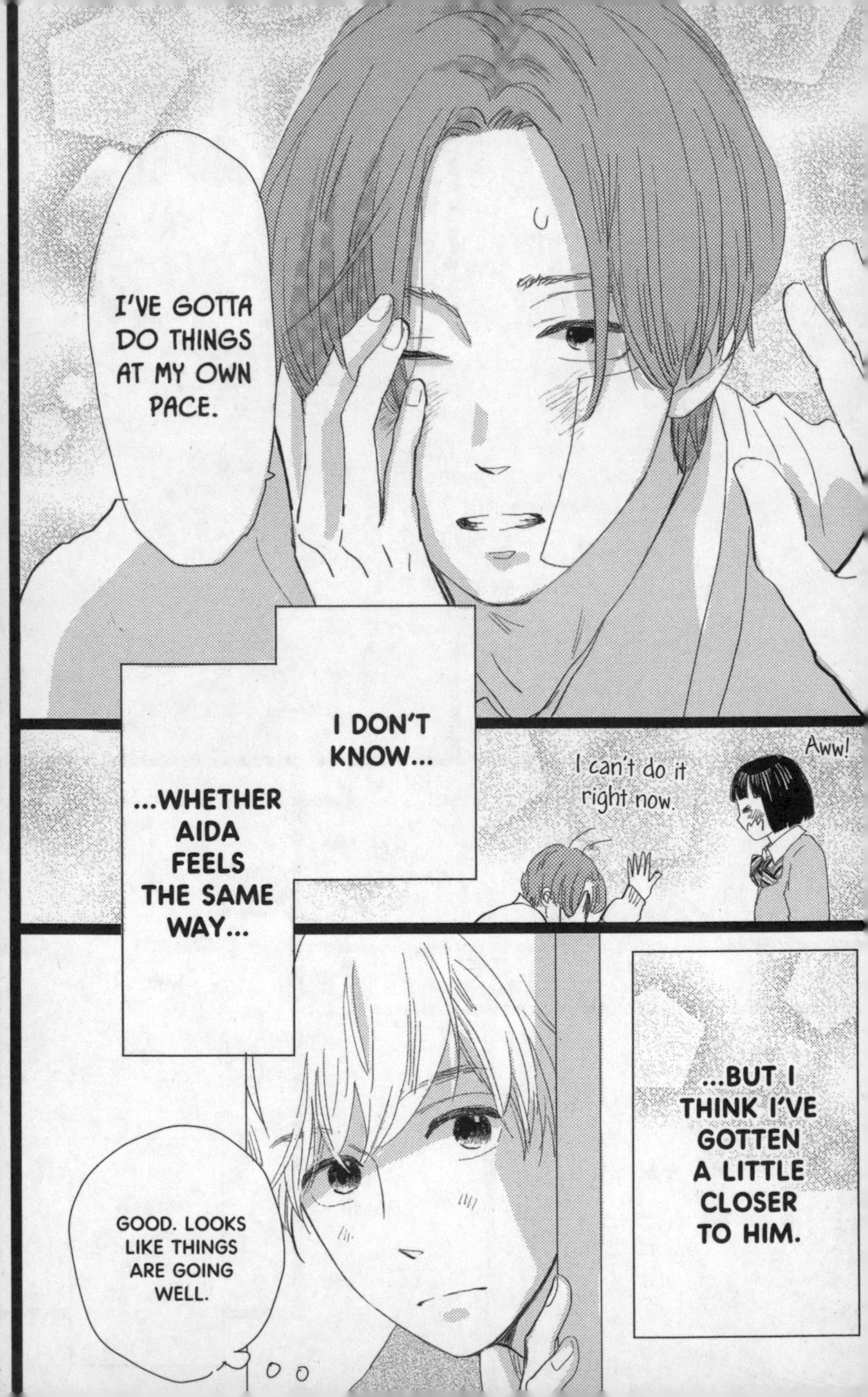
I'VE GOTTA DO THINGS AT MY OWN PACE.
Aww!
I can't do it right now.
I DON'T KNOW...
...WHETHER AIDA FEELS THE SAME WAY...
...BUT I THINK I'VE GOTTEN A LITTLE CLOSER TO HIM.
GOOD. LOOKS LIKE THINGS ARE GOING WELL.

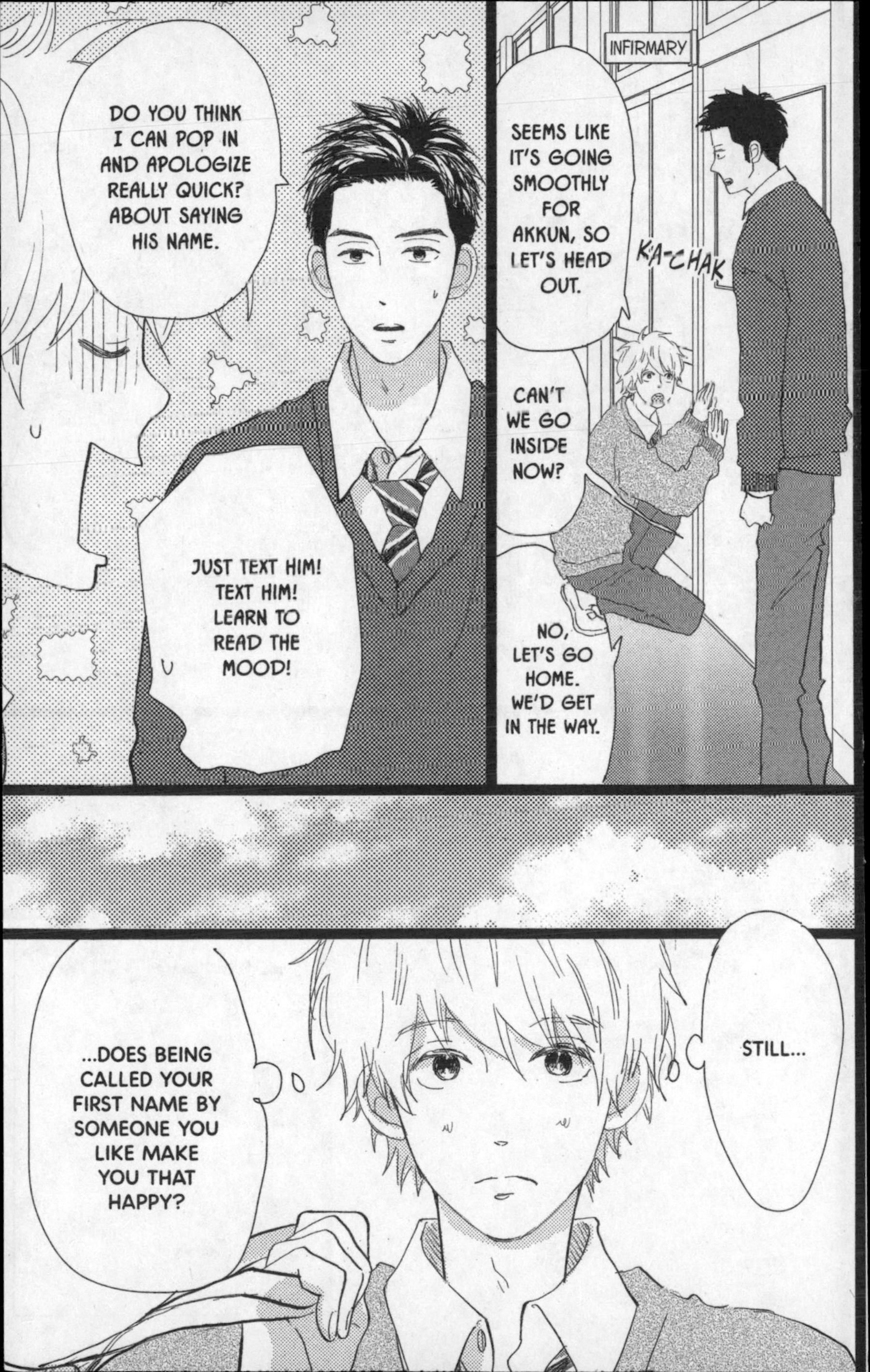
INFIRMARY
SEEMS LIKE IT'S GOING SMOOTHLY FOR AKKUN, SO LET'S HEAD OUT.
KA-CHAK
CAN'T WE GO INSIDE NOW?
NO, LET'S GO HOME. WE'D GET IN THE WAY.
DO YOU THINK I CAN POP IN AND APOLOGIZE REALLY QUICK? ABOUT SAYING HIS NAME.
JUST TEXT HIM! TEXT HIM! LEARN TO READ THE MOOD!
STILL...
...DOES BEING CALLED YOUR FIRST NAME BY SOMEONE YOU LIKE MAKE YOU THAT HAPPY?

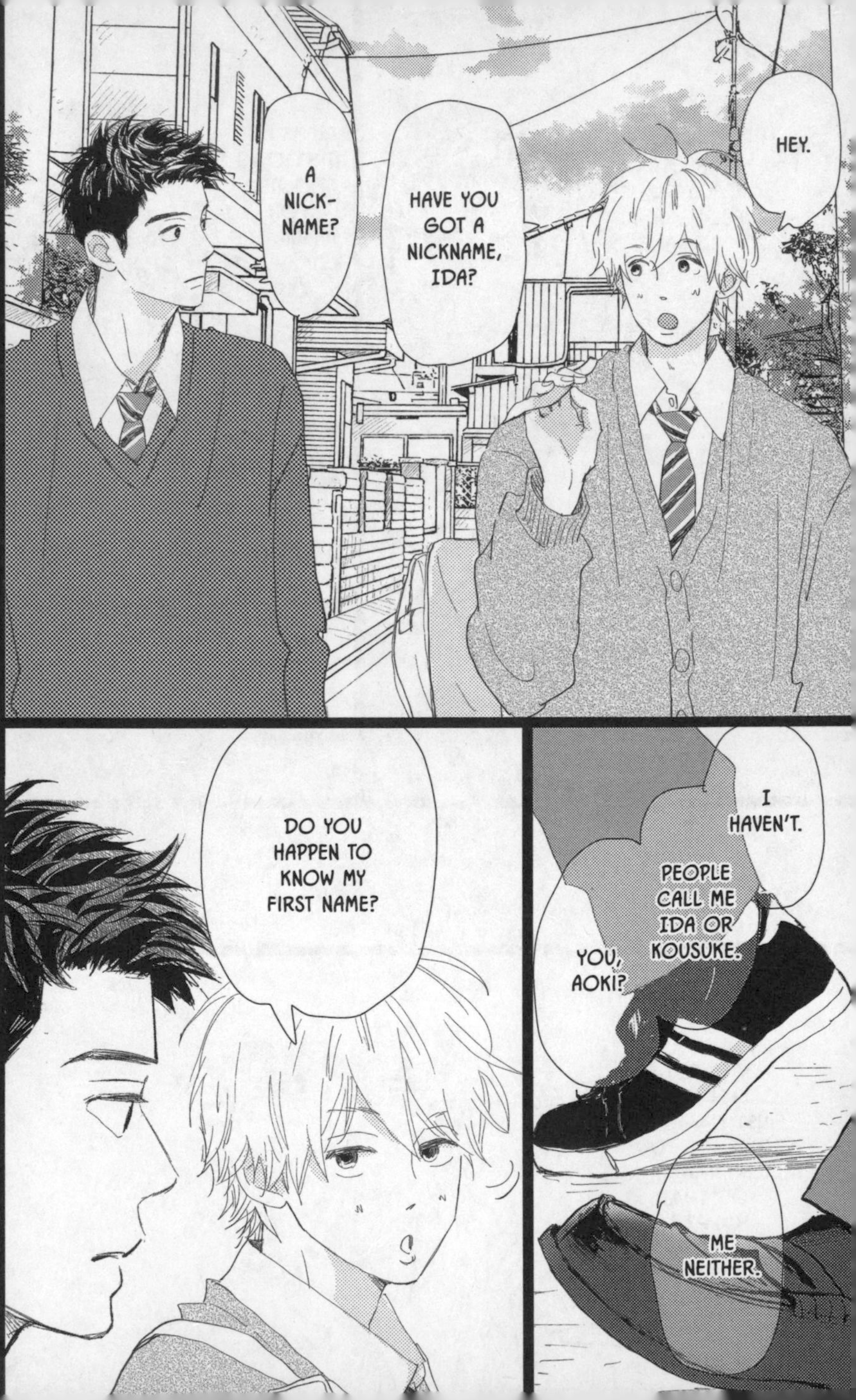
HEY.
HAVE YOU GOT A NICKNAME, IDA?
A NICK-NAME?
I HAVEN'T.
PEOPLE CALL ME IDA OR KOUSUKE.
YOU, AOKI?
ME NEITHER.
DO YOU HAPPEN TO KNOW MY FIRST NAME?

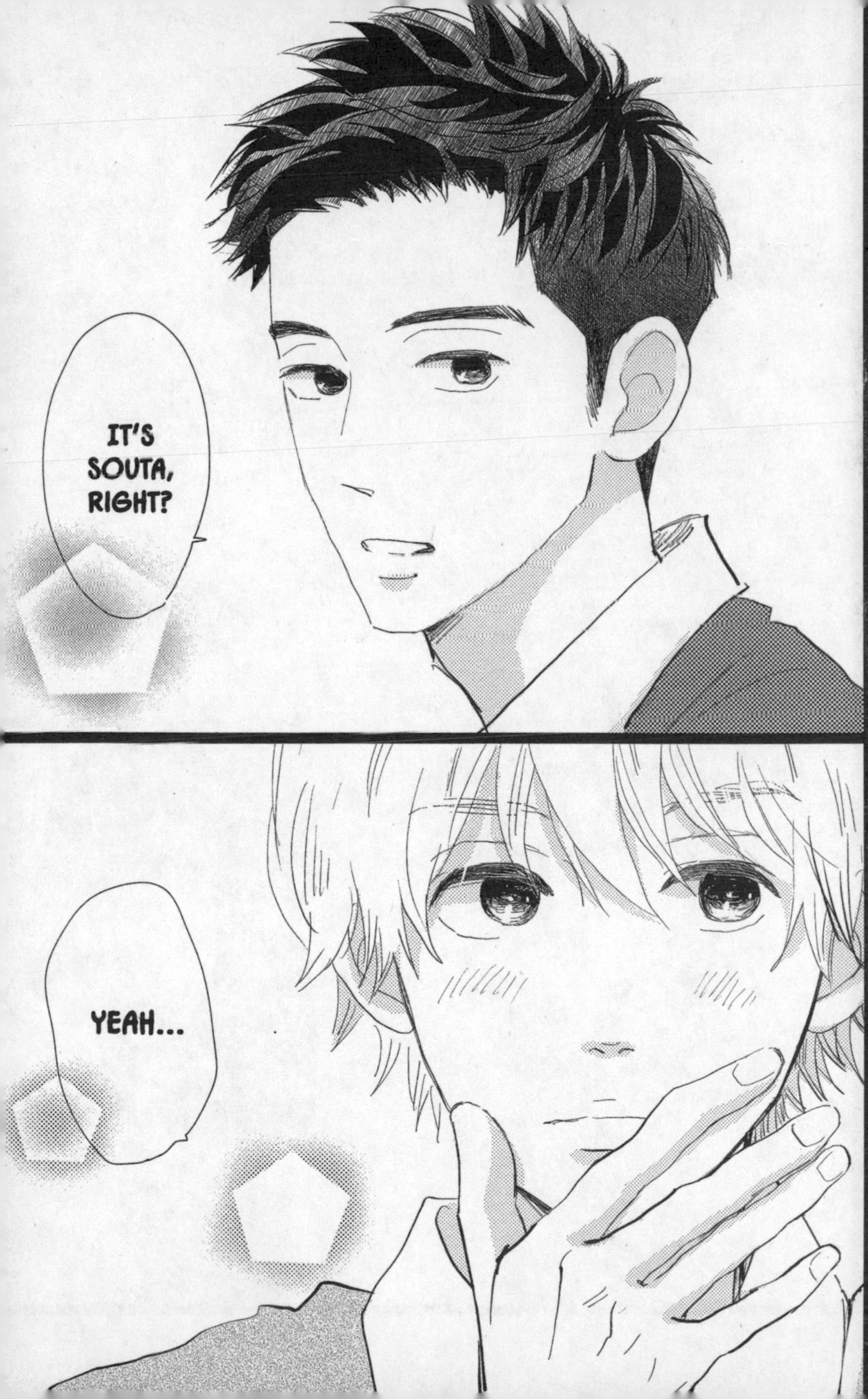
IT'S SOUTA, RIGHT?
YEAH...

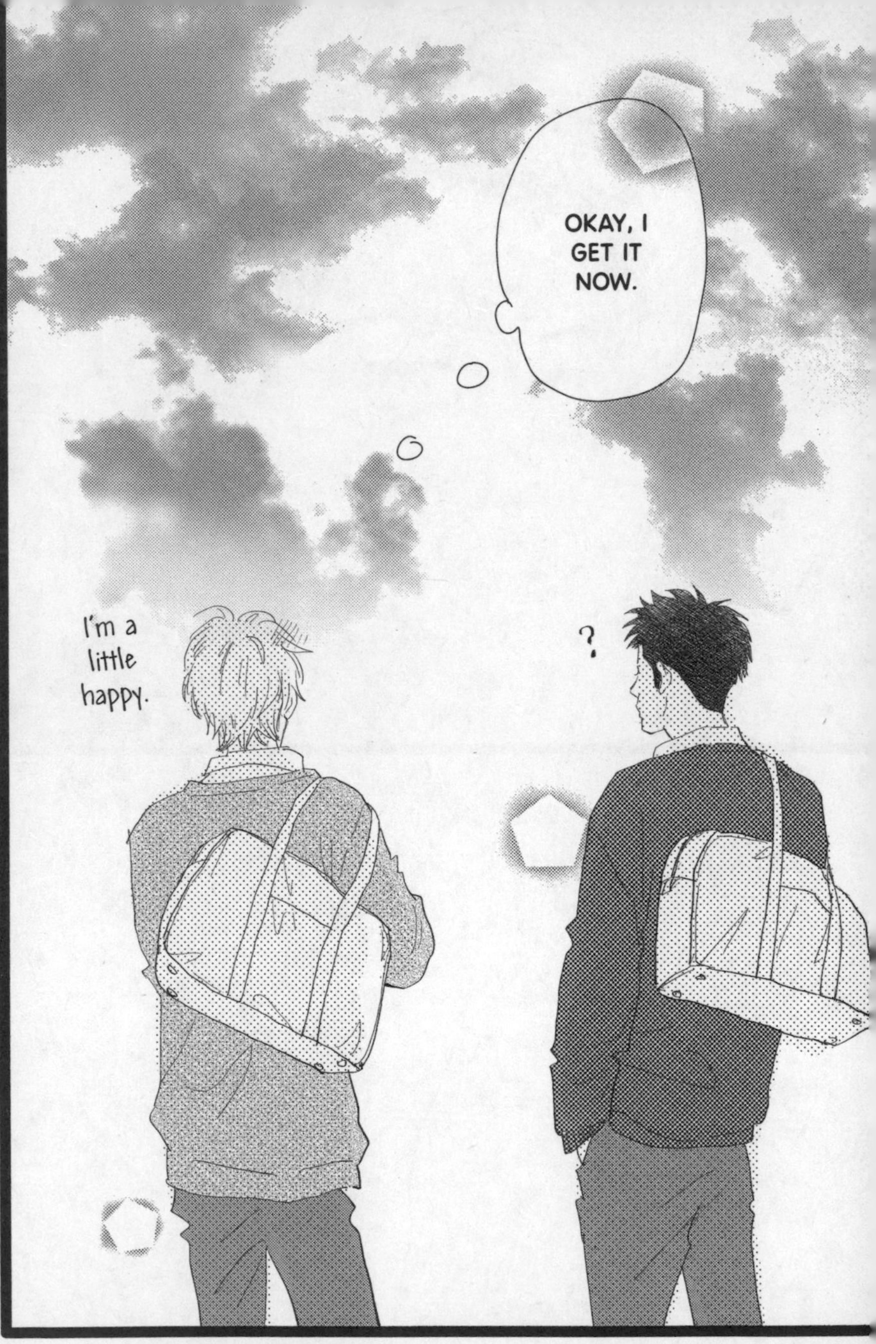
OKAY, I GET IT NOW.
?
I'm a little happy.

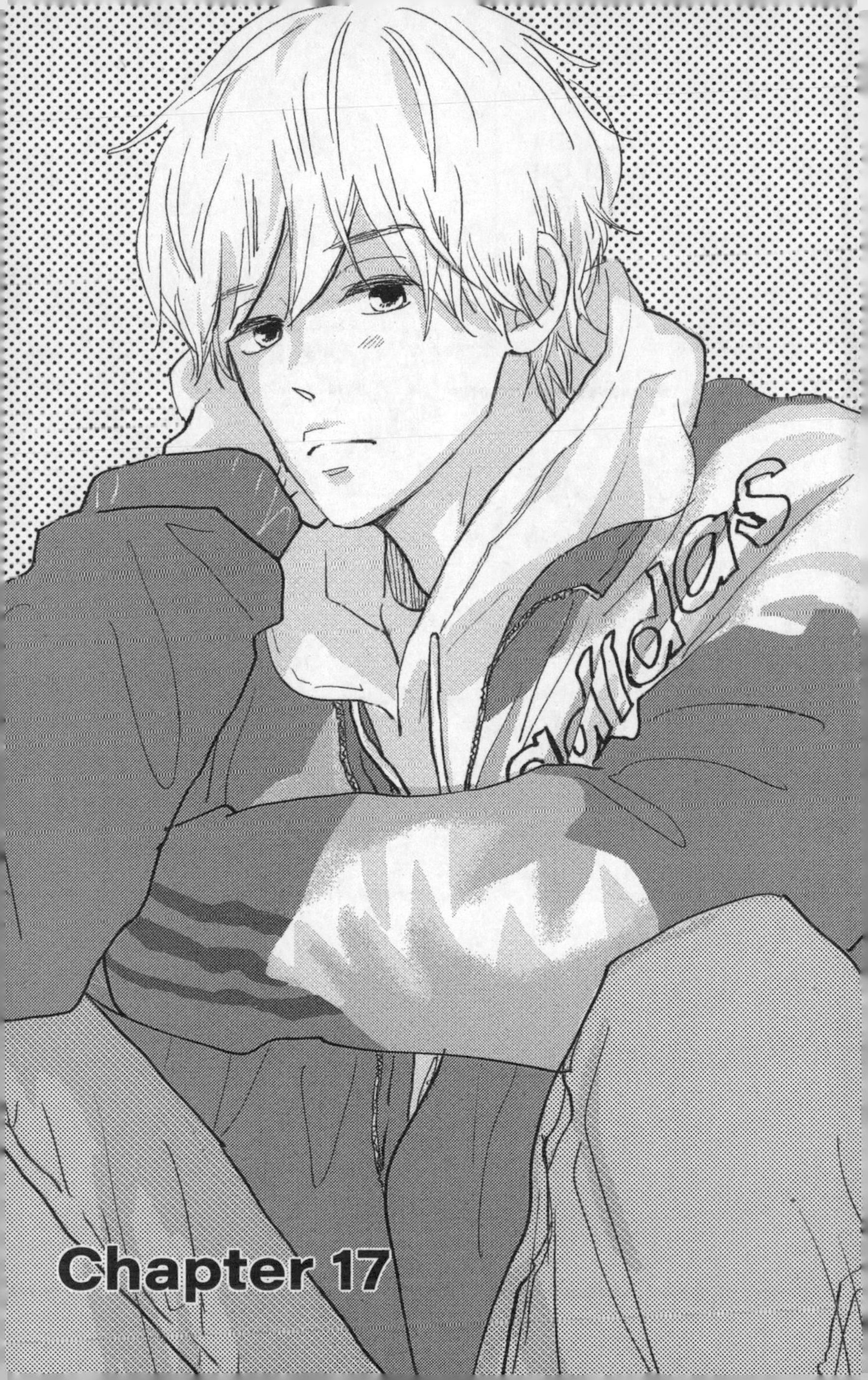

Chapter 17

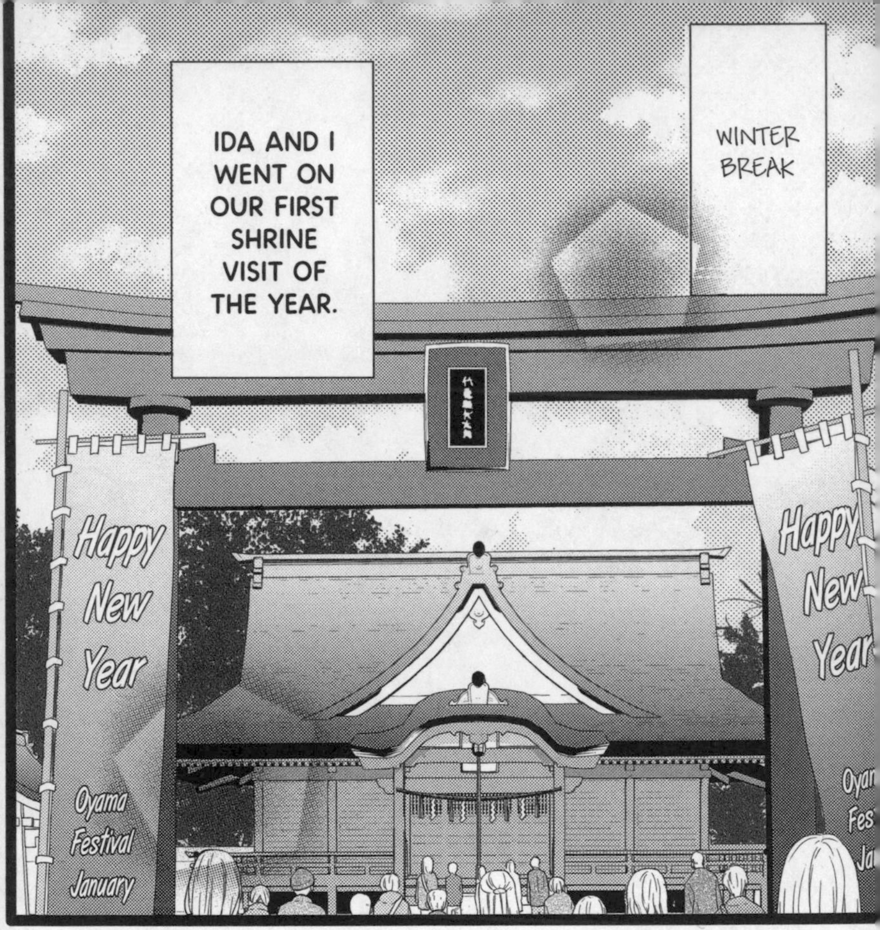
WINTER BREAK
IDA AND I WENT ON OUR FIRST SHRINE VISIT OF THE YEAR.
Happy New Year
Happy New Year
Oyama Festival January

My Love Mix-Up!

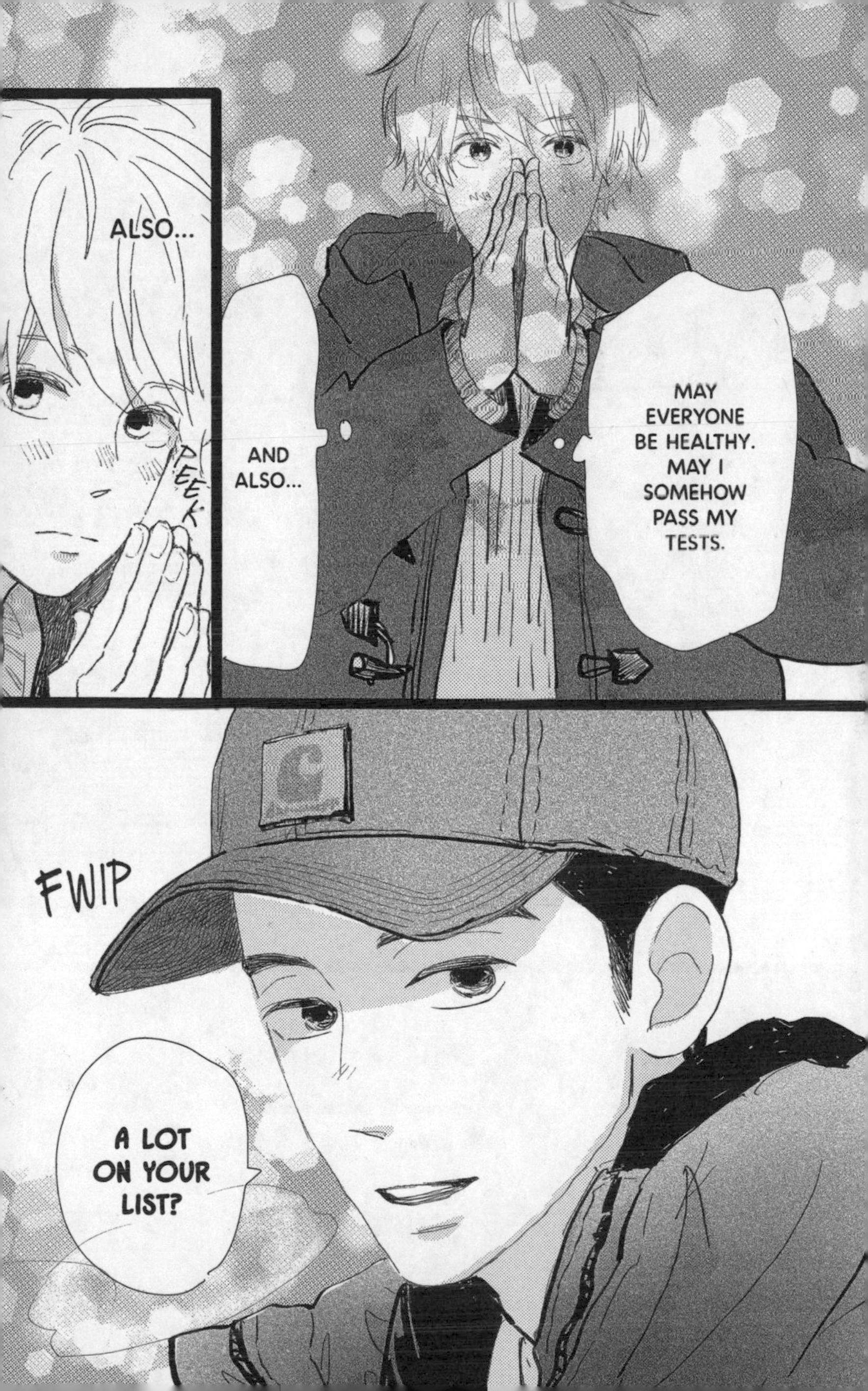
MAY EVERYONE BE HEALTHY. MAY I SOMEHOW PASS MY TESTS.
AND ALSO...
ALSO...
PEEK
FWIP
A LOT ON YOUR LIST?

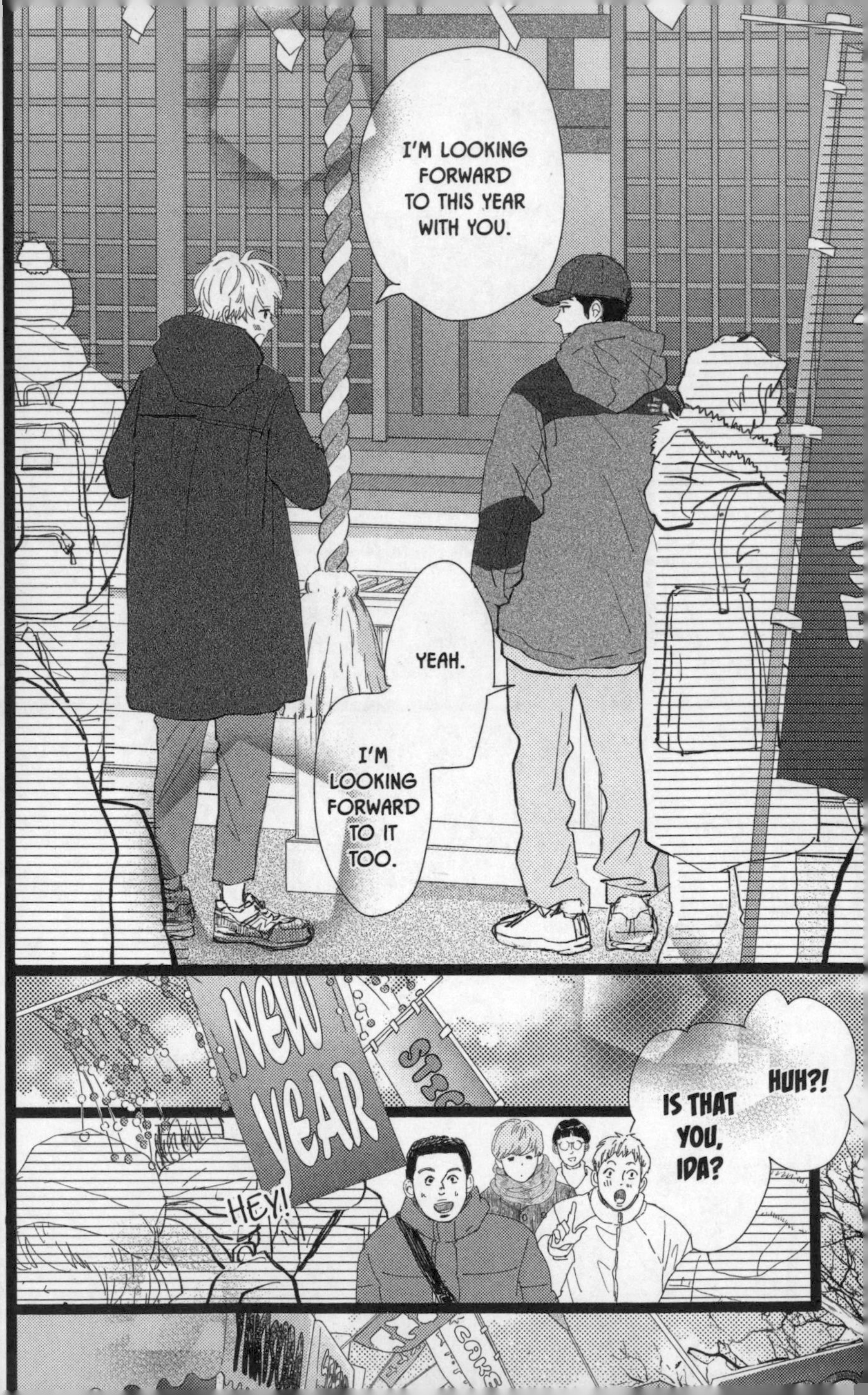
I'M LOOKING FORWARD TO THIS YEAR WITH YOU.
YEAH.
I'M LOOKING FORWARD TO IT TOO.
HUH?!
IS THAT YOU, IDA?
NEW YEAR
HEY!

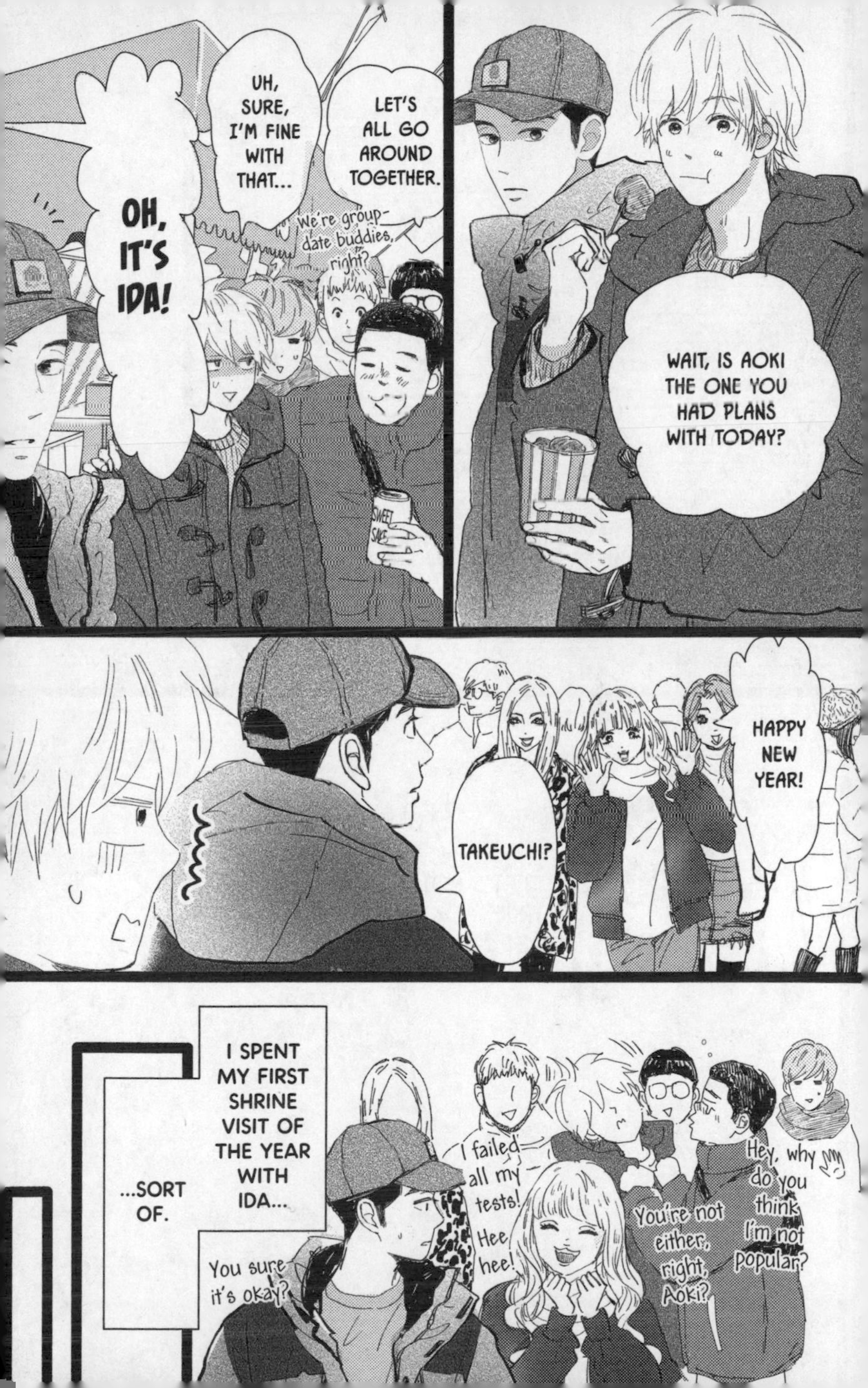
WAIT, IS AOKI THE ONE YOU HAD PLANS WITH TODAY?
LET'S ALL GO AROUND TOGETHER.
UH, SURE, I'M FINE WITH THAT...
We're group-date buddies, right?
OH, IT'S IDA!
HAPPY NEW YEAR!
TAKEUCHI?
Hey, why do you think I'm not popular?
You're not either, right, Aoki?
I failed all my tests!
Hee hee!
I SPENT MY FIRST SHRINE VISIT OF THE YEAR WITH IDA...
...SORT OF.
You sure it's okay?

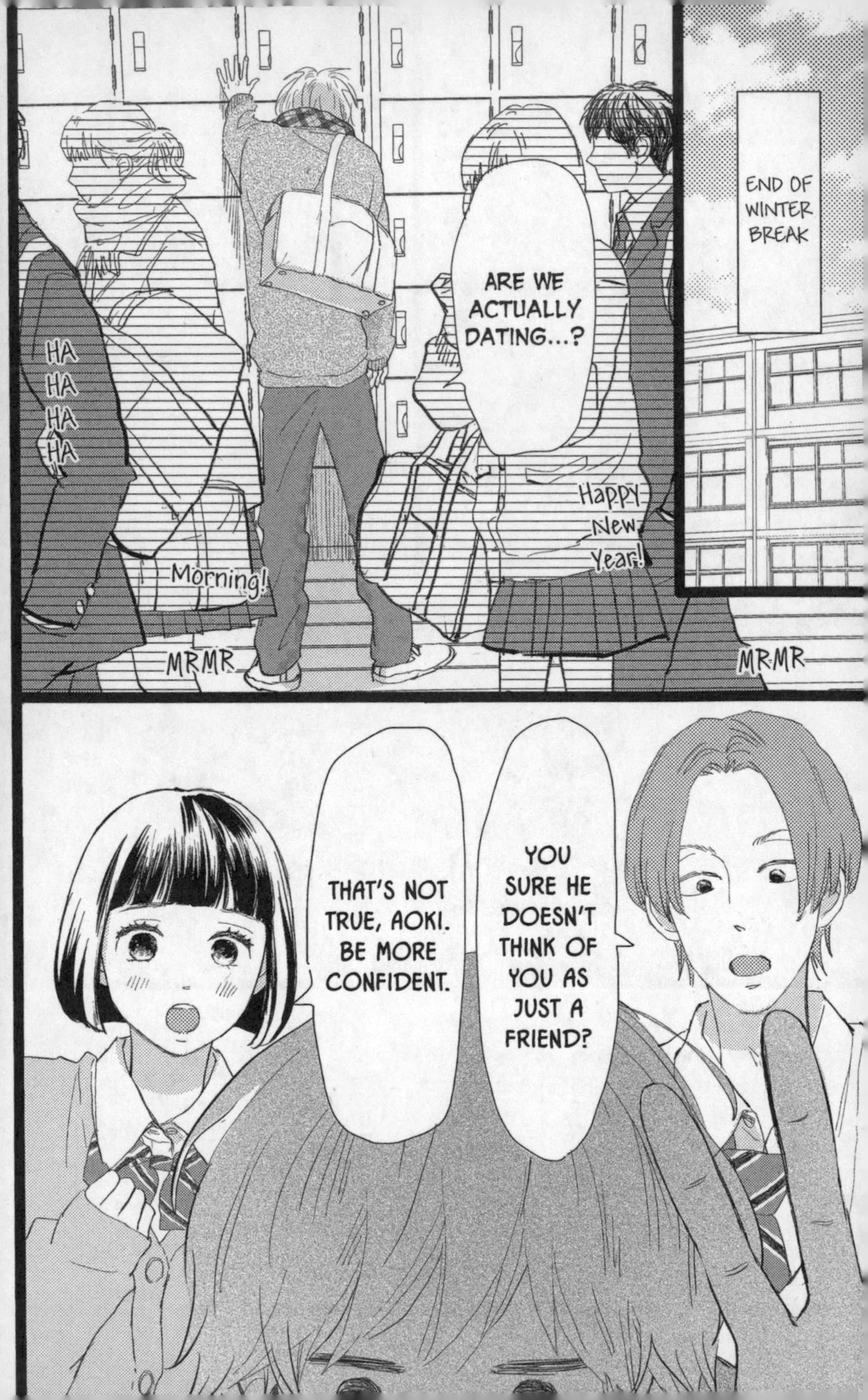
END OF WINTER BREAK
ARE WE ACTUALLY DATING...?
Happy New Year!
HA HA HA HA
Morning!
MRMR
MRMR
YOU SURE HE DOESN'T THINK OF YOU AS JUST A FRIEND?
THAT'S NOT TRUE, AOKI. BE MORE CONFIDENT.

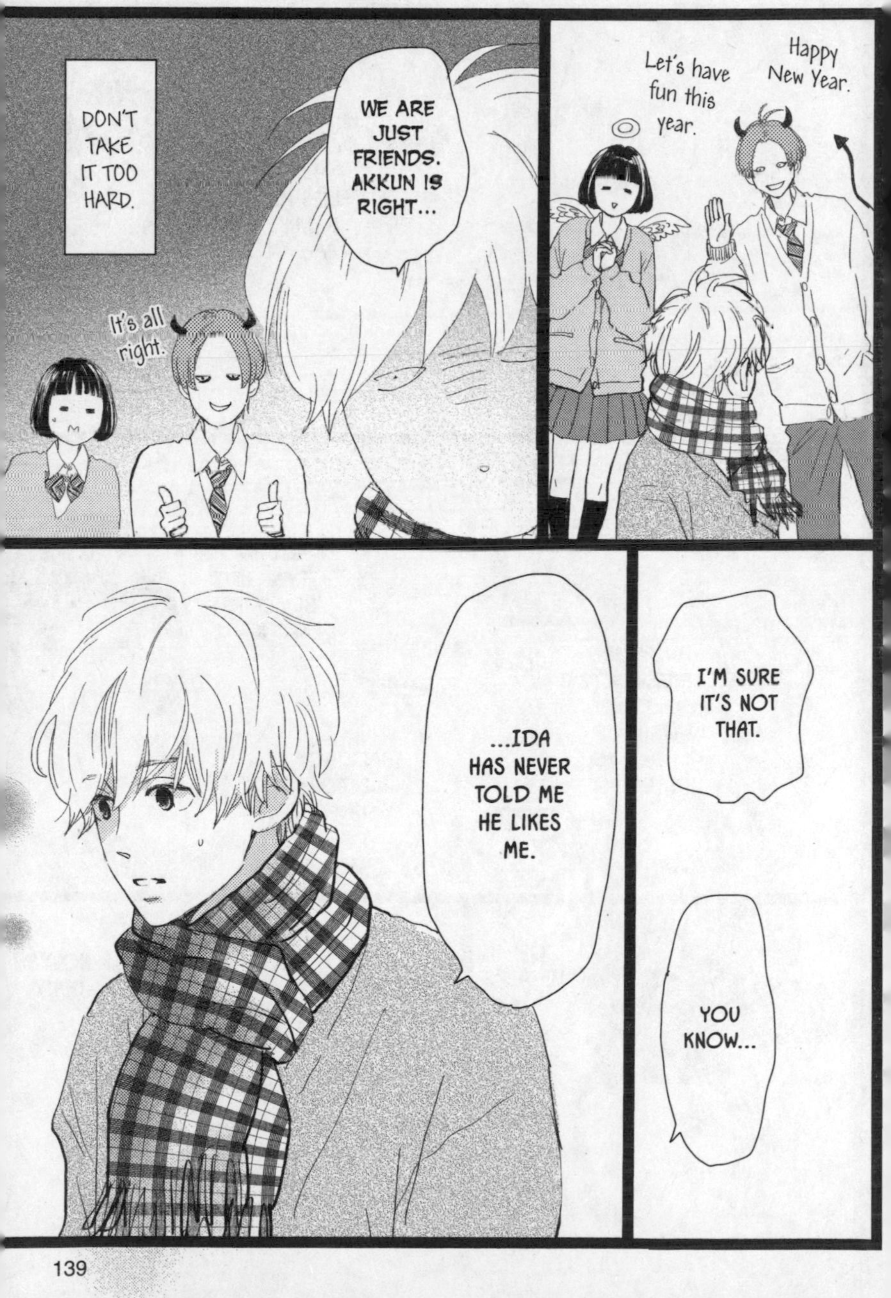
Happy New Year.
Let's have fun this year.
WE ARE JUST FRIENDS. AKKUN IS RIGHT...
DON'T TAKE IT TOO HARD.
It's all right.
I'M SURE IT'S NOT THAT.
YOU KNOW...
...IDA HAS NEVER TOLD ME HE LIKES ME.

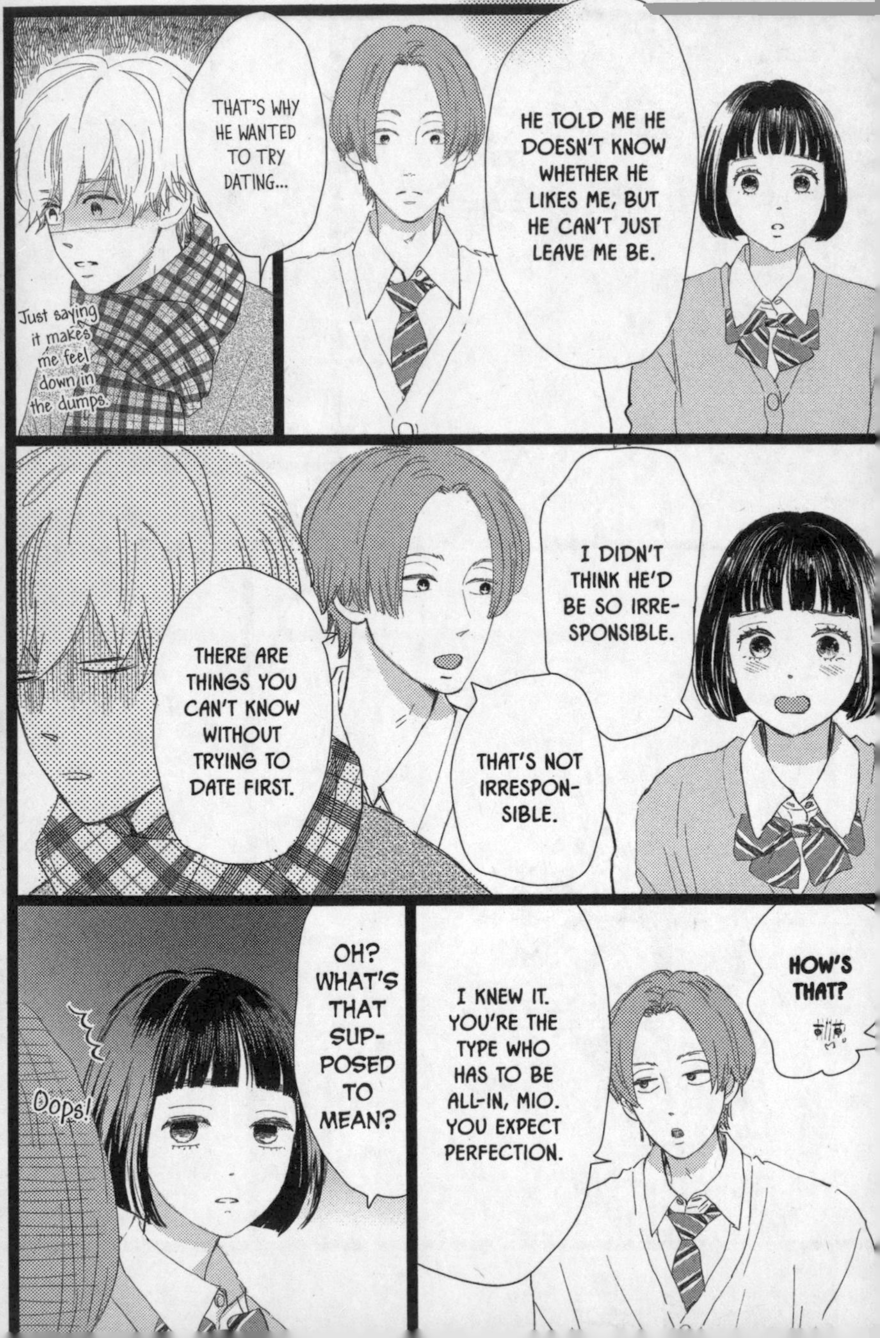
HE TOLD ME HE DOESN'T KNOW WHETHER HE LIKES ME, BUT HE CAN'T JUST LEAVE ME BE.
THAT'S WHY HE WANTED TO TRY DATING...
Just saying it makes me feel down in the dumps.
I DIDN'T THINK HE'D BE SO IRRESPONSIBLE.
THAT'S NOT IRRESPONSIBLE.
THERE ARE THINGS YOU CAN'T KNOW WITHOUT TRYING TO DATE FIRST.
HOW'S THAT?
I KNEW IT. YOU'RE THE TYPE WHO HAS TO BE ALL-IN, MIO. YOU EXPECT PERFECTION.
OH? WHAT'S THAT SUPPOSED TO MEAN?
Oops!

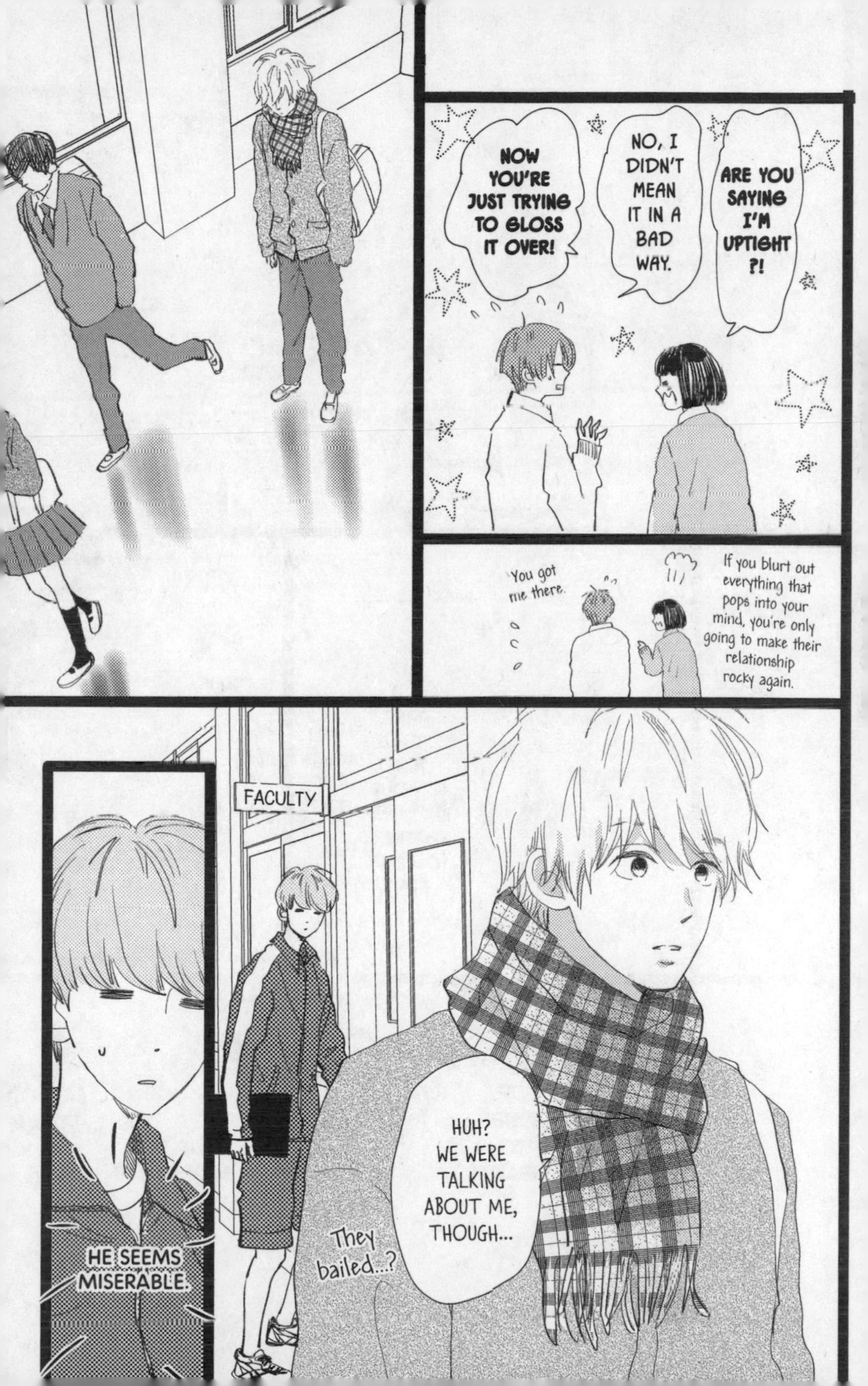
ARE YOU SAYING I'M UPTIGHT ?!
NO, I DIDN'T MEAN IT IN A BAD WAY.
NOW YOU'RE JUST TRYING TO GLOSS IT OVER!
If you blurt out everything that pops into your mind, you're only going to make their relationship rocky again.
You got me there.
HUH? WE WERE TALKING ABOUT ME, THOUGH...
They bailed...?
FACULTY
HE SEEMS MISERABLE.

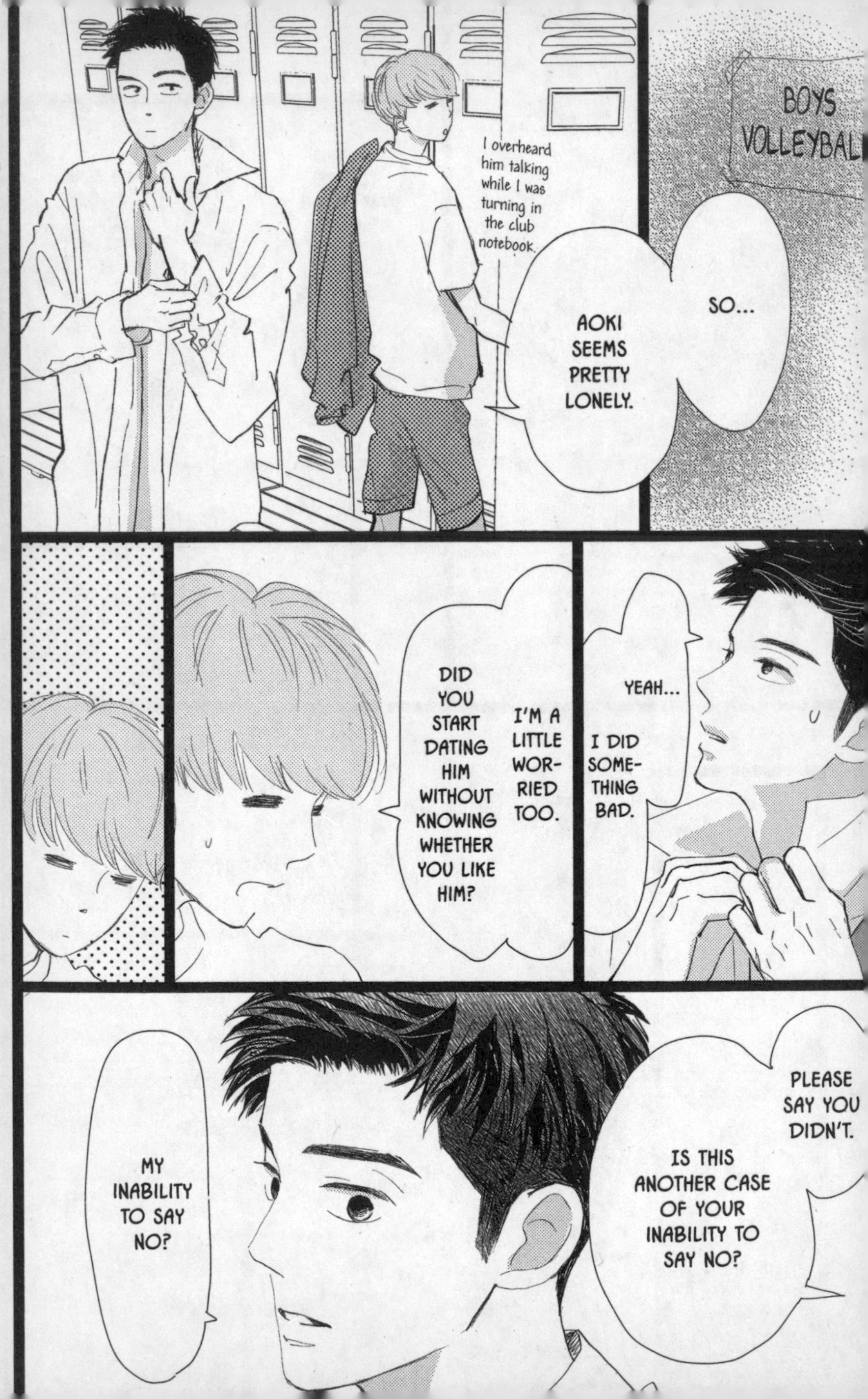
BOYS VOLLEYBAL
SO... AOKI SEEMS PRETTY LONELY.
I overheard him talking while I was turning in the club notebook.
YEAH... I DID SOMETHING BAD.
I'M A LITTLE WOR-RIED TOO.
DID YOU START DATING HIM WITHOUT KNOWING WHETHER YOU LIKE HIM?
PLEASE SAY YOU DIDN'T.
IS THIS ANOTHER CASE OF YOUR INABILITY TO SAY NO?
MY INABILITY TO SAY NO?

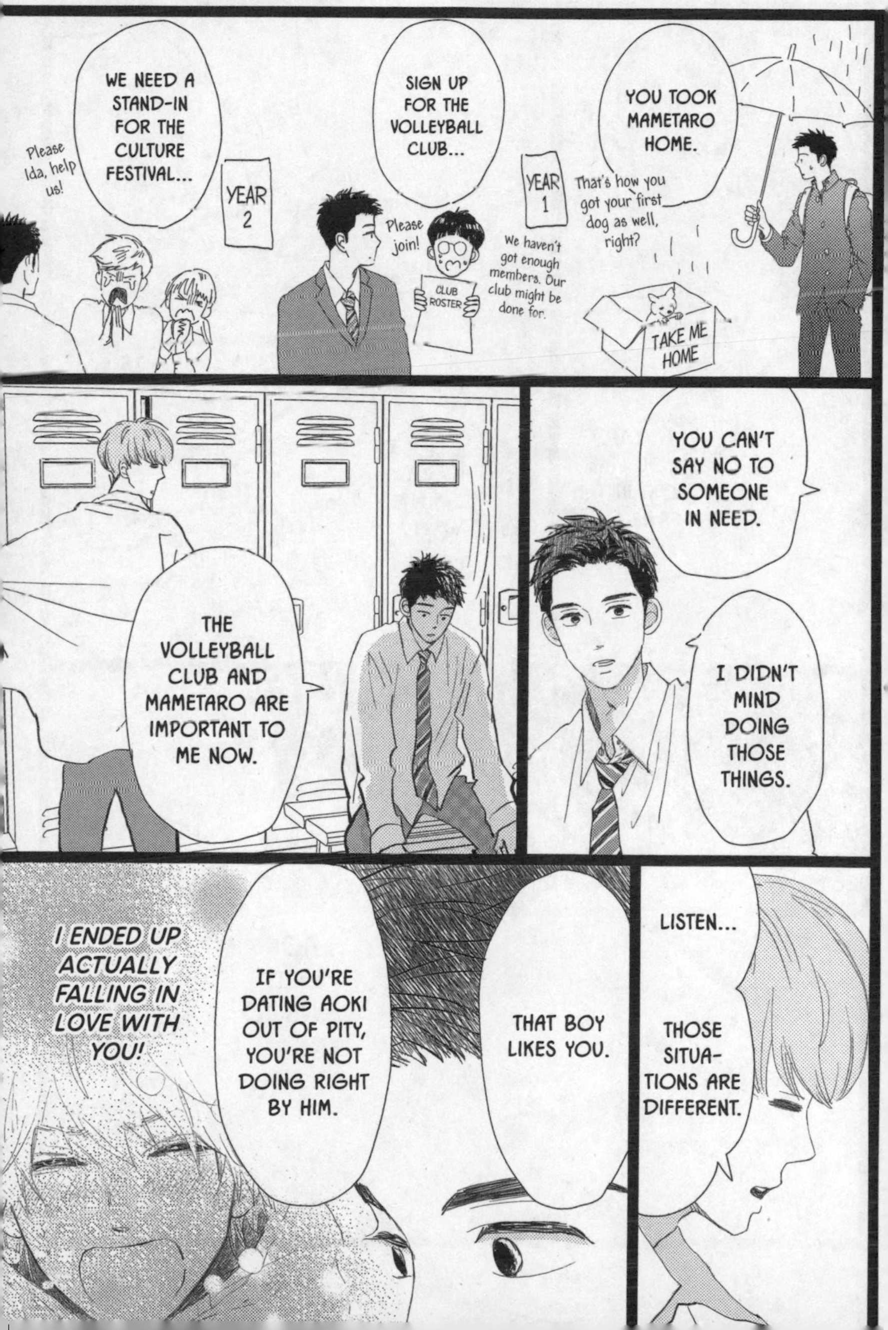
YOU TOOK MAMETARO HOME.
That's how you got your first dog as well, right?
TAKE ME HOME
SIGN UP FOR THE VOLLEYBALL CLUB...
YEAR 1
We haven't got enough members. Our club might be done for.
Please join!
CLUB ROSTER
WE NEED A STAND-IN FOR THE CULTURE FESTIVAL...
YEAR 2
Please Ida, help us!
YOU CAN'T SAY NO TO SOMEONE IN NEED.
I DIDN'T MIND DOING THOSE THINGS.
THE VOLLEYBALL CLUB AND MAMETARO ARE IMPORTANT TO ME NOW.
LISTEN...
THOSE SITUA-TIONS ARE DIFFERENT.
THAT BOY LIKES YOU.
IF YOU'RE DATING AOKI OUT OF PITY, YOU'RE NOT DOING RIGHT BY HIM.
I ENDED UP ACTUALLY FALLING IN LOVE WITH YOU!

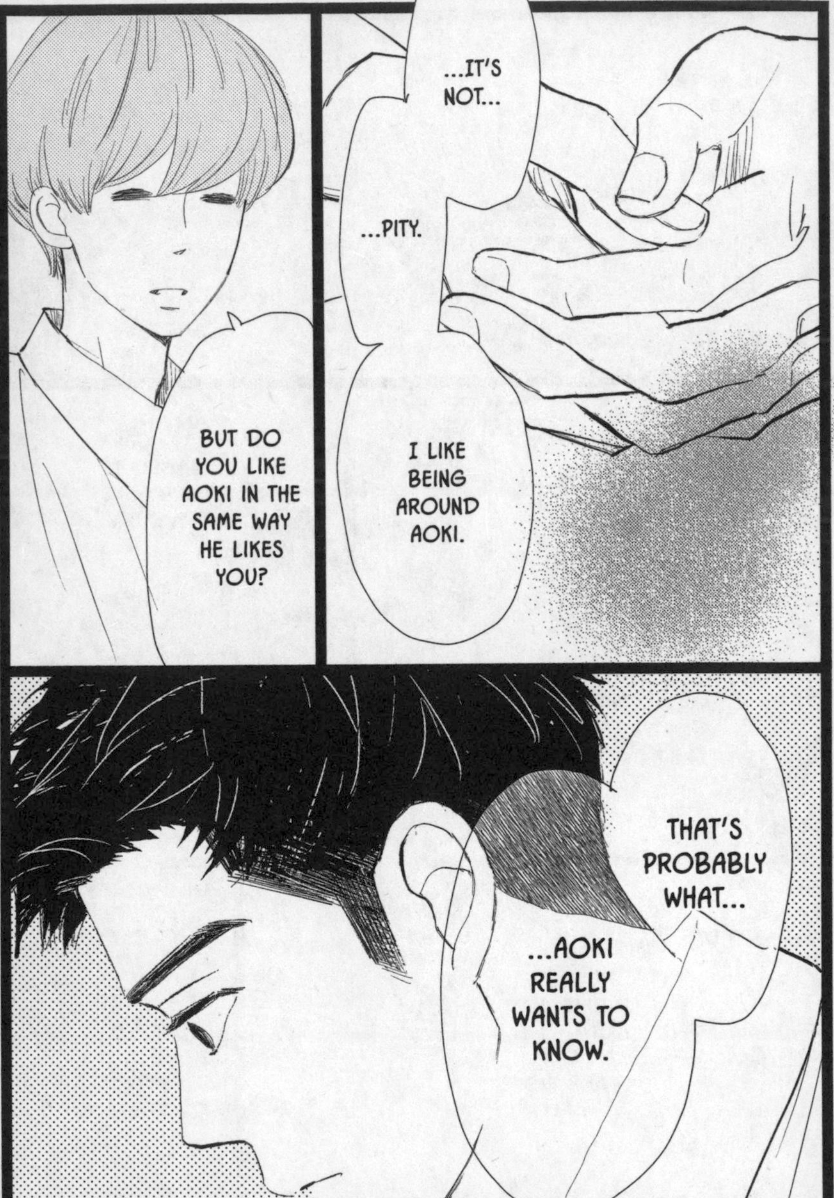
...IT'S NOT...
...PITY.
I LIKE BEING AROUND AOKI.
BUT DO YOU LIKE AOKI IN THE SAME WAY HE LIKES YOU?
THAT'S PROBABLY WHAT...
...AOKI REALLY WANTS TO KNOW.

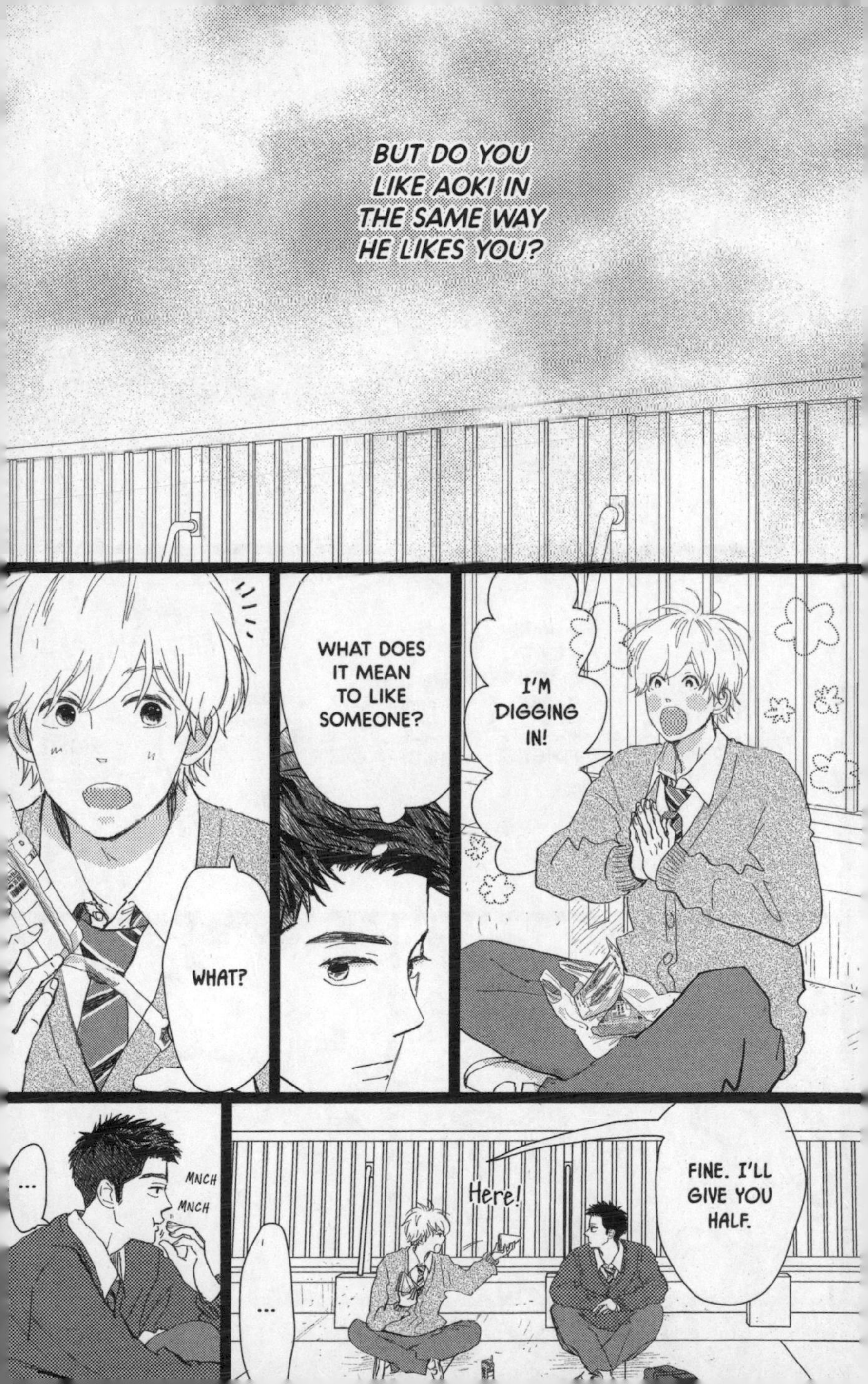
BUT DO YOU LIKE AOKI IN THE SAME WAY HE LIKES YOU?
I'M DIGGING IN!
WHAT DOES IT MEAN TO LIKE SOMEONE?
WHAT?
FINE. I'LL GIVE YOU HALF.
Here!
...
MNCH MNCH
...

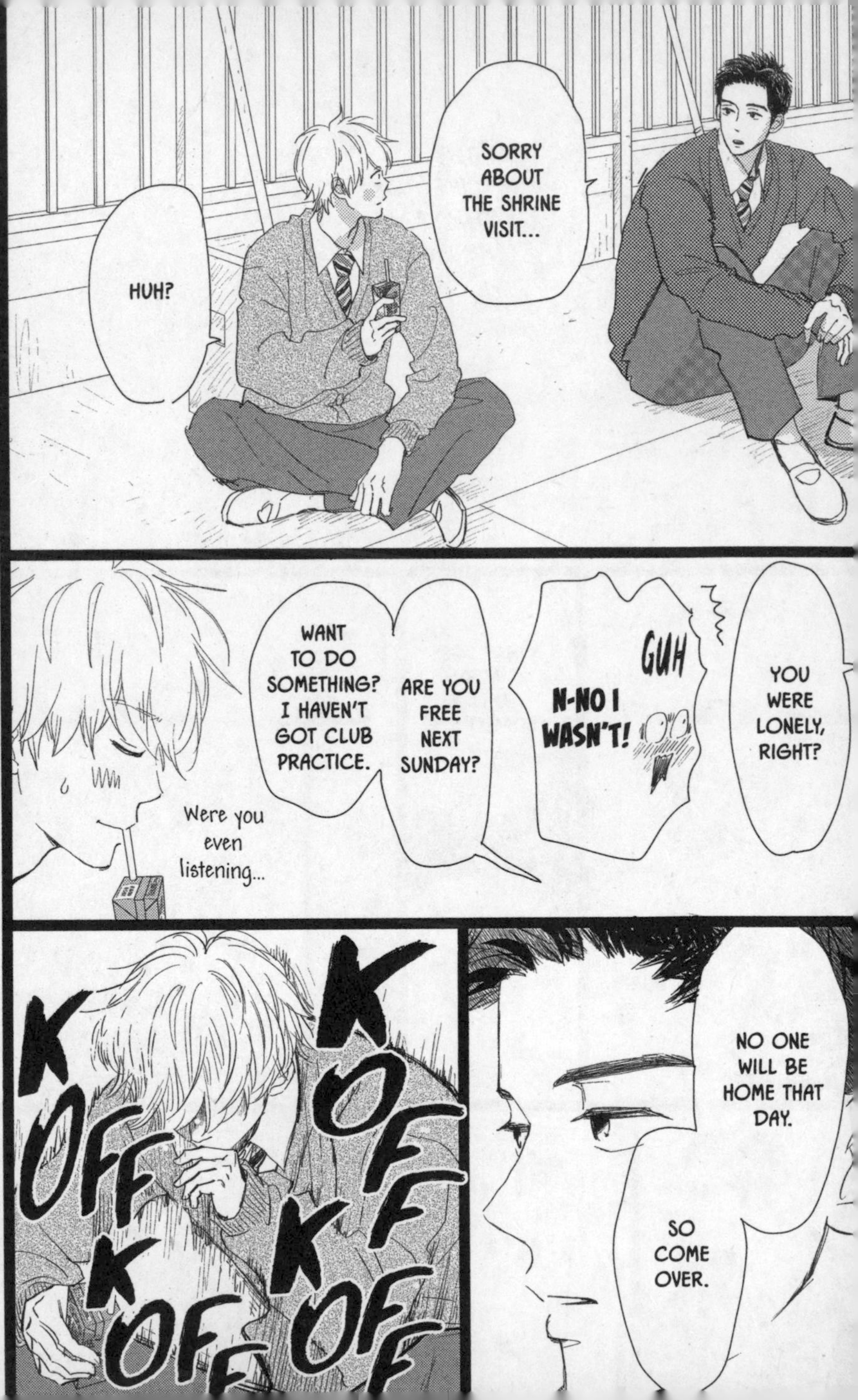
SORRY ABOUT THE SHRINE VISIT...
HUH?
YOU WERE LONELY, RIGHT?
GUH
N-NO I WASN'T!
ARE YOU FREE NEXT SUNDAY?
WANT TO DO SOMETHING? I HAVEN'T GOT CLUB PRACTICE.
Were you even listening...
NO ONE WILL BE HOME THAT DAY.
SO COME OVER.
KOFF KOFF
KOFF KOFF

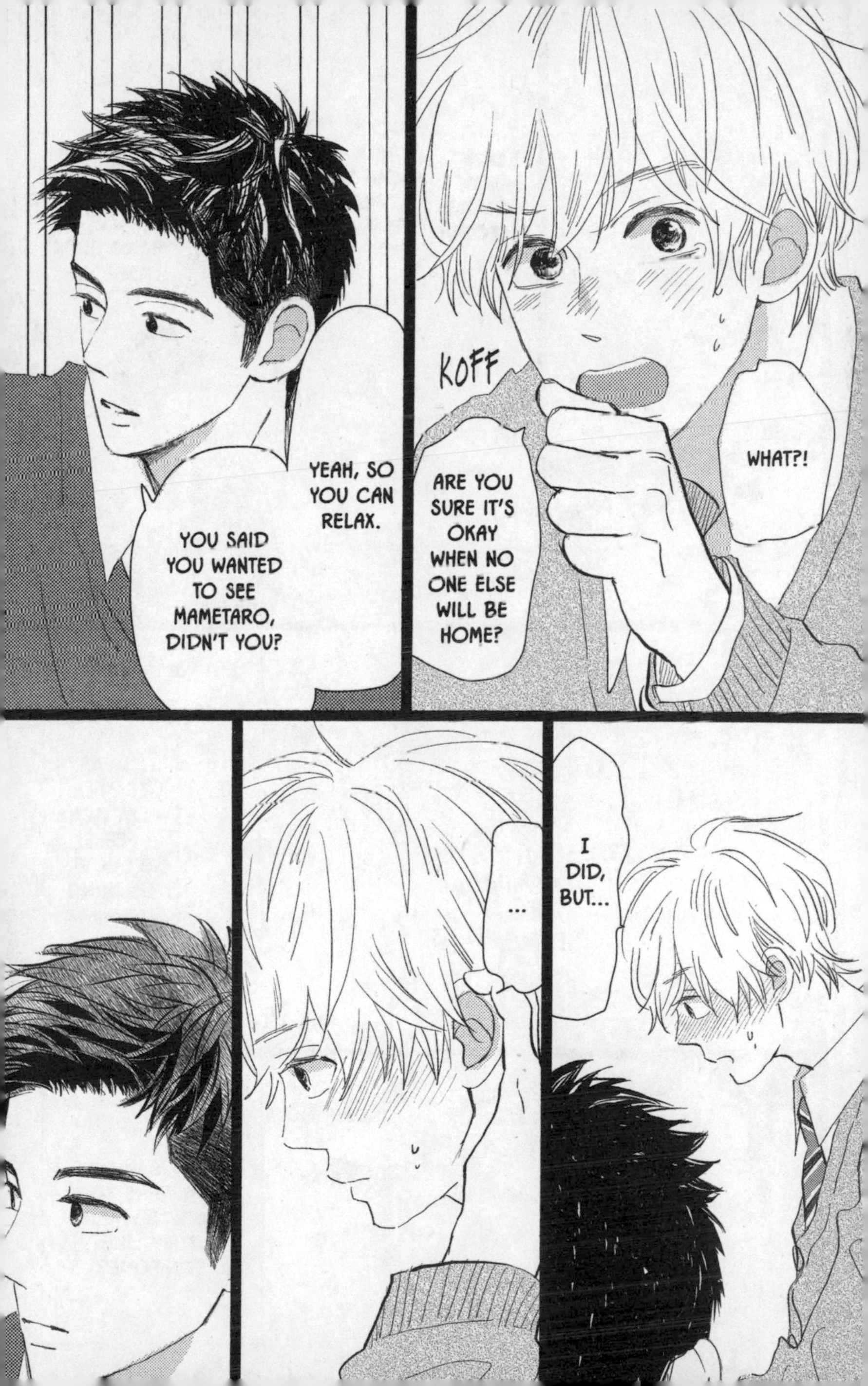
WHAT?!
KOFF
ARE YOU SURE IT'S OKAY WHEN NO ONE ELSE WILL BE HOME?
YEAH, SO YOU CAN RELAX.
YOU SAID YOU WANTED TO SEE MAMETARO, DIDN'T YOU?
I DID, BUT...
...

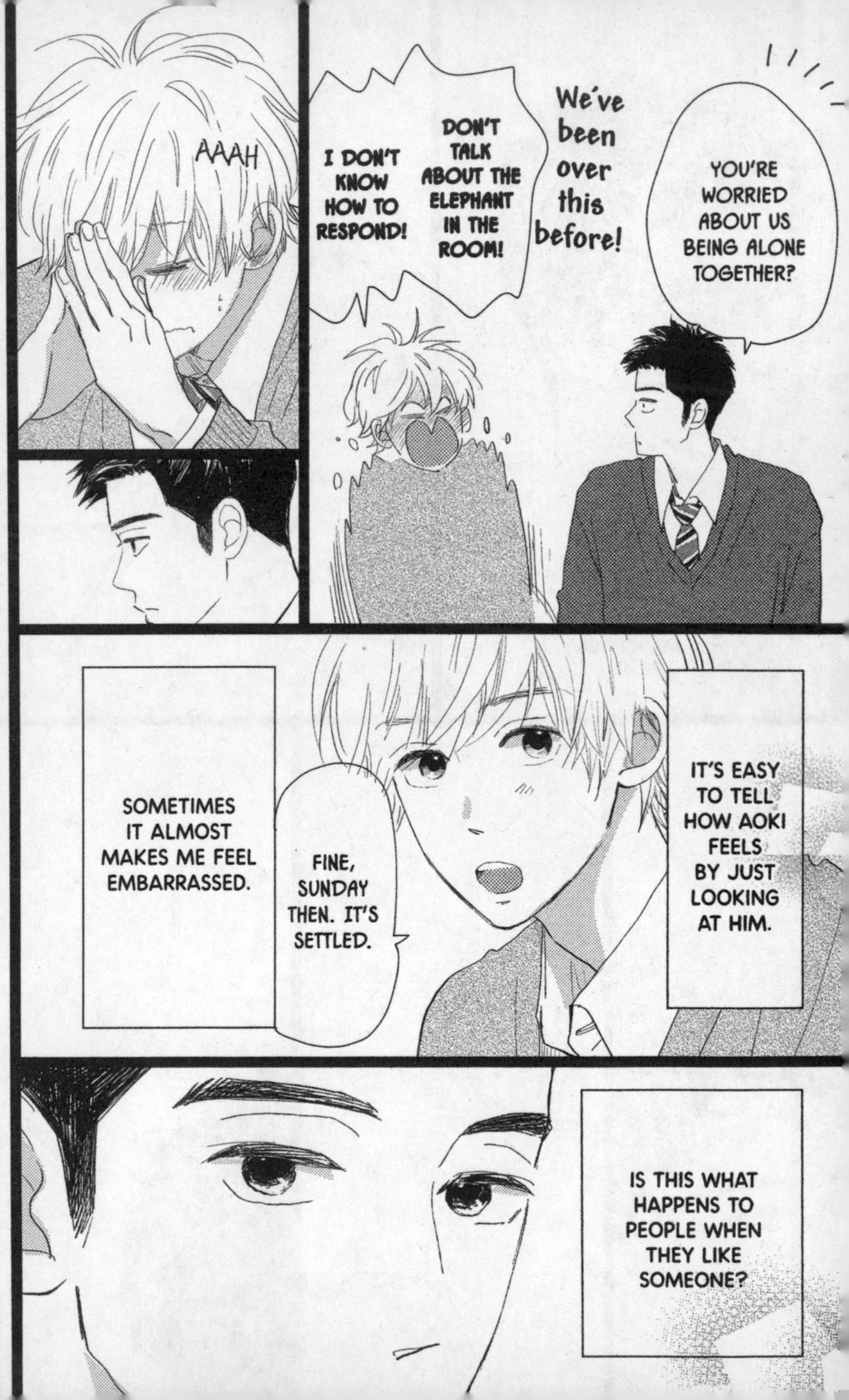
YOU'RE WORRIED ABOUT US BEING ALONE TOGETHER?
We've been over this before!
DON'T TALK ABOUT THE ELEPHANT IN THE ROOM!
I DON'T KNOW HOW TO RESPOND!
AAAH
IT'S EASY TO TELL HOW AOKI FEELS BY JUST LOOKING AT HIM.
FINE, SUNDAY THEN. IT'S SETTLED.
SOMETIMES IT ALMOST MAKES ME FEEL EMBARRASSED.
IS THIS WHAT HAPPENS TO PEOPLE WHEN THEY LIKE SOMEONE?

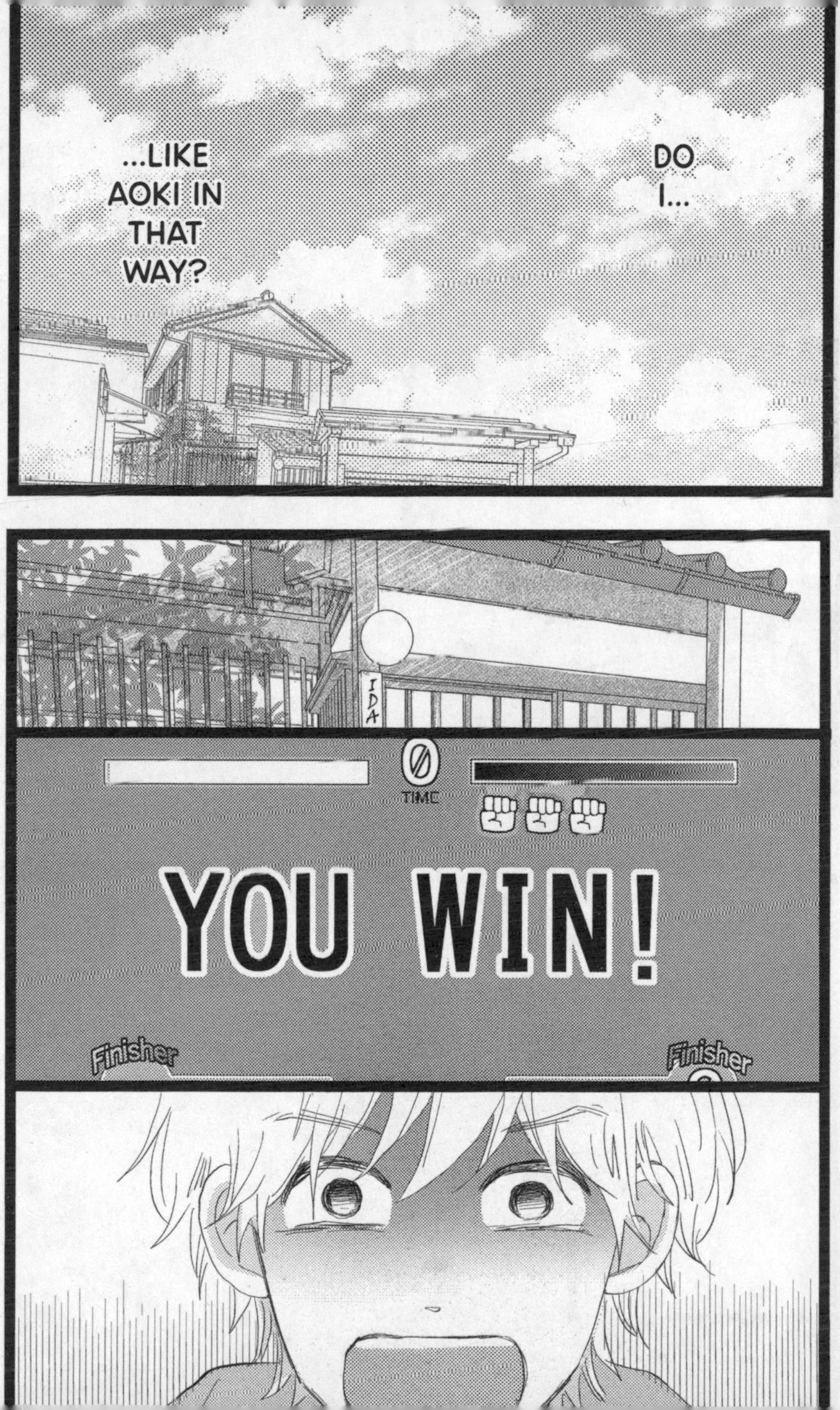
DO I...
...LIKE AOKI IN THAT WAY?
IDA
0
TIME
YOU WIN!
Finisher
Finisher

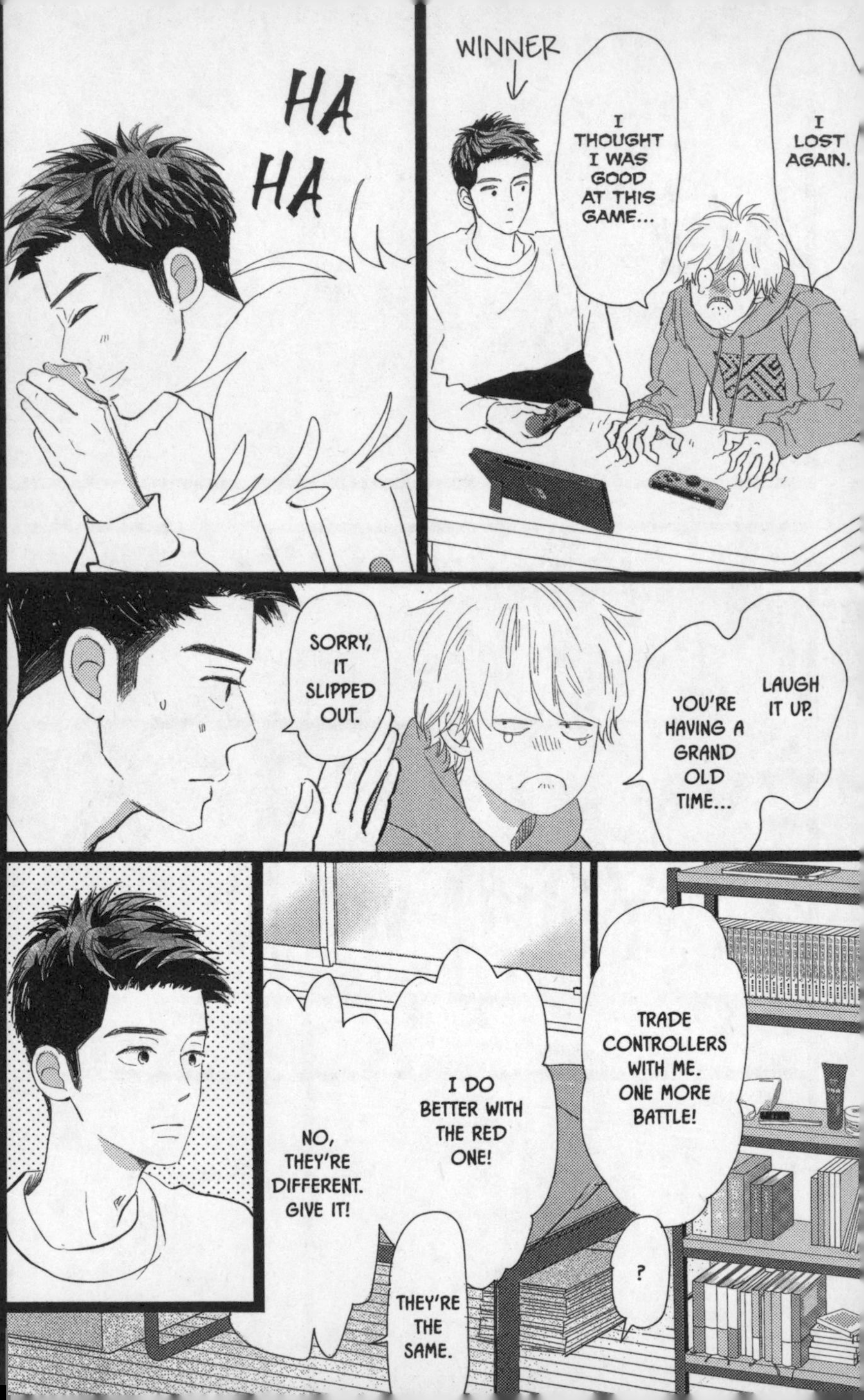
I LOST AGAIN.
I THOUGHT I WAS GOOD AT THIS GAME...
WINNER
HA HA
LAUGH IT UP.
YOU'RE HAVING A GRAND OLD TIME...
SORRY, IT SLIPPED OUT.
TRADE CONTROLLERS WITH ME. ONE MORE BATTLE!
?
I DO BETTER WITH THE RED ONE!
THEY'RE THE SAME.
NO, THEY'RE DIFFERENT. GIVE IT!

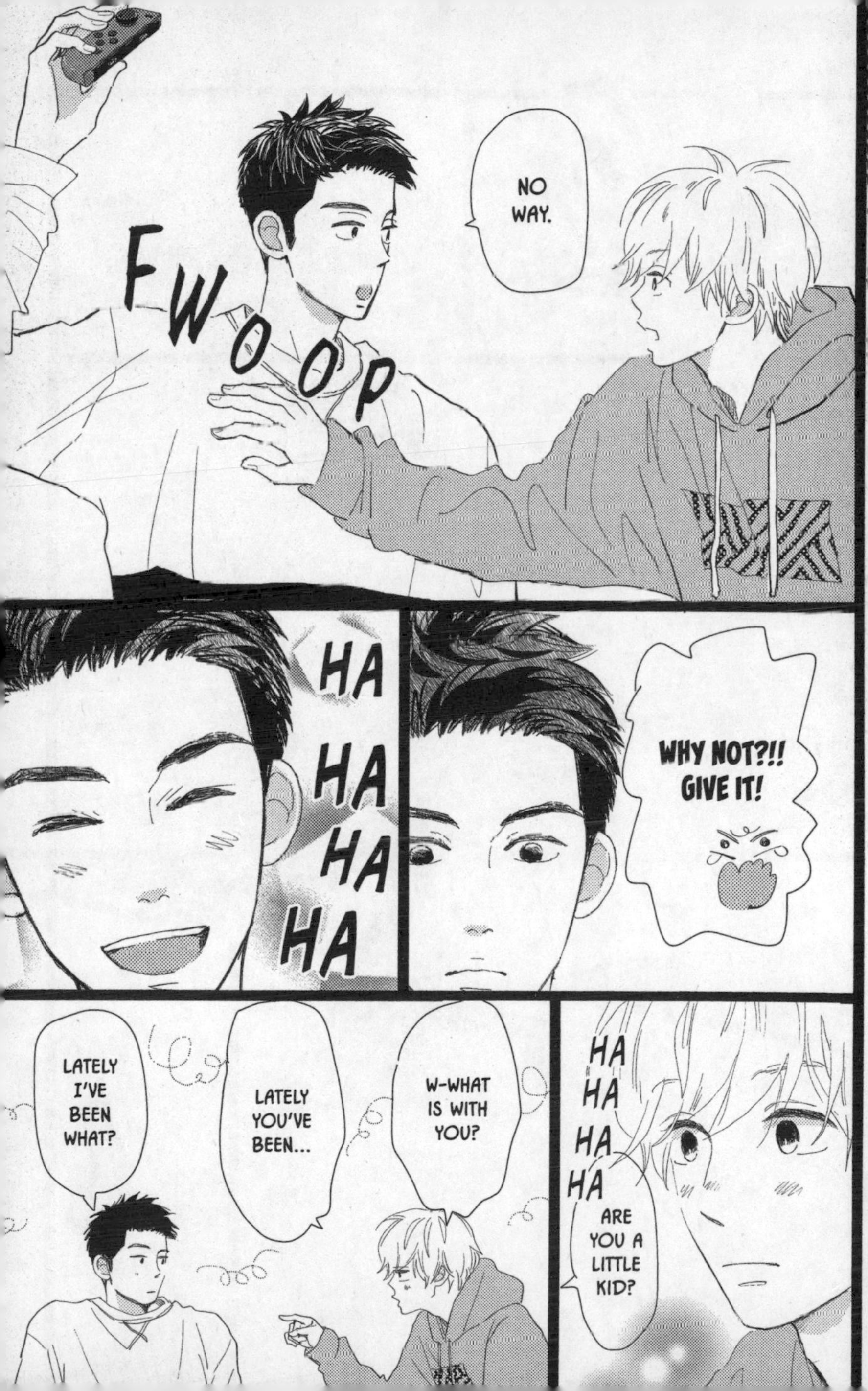
NO WAY.
FWOOP
WHY NOT?!! GIVE IT!
HA HA HA HA HA
HA HA HA HA
ARE YOU A LITTLE KID?
W-WHAT IS WITH YOU?
LATELY YOU'VE BEEN...
LATELY I'VE BEEN WHAT?

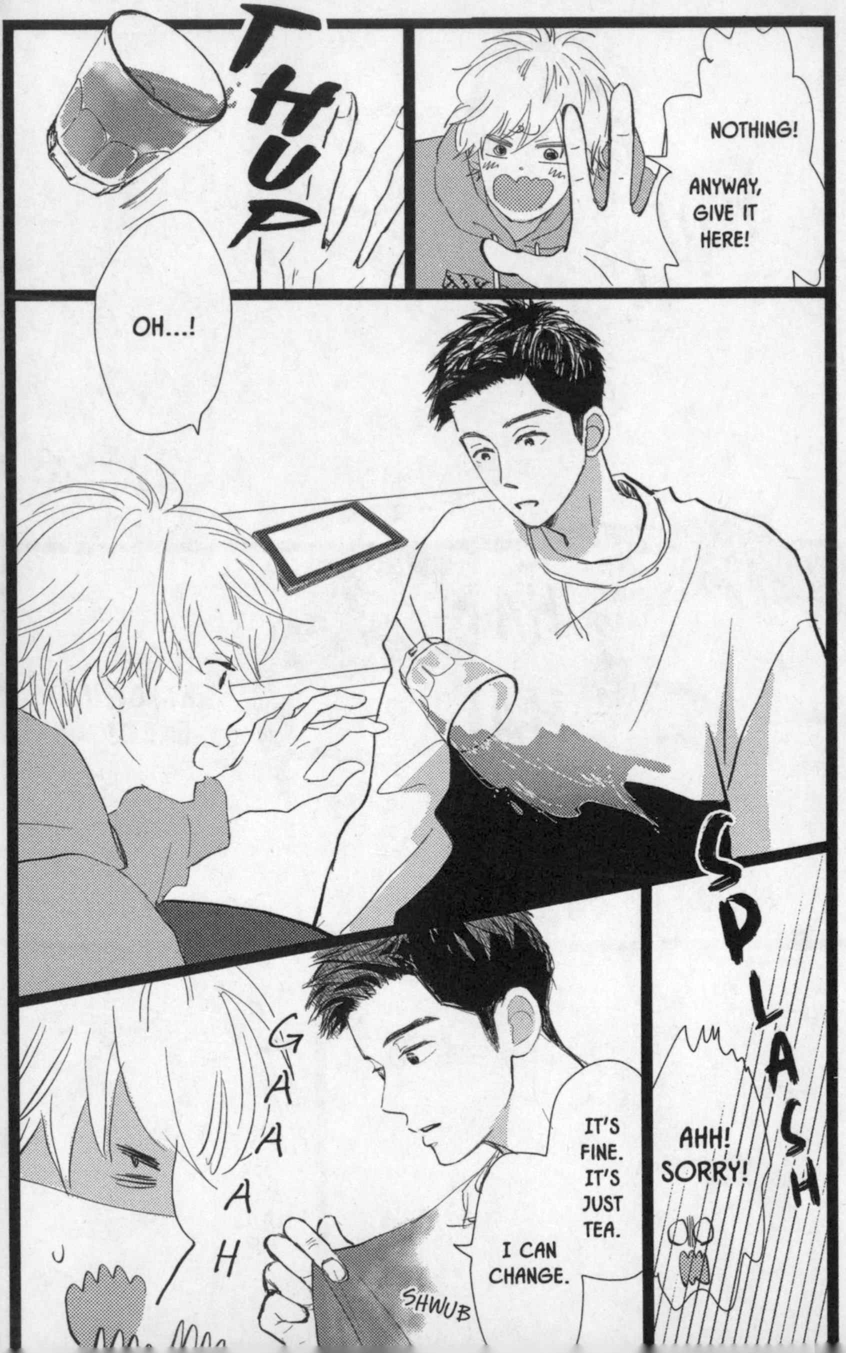
NOTHING!
ANYWAY, GIVE IT HERE!
THUP
OH...!
SPLASH
AHH! SORRY!
IT'S FINE. IT'S JUST TEA.
I CAN CHANGE.
GAAAH
SHWUB

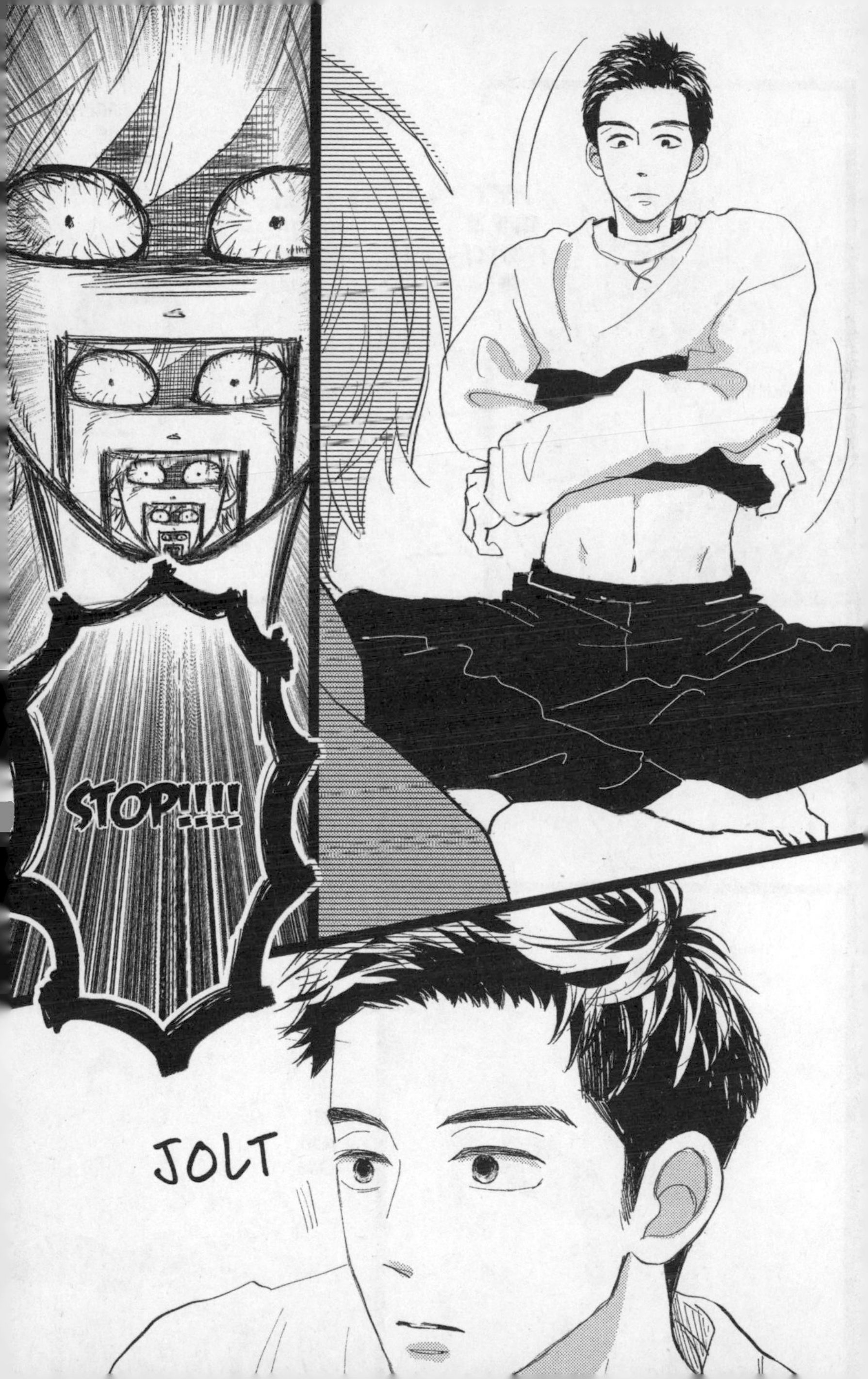
STOP!!!!
JOLT

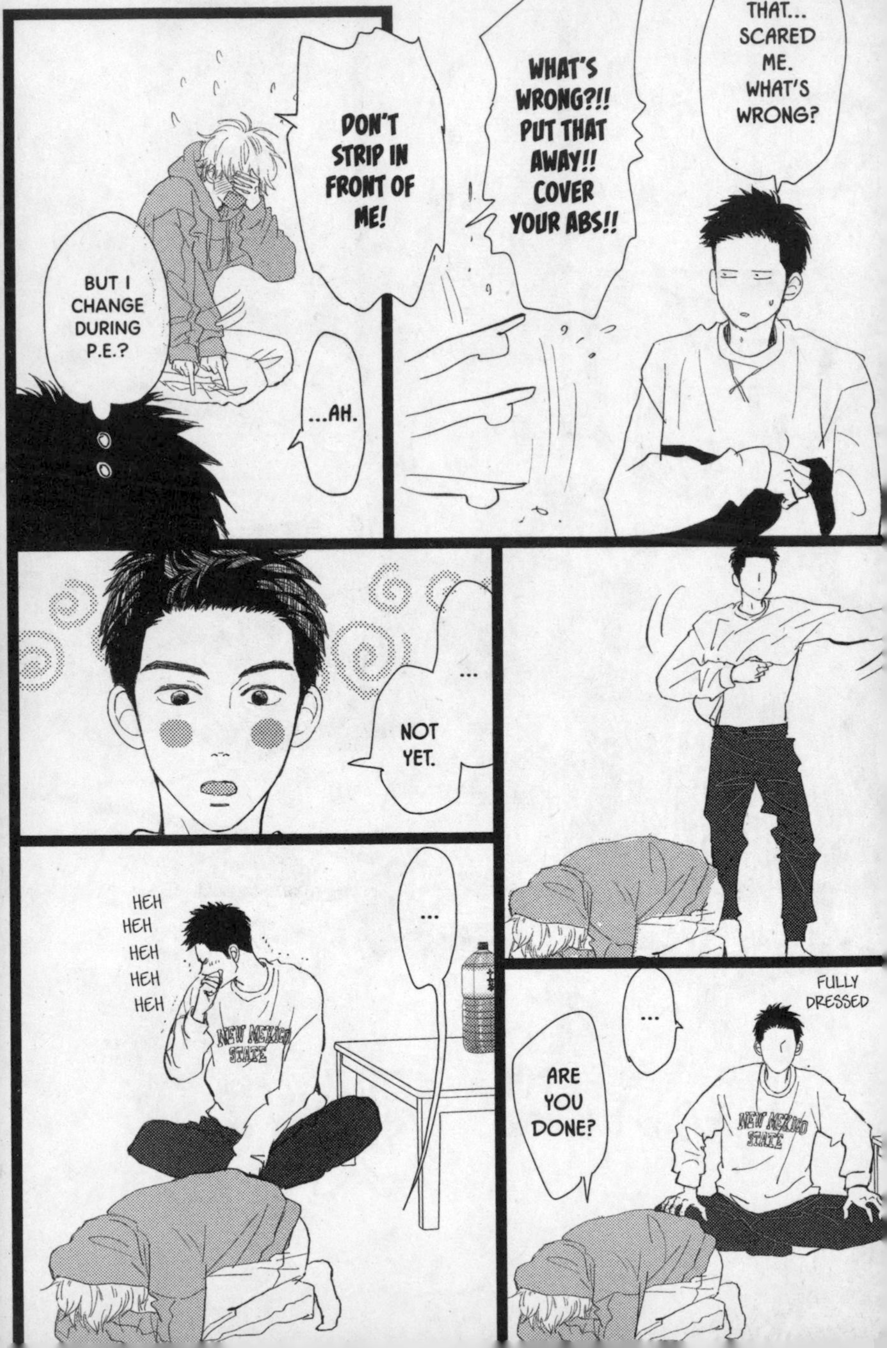
THAT... SCARED ME. WHAT'S WRONG?
WHAT'S WRONG?!! PUT THAT AWAY!! COVER YOUR ABS!!
DON'T STRIP IN FRONT OF ME!
BUT I CHANGE DURING P.E.?
...AH.
... NOT YET.
FULLY DRESSED
...
ARE YOU DONE?
HEH HEH HEH HEH HEH
...

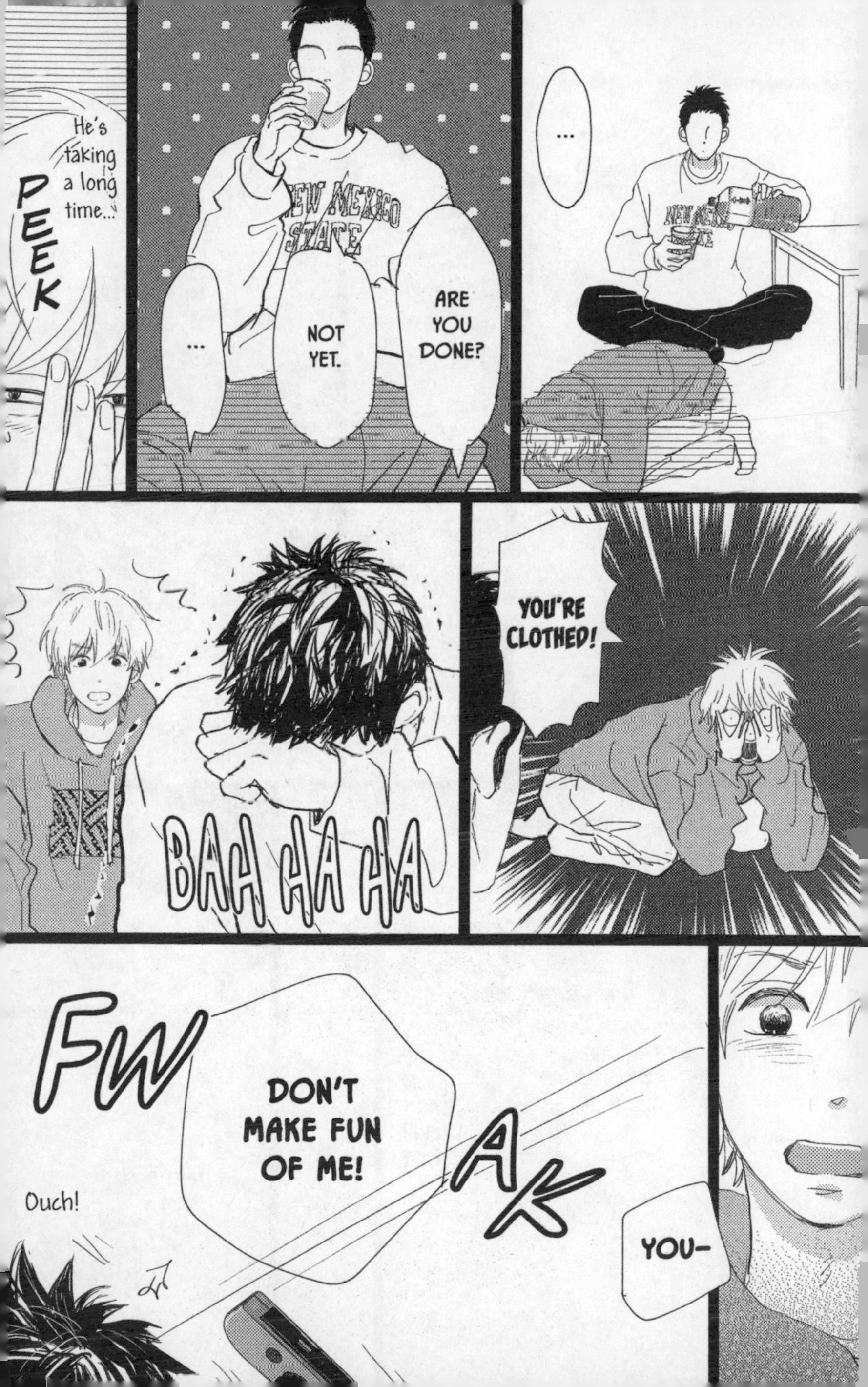
...
ARE YOU DONE?
NOT YET.
...
He's taking a long time...
PEEK
YOU'RE CLOTHED!
BAH HA HA
YOU-
DON'T MAKE FUN OF ME!
FWAK
Ouch!

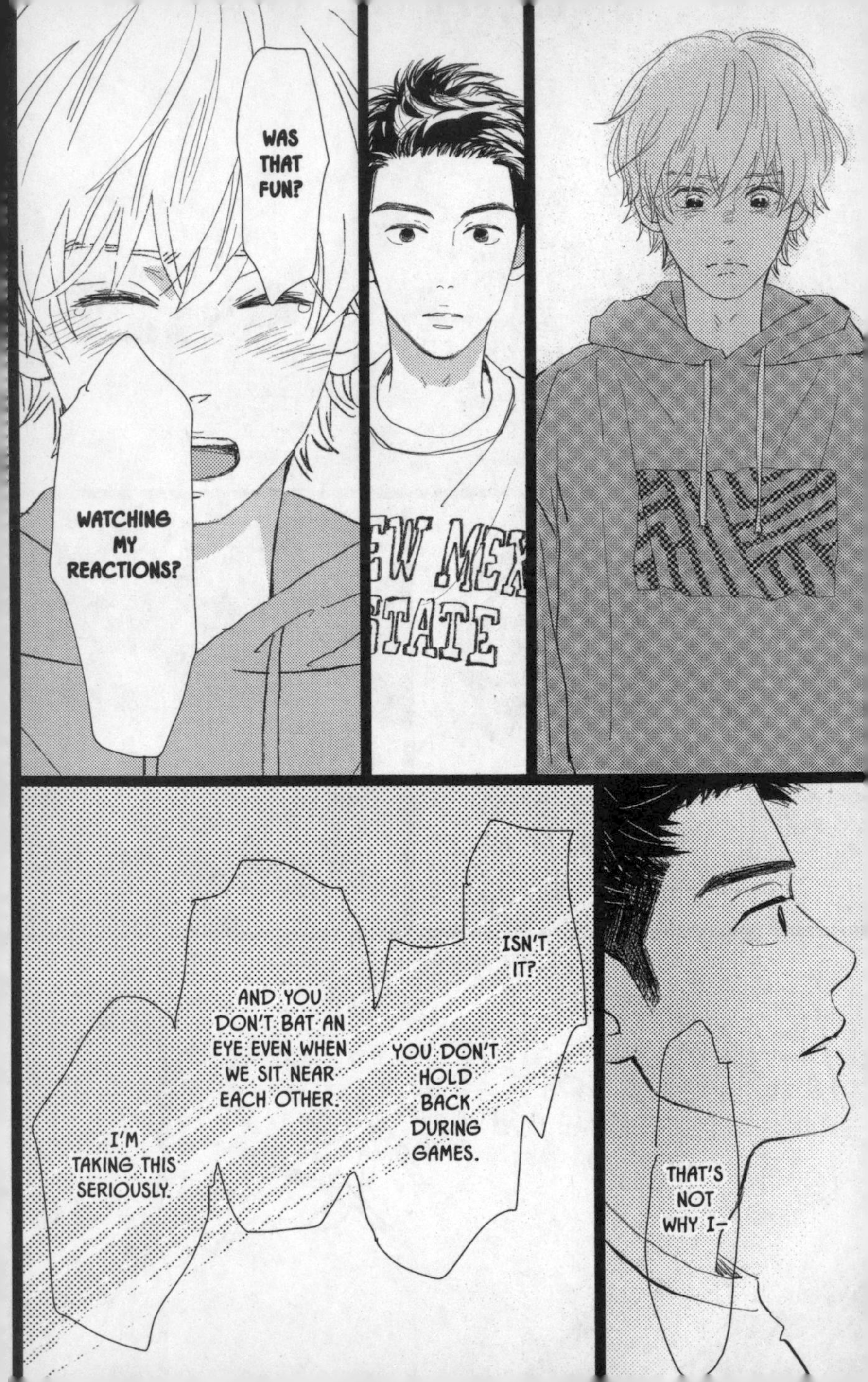
EW MEX
STATE
WAS THAT FUN?
WATCHING MY REACTIONS?
THAT'S NOT WHY I–
ISN'T IT?
YOU DON'T HOLD BACK DURING GAMES.
AND YOU DON'T BAT AN EYE EVEN WHEN WE SIT NEAR EACH OTHER.
I'M TAKING THIS SERIOUSLY.

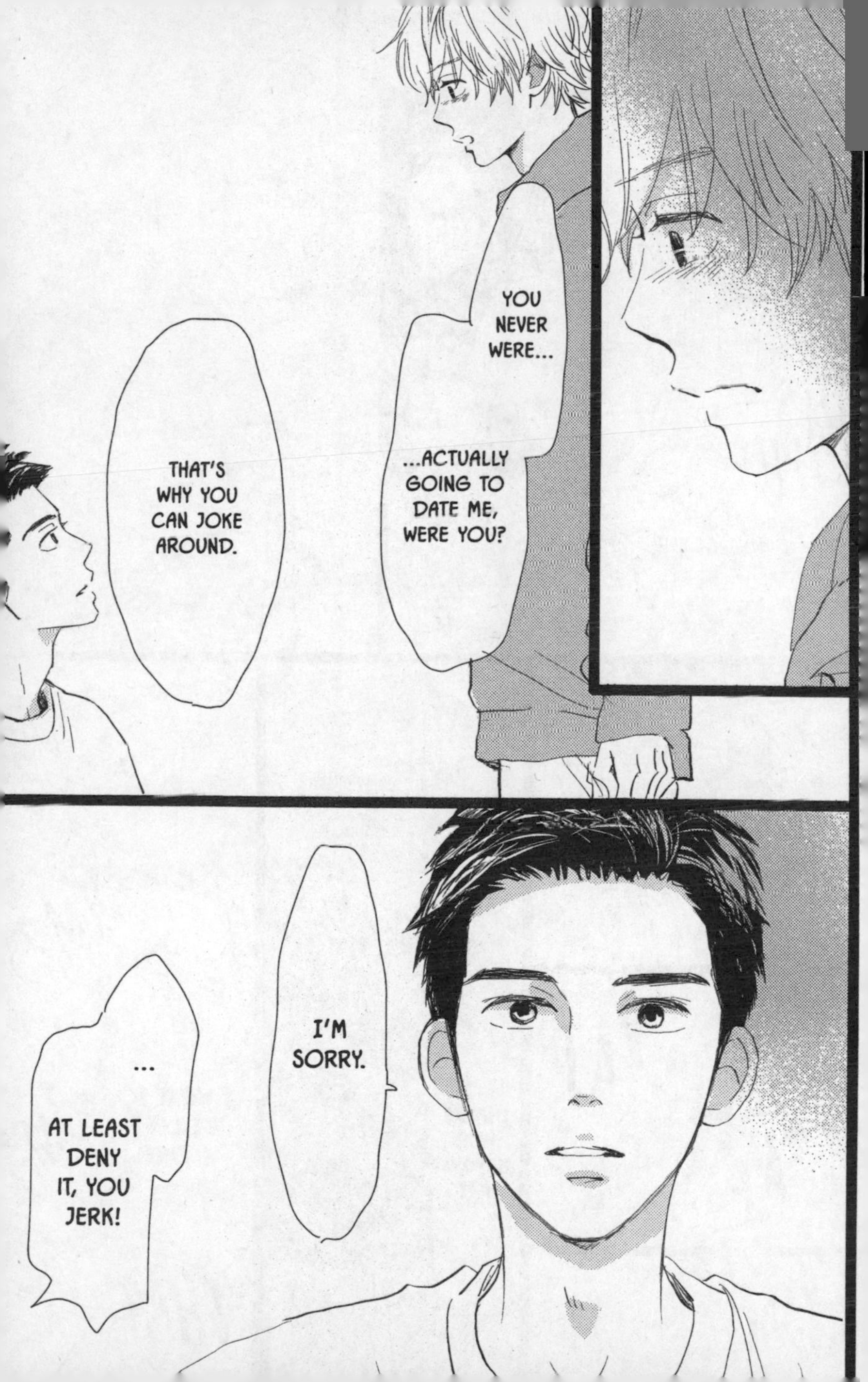
YOU NEVER WERE...
...ACTUALLY GOING TO DATE ME, WERE YOU?
THAT'S WHY YOU CAN JOKE AROUND.
I'M SORRY.
...
AT LEAST DENY IT, YOU JERK!

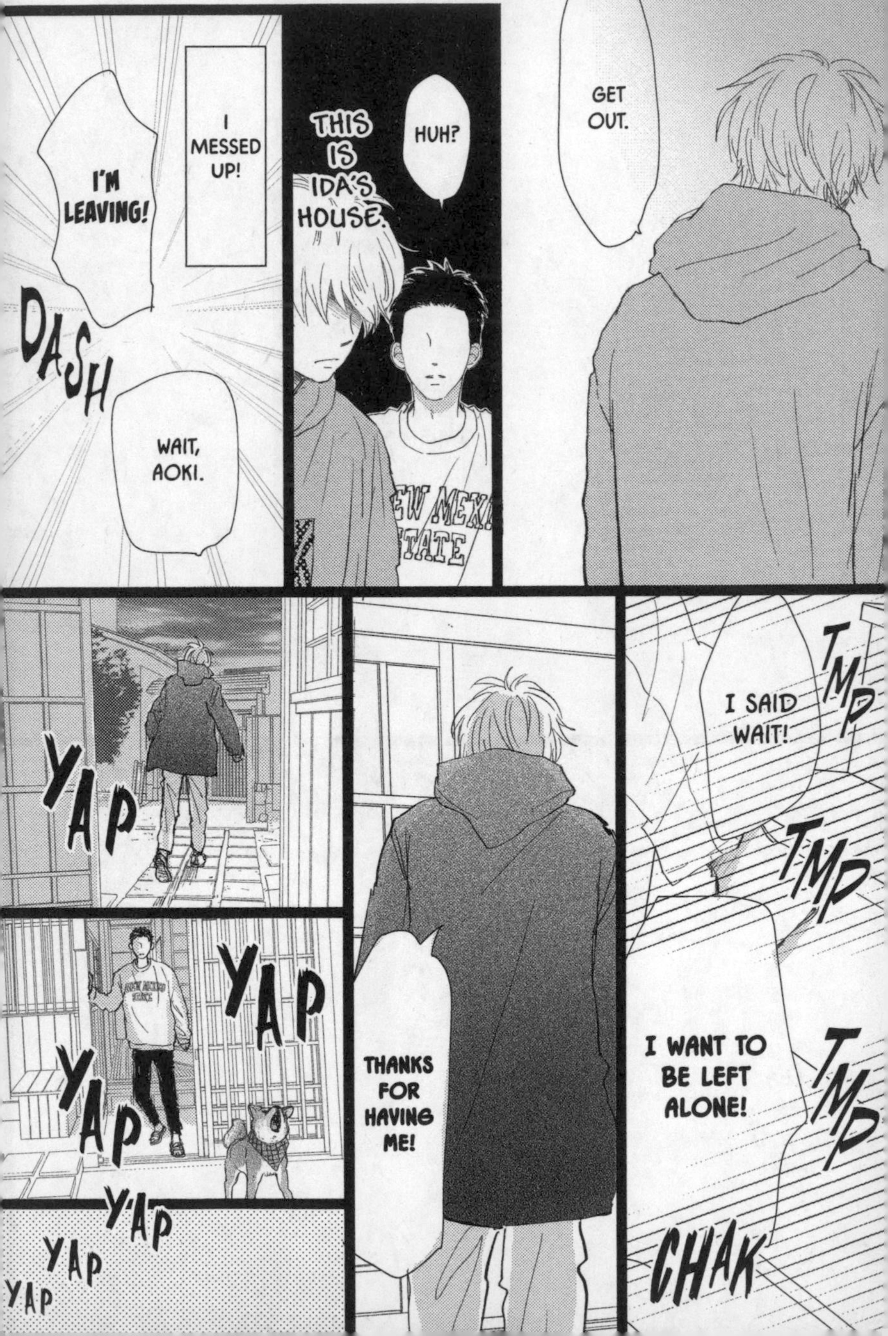
GET OUT.
HUH?
THIS IS IDA'S HOUSE.
I MESSED UP!
I'M LEAVING!
DASH
WAIT, AOKI.
I SAID WAIT!
TMP
TMP
I WANT TO BE LEFT ALONE!
TMP
CHAK
THANKS FOR HAVING ME!
YAP
YAP
YAP
YAP
YAP
YAP
YAP

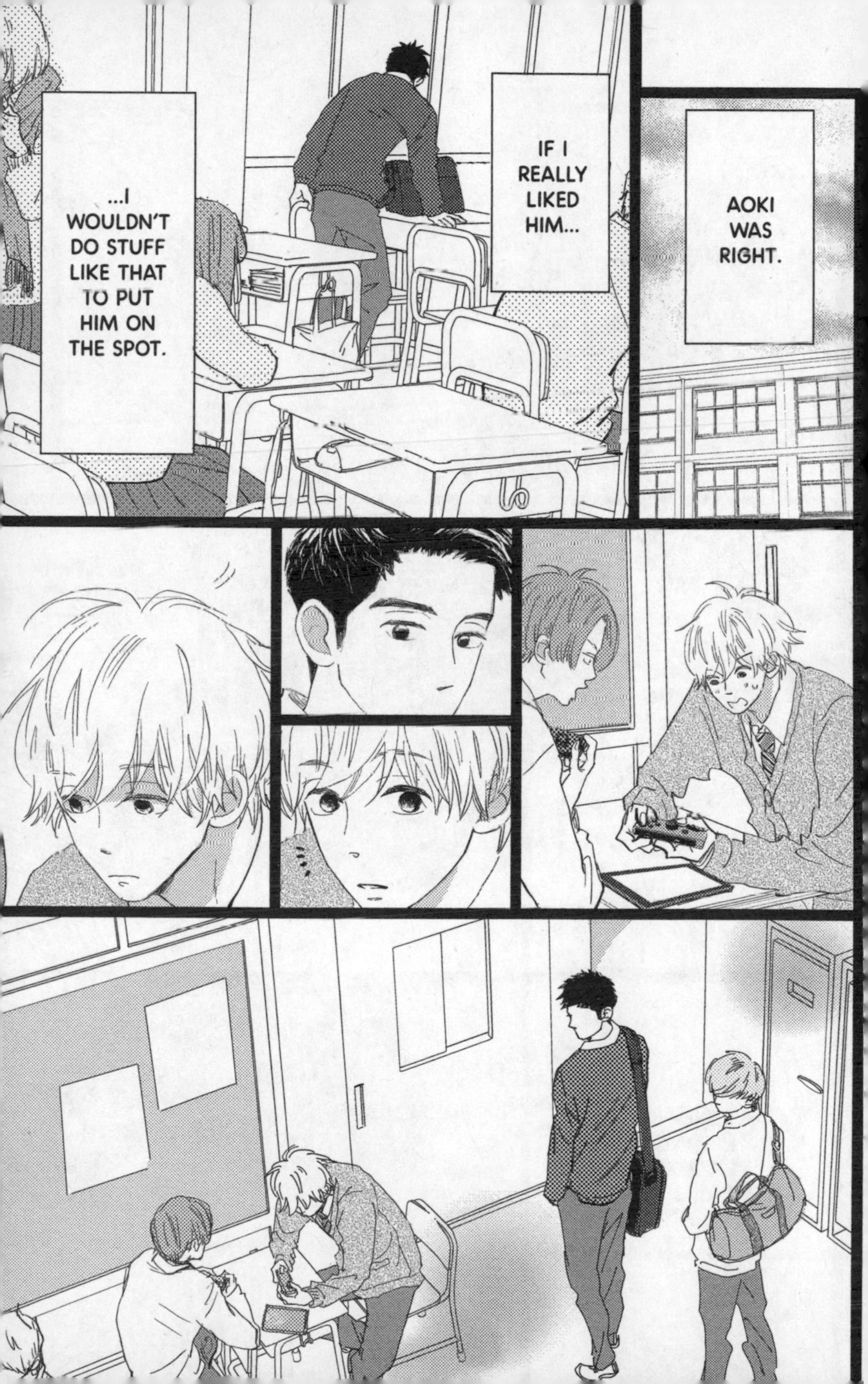
AOKI WAS RIGHT.
IF I REALLY LIKED HIM...
...I WOULDN'T DO STUFF LIKE THAT TO PUT HIM ON THE SPOT.

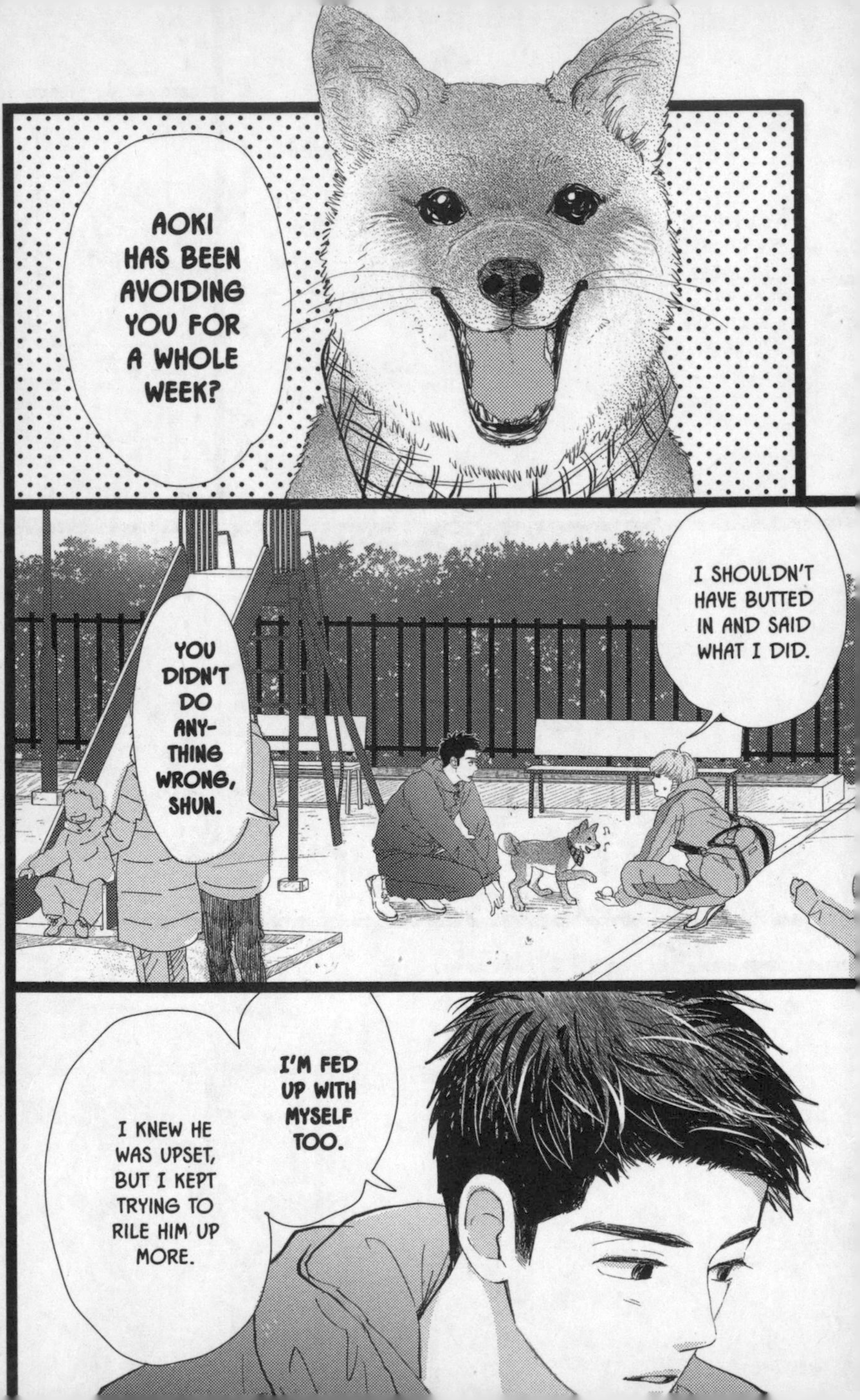
AOKI HAS BEEN AVOIDING YOU FOR A WHOLE WEEK?
I SHOULDN'T HAVE BUTTED IN AND SAID WHAT I DID.
YOU DIDN'T DO ANY-THING WRONG, SHUN.
I'M FED UP WITH MYSELF TOO.
I KNEW HE WAS UPSET, BUT I KEPT TRYING TO RILE HIM UP MORE.

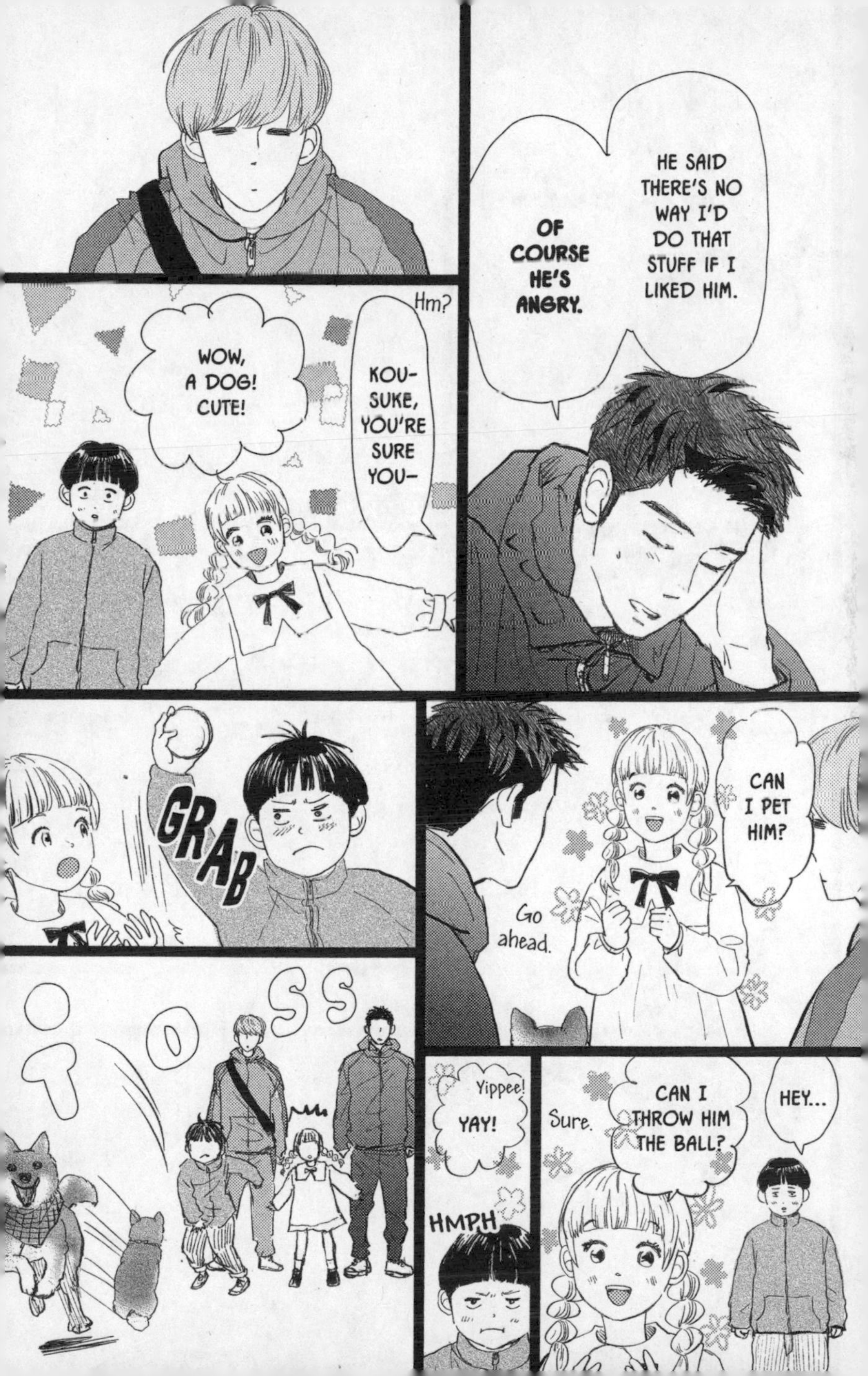
HE SAID THERE'S NO WAY I'D DO THAT STUFF IF I LIKED HIM.
OF COURSE HE'S ANGRY.
Hm?
KOU-SUKE, YOU'RE SURE YOU-
WOW, A DOG! CUTE!
CAN I PET HIM?
Go ahead.
GRAB
HEY...
CAN I THROW HIM THE BALL?
Sure.
Yippee!
YAY!
HMPH
TOSS

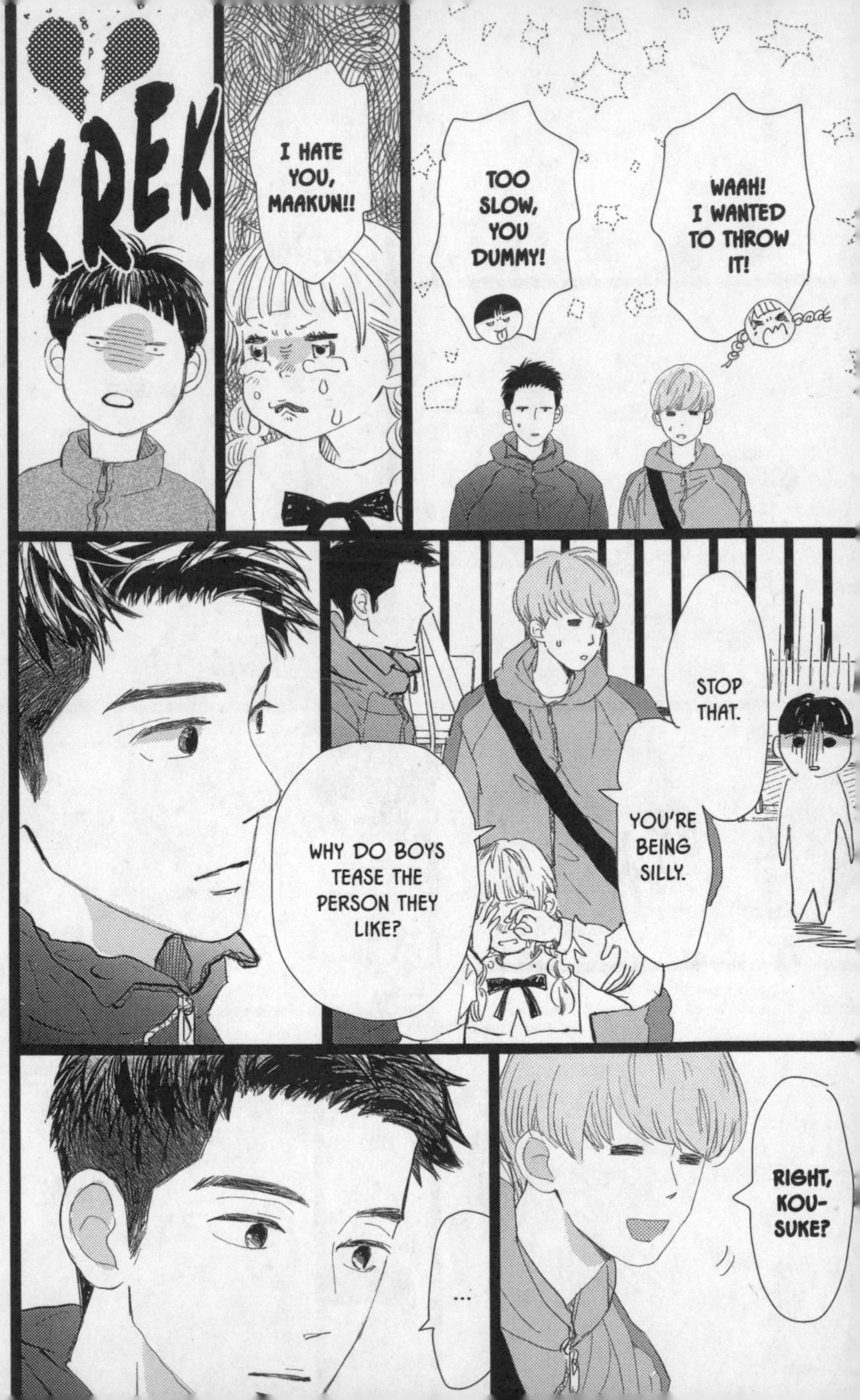
WAAH! I WANTED TO THROW IT!
TOO SLOW, YOU DUMMY!
I HATE YOU, MAAKUN!!
KREK
STOP THAT.
YOU'RE BEING SILLY.
WHY DO BOYS TEASE THE PERSON THEY LIKE?
RIGHT, KOU-SUKE?
...

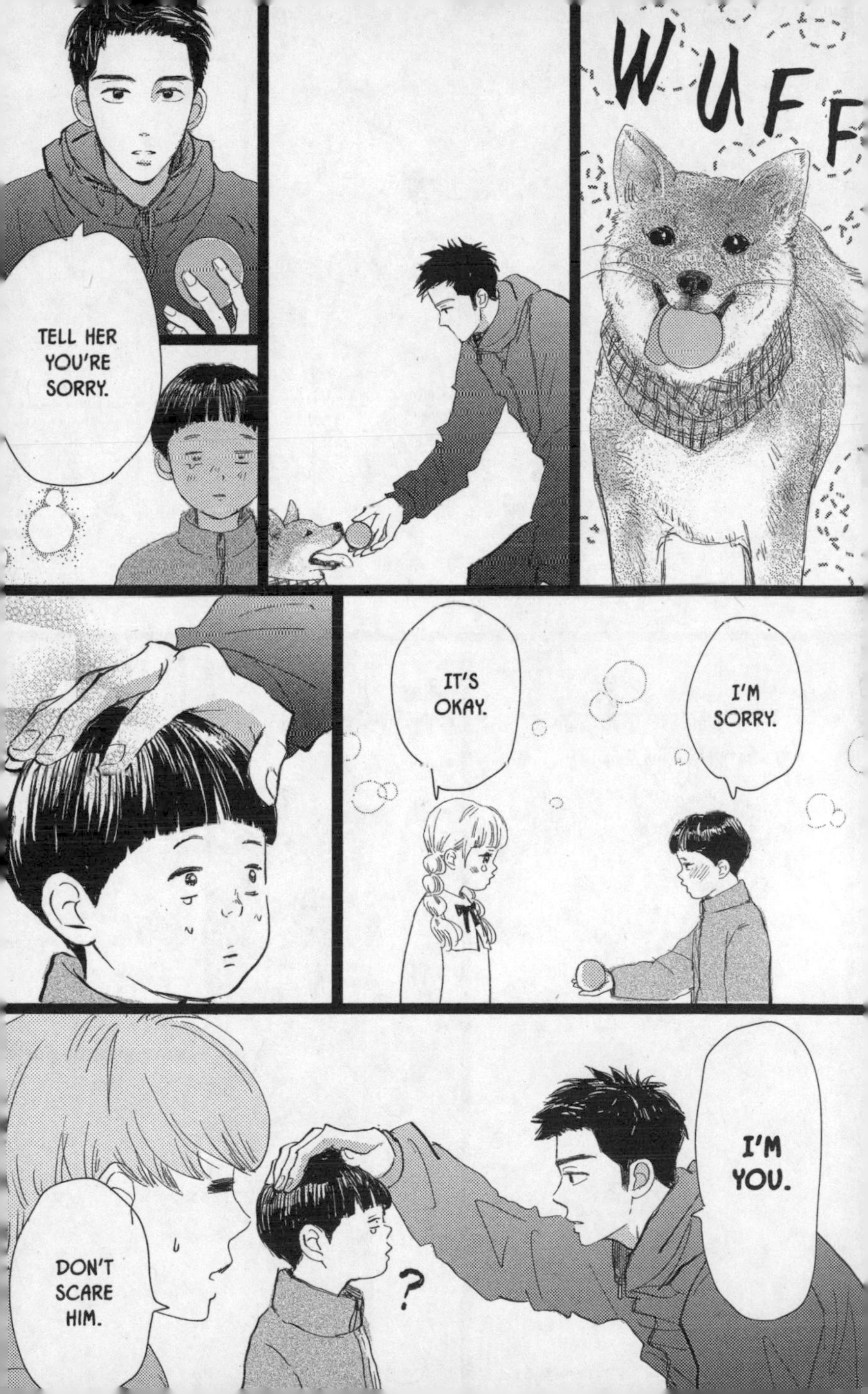
WUFF
TELL HER YOU'RE SORRY.
I'M SORRY.
IT'S OKAY.
I'M YOU.
DON'T SCARE HIM.
?

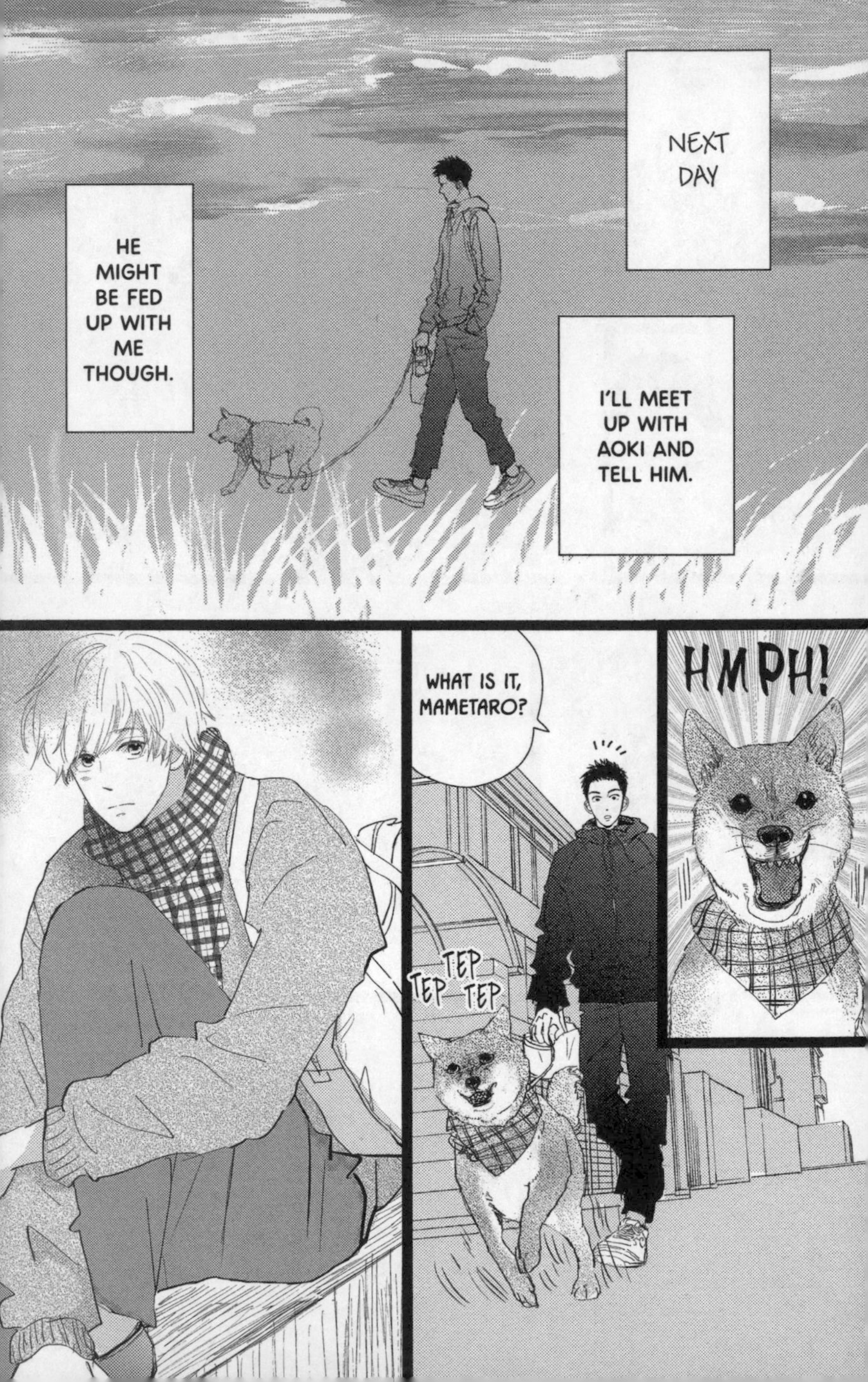
NEXT DAY
I'LL MEET UP WITH AOKI AND TELL HIM.
HE MIGHT BE FED UP WITH ME THOUGH.
HMPH!
WHAT IS IT, MAMETARO?
TEP TEP TEP TEP

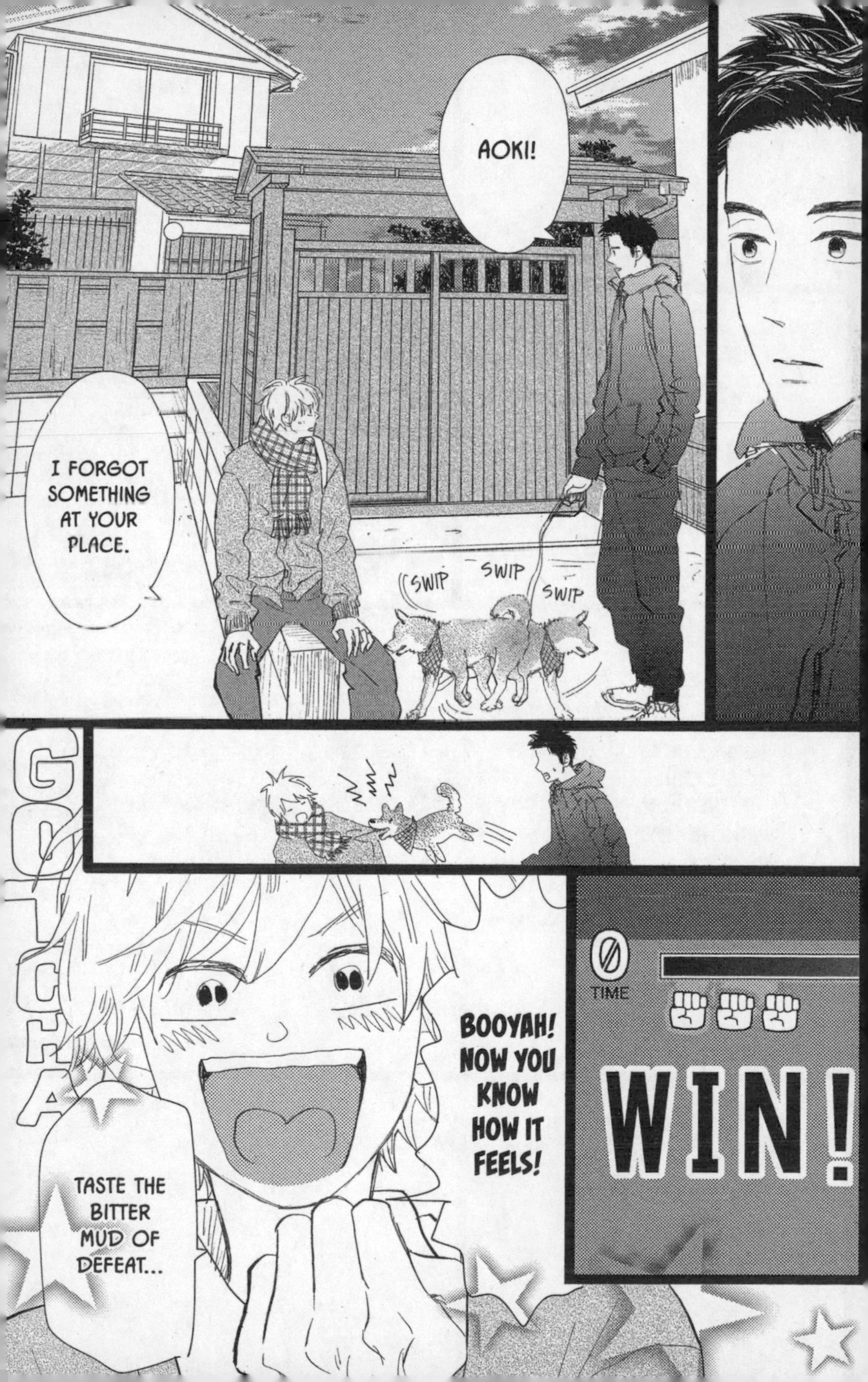
AOKI!
I FORGOT SOMETHING AT YOUR PLACE.
SWIP SWIP SWIP
0
TIME
WIN!
BOOYAH! NOW YOU KNOW HOW IT FEELS!
TASTE THE BITTER MUD OF DEFEAT...
GOTCHA

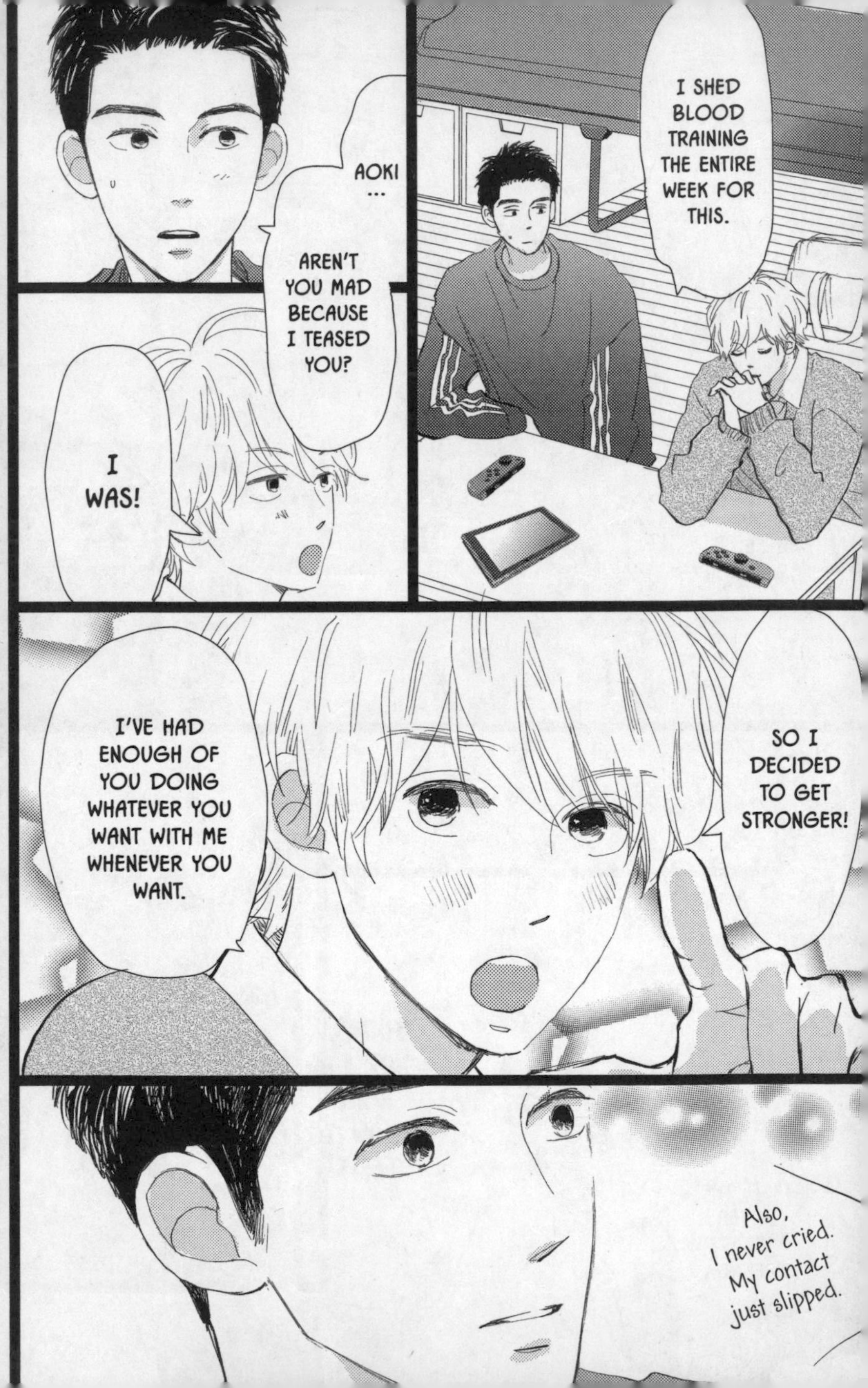
I SHED BLOOD TRAINING THE ENTIRE WEEK FOR THIS.
AOKI ...
AREN'T YOU MAD BECAUSE I TEASED YOU?
I WAS!
I'VE HAD ENOUGH OF YOU DOING WHATEVER YOU WANT WITH ME WHENEVER YOU WANT.
SO I DECIDED TO GET STRONGER!
Also, I never cried. My contact just slipped.

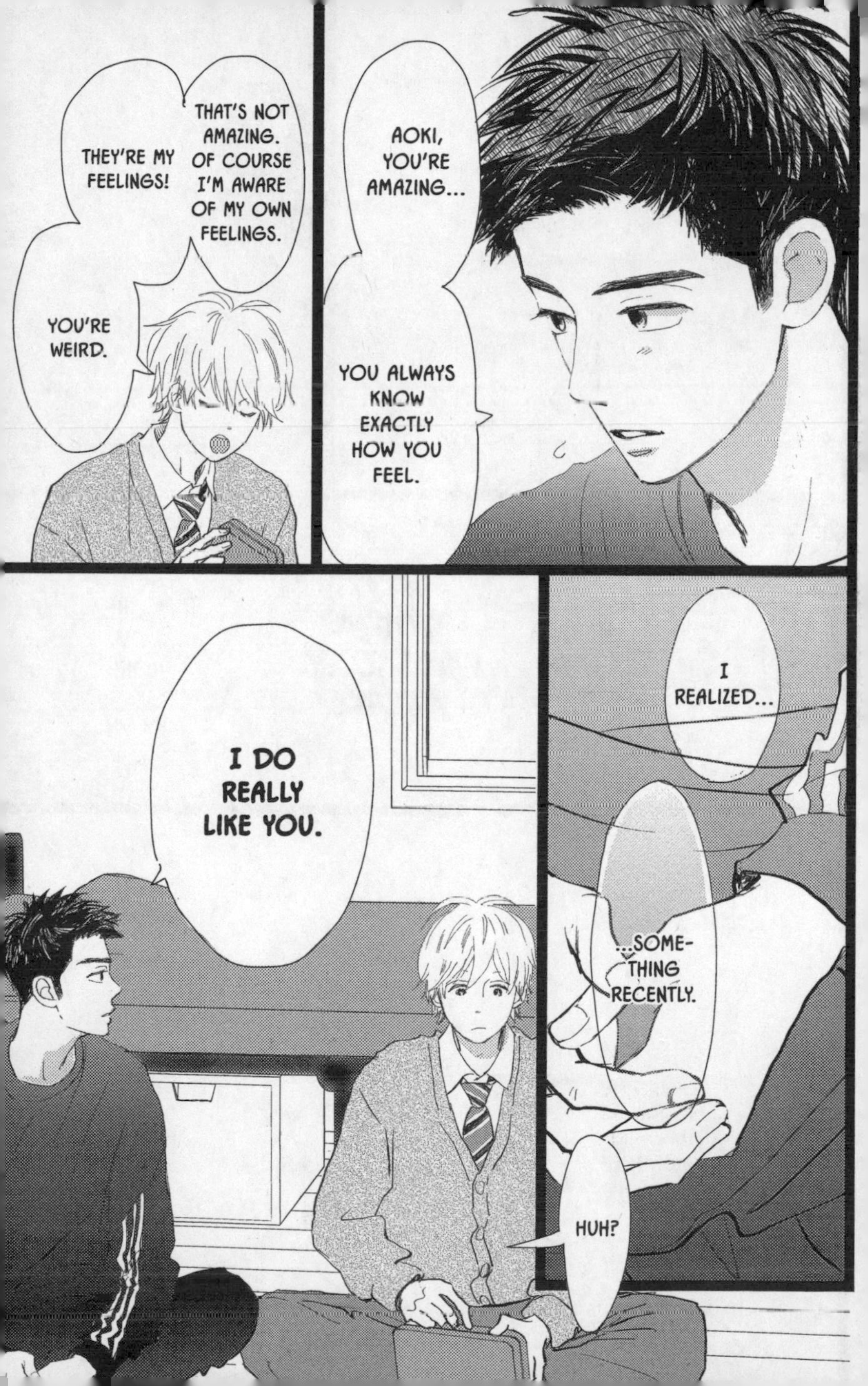
AOKI, YOU'RE AMAZING...
YOU ALWAYS KNOW EXACTLY HOW YOU FEEL.
THAT'S NOT AMAZING. OF COURSE I'M AWARE OF MY OWN FEELINGS.
THEY'RE MY FEELINGS!
YOU'RE WEIRD.
I REALIZED...
...SOMETHING RECENTLY.
HUH?
I DO REALLY LIKE YOU.

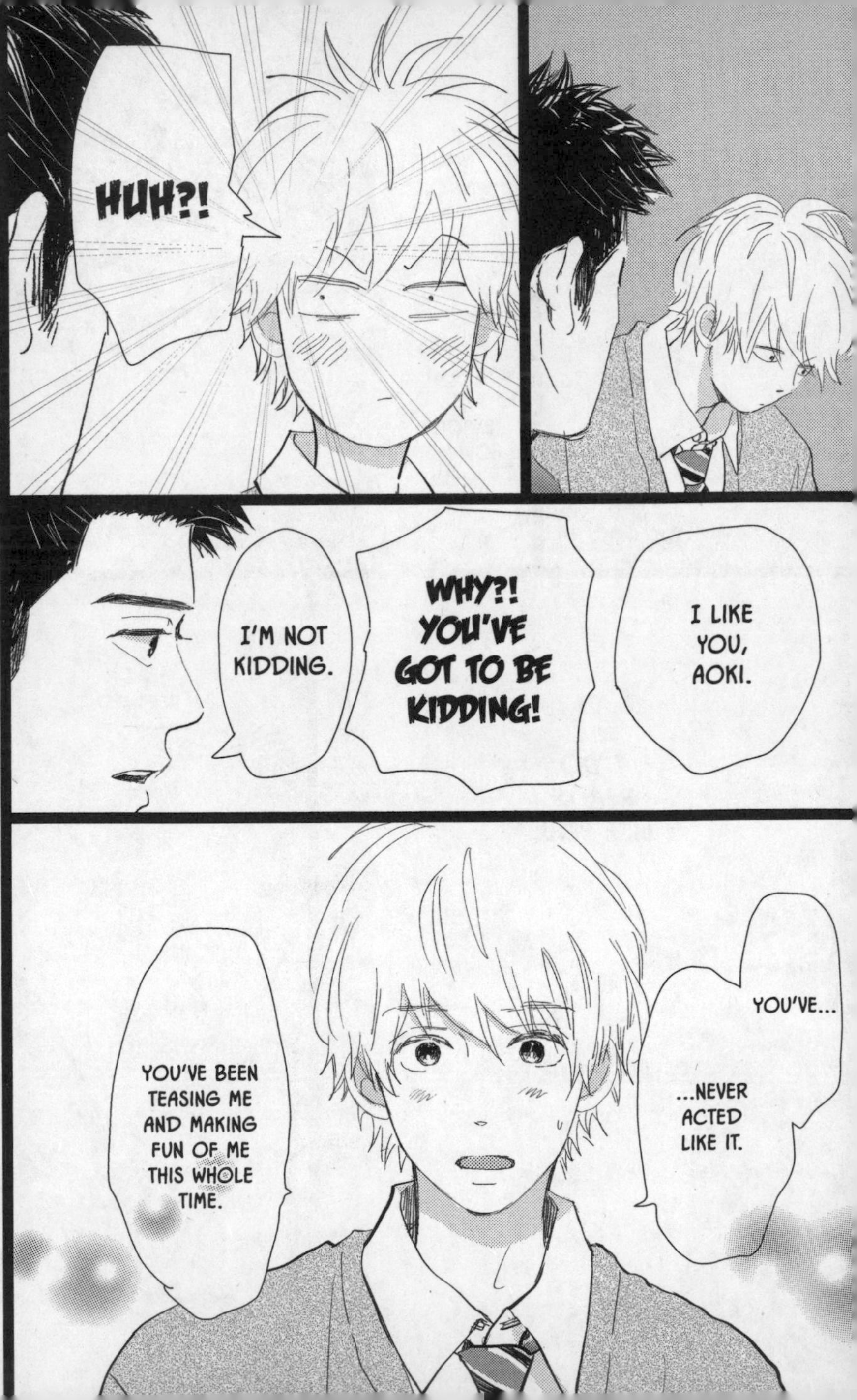
HUH?!
I LIKE YOU, AOKI.
WHY?! YOU'VE GOT TO BE KIDDING!
I'M NOT KIDDING.
YOU'VE...
...NEVER ACTED LIKE IT.
YOU'VE BEEN TEASING ME AND MAKING FUN OF ME THIS WHOLE TIME.

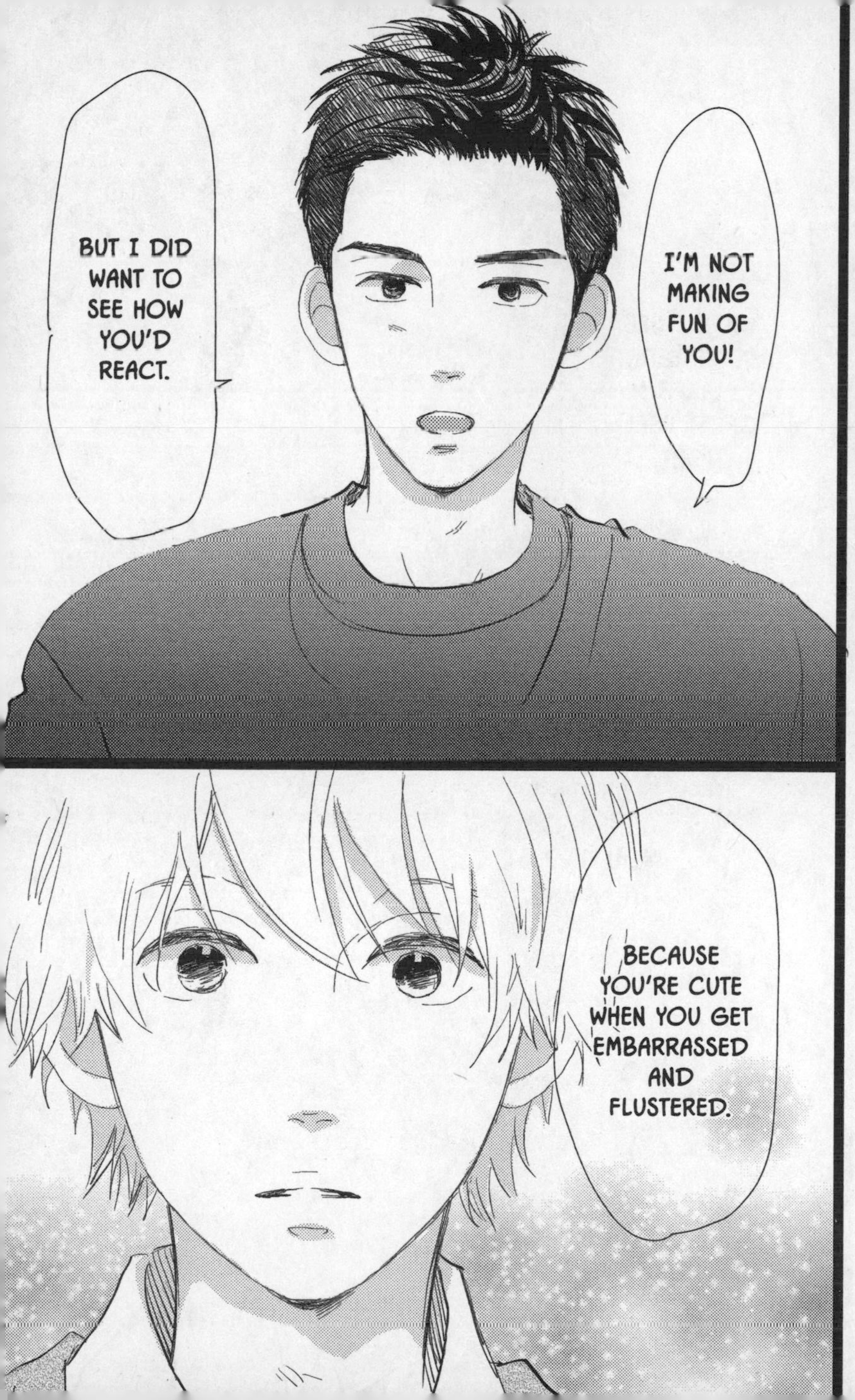
I'M NOT MAKING FUN OF YOU!
BUT I DID WANT TO SEE HOW YOU'D REACT.
BECAUSE YOU'RE CUTE WHEN YOU GET EMBARRASSED AND FLUSTERED.

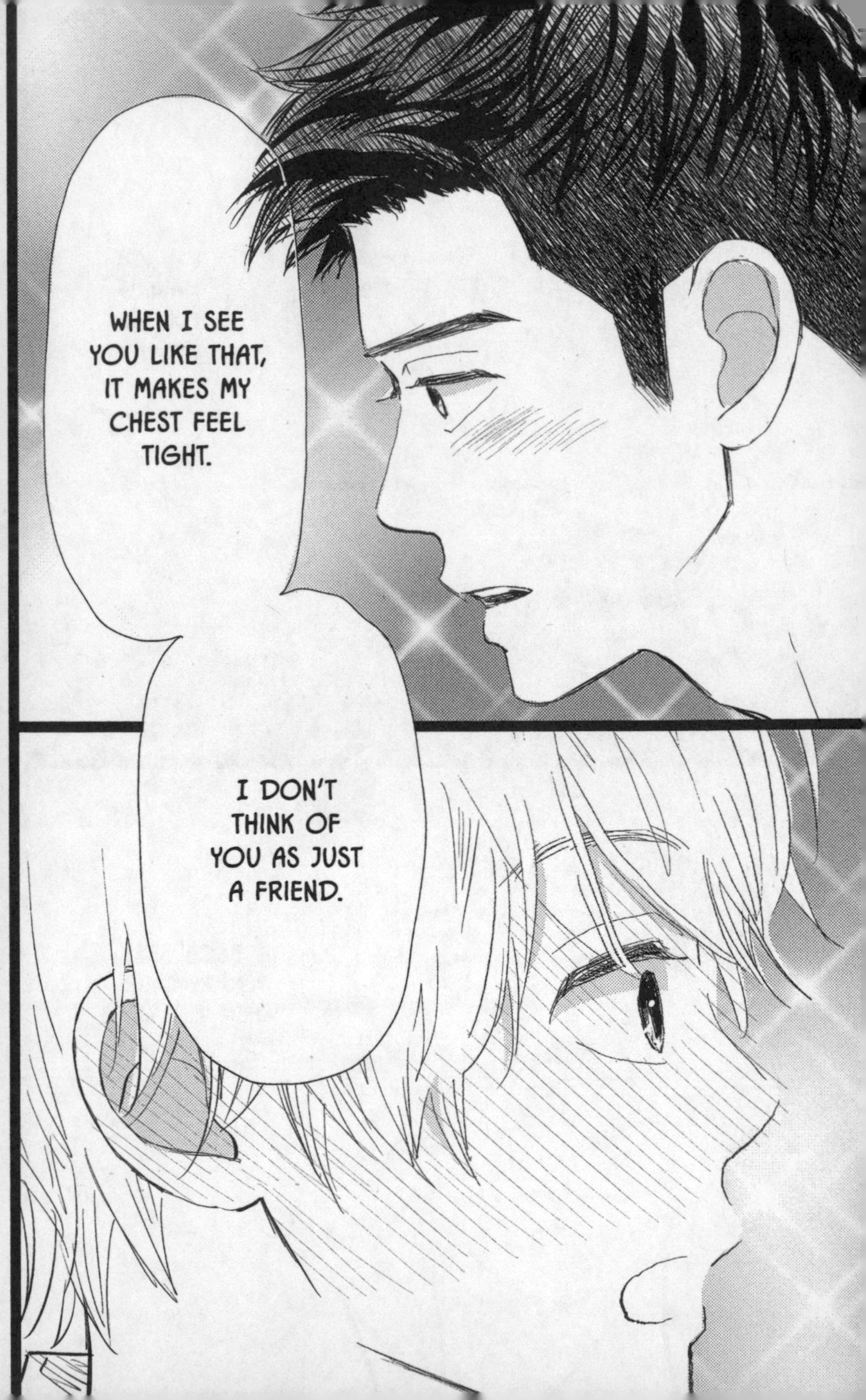
WHEN I SEE YOU LIKE THAT, IT MAKES MY CHEST FEEL TIGHT.
I DON'T THINK OF YOU AS JUST A FRIEND.

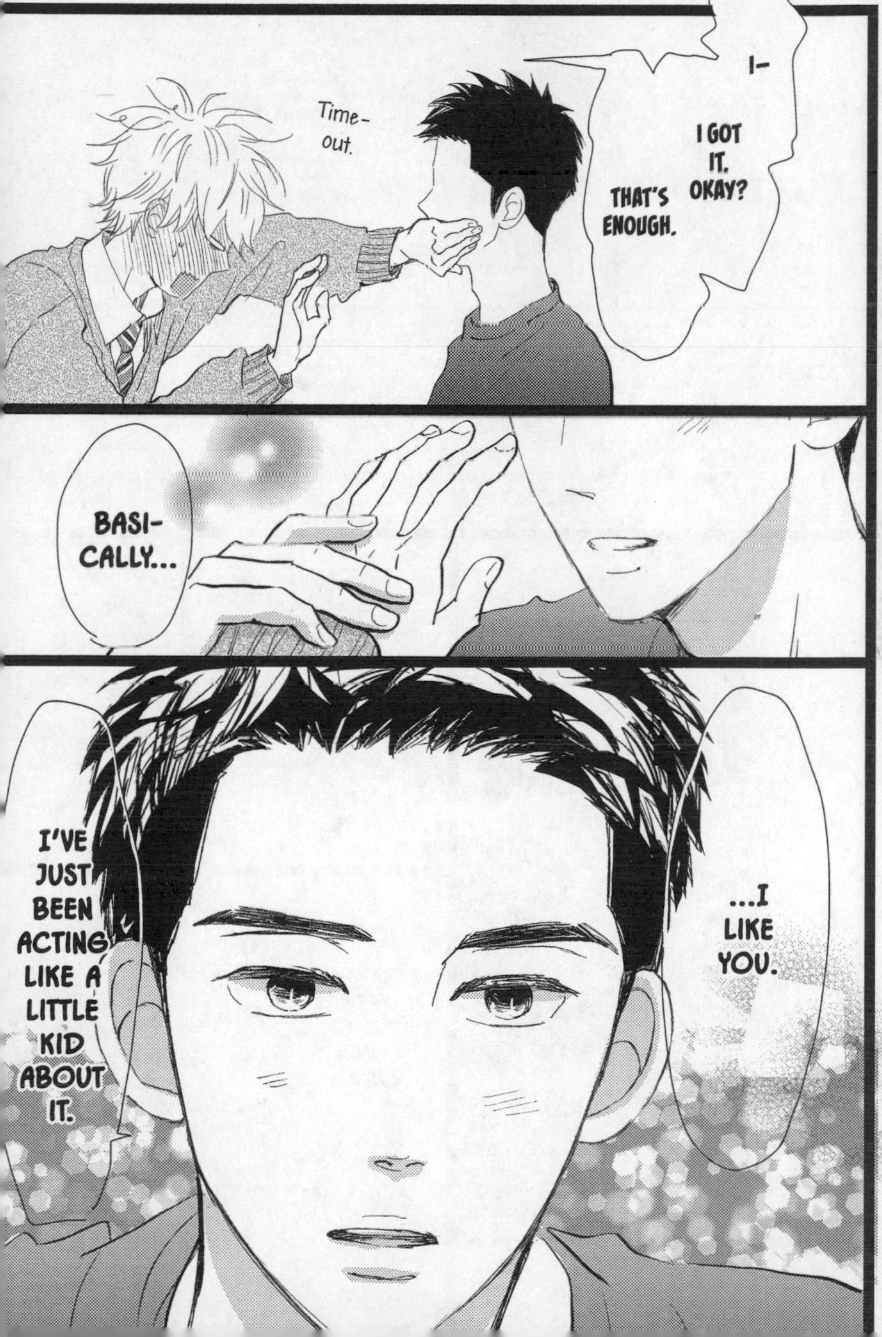
I— I GOT IT. OKAY? THAT'S ENOUGH.
Time-out.
BASI-CALLY...
...I LIKE YOU.
I'VE JUST BEEN ACTING LIKE A LITTLE KID ABOUT IT.

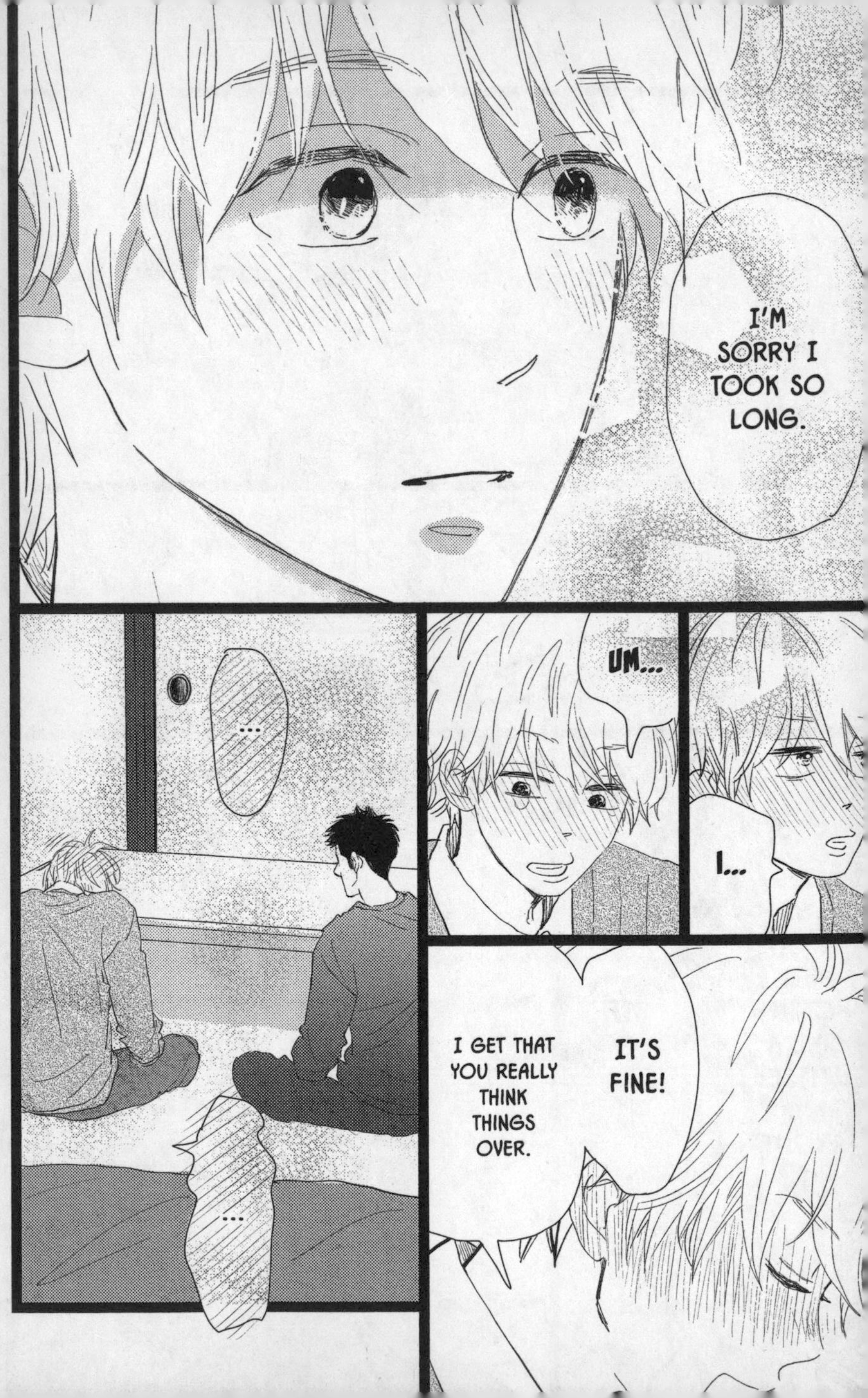
I'M SORRY I TOOK SO LONG.
I...
UM...
IT'S FINE!
I GET THAT YOU REALLY THINK THINGS OVER.
...
...

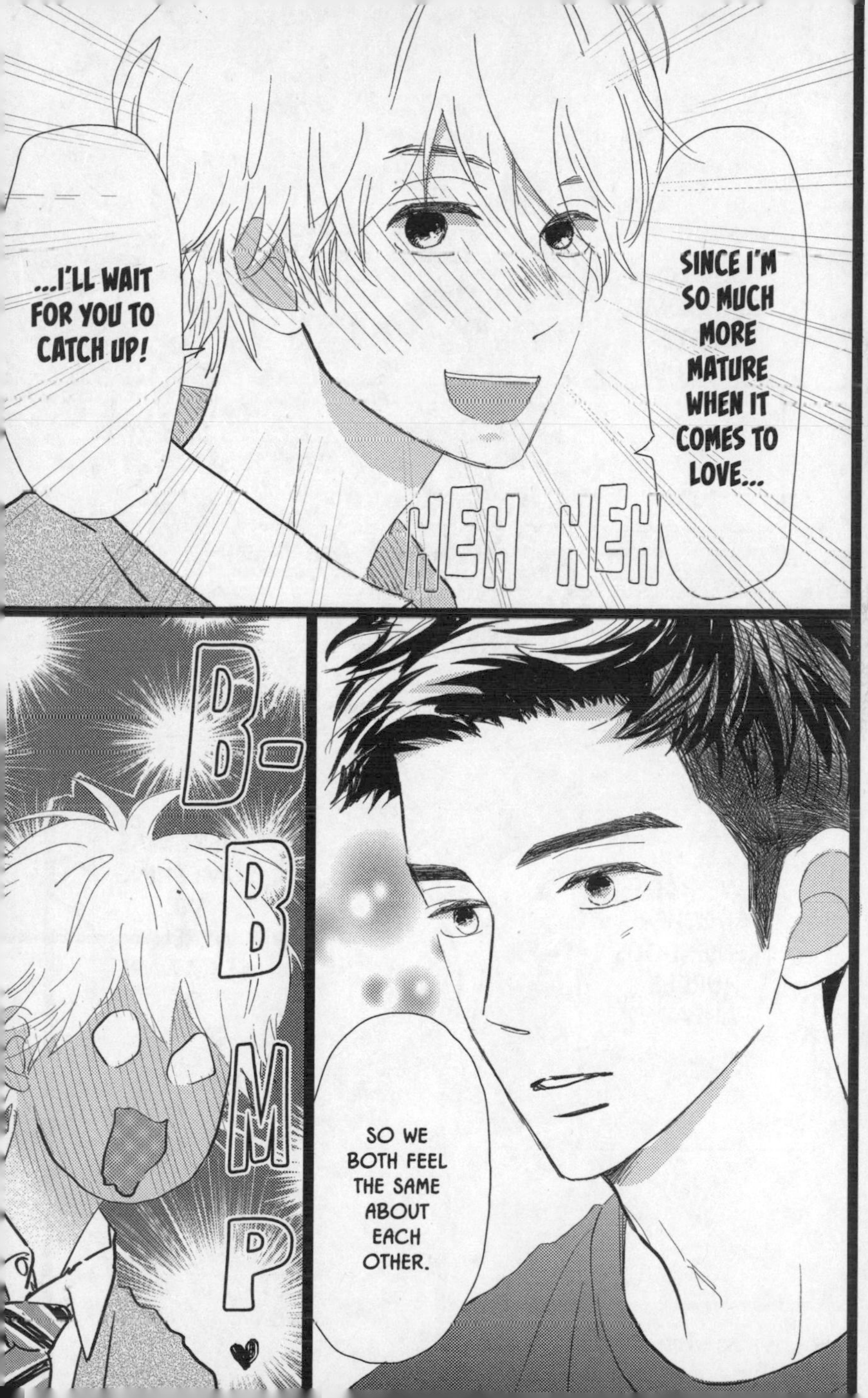
SINCE I'M SO MUCH MORE MATURE WHEN IT COMES TO LOVE...
HEH HEH
...I'LL WAIT FOR YOU TO CATCH UP!
SO WE BOTH FEEL THE SAME ABOUT EACH OTHER.
B-BMP

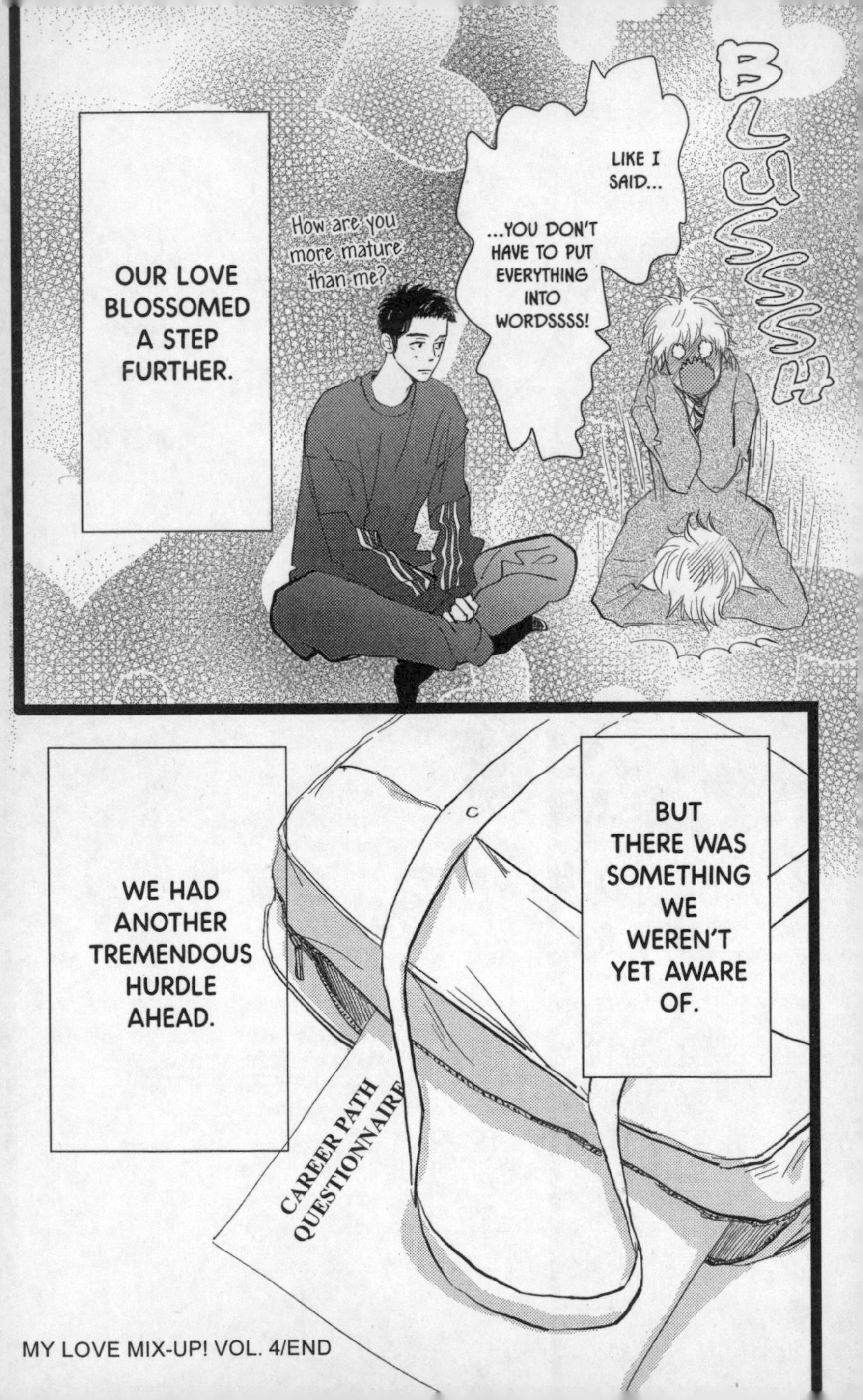
BLUSSSSH
LIKE I SAID...
...YOU DON'T HAVE TO PUT EVERYTHING INTO WORDSSSS!
How are you more mature than me?
OUR LOVE BLOSSOMED A STEP FURTHER.
BUT THERE WAS SOMETHING WE WEREN'T YET AWARE OF.
CAREER PATH QUESTIONNAIRE
WE HAD ANOTHER TREMENDOUS HURDLE AHEAD.

MY LOVE MIX-UP! VOL. 4/END

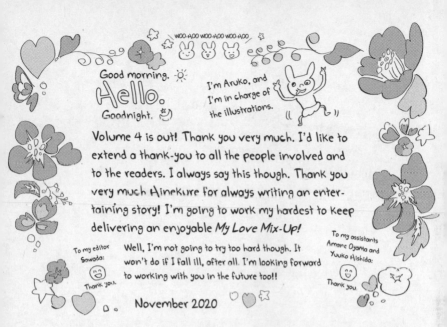

WOO-HOO WOO-HOO WOO-HOO

Good morning. ☀
Hello.
Goodnight. 🌙

I'm Aruko, and I'm in charge of the illustrations.

Volume 4 is out! Thank you very much. I'd like to extend a thank-you to all the people involved and to the readers. I always say this though. Thank you very much Hinekure for always writing an entertaining story! I'm going to work my hardest to keep delivering an enjoyable *My Love Mix-Up!*

To my editor Sawada: 😊 Thank you.

Well, I'm not going to try too hard though. It won't do if I fall ill, after all. I'm looking forward to working with you in the future too!!

To my assistants Amane Oyama and Yuuko Aishida: 😊 Thank you.

November 2020

Thank you for *My Love Mix-Up!* volume 4!

I'm Hinekure Wataru, the one in charge of the manuscript. Lots of things happened in 2020, including the coronavirus, but letting myself get lost in Aruko's drafts on a daily basis cheered me up, as did consulting with my editor in-depth about the story. What especially lifted my spirits was when I'd reflect on the readers' delightful reactions. I am full of gratitude. I'm going to work even harder so I can repay you with stories!

< Digression >

It's hot...

The Christmastime story was published in the middle of the summer in *Bestuma*, but since the volume is going on sale in winter, I think I'll reread it then to enjoy the atmosphere. Aruko, thank you so much for a wonderful depiction of Aoki and the other characters!

Aruko, my editor, the readers: Thank you for everything. I'd be so delighted if you picked up the next volume as well.

I've recently been thinking about how disjointed drumming is cool. I've been watching videos of really good drummers performing.

Aruko

Before I knew it, winter had come to the real world and the manga... Thank you for everything this year! I think I'll eat cake while reading volume 4.

Wataru Hinekure

Aruko is from Ishikawa Prefecture in Japan and was born on July 26 (a Leo!). She made her manga debut with *Ame Nochi Hare* (Clear After the Rain). Her other works include *Yasuko to Kenji*, and her hobbies include laughing and getting lost.

Wataru Hinekure is a night owl. *My Love Mix-Up!* is Hinekure's first work.

My Love Mix-Up!

Vol. 4
Shojo Beat Edition

STORY BY
Wataru Hinekure

ART BY
Aruko

Translation & Adaptation/Jan Cash
Touch-Up Art & Lettering/Inori Fukuda Trant
Design/Yukiko Whitley
Editor/Nancy Thistlethwaite

KIETA HATSUKOI © 2019 by Wataru Hinekure, Aruko
All rights reserved.
First published in Japan in 2019 by SHUEISHA Inc., Tokyo.
English translation rights arranged by SHUEISHA Inc.

The stories, characters, and incidents mentioned in this
publication are entirely fictional.

Printed in the U.S.A.

Published by VIZ Media, LLC
P.O. Box 77010
San Francisco, CA 94107

10 9 8 7 6 5 4 3 2 1
First printing, July 2022

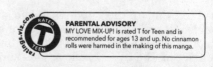

PARENTAL ADVISORY
MY LOVE MIX-UP! is rated T for Teen and is
recommended for ages 13 and up. No cinnamon
rolls were harmed in the making of this manga.

viz.com

shojobeat.com

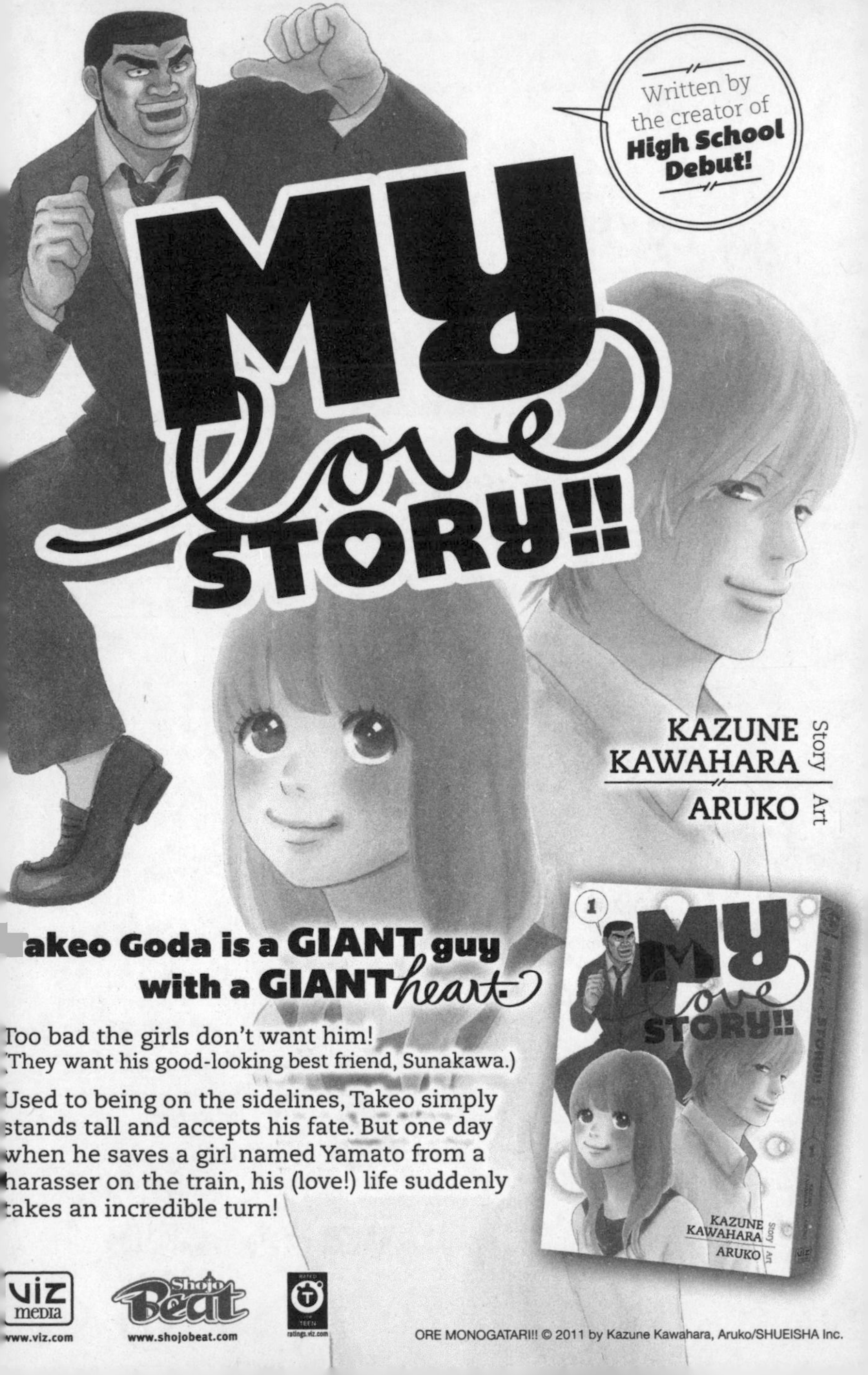
Written by the creator of High School Debut!
MY Love STORY!!
KAZUNE KAWAHARA Story
ARUKO Art
Takeo Goda is a GIANT guy with a GIANT heart
Too bad the girls don't want him!
(They want his good-looking best friend, Sunakawa.)
Used to being on the sidelines, Takeo simply stands tall and accepts his fate. But one day when he saves a girl named Yamato from a harasser on the train, his (love!) life suddenly takes an incredible turn!
1
MY Love STORY!!
KAZUNE KAWAHARA Story
ARUKO Art
viz media
www.viz.com
Shojo Beat
www.shojobeat.com
RATED T TEEN
ratings.viz.com
ORE MONOGATARI!! © 2011 by Kazune Kawahara, Aruko/SHUEISHA Inc.

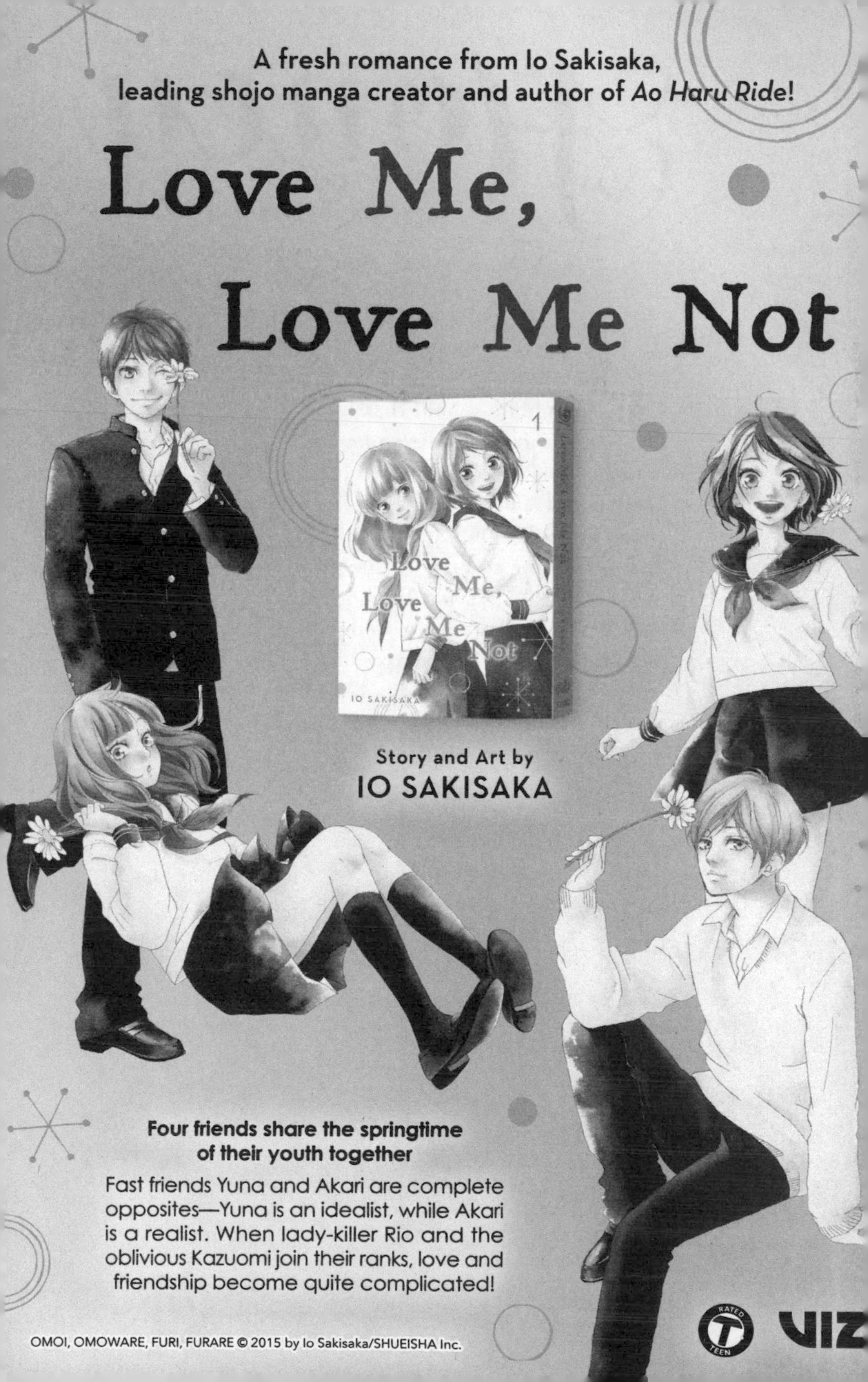

A fresh romance from Io Sakisaka,
leading shojo manga creator and author of *Ao Haru Ride*!
Love Me, Love Me Not
1
Love Me, Love Me Not
IO SAKISAKA
Story and Art by
IO SAKISAKA
Four friends share the springtime
of their youth together
Fast friends Yuna and Akari are complete opposites—Yuna is an idealist, while Akari is a realist. When lady-killer Rio and the oblivious Kazuomi join their ranks, love and friendship become quite complicated!
RATED T TEEN
VIZ
OMOI, OMOWARE, FURI, FURARE © 2015 by Io Sakisaka/SHUEISHA Inc.

Honey So Sweet

Story and Art by Amu Meguro

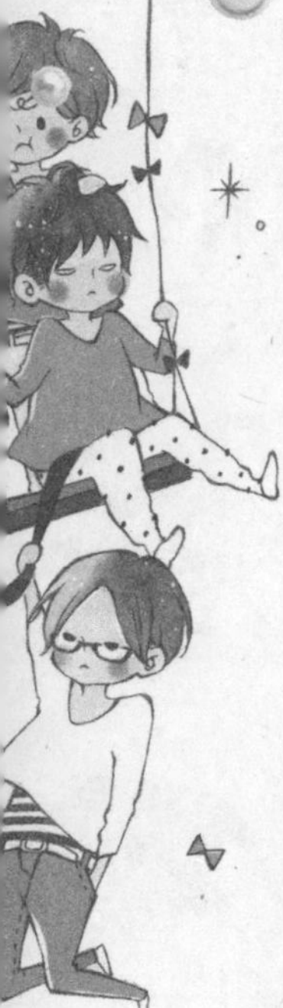

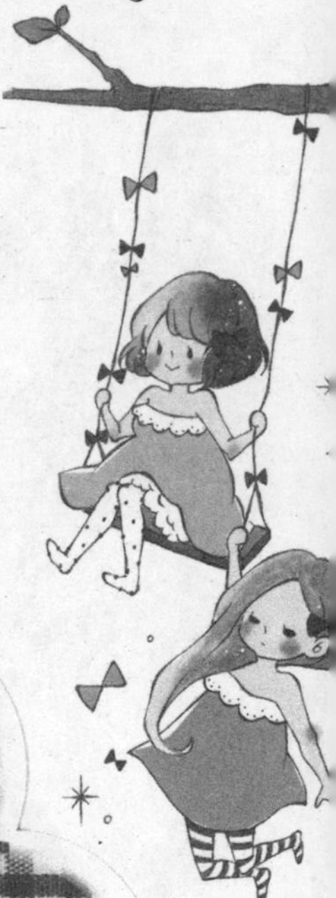

Little did Nao Kogure realize back in middle school that when she left an umbrella and a box of bandages in the rain for injured delinquent Taiga Onise that she would meet him again in high school. Nao wants nothing to do with the gruff and frightening Taiga, but he suddenly presents her with a huge bouquet of flowers and asks her to date him—with marriage in mind! Is Taiga really so scary, or is he a sweetheart in disguise?

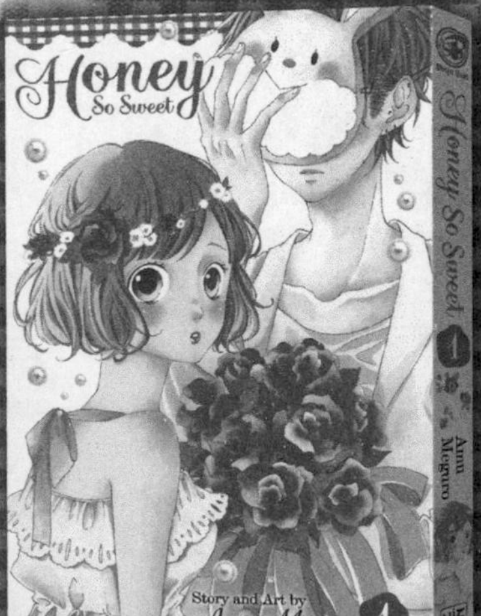
Honey So Sweet
Story and Art by Amu Meguro
1
Honey So Sweet
1
Amu Meguro

Shojo Beat

RATED T TEEN
ratings.viz.com

VIZ MEDIA
viz.com

SHORTCAKE CAKE

CAKE

STORY AND ART BY
suu Morishita

An unflappable girl and a cast of lovable roommates at a boardinghouse create bonds of friendship and romance!

When Ten moves out of her parents' home in the mountains to live in a boardinghouse, she finds herself becoming fast friends with her male roommates. But can love and romance be far behind?

VIZ

DAYTIME SHOOTING STAR

Story & Art by
Mika Yamamori

Small town girl Suzume moves to Tokyo and finds her heart caught between two men!

After arriving in Tokyo to live with her uncle, Suzume collapses in a nearby park when she remembers once seeing a shooting star during the day. A handsome stranger brings her to her new home and tells her they'll meet again. Suzume starts her first day at her new high school sitting next to a boy who blushes furiously at her touch. And her homeroom teacher is none other than the handsome stranger!

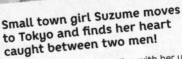

Stop!

You may be reading the wrong way.

In keeping with the original Japanese comic format, this book reads from right to left—so action, sound effects, and word balloons are completely reversed to preserve the orientation of the original artwork. Check out the diagram shown here to get the hang of things, and then turn to the other side of the book to get started!

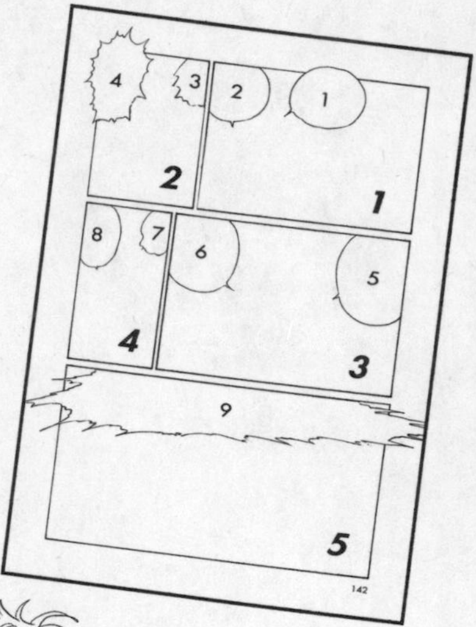
1
2
3
4
1
2
5
6
7
8
3
4
9
5
142

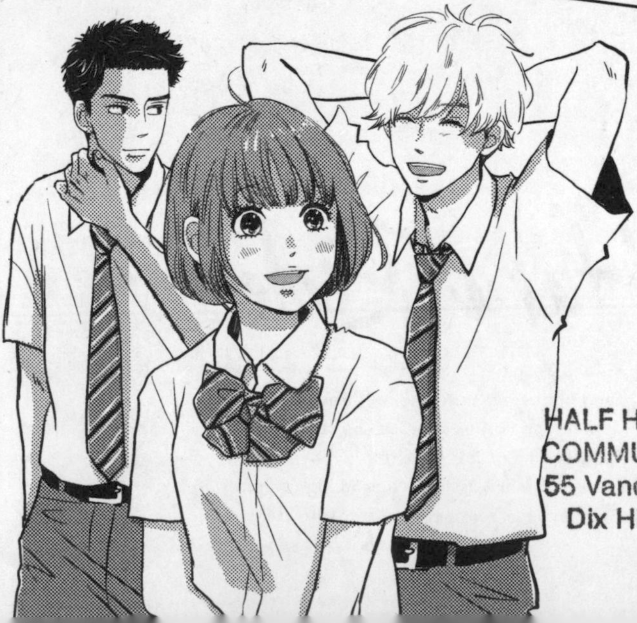